The authors

Pamela Fitzpatrick is a welfare rights worker at the CPAG's Citizens' Rights Office, a co-author of CPAG's *Welfare Benefits and Tax Credits Handbook* and a contributing author to CPAG's *At Greatest Risk*.

Fiona Ripley is a solicitor specialising in immigration and asylum work at Southwark Law Centre in London.

Anne Singh is a solicitor in the litigation team at the Refugee Legal Centre in London.

Acknowledgements

The authors would like to thank everyone who has contributed to this book. We would, in particular, like to thank Colin Yeo, Lisa Woodall, Angus King, David Burgess, Beth Lakhani and Terry Patterson for their invaluable comments. Thanks also go too to the previous authors for their contribution to the book.

Thanks are due to James Marsh for setting up this edition and Nicola Johnston for editing and managing the production of the book. Thanks to Helen Treacy for proofreading the text and the index.

Migration and Social Security Handbook

4th edition

Pamela Fitzpatrick, Fiona Ripley and Anne Singh

hild Pove

CPAG promotes action for the relief, directly or indirectly, of poverty among children and families with children. We work to ensure that those on low incomes get their full entitlements to welfare benefits. In our campaigning and information work we seek to improve benefits and policies for low-income families in order to eradicate the injustice of poverty. If you are not already supporting us, please consider making a donation, or ask for details of our membership schemes and publications.

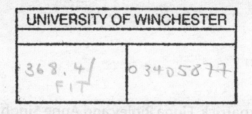
Published by Child Poverty Action Group
94 White Lion Street, London N1 9PF
020 7837 7979

Registered Company No. 1993854
Charity No. 294841

© Child Poverty Action Group 2007

A CIP record for this book is available from the British Library

ISBN: 978 1 901698 770

Design by Devious Designs 0114 275 5634
Cover photo by Peter Olive/Photofusion
Typeset by David Lewis XML Associates Limited
Printed by Clowes Group, Beccles, Suffolk

Contents

Glossary of terms used

A2 countries The two states which joined the EU on 1 January 2007 (Bulgaria and Romania) are referred to as the A2 countries.

A8 countries The eight states which joined the EU on 1 May 2004 (Czech Republic, Estonia, Hungary, Latvia, Lithuania, Poland, Slovakia and Slovenia) are referred to as the A8 countries.

Adjudicator The person who hears and decides an immigration appeal in the first instance.

Administrative removal A form of enforced departure used to remove those who have breached their conditions of leave, overstayed their leave or who have obtained leave by deception.

Applicable amount A figure representing your weekly needs for the purpose of calculating your benefit. For income support your applicable amount is the amount you are expected to live on each week. For housing benefit and council tax benefit it is the amount used to see how much help you need with your rent or council tax. For full details, see CPAG's *Welfare Benefits and Tax Credits Handbook*.

Application registration card The form of identification for those who have claimed asylum, replacing the standard acknowledgement letter.

Association agreement A treaty signed between the European Community and another country which gives nationals of the other country (mainly business and self-employed people) preferential access to the countries of the European Economic Area.

Asylum A place of refuge; allowing a person to stay in one country because of the danger s/he would face if returned to the country from which s/he has fled.

Asylum and Immigration Tribunal Hears and decides appeals against decisions made by the Home Office in matters of asylum, immigration and nationality.

Asylum seeker A person who makes a claim to the immigration authorities to be a refugee, as defined in the United Nations Convention on Refugees 1951. The status of asylum seeker ends when the person is given permission to stay in the

UK, or when any rights of appeal against refusal some to an end. For benefit and asylum support purposes, someone who claims that removing her/him from the UK would violate rights under Article 3 of the European Convention on Human Rights is also treated as an asylum seeker.

Asylum support Support given to asylum seekers instead of welfare benefits and support under the National Assistance Act 1948. An 'interim' system of asylum support administered by local authorities was introduced in December 1999 (and still applies to some asylum seekers). A more permanent scheme administered by the National Asylum Support Service was introduced in April 2000.

Certificate of entitlement A certificate of entitlement to the right of abode demonstrates that a person has the right of abode (right to travel freely to and from the UK). British citizens have the right of abode and can demonstrate this by producing their passports. However, a few Commonwealth nationals also have the right of abode and can obtain a certificate of entitlement, endorsed in their own national passport, to demonstrate this.

Certified case There are many different 'certificates' used in immigration and asylum law – eg, some claims for asylum are 'certified' on the grounds that the asylum seeker can be sent to a safe 'third country' of asylum. The new Nationality, Immigration and Asylum Bill 2002 proposes to allow 'clearly unfounded' certificates to be issued in asylum cases which will deny those asylum seekers a right of appeal until after they have left the UK. At present, the term is most used to describe certificates used to prevent asylum seekers and those making human rights claims from appealing beyond the first tier of appeal to the Immigration Appeal Tribunal.

Civil partner The Civil Partnership Act 2004 came into force on 5 December 2005, enabling same-sex couples to obtain legal recognition of their relationship. Couples who form a civil partnership have a new legal status, that of 'civil partner'.

Common Travel Area The UK, Republic of Ireland, Isle of Man and the Channel Islands, between which there are no immigration controls. Following the events of 11 September 2001, however, some airlines are demanding to see travel documents/passports.

Commonwealth countries Antigua and Barbuda, Australia, Bahamas, Bangladesh, Barbados, Belize, Botswana, Brunei Darussalam, Cameroon, Canada, Cyprus, Dominica, Fiji Islands, Gambia, Ghana, Grenada, Guyana, India, Jamaica, Kenya, Kiribati, Lesotho, Malawi, Malaysia, Maldives, Malta, Mauritius, Mozambique, Namibia, Nauru, New Zealand, Nigeria, Pakistan, Papua New

Guinea, Samoa, Seychelles, Sierra Leone, Singapore, Solomon Islands, South Africa, Sri Lanka, St Kitts and Nevis, St Lucia, St Vincent and the Grenadines, Swaziland, Tanzania, Tonga, Trinidad and Tobago, Tuvalu, Uganda, United Kingdom, Vanuatu and Zambia.

Couple For means-tested benefits, you and your partner are considered to be a 'couple' if you are:
- married and living in the same household;
- not married but 'living together as husband and wife';
- of the same sex, registered as civil partners and living in the same household; *or*
- of the same sex, not registered as civil partners but 'living together as if you were civil partners'.

Deportation (order) Sending a person out of the UK under an order signed by the Home Secretary after the person has been convicted of a serious criminal offence, or because the Home Secretary has decided on public policy or national security grounds that the person's presence is 'not conducive to the public good'. The person cannot return unless and until the order has been revoked.

Discretionary leave A person who would be excluded from a grant of refugee leave under Article 1F(b) of the Refugee Convention or from humanitarian protection under the exclusion criteria would qualify for a grant of discretionary leave if her/his removal would involve a breach of the ECHR.

Enforcement A term used to refer to any of the different ways in which a person can be forced to leave the UK for immigration reasons: having been refused entry at port, having been declared an illegal entrant, or having been notified that s/he is someone who is liable for administrative removal, or who is being deported.

Entry clearance officer An official at a British post overseas who deals with immigration applications made to the post.

European Community (EC) In this book we refer to the legislation of the European Union (previously known as the European Community and before that the European Economic Community) as EC law.

European Convention on Human Rights An international instrument agreed by the Council of Europe. The rights guaranteed by it have now largely been incorporated into UK law by the Human Rights Act 1998.

European Convention on Social and Medical Assistance (ECSMA) An agreement signed by all the EEA states, plus Malta and Turkey, requiring that ratifying states provide assistance in cash and kind to nationals of other ratifying states, who are lawfully present in their territory and without sufficient resources, on the same conditions as their own nationals. It also prevents ratifying states repatriating lawfully present nationals of other ratifying states simply because the person is in need of assistance. If you are a person who is covered by the Convention you are not a 'person subject to immigration control' for means-tested benefits.

European Economic Area (EEA) covers European Union states plus Iceland, Liechtenstein and Norway. EEA nationals have free movement within these and all European Union member states. From 1 June 2002, the right to free movement also applies to Switzerland

European Union (EU) member states are Austria, Belgium, Bulgaria, Cyprus, Czech Republic, Denmark, Estonia, Finland, France, Germany, Greece, Hungary, Ireland, Italy, Latvia, Lithuania, Luxembourg, Malta, the Netherlands, Portugal, Romania, Slovakia, Slovinia, Spain, Sweden and the UK (the UK includes Gibralter for this purpose).

EU/EEA national In this book we use this term to describe citizens of EU member states and EEA countries.

Exceptional leave Used in two senses: either to refer to any leave given to a person outside the immigration rules or to the leave given to a person who is refused asylum but is allowed to stay in the UK under the European Convention on Human Rights or for other humanitarian reasons.

Family For benefit purposes, under British law your family is yourself, your partner and any dependent children who are members of your household (for definition of household, see CPAG's *Welfare Benefits and Tax Credits Handbook*). Under EC law, family members include a wider range of relatives.

Great Britain comprises Wales, Scotland, England and adjacent islands (but not the Isle of Man or Channel Islands).

Habitual residence In order to be entitled to income support, income-based jobseeker's allowance, pension credit, housing benefit and council tax benefit, a claimant must be habitually resident in the Common Travel Area. Some people are automatically treated as habitually resident and are exempt from the test. The term 'habitually resident' is not defined in the benefit regulations and will therefore be determined by looking at all the circumstances in each case. Habitual residence has a different meaning in EC law.

Humanitarian protection Leave granted to a person who, if removed, would face a serious risk to life or person arising from the death penalty, unlawful killing or torture or inhuman or degrading treatment or punishment in the country of return. That is, while they do not satisfy the criteria laid down in Article 1(A)2 of the Refugee Convention, they would be at risk of treatment in violation of Articles 2 or 3 of the ECHR.

Illegal entrant A person who immigration officials decide has *entered* the UK in breach of the immigration law – this could be by deception.

Immigration appellate authority The courts, tribunals and adjudicators that make decisions in immigration and asylum appeals.

Immigration officer An official, usually stationed at a British port of entry, who decides whether to grant or refuse leave to enter. Immigration officers also, however, have responsibility for enforcing immigration control.

Immigration rules Rules of practice made under the Immigration Act 1971 which set out the requirements for granting or refusing entry clearance, leave to enter and leave to remain to people applying in the various different categories.

Indefinite leave Leave which has no time limit.

Lawful presence This is not defined in social security law. However, for housing law it has been decided that a person is not lawfully present if s/he has been given temporary admission to the UK. It has yet to be decided whether or not this applies to social security.

Limited leave Leave which is given for a certain period of time only.

Maintenance undertaking A formal statement signed by a sponsor in the UK that s/he will support a relative or other person applying to come to or stay in the UK. The relative is not eligible to claim non-contributory welfare benefits for five years after it was signed, or after the person has been given leave to enter or remain in the UK on this basis (whichever is the later), unless the sponsor dies.

National Asylum Support Service Financial support and accommodation for asylum seekers. Both this support and the organisation that administers it are currently known as NASS.

Ordinarily resident You must be ordinarily resident in Great Britain to be entitled to tax credits, disability living allowance, attendance allowance, carer's allowance, severe disablement allowance and Category D retirement pension. There is no definition in the benefits regulations of ordinary residence. This means that 'ordinary residence' should be given its ordinary and natural meaning.

Partner See 'Couple'.

Person from abroad A statutory definition that refers to a person who has failed the habitual residence test. It is not linked to a person's immigration status and even a British citizen can be termed a person from abroad for social security purposes.

Person subject to immigration control A social security term. A person subject to immigration control is excluded from entitlement to most social security benefits.

Public funds For immigration purposes these are: housing provided by local authorities – either as a homeless person or allocated from its housing register; attendance allowance; severe disablement allowance; carer's allowance; disability living allowance; income support; working tax credit; council tax benefit; child tax credit; housing benefit; income-based jobseeker's allowance; child benefit.

Refugee A person who satisfies the definition of those who need international protection under Article 1A(2) of the 1951 Convention relating to the status of refugees.

Removal The final procedure for sending a person refused entry, or who is being treated as an illegal entrant, or who is subject to the 'administrative' removal or deportation process, away from the UK.

Right of abode The right to enter, remain, leave and return freely to the UK without the need to obtain 'leave' from the immigration authorities. All British citizens have the right of abode. Some Commonwealth nationals also have the right of abode.

Right to reside A complex residence test introduced in 2004 for certain social security benefits and child tax credit.

Settlement/settled status Defined in immigration law as being 'ordinarily resident' in the UK without any restrictions on the time the person is able to remain here. Those with indefinite leave are generally accepted as being 'settled' in the UK.

Social Charter The 1961 Council of Europe Social Charter has been signed by all the EEA countries, plus Turkey. If you are a national of one of these states and you are lawfully present you are not a 'person subject to immigration control' for means-tested benefits.

Subject to immigration control People often use this term to refer to those who need 'leave' to enter or remain in the UK – and this is the definition given in the Asylum and Immigration Act 1996. However, the Immigration and Asylum Act

1999 gives the same phrase a different, narrower, definition, which is used to exclude people from non-contributory welfare benefits and certain services provided by local authorities' social services departments. In this book, we use the term as it is defined in the 1999 Act for welfare purposes.

Temporary admission A temporary licence given to people to be in the UK while they are waiting for a decision to be made on their immigration status or while they are waiting to be removed from the UK. The alternative to temporary admission, used particularly where a person is waiting to be removed, is detention.

Third country Usually used to refer to a country, other than that of which an asylum seeker is a national, to which the Home Office wishes to send an asylum seeker in order for her/his claim to be decided there, rather than in the UK. Third country nationals is also used to refer to nationals of a country, other than an EU/EEA state, who do not (unless they are family members of an EU/EEA national) enjoy EU rights of free movement.

The United Kingdom comprises England, Wales, Scotland and Northern Ireland.

Visa nationals People who always need to get entry clearance in advance of travelling to the UK, for whatever purpose they are coming here, unless they are returning residents returning within two years or are returning within a period of earlier leave granted for more than six months, or certain refugees and all asylum seekers. For a list of countries covered, see Appendix 7.

Work permit A formal document issued to employers allowing them to employ a named individual in a particular job. They are issued by Work Permits (UK), which is part of the Home Office. This is different from the Home Office 'granting permission' to work, for example, to an asylum seeker. When the immigration authorities do this, technically they simply remove the condition on the asylum seeker's temporary admission prohibiting her/him from working.

Abbreviations

AA	Attendance allowance	GB	Great Britain
AWC	Accession work card	HB	Housing benefit
AIT	Asylum and Immigration Trubunal	HP	Humanitarian protection
		HRT	Habitual residence test
ARC	Application registration card	HSMP	Highly Skilled Migrants Programme
AST	Asylum Support Tribunal		
BDTC	British dependent territories citizen	IB	Incapacity benefit
		ILR	Indefinite leave to remain
BL	Budgeting loan	IND	Immigration and Nationality Directorate
BNO	British national (overseas)		
BOC	British overseas citizen	IS	Income support
BOTC	British overseas territories citizen	JSA	Jobseeker's allowance
		MA	Maternity allowance
BPP	British protected person	NASS	National Asylum Support Service
BS	British subject		
CA	Carer's allowance	NAM	New asylum model
CCG	Community care grant	NI	National insurance
CL	Crisis loan	NINO	National insurance number
CSA	Child Support Agency	PC	Pension credit
CTA	Common Travel Area	PSIC	Person subject to immigration control
CTC	Child tax credit		
CTB	Council tax benefit	REA	Reduced earnings allowance
CUKC	Citizen of the United Kingdom and colonies	SAL	Standard acknowledgement letter
DL	Discretionary leave	SAP	Statutory adoption pay
DLA	Disability living allowance	SDA	Severe disablement allowance
DWP	Department for Work and Pensions	SEF	Statement of evidence form
		SF	Social fund
EC	European Community	SIAC	Special Immigration Appeals Commission
ECHR	European Convention on Human Rights		
		SMP	Statutory maternity pay
ECtHR	European Court of Human Rights	SPP	Statutory paternity pay
		SSHD	Secretary of State for the Home Department
ECJ	European Court of Justice		
EEA	European Economic Area	SSP	Statutory sick pay
ELE	Exceptional leave to enter	UK	United Kingdom
ELR	Exceptional leave to remain	WRS	Workers registration scheme
EU	European Union	WTC	Working tax credit

About this *Handbook*

This *Handbook* is intended to bridge the gap between guides on welfare rights and those on immigration. It is designed to be used by migrants and their advisers wanting advice on benefit entitlement. By 'migrants' we mean people who have come or returned to Great Britain from abroad and people who have left Great Britain to live abroad or are temporarily abroad.

The *Handbook* covers the benefit rules that are most likely to affect migrant claimants and their families, and the practical problems they are likely to face. It is not a complete guide to the benefit rules and should be used together with general guides such as CPAG's *Welfare Benefits and Tax Credits Handbook*.

How to use this book

Your benefit rights may depend upon your immigration status. In Part 1 we outline the immigration system and explain the terms used in immigration law which appear in the rest of the book. Part 1 aims to provide welfare rights advisers with a framework of immigration law. In some cases Part 1 may contain enough information for you to use the rest of the *Handbook* to work out your benefit entitlement. However, if you are unclear about your immigration status or the effects of claiming benefit, you should ask a specialist immigration adviser for immigration advice.

If your immigration status is clear, you should use Part 2 to work out your entitlement to benefits and tax credits. Use the chapter relevant to your immigration status.

If you are abroad, use Part 3. If you are planning to go abroad, use Parts 2 and 3.

Part 4 deals with European Community rules as they affect benefits here and in Europe. Part 5 deals with international agreements with certain other countries that can be used by their nationals and residents.

Part 6 covers the National Asylum Support Service which is responsible for the provision of support and accommodation to destitute asylum seekers.

The law covered was correct at 1 February 2007 and includes regulations up to that date.

Part 1

Immigration law

Chapter 1
Immigration control

This chapter covers:
1. Immigration control (below)
2. The effect of immigration control (p5)
3. How immigration control operates (p11)

The intention of Part 1 of the book is to set out the framework and mechanics of immigration control so that the system of control can be understood and so that welfare advisers can more readily identify and understand a person's immigration status and advise on her/his benefit entitlement. There is not space in this book to set out and explain the conditions which need to be satisfied under the immigration rules (see p14) under which 'leave' (permission) to enter or remain in the UK may be granted; nor the criteria applied when deciding whether to grant a work permit; nor the general grounds for refusal of leave. The criteria contained in the immigration rules for admission as a student and a spouse (Chapter 4) are given as examples only. If you want to know more about the criteria for the different admission categories, they are set out in the immigration rules in accessible language (the immigration rules are not legislation).[1] It is also possible to obtain guidance from organisations such as UK Visas, the Immigration and Nationality Directorate (both branches of government), the Immigration Advisory Service and the Joint Council for the Welfare of Immigrants.[2] The criteria applied when determining whether a work permit can be issued to an employer for someone who wishes to obtain leave to enter and remain is updated regularly. Information, including guidance notes on making applications, can be found at www.workingintheuk.gov.uk.

The requirements of the rules which relate to 'maintenance and accommodation without recourse to public funds' (which apply to many of the categories to which leave can be granted) are, however, explained in Chapter 7.

In addition, a list of all the categories of entry, together with the specific 'maintenance and accommodation' requirements which apply to each one, can be found in the tables in Appendix 4 and Appendix 5.

It is prudent to state at the outset that it is a criminal offence for anyone to give immigration advice unless registered as an immigration adviser or exempt from the requirement to register.[3] Nonetheless, welfare benefits advisers often need to establish someone's immigration status before they can advise on benefit entitlement. They may also identify a need for immigration advice. Details of potential regulated advisers for referral can be found in Appendix 1.

1. Immigration control

The term '**immigration control**' refers to the system by which people's ability to enter, stay and live in the UK for different purposes is restricted and regulated by the government. Control particularly takes place by examining passengers at ports of entry into the UK and continues to operate after a person has been admitted to the country. The body largely responsible for immigration control is the Immigration and Nationality Directorate (IND), a part of the Home Office.

However, in many cases, immigration control begins overseas at designated posts – eg, at British embassies and high commissions. Visa sections at these posts are run by 'UK Visas' – a joint section of the Home Office and the Foreign and Commonwealth Office.

Some people are barely affected by immigration control and may freely come to, and go from, the UK without any restrictions. The largest group of people who fall into this category are those with the 'right of abode' in the UK (chiefly British citizens – see p5). Immigration control has its greatest impact on people who require specific permission (called 'entry clearance' and often referred to colloquially as a visa) to come to the UK. Rights, such as access to social security and employment, are very much determined by the immigration status that a person has as a result of immigration controls. There are other groups of people who are subjected only to reduced forms of immigration control or who enjoy certain advantages in relation to immigration control as a result of being nationals of certain countries other than the UK, or even the particular nature of their employment (see p6).

'Citizenship' or 'nationality' is connected, but not equivalent, to immigration status. In many countries nationality law determines whether a person may freely come to and go from the territory – ie, if the person is a national of the country s/he may freely come and go. The relationship between nationality law and immigration law in the UK is more complex because there are different classes of British national, some of which are greatly affected by immigration control (see Chapter 2).

Who is affected by immigration control

Everyone must undergo some form of examination by the immigration authorities when they arrive in the UK, but the extent of immigration control varies greatly between different groups. There are two main groups.

- Those who require specific permission to come into and stay in the UK; this permission is technically known as **leave to enter** and **leave to remain** in the UK and that is how we will refer to it (sometimes shortened simply to 'leave').

- Those who do not require leave to enter or remain.

The Immigration and Asylum Act 1999 introduced the use of the term '**persons who are subject to immigration control**' (PSIC).[4] The purpose of the creation of this category and associated definition is to determine entitlement to social security benefit and access to certain community care services (see p154). The group of people who are included within this definition is narrower than those who require leave to enter/remain in the UK. For this reason, we will only use the term 'subject to immigration control' when talking about access to welfare under this new definition. For immigration purposes, we will refer to those who require, and who do not require, leave to enter or remain in the UK, but you should be generally aware that the term may be used more loosely by other people. Home Office publications, for example, may refer to people being subject to immigration control when they require leave to enter the UK.[5]

Leave to *enter* is that leave given when a person is coming into the UK from another country whereas leave to *remain* is that given to those who have already entered. There is no practical difference between the two types of leave, the difference is simply in whether the leave was granted on entry or granted following entry.

In addition to granting or refusing leave, the immigration authorities can impose conditions and limitations (eg, access to work and time limits) on leave. They may also curtail leave and, in many circumstances, can enforce a person's departure (see Chapter 6) from the UK.

Movement within the common travel area

The Common Travel Area (CTA) consists of the UK, the 'Islands' (Channel Islands and the Isle of Man) and the Republic of Ireland.[6] Normal immigration control does not apply to journeys within the CTA and, as a result, leave is not generally required for such a journey. However, there are exceptions to this general rule of freedom of travel within the CTA. For example, people who simply pass through the Republic of Ireland on their way to the UK still need leave to enter the UK.[7] The existence of the CTA means that citizens of the Irish Republic may travel to the UK without requiring leave to enter.

2. **The effect of immigration control**

The right of abode in the UK

People who have the '**right of abode**' do not need leave to enter or remain in the UK. They are 'free to live in, and to come and go into and from, the United Kingdom without let or hindrance'.[8] They may stay in the UK for as long as they like and there are no conditions restricting what they may do while in the UK, although in certain circumstances, the power to deprive citizenship and the right of abode extends to cases where the Secretary of State for the Home Department (SSHD) is satisfied that deprivation is conducive to the public good.[9] Those with the right of abode are:[10]

- British citizens;
- certain citizens of Commonwealth countries (for a list of Commonwealth countries, see pxiii).

Commonwealth citizens who have the right of abode are those who, before 1 January 1983, were either:

- Commonwealth citizens with a parent born in the UK; *or*
- women who had become 'patrial' (see p21) through marriage.

For more information about nationality and the right of abode, see Chapter 2.

If you fall into one of these groups, you do not require leave to enter or remain in the UK. However, you are still required to undergo a very limited form of examination sufficient for you to demonstrate that you do hold the status claimed.[11] The passports of those who do not require leave to enter are routinely checked by immigration officers on entry to the UK.[12] You can prove that you have the right of abode by producing:[13]

- a UK passport describing you as a British citizen or as a citizen of the UK and Colonies having the right of abode in the UK; *or*
- a certificate of entitlement (see p108) issued by the UK government certifying that you have the right of abode.

People who do not have the right of abode in the UK

If you are not in one of the above groups (ie, with the right of abode), you generally need leave to enter or remain in the UK. This means that to enter or remain in the UK you must satisfy the requirements of the immigration rules. However, there are certain special groups of people, some of whom do not need leave to enter or remain, even though they do not have the right of abode (see below).

Special groups

No leave required

There are certain special groups of people who do not fit easily into the division between those who need leave and those who do not. The following groups do not need leave, but their ability to enter and remain without leave may depend upon their satisfying, or continuing to satisfy, certain conditions:

- nationals of states which are members of the European Economic Area (EEA) and Swiss nationals (see p7);
- family members of EU/EEA and Swiss nationals who would otherwise require leave to enter the UK (see p7);

- diplomats, embassy staff and others (see p8);
- armed forces personnel (see p8);
- ship and air crews (see p9).

EEA nationals and their family members

EEA nationals are nationals of countries which are members of the EU (Austria, Belgium, Bulgaria, Denmark, Finland, France, Germany, Greece, Ireland, Italy, Luxembourg, Netherlands, Portugal, Romania, Spain, Sweden, United Kingdom, Cyprus, the Czech republic, Estonia, Hungary, Latvia, Lithuania, Malta, Poland, Slovakia, Slovenia, Bulgaria and Romania) and nationals of Norway, Iceland and Liechtenstein. For freedom of movement purposes, Swiss nationals are also treated by EEA members as if Switzerland was also an EEA member. The source of the legal rights of EEA nationals to enter and remain in the UK derives ultimately from the EC Treaty and several EC Directives and not from UK domestic law. It is for this reason that the rights cannot be made subject to the need to obtain any permission (leave) from the immigration authorities before they can be exercised.[14] The residence directives have been consolidated in Directive 2004/38/EC, often referred to as the 'Citizens' Directive', and are transposed in the Immigration (European Economic Area) Regulations 2006.[15]

Generally, the **family members** of an EEA national (including nationals of a non-EEA country, known as 'third country' nationals) are the spouse/civil partner, the descendants (ie, children or grandchildren) of the EEA national or the EEA national's spouse or civil partner who are either under 21 years or, if over 21 years, dependent on the EEA national or her/his spouse/civil partner; and the dependent relatives in the *ascending* line (parents, grandparents) of the EEA national or her/his spouse or civil partner.[16] Other extended family members may also qualify (see p34).[17]

There is a right to reside in the UK for EEA nationals and family members for three months but after this, the right of residence is dependent upon the EEA national exercising rights of free movement which are recognized by EC law, namely as a workseeker, a worker, a self-employed person, a self-sufficient person or a student, or as a worker or self-employed person who has ceased activity. The regulations that implement (sic transpose) EEA freedom of movement rights refer to these EEA nationals as being *qualified persons*.[18] The right to reside has become much more important for EEA nationals and their family members since the changes to the benefit regulations introduced on 1 May 2004 (see Chapter 11). As from 1 May 2004, most workers from eight of the recent ascension countries (the A8 countries – the Czech republic, Estonia, Hungary, Latvia, Lithuania, Poland, Slovakia and Slovenia) are also required to register their first year of employment with the Home Office.[19] More restrictive provisions apply to nationals of the A2 countries (Bulgaria and Romania) as of 1 January 2007. People who would otherwise enjoy rights to reside or freedom or movement rights may be removed from the UK if they cease to be a qualified person or the family member of a qualified person and do not retain the right to reside[20] and they may also not be admitted to the UK, or removed, if the Secretary of State determines that such action is justified on the grounds of public policy, public security or public health.[21] Nationals of certain other countries may also seek to enter or remain in the UK in order to establish themselves in business pursuant to 'association agreements' agreed between the EU and those countries (see p381).

Diplomats and staff of embassies, high commissions and international agencies

Diplomats and certain staff of embassies and high commissions and their families who form part of their household are exempt from immigration controls and so do not require leave.[22] Unless you are actually a diplomat, you cannot benefit from this exemption unless you were out of the country when you were offered the position.[23]

There are further exemptions or partial exemptions from immigration control for:[24]

- consular officers or employees in the service of a foreign government;
- members of foreign governments or their representatives in the UK on official business;
- officials of international organisations such as the International Monetary Fund;
- people attending certain international conferences in the UK and certain Commonwealth officials.

In practical terms, if you fall into any of the above categories you are entitled to benefit from your exemption as soon as you arrive in the UK. However, the exemption only applies for as long as you retain the status for which it was granted.[25] If a person ceases to be exempt from control because, for example, s/he loses her/his job, then s/he is treated as having been granted a period of leave of 90 days from the date s/he ceased to be exempt[26] unless s/he, before becoming exempt, had an existing period of leave which would expire before the end of that 90-day period, in which case s/he is treated only as having that existing leave.[27] This provides the person with a period of grace in which to leave the UK without having remained in the UK unlawfully or to make an 'in-time' (see p41) application for further leave.

Armed forces

The following are exempt from all immigration controls except deportation:[28]

- members of UK armed forces;
- members of a Commonwealth or similar force undergoing training in the UK with the UK armed forces;
- members of a visiting force coming to the UK at the invitation of the government.

In addition, a person who wishes to return to the UK as a returning resident (ie, who had indefinite leave when s/he last left the UK) and who has been away accompanying her/his spouse on duty abroad where her/his spouse is a member of the armed forces, a diplomat or a member of the British Council, does not need to show that s/he has not been away from the UK for more than two years as other returning residents do.[29] Also, a person of any of the occupations listed above is treated as 'present and settled in the UK' (one of the requirements of the immigration rules relating to married couples) even though s/he is serving overseas, for the purposes of applications by her/his spouse for leave to enter, remain or settle in the UK.[30] A Gurkha or armed forces personnel discharged from HM forces after four years' service and her/his spouse/civil partner and children also qualify for settlement.[31]

Ship and air crews

If you arrive in the UK as a member of the crew of a ship or aircraft, hired or under orders to depart as part of that ship's crew or to depart on the same or another aircraft within seven days of arrival, then you may enter the UK without leave.[32] You may also remain in the UK without leave until the ship or aircraft is ready to leave. In order to be a crew member you must be employed to carry out functions necessary to the running of the ship or aircraft.[33]

You will not benefit from this exemption if:[34]
- there is a deportation order against you;
- you have, at any time, been refused leave to enter the UK and have not since been given leave to enter or remain in the UK; *or*
- an immigration officer requires you to submit to examination.

People who require leave but have certain immigration advantages

A second group of people require leave to enter or remain in the UK but due to their nationality, place of birth or employment, enjoy certain advantages in immigration control. They are:
- British nationals who are not British citizens. Not everyone who possesses British nationality has the right of abode (see p6) which comes only with British citizenship. Other British nationals have to obtain leave but they do have certain immigration advantages (see Chapter 2);
- non-visa nationals (see below);
- nationals of certain countries (see p10);
- non-British citizen children born in Britain on or after 1 January 1983 (see p11).

Non-visa nationals

The immigration rules distinguish between **visa nationals**, who require prior 'entry clearance' obtained overseas in order to come to the UK in any category (ie, for any purpose) and **non-visa nationals**, who do not require entry clearance if they are planning to enter the UK for a period of less than six months (eg, as a visitor or short-term student), or for a purpose for which entry clearance is not required under the relevant immigration rule. Entry clearance is now required in all other circumstances even for non-visa nationals.[35] The list of visa national countries changes from time to time and is to be found in Appendix 1 to the immigration rules themselves.[36] A current list is in Appendix 7.

Nationals of certain countries

Depending upon the category in which you seek to enter, the requirements for admission can vary according to nationality. So, in certain circumstances, a national of one country may be in a better position than a national of another country. EEA nationals, of course, benefit from European rights of free movement as discussed on p7. These other circumstances are very much the exception rather than the rule.

- Admission for an au pair placement can only be granted under the rules to citizens of Andorra, Bosnia-Herzegovina, Croatia, the Faroes, Greenland, Macedonia, Monaco, San Marino and Turkey.[37]
- Admission in the capacity of 'working holidaymaker' is only open to nationals in Appendix 3 of the immigration rules and to British nationals without the right of abode.
- If a Commonwealth citizen wishes to seek employment, then s/he may be admitted on the basis of her/his having a grandparent who was born in the UK, thereby avoiding the far more restrictive rules relating to work permits for other people who require leave to enter and remain.[38]
- Nationals of Bulgaria and Romania (and their dependants) may have been granted leave to enter or remain in the UK under the immigration rules as people establishing themselves in business, in self-employment or partnership and have yet to be granted indefinite leave. Nationals of these countries may also have obtained leave to establish themselves in a company which they control.[39] The source of these rights, although they are written into the immigration rules, is EC law in the form of 'association agreements' made between the EC and those countries. There are also other association agreements which give nationals of certain other countries less valuable immigration benefits and which are not referred to in the immigration rules.
- Nationals of Turkey can benefit from an association agreement which is very differently worded to those for Bulgaria and Romania. If certain criteria are satisfied, the agreement, often referred to as the 'Ankara Agreement', progressively extends the right to work in the UK, and with it the right to stay in the UK, to Turkish nationals who have otherwise obtained lawful access to the labour market or have established themselves in self-employment or business.[40] However, it provides for no right of entry for the worker concerned as opposed to those seeking entry for self-employment.

There are rights to enter the UK for business purposes under the immigration rules which nationals of *all* countries can use, but they are more restrictive – eg, they require that the applicant has £200,000 to invest in the business.

Non-British citizen children born in Britain on or after 1 January 1983

Since the British Nationality Act 1981 came into force on 1 January 1983, certain children (see p25) born in the UK are not automatically born British citizens. They therefore require leave to enter and remain in the UK. If they were to leave the UK, they may seek leave to enter to accompany or join a parent and do not have to satisfy the usual maintenance and immigration requirements.[41] Alternatively, they may qualify for re-entry under the ordinary provisions of the immigration rules if they wished to return. However, because they have never actually been granted leave to remain they cannot be:

- removed from the UK as 'overstayers' or as in breach of their conditions of leave;[42] *or*
- removed from the UK as a person who has been refused leave to enter or as an illegal entrant.[43]

These people can, however, be forced to leave the UK if they are removed as part of the family to which they belong.[44]

For more details about enforcement of immigration controls, removal and deportation, see Chapter 6.

---

3. **How immigration control operates**

This section is relevant to people who require leave to enter/remain in the UK (for who requires leave, see Chapter 4). It summarises the basic mechanics of immigration control, the decision making process and the personnel involved at different stages of the immigration process. Further details of relevant immigration controls and how they operate in practice are given in Chapter 3.

Types of leave

There are two kinds of leave:[45]

- limited leave to enter or remain (meaning limited in terms of time – eg, six months or two years);
- indefinite leave to enter or remain (with no restriction on time).

Depending on your circumstances, it is probable that certain conditions will be attached to your limited leave to enter or remain. The conditions may relate to:[46]

- your employment or occupation;

- maintaining yourself in the UK 'without recourse to public funds' (see p84);
- registering with the police.[47]

No conditions may be attached to indefinite leave.[48]

Personnel

The main office of the Immigration and Nationality Directorate of the Home Office (IND) is in Croydon,[49] but the IND also has regional offices in Leeds, Liverpool, Solihull and Glasgow. The officers who work there are all ultimately responsible to the Secretary of State for the Home Department. The following personnel play a significant part in the system of immigration control:

- **Entry clearance officers** are stationed in overseas posts with responsibility for control prior to entry. They are responsible for issuing entry clearance (visas) to those who wish to come to the UK. Following changes made by the Immigration and Asylum Act 1999 (see p14), entry clearance now qualifies as leave to enter when a person arrives in the UK. Entry clearance officers are also responsible for issuing family permits to family members of European Economic Area (EEA) nationals who want to come to the UK and certificates of entitlement to the right of abode.

- **Immigration officers**, including chief immigration officers and immigration inspectors. They are generally responsible for 'on entry' immigration control and are mainly to be found at the ports of entry into the UK.[50] Following changes made by the 1999 Act (see p14), immigration officers may grant a person leave to enter before s/he has actually arrived in the UK. Immigration officers also have wide powers of detention. They may detain people after their arrival in the UK while a decision is made as to whether leave should be granted and they may detain people who are in the process of being removed from the UK.[51] Connected to their powers of detention, immigration officers are also largely responsible for actually operating the process of enforcing the departure from the UK of those who cannot show that they have any entitlement to remain. There are different enforcement procedures which depend upon the category into which the case falls. Immigration officers may 'remove' those refused leave to enter (see p71), those unlawfully in the UK (see p74) and 'illegal entrants' (see p74). In a separate enforcement procedure called 'deportation' (see p71), immigration officers can make initial decisions to deport people on behalf of the Secretary of State,[52] but the later making of the deportation order itself is the responsibility of the Secretary of State. Immigration officers also have powers in relation to suspected immigration criminal offences. They may exercise powers of arrest without warrant and, with a warrant issued by a magistrate, may enter and search premises and search suspects.[53]

- **The Secretary of State** and her/his officers at the Home Office are, in general, responsible for immigration control after entry (see p41).[54] Applications for extensions of leave to remain in the UK after a person has already entered are generally determined by the Secretary of State.[55] The Secretary of State is also responsible for:
  - considering whether there are sufficient compassionate factors to enable those who have overstayed their leave (see p71) or have breached conditions of their leave (see p73) or who are liable to deportation (see p71) to remain in the UK and for deciding whether a deportation order may be revoked;[56]
  - the detention and removal of those who are being forced to leave the UK by the deportation process;[57]
  - making the immigration rules (see p15).[58]
- **Officials at Work Permits (UK)** are responsible for issuing work permits under the various work permit schemes to those who are not nationals of an EEA country and who would otherwise not be entitled to work in the UK.[59] Work permits are not entry clearances or grants of leave, so once a work permit has been obtained a separate application for entry clearance or leave to remain will be necessary.[60]
- **The Lord Chancellor** is responsible for the appointment of personnel of the Asylum and Immigration Tribunal which hears and decides immigration appeals[61] and is also responsible for making rules of procedure for immigration appeals.[62]
- **Immigration Judges and Senior Immigration Judges in the Asylum and Immigration Tribunal** (appointed as above) are responsible for hearing and determining appeals on decisions of entry clearance officers, immigration officers and the Secretary of State.
- **Asylum support adjudicators** are responsible for determining appeals against decisions refusing all asylum support under the National Asylum Support Service (NASS).[63]
- **Home Office presenting officers** are appointed by the Secretary of State and are responsible for presenting the case for the Home Office at immigration and asylum appeals.
- **Home Office case owners** are responsible for deciding new asylum applications and also represent the Home Office in asylum appeals.
- **Police officers** are responsible for the registration of certain people who require leave to enter and remain in the UK,[64] the arrest of people suspected of having committed criminal offences under immigration law[65] and the arrest and detention of people who are liable to be detained in order to enforce their departure from the UK under immigration law.[66]
- **Detainee custody officers** are a class of officers created by the 1999 Act[67] who, as well as immigration officers, prison officers, prison custody officers and the police, have functions relating to holding people who may be detained in custody under immigration law and escorting them from one place to another.

- **NASS officers**, acting on behalf of the Secretary of State, are responsible for making decisions on asylum support. Similarly local authority officers are responsible for making decisions on interim support under the interim scheme of asylum support.[68] It is intended that Home Office case workers (known as case owners) will make decisions on NASS when the New Asylum Model is fully operational.

Immigration legislation

The Immigration Act 1971 contains the basic provisions setting out the framework for immigration control. Subsequent Acts of Parliament, the Immigration Act 1988, Asylum and Immigration Appeals Act 1993, Asylum and Immigration Act 1996, Immigration and Asylum Act 1999, Nationality, Immigration and Asylum Act 2002, Asylum and Immigration (Treatment of Claimants, etc) Act 2004, Immigration, Asylum and Nationality Act 2006 and other legislation passed since 1971 have substantially modified the 1971 Act and have added many new aspects.

The main provisions of the newest legislation, the Immigration, Asylum and Nationality Act 2006, are:

- the withdrawal of all entry clearance appeal rights save for family visitors, those classed as 'dependants' (this group is currently unclear) or those that raise human rights or race discrimination issues;
- the withdrawal of all remaining in-country appeal rights to those without entry clearance refused leave to enter on arrival (except for asylum appeals) and most out of country appeal rights to those refused leave to enter as well, except for those that raise human rights or race discrimination issues;
- the withdrawal of an in-country appeal right dealing with the national security aspects of a deportation appeal – an in-country appeal right will remain for the human rights aspects of the appeal unless the Home Secretary certifies the individual's human rights will not be breached. In these latter circumstances an appeal will lie to the Special Immigration Appeals Commission;
- the introduction of a civil penalty for employing persons illegally and an on-going obligation to check the status of employees;
- new powers to fingerprint those not detained, detain embarking passengers for up to 12 hours and for private contractors to search and detain at ports;
- the extension of grounds upon which people can be deprived of citizenship;
- the application of a requirement of 'good character' to all applications for registration.

However, at the time of writing many of these provisions have not yet been introduced and the commencement dates are still unknown.

In January 2007 the UK Borders Bill was introduced. The main features of this proposed legislation are:

- new powers for immigration officers including the ability to:

- arrest smugglers or traffickers even if their crimes were committed outside of the UK;
- detain at ports individuals they suspect of having committed a crime or those with a warrant outstanding against them;
- arrest those they believe to have fraudulently been acquiring asylum support, and to exercise associated powers of entry, search and seizure;
- access Her Majesty's Revenue and Customs data to track down illegal immigrants;
- additional obligations for foreign nationals living in the UK including:
  - having to apply for a 'biometric immigration document' – a compulsory biometric identification for those living in the UK from outside the EEA – helping tackle fraud, illegal working and multiple identities; *and*
  - failure to obtain biometric identification will put the person at risk of losing their leave to remain in the UK and/or a civil penalty of up to £1,000;
- further restrictions on the rights of foreign national prisoners including:
  - facing automatic deportation if they have committed a serious offence (eg, crimes against children, terrorism or drugs offences) and been sentenced to imprisonment or any other offences which resulted in a custodial sentence of 12 months or more; *and*
  - no longer having the right to appeal from within the UK except under very specific circumstances.

The immigration rules

Decisions as to whether or not a person who requires leave:
- should be granted leave to enter or remain in the UK;
- upon what conditions and for how long; *and*
- should be required to leave the UK,

are generally made according to the immigration rules made under the Immigration Act 1971.

The 'immigration rules' are not *legislation* but rules of practice. The rules themselves are made by the Secretary of State and put before Parliament for approval.[69] The Secretary of State frequently issues statements of amendment to the rules and sometimes re-issues the whole of the rules in a different form. The last complete statement of the rules was laid before Parliament on 23 May 1994 and is referred to as 'HC 395'. Those rules came into effect, with transitional provisions for applications made prior to that date, on 1 October 1994.[70] Unlike social security regulations, which are legislation, the immigration rules are drafted in an informal style and the words used must be given their most natural and ordinary meaning.[71]

The rules chiefly set out:

- a series of 'requirements' which a person needs to satisfy in order to be granted entry clearance or leave in any particular category – eg, as a student, visitor or as a refugee (see p51 for an example);
- a set of additional general considerations for determining whether a person should be granted entry clearance or leave to enter the UK in any category;
- the length of time for which a person may expect to be admitted in any category and the conditions which a person is likely to have attached to her/ his leave if granted;
- the process and criteria for deciding whether a person who has breached immigration control should be required to leave the UK; *and*
- which people are required to satisfy the 'maintenance and accommodation' requirements (see p84).

Immigration decisions outside the rules

Certain people are admitted or allowed entry outside the rules. The rules represent the minimum standard of treatment that a person may expect and must be applied by entry clearance officers/immigration officers.[72] However, the Home Office has the discretion to waive any of the requirements of the rules (and to authorise immigration officers and entry clearance officers to do likewise), and therefore to treat any person more favourably than the strict letter of the rules requires. A person who is treated in this special way, is said to be granted leave 'exceptionally'. Leave may be granted exceptionally to a whole range of people in different circumstances who cannot fit the normal requirements of the rules. Exceptional leave can be limited or indefinite. The term **'exceptional leave'** was also used more narrowly to describe leave which was given to a person who had applied for, but been refused, refugee status but was granted leave because the Home Office determined it would not be right to require that person to return to her/his country. Such individuals are now granted either humanitarian protection or discretionary leave to remain (see Chapter 5).

Notes

1 Parts 2-8 HC 395
2 It is important to ensure that any guidance published by these organisations is up to date as immigration law changes constantly. See www.ukvisas.gov.uk, www.ind.homeoffice.gov.uk, www.iasuk.org and www.jcwi.org.uk.
3 Part V IAA 1999

1. Immigration control
4 ss115(3) and (9) and 116-117 IAA 1999
5 See, eg, Immigration and Nationality Directorate website at IDI's Chapter 1, Section 1, paragraph 1
6 s1(3) IA 1971
7 For details of these categories, see s9(4) and (6) IA 1971 and I(CERI)O 1972 (as amended) and para 15 HC 395

2. The effect of immigration control
8 s1(1) IA 1971
9 s57 IANA 2006 replacing s40(2) BNA 1981
10 s2(1) IA 1971 as substituted by s39(2) BNA 1981
11 s3(8) IA 1971; paras 12-13 HC 395
12 s1(1) and Sch 2 paras 2-4 IA 1971
13 s3(8-9) IA 1971
14 s7 IA 1988; R v Pieck C–157/79 [1981] QB 571
15 The Immigration (European Economic Area) Regulations 2006 (SI No.1003)
16 Reg 7 I(EEA) Regs. However if the EEA national is a student, 'family members' are restricted to spouse or civil partner and children: reg 7(2) I(EEA) Regs
17 Reg 10 I(EEA) Regs implementing Art 10(2) EEC Reg 1612/68 and Art 1(2) Dir 73/148/EEC
18 Reg 5 I(EEA) Regs
19 The Ascession (Immigration and Workers Registration) Regulations 2004 (No.1219)
20 Reg 19(3)(a) I(EEA) Regs
21 Regs 19(3)(b) and 21 I(EEA) Regs
22 s8(3) IA 1971; Diplomatic Privileges Act 1964; International Organisations (Immunities and Privileges) Act 1950; International Organisations Act 1968; Commonwealth Secretariat Act 1966 and associated Orders in Council

23 s8(3A) IA 1971 inserted by s6 IAA 1999
24 s8(2) IA 1971; I(EC)O 1972 as amended
25 s8(3) IA 1971
26 s8A(2) IA 1971 inserted by s7 IAA 1999
27 s8A(3) and 8(5) IA 1971 inserted by s7 IAA 1999
28 s8(4) and (6) IA 1971; see also IDIs ch 15
29 para 19A HC 395 inserted by para 6 Cmnd 4581
30 para 281 HC 395 as amended by para 30 Cmnd 4581. From 15.3.05, paras 276AD-276AH also provide for 4 years' leave to enter to be granted to spouses, civil partners and children of exempt armed forces members.
31 paras 276E-276K HC 395 with effect from 25.10.04
32 s8(1) IA 1971
33 s33(1) IA 1971 and Diestel [1976] Imm AR 51 see also IDIs chap 16
34 s8(1) IA 1971
35 para 24 HC395
36 Appendix 1 HC 395
37 paras 88-90 HC 395
38 paras 186-193 HC 395
39 paras 222, dependants at paras 240-245 HC 395
40 Ankara Agreement, 12 September 1963 and Decisions 2/76, 1/80, 3/80 of the Association Council made under the Agreement. A useful explanation is found in the JCWI Handbook 2006 edn pp585-590.
41 paras 304-308 HC 395
42 s10 IAA 1999
43 Sch 2 paras 8 and 9 IA 1971
44 s3(5)(b) IA 1971, s10(1)(c) IAA 1999

3. How immigration control operates
45 s3(1)(b) IA 1971
46 s3(1)(c) IA 1971
47 paras 325-326 HC 395; Immigration (Registration with Police) Regs 1972; and see list of countries/territories whose nationals are required to register with the police in Appendix 2 HC 395
48 s3(1)(c) IA 1971
49 For addresses and telephone numbers of relevant Home Office Sections see JCWI Handbook
50 s4(1) IA 1971
51 Sch 2 IA 1971

52 *R v SSHD ex parte Oladehinde* [1991] AC 254
53 ss28A-K IA 1971 as inserted by ss136-139 IAA 1999
54 s4(1) IA 1971
55 para 32 HC 395
56 paras 364-395D HC 395
57 Sch 3 paras 1 and 2 1971 Act
58 s3(2) IA 1971
59 paras 116-121 and 128-135 HC 395
60 s33(1) IA 1971
61 s81 and Sch 4 NIAA 2002
62 Sch 4 paras 3-4 IAA 1999
63 ss102-103 and Sch 10 IAA 1999
64 s4(3) IA 1971
65 s24(2) IA 1971
66 Sch 2 para 17 and Sch 3 para 2(4) IA 1971
67 s154 IAA 1999
68 Part VI and Schs 8-9 IAA 1999
69 ss1(4) and 3(2) IA 1971
70 para 4 HC 395
71 See *ECO Bombay v Stanley Walter De Noronha* [1995] Imm AR 341
72 Sch 2 para 1(3) IA 1971 and Sch 4 para 21(1)(a) IAA 1999; *R v SSHD ex parte Hosenball* [1977] 1 WLR 766; *Pearson v IAT* [1978] Imm AR 212

Chapter 2

Nationality

This chapter covers:
1. Types of British nationality (below)
2. Ways of acquiring British citizenship (p23)
3. Deprivation of British citizenship and the right of abode (p29)

1. Types of British nationality

Nationality law has evolved considerably in the UK over the last century, which is one reason for its present complexity. Therefore, this *brief* outline of the history and present nationality provisions will necessarily omit detail. The Home Office guidance on the application of nationality law, in particular instructions on the exercise of discretion in naturalisation or registration decisions, is given in the Nationality Instructions (NIs), which can be found on the Immigration and Nationality Directorate website (www.ind.homeoffice.gov.uk). NIs should be consulted for up-to-date information on requirements and discretionary criteria. However, in complex cases, specialist legal advice should be sought.

The right of abode

A key concept in nationality law is the 'right of abode'. The Immigration Act 1971 describes the right of abode as the right to live in and come and go from the UK without hindrance, save for the controls, such as the examination of passports, which are necessary to establish those rights.[1] Those without the right of abode are subject to immigration control, which means they are subject to domestic United Kingdom (UK) immigration control or to the limitations and entitlements conferred by European Community law.

Types of British national[2]

Confusingly, British nationality and British citizenship are not synonymous. There are actually six different forms of British nationality, only one of which is British citizenship. Not all forms of British nationality attract the right of abode in the UK.
- British citizens (BC);

- British overseas territories citizens (BOTC);
- British subjects;
- British protected persons (BPP);
- British nationals (overseas) (BNO);
- British overseas citizens (BOC).

Some of these forms of nationality are very unusual and will eventually disappear, as they cannot be transferred from one generation to the next. The existence of these more esoteric forms of nationality can be ascribed to the complex imperial and post-imperial legacy of the UK.

1948 to 1981

Before 1948 people were divided into three groups. Then, as now, the last two groups had no 'right of abode' in the UK.
- British subjects – born in a territory belonging to the Crown, including the UK;
- BPPs – aliens under the protection of the Crown;
- aliens – non-British subjects.

With the implementation of the British Nationality Act 1948, people were divided into five groups:
- citizens of the United Kingdom and colonies (CUKC) – people born in, or connected with, the UK or a Crown colony;[3]
- Commonwealth citizens – people born in, or connected with, a Commonwealth country which became independent from the UK and who then became citizens of the newly independent country. CUKC status would normally be lost when the colony became independent;
- British subjects without citizenship (BSWC) – people who did not become citizens of the Commonwealth country in which they lived;
- BPPs;
- aliens.

Until 1962, CUKCs, Commonwealth citizens and BSWCs continued to be considered 'British subjects' and therefore had the right of abode and they could freely enter, live and work in the UK. However, the Commonwealth Immigrants Acts of 1962 and 1968 affected the immigration position of CUKCs and Commonwealth citizens. The 1962 Act gave rights of entry to people who had British passports issued in the UK or issued on behalf of the UK government abroad, but denied Commonwealth citizens free entry to the UK. Under the 1968 Act CUKCs who did not have parents or grandparents born in the UK lost the automatic right of entry to the UK. Holding a British passport no longer gave an automatic right to enter and live in Britain. One of the most controversial effects of this legislation was to deny entry to the UK to large numbers of East African Asians who had CUKC status.[4]

The Immigration Act 1971 introduced the concept of 'patriality'. Patrials had the right of abode in the UK and therefore did not require leave to enter or remain, meaning they could come and go to and from the UK freely. Most of the people who obtained patrial status were CUKCs, although some Commonwealth citizens also qualified.[5] Patrial status could derive from the person's ancestry, the nature and duration of their residence in the UK, how their CUKC status was obtained and, for certain women, the status of their husband. The 1971 Act separated 'nationality' from the right of abode and, with it, the right to enter the UK freely.

British Nationality Act 1981

The British Nationality Act 1981 came into force on 1 January 1983. It abolished the status of CUKC and created three new types of nationals out of patrial and non-patrial CUKCs:[6]
- British citizens – ie, partial CUKCs (with the right of abode);
- British dependent territories citizens (BDTC) – ie, non-patrial CUKCs who had a connection with a place which continued to be a colony or 'dependent territory' (now BOTC);
- BOC – ie, non-patrial CUKCs whose connection was with a place which had ceased to be a British dependent territory by 1983.

Under the 1981 Act, British citizens have the 'right of abode'.[7] Until 1 January 1983, some non-patrial CUKCs were entitled to patrial status and obtained the right of abode after five years' ordinary residence in the UK.[8] Non-British citizen British nationals (eg, some CUKC, BPP and British subjects without citizenship resident in the UK for five years) have the right to register as British citizens if they satisfy certain conditions.[9]

Commonwealth citizens who were patrial on 1 January 1983 by virtue of having a parent born in the UK or because they were women married to partials were classed simply as Commonwealth citizens with the right of abode in the UK.[10] After 1 January 1983, a Commonwealth woman marrying a British citizen did not have the right of abode.

Anyone born abroad after 1 January 1983 who would have qualified for the right of abode as a result of parentage, became a British citizen 'by descent'.[11]

Developments since the 1981 Act

Since the 1981 Act, there have been significant developments in British nationality law. However, these changes have generally been introduced by legislation dealing with the 'status' of people from specific 'territories' or, as nationality and immigration law becomes increasingly entwined, changes have been part of general immigration legislative provision. Most recent changes to nationality law and procedure have focused upon exclusion from and deprivation of citizenship.

- Following the war in the Falkland Islands in 1983, legislation was introduced which converted most people born in the Falklands from BDTCs to British citizens by birth.[12]

- Before Hong Kong was returned to the People's Republic of China in 1997, Hong Kong's BDTCs had the chance to register as a new type of national, BNOs.[13] In 1997, status as a BDTC ended for those living in Hong Kong, but BNOs were able to continue to use British travel documents and were able to register as British citizens following five years' residence and having achieved settled status in the UK.[14] Others, who were ordinarily resident in Hong Kong in 1997, and who would have become stateless except for their British nationality, were also permitted to register as British citizens.[15]

- The Secretary of State also registered as British citizens 50,000 residents of Hong Kong who were 'heads of households'.[16] Selection was carried out by the Governor of Hong Kong under the provisions of a well-publicised scheme.[17]

- The British Overseas Territories Act 2002 re-designated BDTCs as BOTCs and stated that all those who were BOTCs when the relevant parts of the Act came into force, would automatically become British citizens with the right of abode.[18] The result is that, anyone who was a BOTC (formally BDTC) on 21 May 2002, became a British citizen.[19] The dependencies themselves have been re-named as 'British Overseas Territories'. These territories are as follows: Anguilla, Bermuda, British Antarctic Territory, British Indian Ocean Territory, British Virgin Islands, Cayman Islands, Falkland Islands, Gibraltar, Montserrat, Pitcairn Islands, St Helena and Dependencies, South Georgia and the South Sandwich Islands, the Turks and Caicos Islands and the Cyprus Sovereign Base Areas of Akrotiri and Dhekelia. However, BOTCs from the Cyprus Sovereign Base Areas do *not* obtain British citizenship under the Act.

Dual nationality

A '**dual national**' is a person who is simultaneously a national of two countries. Some countries (eg, Malaysia) do not allow dual nationality so some people are forced to choose between being a national of one country or a national of another. UK nationality law does not prevent a person from being both a British national and a national of another country.

Special voucher scheme

The special voucher scheme was introduced at the same time as the Commonwealth Immigrants Act 1968 and applied to BOCs. There was an annual quota which caused long waiting lists. There were no formal rules stating who would qualify for a voucher. In practice, the applicant had to: have no other nationality available to her/him; be under pressure to leave the country in which s/he was resident (this has mainly applied to people living in East and Central Africa and people who left those countries to go to India); and be the head of a household (married women are excluded). Under the scheme, if you were a BOC, you could be admitted to the UK for an indefinite period if you had been issued with a 'special voucher' by the immigration authorities.[20] Your spouse and children were also allowed to join you if you could maintain and accommodate them without recourse to public funds.[21] On 5 March 2002, the scheme was abolished without notice and applications for vouchers on or after that date would not be considered. Although the Home Secretary subsequently acknowledged that the UK has a moral obligation towards BOCs, it is known that deportation orders were enforced against BOCs in the mid 1990s. Following changes which came into force on 30 April 2003, in certain defined circumstances, a BOC may now have an entitlement to register as a British citizen.[22]

British nationals, the right of abode and immigration law

As explained above, the possession of British nationality may or may not confer the 'right of abode'. British citizens and some Commonwealth citizens, as defined in the Immigration Act 1971, have the right of abode.

British citizens have the right of abode in the UK and, therefore, on proof of their status, may freely enter the UK and do not require leave to enter or to remain in the UK (see Chapter 1). Other British nationals may have obtained the right of abode. Some British nationals who do not have the right of abode, although they must generally satisfy the various provisions of the immigration rules may have certain advantages over foreign nationals. For example, BOCs granted indefinite leave to enter or remain in the UK by the immigration authorities any time after 1 March 1968 can leave the UK and qualify for indefinite leave to enter on their return. They do not have to satisfy the 'returning residents' rule which applies to those who left the UK when they had indefinite leave.[23]

Any national of the non-British citizen types is entitled to be freely admitted to the UK on production of a UK passport which was issued prior to 1 January 1973 in the UK, Channel Islands, the Isle of Man or Republic of Ireland. The only exceptions are those people whose passports are endorsed to show that they were subject to immigration control and required leave.[24]

2. Ways of acquiring British citizenship

In addition to those who have 'acquired' British citizenship by virtue of the entitlements conferred on them by legislative changes affecting their status (see above), citizenship may be acquired in the following ways:

- birth;
- naturalisation;
- registration.

The *way* in which British citizenship is obtained is important as it determines whether you can pass on your citizenship to your children.

- If you were born abroad and, therefore, acquired British citizenship because of the nationality of your parents (referred to as 'British citizens by descent' in the British Nationality Act 1981), you cannot automatically pass on your citizenship to your own children if they are born abroad.
- If you obtain your citizenship by birth, registration, naturalisation (British citizens otherwise than by descent), you can automatically pass on your citizenship to your children even if they are born abroad although this citizenship passes for one generation only (special provisions are made for children born to those living abroad who are working for the government).[25]
- British overseas citizens, British subjects and British protected persons cannot generally pass on their citizenship.

British citizenship and birth

There are two main factors determining British citizenship according to birth:
- whether you were born before or after 1 January 1983, the date when the British Nationality Act 1981 came into force;
- whether you were born inside or outside the UK.

Born before 1 January 1983

Born in the UK

Children born before 1 January 1983 in the UK are British citizens, as are those who were adopted in the UK by a British parent. Only children born to diplomats and enemy aliens at times of war did not become British citizens.[26]

Born outside the UK

- Children born overseas to British fathers became British citizens if, at the time of the birth, the father was a citizen of the United Kingdom and colonies (CUKC) otherwise than by descent and the parents were married. The father must have registered or naturalised.
- Children born overseas to a British mother and non-British father (or to a British father who was not married to the child's mother) would not become British citizens, but the government has allowed such mothers to register their children as British citizens provided they do this before the child is 18. The last registrations under this provision, therefore, occurred at the end of 2000 (ie, 18 years from 1 January 1983).
- Children born in non-Commonwealth countries whose father's father was British otherwise than by descent are British provided the birth was registered at a British consulate within a year of the birth.

Born on or after 1 January 1983

Born in the UK (or in the British overseas territories, save in Cyprus, since 21 May 2002)

- Children born in the UK after 1 January 1983 are only British citizens if, at the time of their birth, one parent is either a British citizen or is settled (ie, ordinarily resident with no restriction on their stay[27] in the UK).[28] People who are resident in the UK and have indefinite leave are normally accepted as being 'settled'.
- Children adopted under an adoption order made in the UK also become British citizens if either of the adoptive parents are British citizens.[29]
- A child will be a British citizen even if the parent upon whose citizenship the child relies dies prior to the child's birth.[30]
- Children born in the UK who are not British citizens can apply to 'register' as British citizens after they have been in the UK for 10 years or after either of their parents obtains settled status.
- Children who do not have the nationality of any other country and are not born British are stateless. For the immigration position of children born in the UK who are not British, see p28.

'**Parent**' for these purposes always included the mother but excluded the father if he was not married to the mother at the time that the child was born.[31] Section 9 of the Nationality, Immigration and Asylum Act 2002, which came into force on 1 July 2006, abolished this discrimination against the children of unmarried parents born after the commencement date. The Secretary of State may (and does) exercise discretion under section 3(1) of the British Nationality Act 1981 to register as a British citizen the illegitimate child born before 1 July 2006 of a British father. Since March 2000 there has been a policy to register such children where the Home Office is satisfied as to paternity and that the father is British, that there is consent of both parents and that the conditions for registration would have been met if the child had been legitimate, including there being no reason to refuse on character grounds.[32] It is important to note that this policy refers only to British fathers and excludes settled fathers.

Born outside the UK

- Children born outside the UK on or after 1 January 1983 are British citizens by descent if either their father or their mother:
  - is a British citizen by birth, registration or naturalisation (ie, otherwise than by descent);[33] *or*
  - was a CUKC and gained the right of abode by living in the UK for five years or more before 1 January 1983.
- Children born abroad to parents who are themselves British citizens by descent[34] do not generally become British citizens. These children have certain

rights, but the law is complex. Expert advice should be sought in these circumstances.

Applying for citizenship

You may be able to acquire British citizen status either by 'naturalisation' or by 'registration'. If you apply to naturalise, the decision whether or not to grant citizenship will always be discretionary although, in practice, if you meet certain conditions citizenship will be granted. If you apply for registration and satisfy the relevant specified conditions, the Home Office will normally grant you British citizenship, subject to a new good character test introduced under the Immigration, Asylum and Nationality Act 2006 (IANA 2006). However, other forms of registration are discretionary – eg, the registration of the illegitimate child of a British father (see p25).

Applications are made on forms specific to the applicant's circumstances. For example, Form AN(NEW) is for applications for naturalisation as a British citizen under section 6 BNA 1981 and Form MN1 is the application form for the registration of a minor as a British citizen under sections 1(3), 3(1), 3(2), 3(5) BNA 1981. The application forms are available, with guidance notes, on the IND website (www.ind.homeoffice.gov.uk). An application should always be accompanied by the supporting documentation specified in the guidance and the required fee.

Naturalisation

You can apply to the Home Office to be naturalised as a British citizen if you are an adult (over 18) and fulfil all of the following criteria relating to settlement, length of residence, language and knowledge of life in the UK, future intentions and good character.[35]

There are two principal categories of application for naturalisation:
- based on five years' residence in the UK (at least one of which is with no restrictions on your leave to remain, which would usually mean indefinite leave to remain (ILR));
- based on marriage or registered civil partnership to a British citizen and residence in the UK.

Five years' residence

The following requirements must be satisfied:
- you must be of full age (18 or over);
- you must be of 'full capacity';
- there are special provisions for those in Crown Service outside the UK, but in general the following residence requirements must be satisfied:
  - you must have been settled in the UK (usually meaning you must have ILR) for at least a year prior to the date of your application;

- you must have been lawfully in the UK at the beginning of the period of five years ending on the date of the application and have lived lawfully in the UK without absences of more than 450 days over the course of that five year period and, in all cases, not more than 90 days of absence in the 12 months ending on the date of application;
- you must be of good character – among other matters, criminal convictions may be taken into account;
- you must have sufficient knowledge of English, Welsh or Scottish Gaelic and sufficient knowledge of life in the UK (see below);
- you must intend to have your home in the UK.

Marriage or civil partnership

The following requirements must be satisfied:
- you must be of full age (18 or over);
- you must be of 'full capacity';
- you must be married to, or have formed a civil partnership with, a British citizen;
- there are special provisions for those in Crown Service outside the UK, but in general the following residence requirements must be satisfied:
  - you must have been lawfully in the UK at the beginning of the period of three years ending on the date of the application and have lived lawfully in the UK without absences of more than 270 days in that three year period and, in all cases, not more than 90 days of absence in 12 months ending on the date of application;
  - you must not be subject to any restrictions on your stay on the date of application (again, usually meaning you must possess ILR);
- you must be of good character – among other matters, criminal convictions may be taken into account;
- you must have sufficient knowledge of English, Welsh or Scottish Gaelic and sufficient knowledge of life in the UK (see below);
- you must intend to have your home in the UK.

Knowledge of life in the UK

It is now necessary to demonstrate knowledge of life in the UK when applying for naturalisation. There are two routes to fulfilling this requirement:
- sit and pass the *Life in the UK* test. This is based on a publication called *Life in the United Kingdom: A Journey to Citizenship*. The test focuses on Chapters 2, 3 and 4. 24 questions have to be answered in 45 minutes at one of 90 test centres across the UK. Details are available from www.lifeintheuktest.gov.uk.
- successfully undertake an ESOL (English for Speakers of Other Languages) with citizenship course. If you feel you do not possess the necessary language skills to sit the *Life in the UK* test, you can instead undertake this course with one of many course providers across the UK.

The Home Office also retains discretion to waive the requirement in exceptional circumstances – eg, because of age or physical or mental condition.

Citizenship ceremonies

If you apply to naturalise after 1 January 2004 and the Secretary of State decides to grant you citizenship, you are informed of this decision and sent an invitation to attend a citizenship ceremony, normally within a three-month time limit and at your local town hall, to take the required oath or affirmation. The citizenship certificate is given at the ceremony. Exemptions are granted only in exceptional circumstances.

Registration

Since section 58 of the IANA 2006 came into force on 4 December 2006, registration is no longer automatically 'as of right'; the Home Office has a discretion to refuse applications on the grounds of the bad character of the applicant. This applies to both adult and minor applicants aged 10 or over. The following people can apply for registration:

- British nationals who are not British citizens who have had 'settled' status in the UK for a year or more can apply to register as British citizens if they have lived lawfully in the UK for five years.[36] During that time, they must not have been out of the UK for longer than 450 days in total nor for longer than 90 days in the last year.
- Non-British citizen children born in the UK can apply for registration as British citizens if, while they are still minors, one of their parents becomes settled.[37]
- A child born in the UK can be registered if s/he remains in the UK for 10 years and is not absent for more than 90 days in any one year.[38]
- Children born overseas to British citizens (who are British by descent) can register in one of two ways. However, other than in 'special' circumstances an application must be made within a year of birth unless the child and his/her parents have resided in the UK (or a 'qualifying territory') for three years.[39] Specialist advice should be sought if you are in this position.

The Home Office retains the discretion to register all other children.[40] As stated on p24, it has been Home Office policy to register those born abroad before 1 January 1983 to British-born mothers provided the application is made while the child is still a minor. The Home Office may also register children whose parents were not married at the time of their birth and were born before 1 July 2006 and therefore did not obtain citizenship through their British citizen father. It may also register a child who has been living in the UK for a substantial period of time depending on the child's immigration status, her/his connections with the UK and her/his parents' status.

Challenging decisions

From 7 November 2002, the Home Office should give written reasons for refusing all nationality decisions.[41] Where refusals do occur they are usually based on either failure to provide sufficient evidence that the requirements are met or on the grounds of bad character.

There is no right of appeal against the refusal of an application for naturalisation or registration. However, if, for example, it is clear that the Home Office has misapplied the law or stated policy on the exercise of discretion it is worth asking for a review of the decision. The only legal challenge is by way of an application for permission to apply for judicial review in the Administrative Court. Specialist legal advice should be sought on whether there is merit in such a claim.

3. Deprivation of British citizenship and the right of abode

You can lose British citizenship in the following ways:
- renunciation – ie, you renounce your citizenship where you are either a dual national or wish to obtain another nationality. The Secretary of State must be satisfied that you will obtain the nationality of the other country;[42]
- deprivation – ie, if you obtained it by registration or naturalisation or would not become stateless as a consequence, the Secretary of State can make an order depriving you of British citizenship.

Renunciation of citizenship

A British citizen of full age and capacity can make a declaration renouncing British citizenship (Form RN1). Loss of citizenship is at the date of registration of the declaration, however, there is provision that if another citizenship is not acquired within six months, you will be regarded as having remained British.

An application for registration as a British citizen by a person who has renounced citizenship may be made if certain conditions are satisfied.[43] However, the entitlement to register operates only once. If the person again renounces and again seeks to register, the decision is one of discretion for the Secretary of State.

Deprivation of citizenship and the right of abode

Provisions for deprivation of citizenship were formalised by section 40 of the British Nationality Act 1981. However, this section was amended by section 4 of the Nationality, Immigration and Asylum Act 2002 to empower the Secretary of State to deprive British citizens, British overseas territories citizens, British overseas citizens, British nationals overseas, British protected persons or British subjects of their citizenship if s/he is satisfied that they had done anything 'seriously prejudicial to the vital interests of the UK' *and* would not become stateless as a result or they had acquired their citizenship status by registration or naturalisation and did so using fraud, false representations or concealing material facts. Section 56 of the Immigration, Asylum and Nationality Act 2006 came into force on 16 June 2006 and replaces section 40(2) of the British Nationality Act 1981. Consequently, the Secretary of State can deprive a person of citizenship status if satisfied that deprivation is 'conducive to the public good'. That is a far lower threshold which is equivalent to the presumption of deportation for non-citizens.

It is also now possible for the Secretary of State to remove a person's right of abode if s/he 'thinks that it would be conducive to the public good' for the person to be excluded or removed from the UK.[44] This decision attracts a right of appeal.

In certain circumstances, the Home Office may also declare that a person has never been a British citizen. This may happen where citizenship was acquired on an incorrect basis or the authorities made a mistake.

Notes

1. Types of British nationality
1 s1 IA 1971
2 For further details see *Macdonald* and *Fransman* (see Appendix 3)
3 s12 BNA 1948
4 *East African Asians v UK* [1981] EHRR 76
5 s2 IA 1971 as substituted
6 Parts I, II and III BNA 1981
7 s2(1)(a) IA 1971
8 s2(1)(c) IA 1971 as substituted
9 s4(1) BNA 1981
10 s2(1)(b) IA 1971 as substituted
11 s2(1) BNA 1981
12 Falklands Act 1983
13 Hong Kong Act 1985
14 s4(1) BNA 1981
15 British Nationality (Hong Kong) Act 1997
16 British Nationality (Hong Kong) Act 1990
17 Hong Kong Selection Scheme Order
18 s3 British Overseas Territories Act 2002
19 British Overseas Territories 2002 (Commencement) Order 2002

20 paras 249-251 HC 395
21 paras 252-254 HC 395
22 s4(B) BNA 1981
23 para 17 HC 395
24 para 16 HC 395

2. Ways of acquiring British citizenship
25 s2(1)(2) BNA 1981
26 Now s50(3) BNA 1981
27 s50(2),(3) and (4) BNA 1981
28 s1 BNA 1981
29 s1(5) and (6) BNA 1981
30 s48 BNA 1981
31 ss47 and 50(9) BNA 1981
32 NI Chap 9, s9
33 s2(1)(a) BNA 1981
34 s14 BNA 1981 for definition of 'by descent'
35 s6 and Sch 1 BNA 1981
36 s4(1) BNA 1981
37 s1(3) BNA 1981
38 s1(4) BNA 1981

39 s3 BNA 1981. The qualifying territories
    are the British overseas territories save
    those in Cyprus. Only children born
    since 21 May 2002 can benefit from
    residence in the qualifying territories.
40 s3(1) BNA 1981
41 s44 BNA 1981 as amended by s7 NIAA
    2002

3. **Deprivation of British citizenship and
   the right of abode**
42 s12 BNA 1981 (last complete statement
    of immigration rules, 23 May 1994)
43 s13(1) BNA 1981
44 s2A IA 1971, inserted by s57 IANA 2006

3

Chapter 3

Admission to and staying in the UK

This chapter covers:
1. Immigration control before arrival (below)
2. Immigration control on arrival (p37)
3. Immigration control after entry (p41)
4. The future of immigration control (p44)

1. Immigration control before arrival

Entry clearance

Chapter 1 outlines who is 'subject to immigration control' and, therefore, may require 'leave to enter' the UK. In brief, the two main groups who may enter the UK without leave to enter are British citizens and Commonwealth citizens who have the right of abode,[1] or those exempt from the requirement of leave as a European Economic Area (EEA) or Swiss national and their family members.[2]

The rules on which persons subject to immigration control are required to apply for '**entry clearance**' (evidence of your eligibility to enter the UK) from a British post overseas before arriving in the UK, are outlined in Chapter 1 and set out in further detail here. Entry clearance is normally issued in the form of a visa or an entry certificate.

- If you are a '**visa national**', stateless person or refugee, technically the entry clearance issued to you is called a 'visa'.
- If you are a '**non-visa national**' or a British national other than a British citizen, technically your entry clearance is called an 'entry certificate'.[3]

Both visas and entry certificates are 'entry clearance'. They are endorsed in your travel document (usually a passport) in the form of stickers (sometimes referred to as a 'vignette').[4] There are two forms of vignette:

- uniform format visas issued for visits, airside and transit visas which are usually green; *and*
- entry clearance vignettes for all other purposes which are usually red.

The vignette is endorsed with the purpose and length of permitted stay and shows 'valid from' and 'valid to' dates. Entry clearance is only valid for a certain length of time and you must arrive in the UK and present the entry clearance within the period of its validity. The validity dates and the date you arrive in the UK determine the length of leave granted on arrival. Entry clearances also state the conditions that apply to the leave that you obtain on arrival in the UK – eg, 'employment prohibited' and/or 'no recourse to public funds'.

Leave to enter is automatically refused if entry clearance is required but not obtained. However, it is important to note that when the holder of an entry clearance arrives in the UK, admission is not automatic and entry to the UK may still be refused, although only in limited circumstances.[5]

Who needs entry clearance

Whether or not you need an entry clearance mainly depends on your nationality, the period of time for which you are coming to the UK and your reasons for coming to the UK.[6]

- Visa nationals require entry clearance whatever their purpose for coming to the UK. Visa nationals are nationals of all those countries which are listed in Appendix 1 to the immigration rules. Countries are sometimes added to and deleted from this list and it is therefore essential to check whether you are a 'visa national'. Others who need a visa, whatever the reason for their coming to the UK, are: people who hold passports or travel documents issued by the former Soviet Union or the former Socialist Federal Republic of Yugoslavia, stateless people and people who do not hold national documentation.[7]

- Non-visa nationals may require entry clearance depending on the purpose of their travel to/stay in the UK. If the relevant immigration rule requires entry clearance, then, notwithstanding that you are a non-visa national, you must apply for entry clearance in this category. From 13 November 2005, all non-visa (and non-EEA nationals), subject to the 'exceptions' below, require entry clearance to enter the UK for more than six months.

Despite the above rules, however, you do not need an entry clearance if you:

- are returning to the UK within the period covered by a previous grant of leave, which was granted by the immigration authorities for more than six months, as long as you are seeking to return for the same purpose;[8]

- qualify to be admitted to the UK in the category of a returning resident (those who had indefinite leave in the UK when they last left and are returning within two years of departure);[9]

- are a visitor returning to the UK within the period of validity of your visit visa;[10]

- are a national of the People's Republic of China holding a passport issued by the Hong Kong or Macao Special Administrative Region.[11]

EEA, Swiss nationals and family members

An EEA or Swiss national does not require any form of entry clearance in order to be admitted to the UK (see Chapter 8). A non-EEA national who is a 'family member' of an EEA national who is *either* a visa national, *or* is coming to the UK to live with the EEA national rather than just for a visit, is strongly advised to obtain an EEA family permit before travelling (p100). The family permit is therefore, in practice, a form of entry clearance. It can be obtained free of charge from the entry clearance officer. The UKvisas website (www.ukvisas.gov.uk) does include application forms for EEA applications, however, their use is not compulsory as long as the necessaries are proven when entry clearance is optional.

Although you may not need an entry clearance in order to obtain admission under the immigration rules, you can choose to get entry clearance as a precaution before travelling to establish your eligibility for admission.[12] In deciding whether to apply for entry clearance when this is not strictly required, you need to weigh up the additional cost and delay of getting an entry clearance against the risk of being refused on your arrival in the UK if you arrive without it. People who have had immigration problems in the past, but who do not strictly need an entry clearance, often apply for one to avoid problems on entry. You should also be aware that even if you have an entry clearance, admission to the UK on arrival is not guaranteed but if you are refused you may have an in-country appeal by virtue of your entry clearance.

Obtaining entry clearance

You must be outside the UK when you make your application for entry clearance.[13] Applications are usually made to a British embassy, high commission or consulate[14] in the country in which you are living unless:

- there is no such post in that country; *or*
- you are applying to come to the UK as a visitor, in which case you may apply to any post which accepts applications for that category.[15]

In a growing number of countries, applications for entry clearance must be made via a courier company, who process the paperwork and deliver it to the relevant entry clearance post. You may then be called for an interview at the post.

You will not be considered to have made the application until you have paid the appropriate fee,[16] although it is possible to ask for the fee to be waived if you have no means to meet it. The fee should be paid in local currency. Application forms and a list of relevant fees can be downloaded for free from www.ukvisas.gov.uk. Application forms are periodically updated and it is mandatory to use the correct form. It is important to note that these forms are only for applications for entry clearance outside the UK. Applications made to posts in some countries must be accompanied by a record of the applicant's fingerprints[17] and failure to provide these entitles the entry clearance officer to treat the application as invalid. The Government proposes to extend this requirement to all visa applicants by 2008.[18]

Often the entry clearance officer interviews the applicant and may conduct further investigations such as making enquiries of other agencies or even visiting relatives or neighbours.[19] Applications may also be referred back to the Home Office for inquiries to be made in the UK, usually for guidance in a complicated case.

Entry clearance decisions

When deciding whether to grant entry clearance to a person in a particular category, the entry clearance officer should take account of exactly the same requirements as govern leave to enter in that category.[20] The requirements in the rules are applied to the circumstances that exist at the date of the decision on the entry clearance application. The only exception relates to a child applying to join parents for settlement in the UK. In this instance, the child's age is taken to be the age at the date of application rather than the date of the decision.[21] These considerations are important as there can sometimes be a long delay between making an entry clearance application and the making of the decision on it.

The immigration rules relating to each category state that leave may be granted if the particular requirements of the rules relating to the category in question are satisfied. However, even if you satisfy the requirements of the rules for the category in which you seek entry, you may still be refused an entry clearance under the 'general grounds' on which leave may be refused. These 'general grounds' for refusal are set out in two lists – one where entry clearance or leave to enter 'is to be refused'[22] and one where it 'should normally be refused'.[23] If your case is affected by the second list of factors, it would be wise to seek specialist advice and to seek to address any concerns the entry clearance officer might have.

If entry clearance is granted then an entry clearance will be endorsed on your passport. If the entry clearance officer refuses to grant entry clearance and you have a right of appeal against the decision then you will receive a written notice of the refusal which will include details of the reasons for the refusal and how you may exercise your right of appeal (see p76).

Revocation of entry clearance

An entry clearance officer may revoke an entry clearance after it has been granted if s/he believes that it was obtained by false representations or a failure to disclose material facts, or that there has been a change of circumstances since it was issued, or if your exclusion is conducive to the public good.[24] There is no right of appeal against a decision to revoke or cancel entry clearance.[25]

Other documents relating to entry that may be obtained before arrival

Work permit and immigration employment documents

Many categories of entry to work in the UK require you to obtain an immigration employment document (IED) before applying for entry clearance or leave. These documents are necessary for the work permit scheme,[26] and under the highly skilled migrant programme (HSMP) and other employment and self-employment schemes. The IED does not operate as entry clearance so, if you intend to come to the UK you still require an entry clearance in accordance with the above rules.[27] The IED must be obtained before your entry clearance application is granted.[28]

In the era of 'managed migration', there are planned imminent changes to the range of work permit employment, involving the introduction of a all-encompassing points based-system. On 7 November 2006, the Minister for Immigration announced changes to the HSMP points system as the 'first step towards a points-based system for managed migration' and changes have already come into effect. Other features of the proposed new points-based system include it being the prospective employee rather than employer that applies (and pays the fees) for the application.[29] Also, the application for an employment permit is considered at the same time (and by the same entry clearance officer or caseworker) as the application for entry clearance or leave to enter/remain, turning it into a one-step application process.

Certificate of entitlement

If you are a British citizen or other person with the right of abode in the UK, you can obtain a certificate of entitlement to the right of abode by applying to the entry clearance officer at a British post overseas.

Granting leave to enter before arrival in the UK

Increasingly immigration control is becoming extra-territorial,[30] with travellers being subject to UK immigration control before boarding and UK immigration officers granting or refusing leave to enter as if in a UK port. Consequently, leave may be granted or refused by an immigration officer before your departure from your own country or while you are travelling to the UK.[31] For these purposes, an immigration officer may examine you outside the UK, ask questions and ask you to produce documents including an up-to-date medical report.[32] A failure to supply information or to produce such a document is a ground in itself for refusing leave to enter.[33]

2. **Immigration control on arrival**

Examination on arrival

Immigration officers examine you on your arrival at ports of entry to the UK in order to determine whether you:[34]
- are a British citizen or Commonwealth citizen with the right of abode; *or*
- may otherwise enter the UK without leave; *or*
- require leave to enter, already have leave which is still in force and, if not, whether you should be granted leave to enter the UK and, if so, for what period and upon what conditions.

If you do not require leave to enter you are nevertheless required to produce a passport or travel document which demonstrates your identity and nationality together with evidence of your entitlement to enter without leave.[35] Inability to produce such a document may render you liable to prosecution[36] although not an illegal entrant.

It is a criminal offence to refuse to submit to this examination.[37] Certain nationals may be subjected to more vigorous examination.[38]

Who has leave when they arrive in the UK

If you already have leave when you arrive, you may be examined to determine whether or not that leave should be cancelled by the immigration officer.[39] You may already have leave before you arrive in the UK if:
- leave to enter was granted before you arrived in the UK. Where you were given leave orally as a visitor, the burden is upon you to show that you do in fact have leave;[40]
- you arrive in the UK with an entry clearance which operates as leave to enter (see below); *or*
- you still have leave from your previous stay in the UK (see p38).

Entry clearance taking effect as leave to enter

In most cases, entry clearance obtained at a British post abroad operates as advance leave to enter.[41] An entry clearance operates as leave to enter the UK where the entry clearance states the purpose for which it is given[42] and either:
- is endorsed with the conditions to which it is subject; *or*
- contains a statement that it is to have effect as indefinite leave to enter.

The following entry clearance endorsements do not operate as leave to enter: certificates of entitlement, EEA family permits, exempt visas and direct airside transit visas.

The 'period of validity' of a grant of entry clearance is 'the period beginning on the day on which the entry clearance becomes effective and ending on the day on which it expires'.[43] The 'effective date' or 'valid from date' is normally the date of issue but an entry clearance officer may delay this date for up to three months to correspond with the date of travel.[44]

You must arrive during the period of validity. If you are a visitor, leave to enter is for six months where six months or more remain on the period of validity. Where less than six months remain on the period of validity, leave to enter will expire when the entry clearance expires and not six months from the date of entry. Visit visas have effect as leave to enter on an unlimited number of occasions during their period of validity.[45] For purposes other than visits, entry clearance has effect on one occasion during the period of validity,[46] whether the leave is endorsed with conditions[47] or is indefinite.[48] However, such entry clearance operates as leave to enter on every entry during the period of leave which is granted, since leave does not lapse on your departure.

Where entry clearance operates as leave to enter, an immigration officer at the port of arrival may examine you and decide whether the leave should be cancelled.[49] It may be cancelled if you arrive before the 'valid from'/effective date (although the immigration officer may, although cancelling the entry clearance, grant leave to enter in these circumstances[50]) or request leave to enter for a different purpose from that stated on the entry clearance.

Returning to the UK

Leave to enter does not lapse on leaving the Common Travel Area (consisting of the UK, the Republic of Ireland, the Channel Islands and the Isle of Man), if it was conferred by means of an entry clearance (other than a visit visa)[51] or if leave was granted for more than six months.[52] Consequently, in practice, visit visas have effect as leave to enter on an unlimited number of occasions during their period of validity.[53] For purposes other than visits, entry clearance operates as leave to enter on every entry during the period of leave which is granted, since leave does not lapse on your departure.[54] If the leave to enter is indefinite leave, it remains in force while you remain outside the UK for a continuous period of two years but will then lapse if you have not returned to the UK within that period.[55] Where leave remains in force while you are outside the UK, the conditions which are attached to the leave are suspended until you return.[56]

Where you arrive in the UK having been granted leave to enter before your arrival or with leave which did not lapse upon your leaving the UK previously or with an entry clearance which takes effect as leave to enter, the immigration officer may also, by notice in writing, suspend the leave while you are examined further to determine whether to cancel the leave.[57] If appropriate, after that examination, the immigration officer may cancel the leave[58] if any of the following conditions apply:[59]

- there has been a change of circumstances such that leave should be cancelled;

- leave was obtained by providing false information or failing to disclose material facts;
- medical reasons make it undesirable to admit you (unless you are settled in the UK or there are strong compassionate factors);
- exclusion is conducive to the public good; *or*
- you failed to provide information or documents as requested by the immigration authorities.

People who do not have leave when they arrive in the UK

In deciding whether to grant or refuse leave to enter if you arrive in the UK without existing leave (assuming that you are not a person required to possess entry clearance on arrival, as you would automatically be refused leave as discussed above), the immigration officer must apply the criteria in the immigration rules as to whether or not you satisfy the requirements in the category for which you have applied. The immigration officer must also be satisfied that none of the *general* grounds upon which leave can be refused to a person seeking entry in any category apply – eg, previous breaches of immigration control, refusal of a sponsor to give, when requested, an undertaking to be responsible for your support in the UK or where the Secretary of State has directed that your exclusion from the UK is conducive to the public good.[60]

Decision to grant or refuse leave or to cancel existing leave

Those passengers with advance leave to enter (eg, entry clearance) do not generally have any other passport stamp showing leave to enter has been granted by an immigration officer following 'examination'. Others should be given some form of notice of the decision to grant, refuse or vary leave to enter. If an immigration officer considers refusing leave to enter, this should be authorised by a chief immigration officer or an immigration inspector.[61] If leave to enter is refused, even if initially orally, a notice in writing must be given as soon as practicable giving the reasons for refusal.[62] If the refusal attracts a right of appeal (see p76), written notice must be given of this.[63]

Right of appeal against refusal of entry clearance and leave to enter

Not all decisions relating to refusal of entry clearance or leave to enter attract a right of appeal. The Nationality, Immigration and Asylum Act 2002 (NIAA 2002) sets out an exhaustive list of the situations in which an appeal right exists. Where there is no right of appeal an application for judicial review may be possible but specialist legal advice will be necessary. As discussed below, major restrictions on rights of appeal in the employment and student categories will be introduced when the relevant parts of the Immigration, Asylum and Nationality Act 2006 (IANA 2006) come into effect.

Right of appeal against a refusal of entry clearance

At present there is a right of appeal against refusal of entry clearance except in specified circumstances:[64]

- refusal is on the grounds that you do not satisfy an age or nationality requirement of the immigration rules;
- you do not have an immigration document;
- you seek to be in the UK for a period longer than permitted by the immigration rules;
- you seek to be in the UK for a purpose not covered by the immigration rules;
- you are seeking entry as a non-family visitor;
- you are seeking entry for a short course or as a prospective student;
- where you have been refused on the ground that you have failed 'to supply a medical report or certificate in accordance with a requirement of the immigration rules'.[65]

Section 4 of the IANA 2006 (as yet no date is fixed for implementation nor are there any regulations specifying class, descriptions, categories etc) will replace sections 88A, 90 and 91 of the NIAA 2002 with the effect that an appeal may only be brought against refusal of entry clearance in the following circumstances:

- where entry clearance was sought to visit a person of a class or description to be prescribed by regulations (likely to be specified family members);
- where entry clearance was sought for the purpose of entry as a dependant of a person in circumstances prescribed in regulations;
- where an appeal is to be brought on race discrimination grounds;
- where an appeal is to be brought on the ground that the decision is incompatible with your human rights.

It is anticipated that this statutory provision (and the implementing regulations) will limit the right of appeal against refusal of entry clearance to close family members or dependants of a person in the UK. Consequently, there will be no right of appeal against refusal of entry clearance, for example, for students or workers.

Right of appeal against refusal of leave to enter

The only circumstances in which an appeal may be brought against refusal of leave to enter as a person who has entry clearance is where the purpose specified in the entry clearance is the same as that specified in your application for leave to enter or where the appeal is on refugee or human rights or race discrimination grounds.[66]

When the immigration officer cannot make an immediate decision

In many cases, in particular where you are seeking leave to enter as a refugee, the final decision on whether to grant leave to enter cannot be made immediately. While the decision is pending, the immigration officer has two options: either you may be detained pending a decision to give or refuse leave to enter or to cancel an existing leave to enter, or you may be granted **'temporary admission'** to the UK. Temporary admission is not leave to enter or remain in the UK, it is a restricted 'licence' to be in the UK and, subject to certain procedural safeguards, it can be revoked in favour of detention at any time.[67] People who are initially detained under these powers may later be released on temporary admission by the immigration officer[68] or, in most cases, may seek bail from an immigration judge.[69] Temporary admission may be granted subject to conditions as to residence, employment and reporting to the police or an immigration officer.[70]

3. **Immigration control after entry**

Responsibility for control after entry

Once you have entered the UK, in most cases responsibility for regulating your immigration position passes from the immigration service to the Secretary of State for the Home Department (the Home Secretary acting through the Home Office).[71] For immigration purposes, you have technically not 'entered' the UK while you are on temporary admission or you are detained pending a decision by the immigration officer following your arrival in the UK.[72] Therefore some people, in particular asylum seekers, may be in the UK for a very extended period but immigration law does not recognise them as having 'entered' the UK. Once you have entered the UK, any application for leave is termed an application to 'vary' leave or leave to remain rather than leave to 'enter'.[73]

Residence permits

The UK has opted into the European Community Residence Permit Scheme.[74] Since February 2004, leave to remain for more than six months is in the form of a residence permit.

Applying for leave to remain

Leave to enter or remain can be for a limited or indefinite period.[75] Where you have been granted indefinite leave to enter or remain you do not need to apply while you are in the UK to extend or vary your leave because:
- it is indefinite and therefore has no time limit attached to it (although it may lapse[76]);
- no conditions can be attached to an indefinite leave to enter or remain in the UK and so there are no conditions that can be lifted.[77]

If you have been granted only limited leave to enter (or remain) in the UK, you may decide that you want to stay for a longer period. Alternatively, you may wish to change the conditions on which your leave has been granted. These applications may be described as applications for leave to remain or applications to 'vary' leave.

If your leave has already expired by the time you come to apply for further leave, then you should obtain legal advice about making a further application without delay. The consequences of not applying for further leave in time are very serious. If you do not apply in time:

- as a person who becomes 'subject to immigration control',[78] you may lose entitlement to social security benefits and/or support from a local authority social services department;[79]
- your application for further leave may be refused under the immigration rules[80] and on the grounds that you have failed to comply with the conditions of your leave;[81]
- the right of appeal is lost;[82]
- you become liable for removal from the UK as an overstayer;[83] *and*
- you are liable to criminal prosecution.[84]

It is, therefore, very important that an application is made before your existing leave expires. In many cases, the application is made before the leave expires, but it is not possible for the Home Office to make a decision on the application before the leave expires. The Immigration Act 1971 provides for leave to be extended beyond its original duration where an in time variation application is made, the application is still being considered, an appeal could be brought against a refusal of an application or an appeal is pending.[85] The Immigration, Asylum and Nationality Act 2006 (brought into force on 31 August 2006) amends the provision for the continuation of leave. Leave is statutorily extended while an application is pending and while an appeal could be brought or is pending and 'whilst the appellant is in the UK', thereby preventing those who appeal out of country from having statutorily extended leave.[86]

Making the application for leave to remain

Completion of an application form is compulsory for most applications to stay in the UK (except applications for asylum or under Article 3 of the European Convention on Human Rights). Forms are also available for applications under European law and under European Community Association Agreements. You should always apply, on the prescribed form[87] and with the fee (if not in an exempt category of applicants[88]), to the Home Office before your current leave expires to extend your leave.[89] An application not completed as required is invalidated in the absence of a 'satisfactory' explanation or if not completed and returned within 28 days where evidence was omitted or the form was incomplete.[90] Applications that are invalidated are treated as not being made.[91] It may then be that your leave expires before you are able to re-submit a valid application.

Application forms are updated and amended regularly. Using the correct application form for the purpose for which further leave is being requested is vital. You are, of course, always best advised to seek professional advice in making your application. You can get the appropriate application form by telephoning the Application Forms Unit at the Home Office or current forms can be downloaded from www.ind.homeoffice.gov.uk. The application form gives details of all the documents, photographs and any other information you will need to provide with your application. If you are sending your application by post you should copy it and send it by recorded or special delivery. If your application is straightforward, it is possible to make an appointment to apply in person at the Home Office Public Enquiry Office. The fee is considerably more but it is usually possible to have a 'same day service'.

In general, there have been very serious delays in dealing with applications by the Home Office over the past few years. Consideration times fluctuate, usually depending on the nature of the application and whether the Home Office is focusing staff and other resources in particular departments. For example, in 2006 there was a 'diversion' of resources to deal with foreign national prisoners and enforcement of deportations and also to facilitate the implementation of the New Asylum Model. The Home Office has recently stated that it may take up to five years to deal with some other applications – eg, those applying to vary leave from humanitarian protection/discretionary leave.

In order to make an application for leave to remain, the Home Office requires that you send in your passport. If you request the return of your passport in order to travel outside the CTA while your application is still outstanding, your application is treated as withdrawn when the passport is returned to you.[92] The Home Office will only speed up an application for leave so that you can travel if there is an emergency, such as a family illness. It is possible, however, to make arrangements with the Home Office for the return of your passport for other reasons without affecting your application – eg, opening a bank account or obtaining a driving licence. If you do this you must make it clear that you are not requesting your passport in order to travel.

Decisions made by the Home Office where no application has been made

In certain circumstances, the Home Office can curtail limited leave to enter or remain (ie, bring your leave to an end before it is otherwise due to expire) without your making any application to the Home Office. When your leave is curtailed, you become a person with no leave (an overstayer) which may have benefit implications as such a person is 'subject to immigration control'. However, if you appeal against the variation, then the variation will not take effect during the time that you are appealing which may preserve your position as a person not 'subject to control' if you were not one before.

Leave may be curtailed in the following circumstances:[93]

* false representations are made or there is a failure to disclose a material fact for the purpose of obtaining leave to enter or a previous variation of leave;

- failure to comply with any conditions attached to the grant of leave to enter or to remain;
- failure to continue to meet the requirements of the immigration rule under which leave was granted;
- failure to maintain or accommodate yourself and any dependants without recourse to public funds;
- it is undesirable to allow you to remain in the UK in the light of your character, conduct, associations or the fact that you represent a threat to national security.

If leave is curtailed so that there is no leave remaining, this is an 'immigration decision' and so attracts a right of appeal.

In addition, the Home Office may add, vary or revoke conditions attached to your leave without you making any application for this to be done.[94] There are no specific rules as to when this can be done. There is no right of appeal against a decision to vary conditions.

Notice of decisions

If you apply to the Home Office for a variation of your leave and the application is successful, the Home Office will endorse the further leave/conditions in your passport or travel document and may also inform you in writing of the decision.[95] If you are unsuccessful in your application, or the Home Office has varied or curtailed your leave without your applying, then you will also be informed of this in writing,[96] and you will be informed of any right of appeal that you have against this decision.[97]

Enforcement, registration and complying with conditions

Decisions to enforce departures from the UK are also, of course, an important part of immigration control and involve both the immigration service and officials at the Home Office. There are other forms of immigration control which also operate after your arrival in the UK. You may be required to register with the police, or to comply with certain conditions upon which temporary admission or bail is granted. Enforcement and the other forms of control are dealt with separately (see p70).

4. **The future of immigration control**

On 7 February 2005, the Government published a five-year strategy for reforming the immigration and asylum system.[98] The focus is on control, with stronger 'border controls', increased detention and removal of failed asylum seekers and limits on rights to settlement in the UK.

Various provisions of the Immigration, Asylum and Nationality Act 2006 have now been implemented, although some of the most profound changes, including the removal of various appeal rights (eg, people refused entry clearance to come to the UK as fiancées, carers, students, work permit holders, business persons, etc) have yet to be introduced.

Many of the proposals do not require statutory provisions – eg, the proposed points-based system (see p36) will be 'rolled-in' by a series of changes to rules and procedures.

In 2006, regulatory changes transposed EC Directives into UK domestic immigration law. These included The Immigration (European Economic Area) Regulations 2006 which transpose Directive 2004/38/EC on the free movement of persons and also the Refugee or Person in Need of International Protection (Qualification) Regulations 2006, designed to give effect to Council Directive 2004/83/EC on minimum standards for the qualification of third country nationals and stateless persons as refugees or as persons who otherwise need international protection and the content of the protection granted – known as the 'Qualification Directive'. The immigration rules have also been changed to incorporate these regulations.

Notes

1. Immigration control before arrival

1 ss3(1), 2(1)(b), 2(2) IA 1971
2 s7 IA 1988 as set out in I(EEA) Regs 2000 as amended by SI 2003/549 and SI 2003/3188 (extending the definition of family members) and modified by SI 2002/1241 (extending EEA free movement rights to Swiss nationals, regs 12 and 14).
3 para 25 HC 395
4 para 24 HC 395
5 paras 30A and 321 HC 395
6 para 24 HC 395
7 para 1(a)-(d) Appendix 1 HC 395
8 para 2(b) Appendix 1 HC 395; Art 13(2)-(4) I(EEA) Regs
9 para 2 Appendix 1 HC 395
10 Art 4(1) I(LER)O
11 HC 395 as amended, Appendix 1 para 2(d) and (e)
12 para 23A HC 395 inserted by HC 1224
13 para 28 HC 395

14 UKvisas (the joint initiative of the Foreign and Commonwealth Office and the Home Office) publishes a list of such designated posts abroad at www.ukvisas.gov.uk.
15 paras 28-29 HC 395
16 para 30 HC 395
17 Immigration (Provision of Physical Data) Regulations 2006 No.1743 made under s126 NIAA 2002
18 *Controlling our borders: Making migration work for Britain: Five year strategy for asylum and immigration,* Cm 6472, Feb 2005
19 This practice was condoned in *R v Immigration Appeal Tribunal, ex p Hoque and Singh* [1988] Imm AR 216, CA.
20 para 26 HC 395
21 para 27 HC 395
22 IDI makes clear that, in practice, there are cases where refusal is not appropriate even on the 'mandatory' grounds.

23 para 320 HC 395
24 para 30A HC 395 added by HC 329 from 3 June 1996
25 It is not an immigration decision for the purposes s82 NIAA 2002.
26 paras 128-199 HC 395
27 Guidance and application forms are available from Work Permits UK helpline or from www.workingintheuk.gov.uk. The requirements of the immigration rules for persons seeking to enter or remain in the UK for employment are at paras 128-199 HC 395.
28 paras 116(i) and 128(i) HC 395
29 *Controlling our borders: Making migration work for Britain: Five year strategy for asylum and immigration*, Cm 6472, Feb 2005
30 Art 7 I(LER)O (made under s3A IA 1971 as inserted)
31 Art 7(1) I(LER)O; para 17A HC 395 as inserted by HC 704
32 Art 7(2)(3) I(LER)O
33 Art 7(4) I(LER)O

2. Immigration control on arrival

34 Sch 2 paras 2(1) and 2A IA 1971
35 s3(8) and (9) and Sch 2 para 4(2)(a) IA1971; paras 11-13 HC 395
36 s2 AI(TC)A 2004
37 s26(1)(a) IA 1971
38 Ministerial authorisation under the s19D Race Relations Act 1976 (inserted by Race Relations (Amendment) Act 2000)
39 Sch 2 para 2A IA 1971
40 Art 11 I(LER)O
41 Art 2-4 I(LER)O as amended by SI 2004/475; para 25A HC 395
42 Art 3(2) I(LER)O
43 Art4(1) I(LER)O
44 IDI Ch 1, s4, para 4.4
45 Art 4(1) I(LER)O
46 Art 4(3) I(LER)O
47 Art 4(3)(b) I(LER)O
48 Art 4(3)(a) I(LER)O
49 Sch 2, para 2A IA 1971 (inserted IAA 1999, amended NIAA 2002)
50 IDI, Ch 1, s4, para 10.3
51 Art 13(2)(a) I(LER)O
52 Art 13(2)(b) and (3) I(LER)O
53 Art 4(1) I(LER)O
54 Art 13 I(LER)O
55 Art 13(4)(a) I(LER)O; paras 20 and 20A HC 395
56 Art 13(4)(b) I(LER)O
57 Sch 2 para 2A(7) and (10) IA 1971; para 10A HC 395 inserted by HC 704

58 Sch 2 para 2A(8) IA 1971; Art 6(1) I(LER)O read also with Art 13(5); para 10B HC 395 inserted by HC 704
59 Sch 2 para 2A(2)-(4) IA 1971; para 321A HC 395 inserted by HC 704
60 paras 320-322 HC 395
61 para 10 HC 395
62 Art 10(1) I(LER)O
63 For decisions attracting right of appeal see s82 NIAA 2002; for requirement to given written notice see Immigration (Notices) Regulations 2003 (No.658)
64 ss88,89, 90 and 91 NIAA 2002
65 s5 IANA 2006 (although there is no such requirement in the immigration rules as yet)
66 s89 NIAA 2002 (as amended)
67 Sch 2 para 21(1) IA 1971
68 Sch 2 para 21(1) IA 1971
69 Sch 2 para 22 IA 1971
70 Sch 2 para 21(2) IA 1971

3. Immigration control after entry

71 s4(1) IA 1971
72 s11 IA 1971
73 *Davoren* [1996] Imm AR 307 CA
74 EC Reg 1030/2002 (13 June 2002)
75 s3(1)(b) IA 1971
76 Art 13(4)(a) I(LER)O
77 s3(1)(c) IA 1971 which applies only to limited leave
78 s115 IAA 1999
79 ss116-118 IAA 1999
80 See eg, paras 284(i) and 322(3) HC 395
81 s10 IAA 1999; para 322(3) HC 395
82 s82(2)(e) and (f) NIAA 2002; s14 IA 1971
83 s3(5)(a) IA 1971
84 s24 IA 1971
85 s3C(2) IA 1971
86 s11 IANA 2006
87 s31A IA 1971 inserted by s165 IAA 1999 from 1 August 2003 (SI 2003/1862) and amended by s121 NIAA 2002 from 1 February 2003; I(LR)(PFP) Regs
88 Reg 5(e), (3)(a) and (b) Immigration Employment Document (Fees) Regulations 2003 No.541. See also 'Information about charges' on the IND website in the section on 'making an application'.
89 para 32 HC 395
90 Regs 14 and 15 I(LR)(PFP) Regs
91 Reg 14 Immigration (Leave to Remain) (Prescribed Forms and Procedures) Regulations 2005 (No.771)
92 para 34 HC 395

93 para 323 HC 395
94 s3(3)(a) IA 1971
95 s4(1) para 31 IA 1971
96 s4(1) para 31 IA 1971
97 Regs 4(1) and 5 IAA(N) 2000

4. **The future of immigration control**

98 *Controlling our borders: Making
    Immigration Work for Britain: five year
    strategy for asylum and immigration,
    Cm 6472, Feb 2005*

Chapter 4

Leave and settlement

This chapter covers:
1. Leave to enter or remain (below)
2. Categories of leave and switching category (p50)

---

1. Leave to enter or remain

As discussed in previous chapters, people who do not have the right of abode in the UK and who are therefore subject to immigration control require leave to enter (on arrival) and leave to remain (after entry), and special rules apply to certain special groups.[1] Leave is of two kinds:[2]
- limited leave to enter or remain;
- indefinite leave to enter or remain.

Limited leave

If you have limited leave, you can only remain in the UK for a certain period of time. In order to lawfully remain in the UK after the time permitted, you must obtain further leave to remain and the application *must* be made to the Home Office before the existing leave ends. Certain conditions can be attached to a limited leave to enter or remain which may:[3]
- restrict or prohibit the employment or occupation you can take in the UK;[4]
- require you to maintain and accommodate yourself and any dependants without recourse to public funds;[5]
- in certain circumstances, require you to register with the police if you are not a citizen of a Commonwealth country or a European Economic Area national;
- require you to report to a medical officer at a specified time and date.

The immigration rules indicate the length of limited leave normally granted to a successful applicant in the different categories and, in some cases, the conditions that will be imposed upon that leave.

Employment conditions

The rules distinguish between:

- a prohibition upon employment (eg, visitors are usually prohibited from working);[6] *and*
- a restriction upon the freedom to take employment (eg, given to students).[7]

While you can apply to the Home Office to get working restrictions lifted in order to work legally, if you have a prohibition on working you must apply to the Home Office for the terms of your leave to be varied. In the case of students, from 21 June 1999, the Home Office has operated a concession whereby students are automatically deemed to have been granted permission to work for not more than 20 hours a week during term time and full time during vacations.[8]

Overstaying leave and breaching conditions of leave

The consequences of overstaying your leave or otherwise breaching the conditions of your leave are that:

- you may be removed from the UK;[9]
- you are liable to be prosecuted for a criminal offence (although prosecutions are rare);[10]
- your existing leave to enter or remain in the UK may be curtailed (if you are in breach of conditions of leave);[11]
- any future applications under the immigration rules for entry clearance, leave to enter and leave to remain are less likely to succeed.[12]

Indefinite leave to remain (settlement)

Indefinite leave to enter or remain in the UK is leave without a time restriction. No conditions relating to employment, public funds etc can be attached to indefinite leave.[13] This is important for welfare benefit purposes, as a person given a condition on her/his leave not to have recourse to public funds is 'subject to immigration control' and excluded from non-contributory benefit.[14] The only way in which a person who has indefinite leave can be subject to immigration control is where it was given on the basis of a maintenance undertaking of another person to provide for her/him.[15] Indefinite leave amounts to a right of permanent residence in the UK. Indefinite leave to remain is therefore often referred to as permanent residence or settlement.

However, a person who has indefinite leave can still, in limited circumstances, have their indefinite leave to remain 'revoked' and be required to leave the UK. Such people may be deported on grounds that their presence is not conducive to the public good (usually following a criminal conviction) and on national security grounds.

If you had indefinite leave when you left the UK you can seek to re-enter as a returning resident[16] provided you:

- wish to return to settle in the UK;

- have been away from the UK for no more than two years (unless there are special circumstances – eg, previous long residence);
- did not receive assistance from public funds towards the cost of leaving the UK (this refers to the special scheme which operates to enable people to ask for their costs of re-settling in their country of origin to be reimbursed; it does not refer to obtaining welfare benefits).

A person who has indefinite leave is usually also 'settled' in the UK. To be settled, you have to be lawfully 'ordinarily resident' in the UK without your stay being time-limited.[17] In practice, therefore, the terms 'indefinite leave to remain' and 'settlement' are often used interchangeably.

You must be settled in order:
- to naturalise or register as a British citizen (see pp26 and 28);[18]
- for your children born in the UK to become British citizens by birth[19] (see Chapter 2);
- to bring members of your family to the UK under the immigration rules with a view to their living permanently in the UK with you.

The following are the most important routes to settlement.
- Certain categories of admission under the immigration rules lead to obtaining indefinite leave to remain and settled status, usually but not always after a period of limited leave in that capacity. Other more temporary categories do not lead to settlement.
- Members of the family of a person (the 'sponsor') settled in the UK are also admitted with a view to settlement under the rules.
- If you have lived lawfully (continuous residence with leave to remain) in the UK for 10 years or more.
- If you have lived (continuous residence either lawfully or unlawfully) in the UK for 14 years or more (prior to any notice of liability to removal or other enforcement action).

From 2 April 2007, the *Life in the UK* test, which is currently required for those applying for naturalisation, will also be applied to applications for indefinite leave (see p27).

2. **Categories of leave and switching category**

Purpose for entering or staying in the UK

An application for leave is generally made for a particular purpose. If you do not state a purpose, the immigration authorities will ask you to say why you wish to enter the UK. For applications for leave to remain, the form used[20] indicates the nature of the application.

The immigration rules divide people into different categories according to the reason for seeking leave to enter or remain in the UK. In order to succeed in an application for entry clearance, leave to enter or an extension of leave you have to satisfy the appropriate requirements. It is not within the scope of this book to set out the requirements of all the immigration rules. The updated immigration rules can be found at www.ind.homeoffice.gov.uk/lawandpolicy/immigration-rules. Each paragraph or rule details the requirements to be satisfied for entry clearance and leave to remain and the period of leave to be granted. Home Office policy and guidance on the application of the rules can be found in the Immigration Directorates' Instructions (IDIs), Asylum Policy Instructions, European Casework Instructions and the Operational Enforcement Manual which can all be found under Law and Policy, Policy Instructions, on the Immigration and Nationality Directorate website (www.ind.homeoffice.gov.uk).

An example of how the immigration rules set out the requirements to be satisfied can be seen at *Part 3: persons seeking to enter or remain in the United Kingdom for studies*. Paragraphs 57 to 87F describe the requirements for different categories of students and their families.

Example: Requirements for leave to enter as a student

57. The requirements to be met by a person seeking leave to enter the United Kingdom as a student are that he:

    (i) has been accepted for a course of study which is to be provided by an organisation which is included on the Department for Education and Skills' Register of Education and Training Providers, and is at either;

        (a) a publicly funded institution of further or higher education; or

        (b) a bona fide private education institution which maintains satisfactory records of enrolment and attendance; or

        (c) an independent fee paying school outside the maintained sector; and

    (ii) is able and intends to follow either:

        (a) a recognised full time degree course at a publicly funded institution of further or higher education; or

        (b) a weekday full time course involving attendance at a single institution for a minimum of 15 hours organised daytime study per week of a single subject, or directly related subjects; or

        (c) a full time course of study at an independent fee paying school; and

    (iii) if under the age of 16 years is enrolled at an independent fee paying school on a full time course of studies which meets the requirements of the Education Act 1944; and

    (iv) intends to leave the United Kingdom at the end of his studies; and

    (v) does not intend to engage in business or to take employment, except part time or vacation work undertaken with the consent of the Secretary of State for Employment; and

> (vi) is able to meet the costs of his course and accommodation and the maintenance of himself and any dependants without taking employment or engaging in business or having recourse to public funds.

The rules relating to students are a good example of a category in which it is necessary to refer to the policy instructions as well as the relevant paragraphs of the immigration rules. The IDIs regarding students give details of the evidence regarding courses, funding and so on to which an entry clearance officer will have regard when considering an application. For example, although paragraph 57(iv) states that you must satisfy the entry clearance officer that you intend to leave the UK at the end of your studies, Chapter 3, paragraph 3.20.2 *(Intention to leave)* states that those on a recognised UK degree course will be permitted to apply in country to vary their leave to work permit employment and therefore the intention to leave requirements should be disregarded at the initial application stage. If entry clearance is granted, you may be admitted to the UK for a period appropriate to your course. You could still be refused leave even if you meet the above criteria if certain 'general grounds' of refusal (which apply to all cases except asylum applications) apply.[21] If you do not meet the rules for students you will not usually be given leave to enter.[22] As a student, you will probably have a condition attached to your leave that you maintain and accommodate yourself without recourse to public funds.[23]

Family members

Family members may apply to stay permanently with someone who is settled in the UK. You may also, however, be admitted as a family member to join a person in the UK who is not here in a settled capacity. The conditions you must satisfy vary according to the status of the person you are joining. For example, a child joining a working holidaymaker must be under 5, rather than under 18 (the usual criteria)[24] and to count as a spouse/civil partner under the immigration rules, you and your spouse/civil partner must be aged 18 or over.

Temporary and permanent/settled purposes

Some people are only admitted for temporary purposes which do not lead to settlement. In these cases, the leave granted is always time-limited and applicants are expected to leave the UK when the purpose for which leave was granted has been fulfilled. Other people are admitted for longer term or permanent purposes which lead to indefinite leave and settlement in the UK. For some permanent/settled purposes, such as for children or other dependent relatives, indefinite leave can be granted immediately. For others, such as fiancé(e)s, spouses, civil partners and unmarried partners, indefinite leave is usually only granted after completion of a period of limited leave in the UK.

For example, if you are applying for entry clearance as the spouse of a person who is present and settled in the UK or being admitted on the same occasion for settlement, paragraph 281 of the immigration rules applies. Paragraphs 281-282 of the rules are set out below.

Spouses or civil partners of persons present and settled in the United Kingdom or being admitted on the same occasion for settlement

Requirements for leave to enter the United Kingdom with a view to settlement as the spouse or civil partner of a person present and settled in the United Kingdom or being admitted on the same occasion for settlement

281. The requirements to be met by a person seeking leave to enter the United Kingdom with a view to settlement as the spouse or civil partner of a person present and settled in the United Kingdom or who is on the same occasion being admitted for settlement are that:

    (i) (a) the applicant is married to or the civil partner of a person present and settled in the United Kingdom or who is on the same occasion being admitted for settlement; or

    (b) the applicant is married to or the civil partner of a person who has a right of abode in the United Kingdom or indefinite leave to enter or remain in the United Kingdom and is on the same occasion seeking admission to the United Kingdom for the purposes of settlement and the parties were married or formed a civil partnership at least 4 years ago, since which time they have been living together outside the United Kingdom; and

    (ii) the parties to the marriage have met; and

    (iii) each of the parties intends to live permanently with the other as his or her spouse and the marriage is subsisting; and

    (iv) there will be adequate accommodation for the parties and any dependants without recourse to public funds in accommodation which they own or occupy exclusively; and

    (v) the parties will be able to maintain themselves and any dependants adequately without recourse to public funds; and

    (vi) the applicant holds a valid United Kingdom entry clearance for entry in this capacity.

For the purposes of this paragraph and paragraphs 282-289 a member of HM Forces serving overseas, or a permanent member of HM Diplomatic Service or a comparable UK-based staff member of the British Council on a tour of duty abroad, or a staff member of the Department for International Development who is a British Citizen or is settled in the United Kingdom, is to be regarded as present and settled in the United Kingdom.

Leave to enter as the spouse or civil partner of a person present and settled in the United Kingdom or being admitted for settlement on the same occasion

282. A person seeking leave to enter the United Kingdom as the spouse or civil partner of a person present and settled in the United Kingdom or who is on the same occasion being admitted for settlement may, in the case of a person within paragraph 281(I)(a), be

admitted for an initial period not exceeding 2 years or, in the case of a person within paragraph 281(I)(b), indefinite leave to enter may be granted provided a valid United Kingdom entry clearance for entry in the appropriate capacity is produced to the Immigration Officer on arrival.

As can be seen from para 281(b) above, if the parties have lived together abroad for four years since the marriage/civil partnership then they can apply for indefinite leave. If not, spouses/civil partners qualify for 24 months' leave.

Additionally, you cannot qualify as a spouse if your marriage is polygamous and there is another wife or husband alive who has *either*:[25]

- been in the UK since her/his marriage; *or*
- been recognised as having (by the issue of a certificate of entitlement) the right of abode, or has been granted entry clearance to enter the UK as the spouse of your wife or husband.

However, if another spouse was here as a visitor or entered illegally or did not disembark from the ship or aircraft this does not affect your rights as the spouse. You also still qualify as the spouse if you:[26]

- were in the UK before 1 August 1988 having been admitted for settlement as the spouse of your present wife or husband; *or*
- have, since your marriage, been in the UK at any time since your wife or husband's other spouse died.

Switching categories

'Switching' or changing between immigration categories while in the UK, technically an extension of your leave but often referred to as a variation, has been made more difficult in recent years by changes in the immigration rules. Many of the immigration rules prevent switching by imposing a requirement that the applicant entered the UK with a valid entry clearance in the same capacity in which leave to remain is sought.

Whether you can switch depends on the immigration rule into which you want to switch. For example, if you want to apply to remain in the UK as a spouse, it is the spouse rules you will need to check, not the rule for your current status (such as visitor or student). Whatever your new category, you must show that you satisfy the requirements of the immigration rules for being here in that capacity. The Home Office can treat an application to switch as evidence that you did not genuinely enter for the purpose for which you were granted leave. Under these circumstances, you may be refused leave to remain.

It is often possible to ask for further leave in the same capacity. However, some categories (eg, visitors) have a maximum period it is permitted to spend in total before you are required to leave.[27] In many permanent categories, the rules require you to remain in the UK with limited leave for a period of continuous years before applying for settlement.

You should consider seeking professional advice before making your application to remain or to change status. Remember, even if you may not switch under the immigration rules, you may ask for the entry clearance requirement to be waived as the Home Office does have a discretion to allow switches outside the rules where circumstances merit it, although this discretion is rarely exercised. The Home Office will generally not view financial circumstances (eg, relating to your job or prospective employment) as exceptional and only circumstances relating to the individual which would make it unduly harsh to return to your country of residence and make an entry clearance application may be considered as exceptional.

Notes

1. **Leave to enter or remain**
   1 ss1 and 3 IA 1971
   2 s3(1)(b) IA 1971
   3 s3(1)(c) IA 1971; para 8 HC 395 as amended
   4 The employment requirements and conditions are relevant to the 'available for and actively seeking work' test which affects access to JSA.
   5 Although this has been a requirement in the rules for a long time, it is only since 1 November 1996 that it has been elevated into a *condition* upon which leave may be granted – see para 8 HC 395 as amended by para 3 Command Paper 3365 (August 1996) and s3(1)(c) IA 1971.
   6 paras 42 and 45 HC 395
   7 paras 58 and 61 HC 395
   8 IDIs ch 3 para 3.18.1
   9 s10 IAA 1999
   10 s24(1)(b) IA 1971
   11 para 323 HC 395
   12 paras 320(11) and (17) and 322(3) HC 395
   13 s3(3)(a) IA 1971
   14 s115(9)(b) IAA 1999
   15 s115(9)(c) IAA 1999
   16 paras 18-19 HC 395
   17 s33(2A) IA 1971 as amended; see also para 6 HC 395

   18 ss4 and 6 and Sch 1 BNA 1981
   19 s1 BNA 1981

2. **Categories of leave and switching category**
   20 para 32 HC 395 as amended
   21 paras 320-322 HC 395
   22 para 59 HC 395
   23 s3(1)(c) IA 1971
   24 paras 101(ii), 102 and 103 HC 395
   25 paras 277-280 HC 395
   26 paras 277-280 HC 395
   27 IDIs

Chapter 5

Asylum seekers and human rights claims

This chapter covers:
1. Consideration of cases (p57)
2. Asylum decisions and refugee status (p63)
3. Humanitarian protection and discretionary leave to remain (p65)

The following is a description of the immigration process as it relates specifically to asylum seekers and human rights claims.

The substantive law governing consideration and determination of asylum claims is the 1951 Convention Relating to the Status of Refugees and its 1967 Protocol, commonly referred to as 'the Refugee Convention'. The substantive law governing the consideration and determination of human rights claims is the European Convention on Human Rights 1950 and the Human Rights Act 1998. There is also a series of statutory provisions, the latest being the Immigration, Asylum and Nationality Act 2006 (IANA 2006) providing for the basis of grants of and revocation of refugee status, rights of appeal etc.

The Qualification Directive

Council Directive 2004/83/EC (known as the 'Qualification Directive') on minimum standards for the qualification of third country nationals and stateless persons as refugees or as persons who otherwise need international protection and the content of the protection granted was (arguably partly) implemented on 9 October 2006 by regulations and changes to the immigration rules.[1] The regulations apply to any pending asylum or humanitarian protection claim or pending appeal as at the date of coming into force.

Home Office policy on how asylum claims are considered is found in the Asylum Policy Instructions available at www.ind.homeoffice.gov.uk.

New Asylum Model

New claims for asylum and human rights protection (but not 'fresh' claims – see p57) are considered under a new asylum process currently referred to in the Home Office as the New Asylum Model (NAM). The Home Office began implementing

NAM in June 2005 with a non-detained process in Liverpool for claims considered 'late and opportunistic'. It is intended that all new asylum and human rights claims will be processed under NAM by April 2007. All claims for asylum made before 2006 and/or 'fresh claims' (that is second or subsequent claims based on fresh evidence) are now referred to in the Home Office as 'legacy cases'. In practice this category includes applications to extend humanitarian protection and discretionary leave to remain (see p65). The Home Office has advised that legacy cases may take up to five years to resolve.

Seeking asylum

An asylum seeker is a person who has asked for leave to enter or remain in the UK as a refugee and is claiming that:
'owing to a well-founded fear of persecution for reasons of race, nationality, membership of a particular social group or political opinion is outside the country of his nationality and is unable or owing to such fear is unwilling to avail himself of the protection of that country; or who, not having a nationality and being outside the country of his former habitual residence is unable or owing to such fear unwilling to return to it.'[2]

It is not possible, under the immigration rules, to apply for an entry clearance to come to the UK as a refugee.[3] Therefore in all but a very few cases, asylum seekers apply for leave as refugees either at the port (known simply as '**port applications**') or from inside the country ('**in-country applications**').

An in-country applicant must claim asylum in person at the Asylum Screening Unit in Croydon or Liverpool, unless you are one of a strictly defined category of vulnerable asylum seekers who must also apply in person but may do so at the nearest enforcement office. Section 12 of the IANA 2006 (not in force at the time of writing) will enable claims for asylum to be made at a non-designated place, which would include postal claims.

In respect of legacy cases, the procedure for considering an asylum application varies depending upon your original nationality, how you travelled to the UK and upon your personal situation – eg, age and health, claims of torture. Practice in the asylum process changes rapidly and, in general, does not need legislation in order to change. For example, some applicants may not be given Statement of Evidence Forms (see p59) but proceed directly to interview. Below is an overview of the procedure for asylum and human rights claims.

1. Consideration of cases

Screening

An application for asylum should be made as soon as reasonably practicable[4] in order for an asylum seeker to be able to qualify for national asylum support –

financial support and accommodation for asylum seekers. Both this support and the organisation that administers it are currently known as NASS (see Part 6). NASS is now usually granted to destitute asylum seekers that claim asylum within 72 hours of arrival. If NASS is refused because of a late claim then you can apply for judicial review on the ground that the refusal breaches your human rights.

The standard process at present if you have been granted temporary admission is that you are initially fingerprinted and given a screening interview, which concentrates on personal details and mode of entry and travel to the UK (said by the Home Office to be intended to address identity and nationality). You are also asked questions regarding your travel document or passport. A failure to produce an 'immigration document' within three days of an in-country screening interview may lead to prosecution.[5] Such prosecutions were brought on a regular basis against asylum seekers who applied on arrival but are likely to be less common following a recent Court of Appeal decision that held that an 'immigration document' refers to a genuine document.[6] If you were never issued with a genuine passport you evidently have a 'reasonable excuse' for failing to provide it.

The New Asylum Model (NAM) procedure involves categorising you into a 'segment' or 'track' defined by level of priority and barriers to removal and in accordance with certain criteria assessed at the initial screening interview. For example, a claim may be defined as 'late and opportunistic' with low barriers to removal if national documentation from your embassy or High Commission may be easily obtained to enable the Home Office to remove you relatively easily should your asylum claim ultimately fail.

The screening interview is also intended to establish whether you may be returned to a 'safe' third country, which has responsibility for determining the claim to asylum. This is usually, although not always, a country through which you have travelled to arrive in the UK.

Third country cases

As an asylum seeker, you cannot normally be removed from the UK while your claim is pending a decision.[7] An exception to this is where the Secretary of State intends to remove you to a third country. The substantive statutory basis for 'third country removals' is the Asylum and Immigration (Treatment of Claimants, etc.) Act 2004[8] which provides for a 'graduated approach to the 'safety' of third countries for Refugee Convention and ECHR purposes'. Schedule 3 allows for four lists of countries and provisions to add or remove countries from these lists.

EEA member states (including A8 and A2 countries) are presumed safe.[9] The member states have established a set of criteria by which they decided which member state has responsibility for substantively considering and determining a person's asylum claim. These criteria are set out in EC Regulation 243/2003 (commonly known as 'Dublin (II)' as it is the successor to the original Dublin

Convention). There are time limits within which the responsibility of the 'third country' (ie, the other EU member state) should be decided but you cannot rely on these and any delay to assert that your claim should be considered in the UK.[10]

There are other lists (and removal arrangements) for other third countries.[11] The Secretary of State may designate certain countries by order (historically the USA, Canada and Switzerland).

Once the third country is identified, your asylum claim is 'certified' by the Secretary of State. This affects your rights of appeal or judicial review. In general there is no 'in-country' or 'out of country' right of appeal on Refugee Convention grounds, although depending on the facts of the case, the designated third country and whether the Secretary of State certifies the case as 'clearly unfounded' there may be a right of appeal or judicial review on human rights grounds.[12] This is a complex area of law and it is best to seek specialist legal advice.

Accelerated procedure cases and 'fast track'

Any claim, whatever your nationality or country of origin, may be fast tracked where after screening it appears to be one that may be decided quickly. Applicants whose claims are deemed suitable for fast track processing are held in detention – at the time of writing, at Oakington, Harmondsworth or Yarl's Wood. The 'Detained Fast Track Countries List' is available at www.ind.homeoffice.gov.uk along with a list of categories of applicant considered unsuitable for the process, including unaccompanied minors, anyone presenting with acute psychosis, any medical condition which requires 24 hour nursing or medical intervention and pregnant women of 24 weeks and above. Presently, those processed through Harmondsworth receive a decision on their claim within three days of arrival and are subject to an expedited appeals procedure.

The next steps in an asylum claim

Asylum seekers who are not detained are on 'temporary admission', bail granted by a Chief Immigration Officer (CIO bail) or bail granted by an Immigration Judge following a period in immigration detention.

The Secretary of State is required to give you a document clarifying your status within three days of your arrival (or date of in-country claim for asylum)[13] and information about benefits and services you may be eligible to receive within 15 days.[14] Following a screening interview, you are usually given some form of induction during which you receive an Application Registration Card (ARC), which contains your personal details and acts as a form of identity. In some cases, for example, where a claim is made at a non-ARC equipped site, a temporary standard acknowledgement letter (see p110) is issued.

You may be given a Statement of Evidence Form (SEF), which is a questionnaire for completion in English and with a deadline for submission (normally 10 working days). The SEF is your first opportunity to give an account of the events which caused you to come to the UK and claim asylum and why you fear persecution. It is generally better if a statement is attached. The SEF must be returned by the deadline on the form. If it is not completed and returned in time, the Home Office may make a decision on the existing evidence without considering the detailed claim that you wish to put forward. This will almost always result in a refusal.

You are required to attend an interview about your claim at the Home Office Immigration and Nationality Department in Croydon, if you are accommodated in the south and Liverpool if you are accommodated in the north. Under NAM interviews will take place at additional locations, including central London, Solihull, Leeds, Cardiff and Glasgow. If a SEF was completed, it usually forms the basis of the interview. A Home Office interpreter can be present if needed. You may have legal representation, although (except in very few cases) the Legal Services Commission (LSC) will not meet the interview attendance costs of a publicly funded representative. If there is no legal representative present, you are entitled to request the tape recording of the interview, although the request needs to be made in advance of the interview. At the time of writing the LSC is funding representatives to attend substantive NAM interviews as part of a pilot in Solihull and this may be expanded in the future.

The key characteristic of NAM is that the same Home Office 'caseowner' has responsibility for all aspects of the claim. The caseowner will interview you and make the decision on the claim and represent at the appeal if the application is refused. The caseowner communicates with you and/or your representative regarding the time frame (within prescribed deadlines) for submission of supporting evidence and consideration of the claim, reporting restrictions etc. The caseowner is responsible for the case to completion – ie, to grant of protection or to removal.

Home Office policy on accepting further representations following the main asylum interview depends upon whether you have been served with a SEF, been through the induction centre process (during which you receive a 'briefing' on your role and responsibilities concerning your asylum application) or been through the fast track process (where legal representatives attendance at the substantive interview may be LSC funded). It is only where you do not fall into any of these categories that the Home Office has agreed to consider further representations within the five days following interview. Notwithstanding this, any problems arising from the substantive interview should be addressed in writing as soon as possible (and before the decision is made) after the interview. NAM allows for a degree of negotiation with the caseowner regarding time limits.

In most cases a decision is reached fairly rapidly following the interview. The Home Office aims to serve decisions around five to seven working days after the substantive asylum interview.

To determine whether you are a refugee, the asylum application is considered by caseworkers at the Home Office who have access to information concerning the particular country from which the asylum seeker has come.[15] Country assessment reports (Country of Origin Information Service reports, referred to as COIS reports) and Operational Guidance Notes (OGNs) are produced by the Home Office. The statutory Advisory Panel on Country Information (APCI)[16] advises the Home Office on the balance and reliability of the information contained in the COIS reports and, in principle, researching and presenting country information for the COIS reports is separate from Home Office policy. The OGNs contain country information which embodies Home Office policy.

The onus is on applicants to show they meet the requirements of the law and immigration rules relating to asylum.[17] Obtaining the necessary evidence and ensuring that there are no misunderstandings, errors or discrepancies in the application is of the utmost importance. Minor discrepancies may be relied upon by the Secretary of State to question the truthfulness of a claimant's account.

The Reception Directive – permission to work

On 4 February 2005, Council Directive 2003/9/EC, known as the Reception Directive came into force and laid down minimum standards for the reception of asylum seekers.[18] It provides that the member state shall determine the period of time during which an asylum seeker shall not have access to the labour market,[19] that if a first instance decision had not been taken in one year from the date of claim (and the delay was not attributable to the applicant) there should be provision for access to the labour market[20] and that permission to work should not be withdrawn during the appeals process (where the procedure has a suspensive effect).[21] The provisions are now to be found in the Immigration Rules.[22]

Human rights claims

All Home Office decisions should comply with the European Convention on Human Rights (ECHR) which is now, effectively, incorporated into UK law.[23] The Qualification Directive (p56) and consequent domestic regulations and rule changes also allow for a new type of international protection called **humanitarian protection** (HP).

Article 3

Article 3 of the ECHR provides that: 'No one shall be subjected to torture or to inhuman or degrading treatment or punishment'.[24] The group of people who fall within the protection of Article 3 ECHR is broader than those who fall within the Refugee Convention. For example, under Article 3 you do not need to show that you will be ill-treated for a particular reason. Article 3 also provides greater protection than the 1951 Refugee Convention for those who are fleeing the effects of civil war.

While the 1951 Refugee Convention contains exclusions for people who are a danger to the host country or who have committed very serious offences against humanity or the principles of the United Nations, Article 3 is an **absolute** right, which means that, even if you are a danger to the country, which you are in, you cannot be returned if you will face torture or inhuman or degrading treatment or punishment. A person claiming protection under Article 3 of the ECHR will need to show that there are 'substantial grounds for believing' that there is a 'real risk' of a breach of this right.[25]

However, only those who fit the criteria under the 1951 Refugee Convention are recognised as refugees. Those who are allowed to remain under Article 3 ECHR may be granted HP or 'discretionary leave' (DL – see p67).

Absolute, limited and qualified human rights

Article 3 is not the only provision of the ECHR by which you may apply to stay in the UK. You may seek to rely upon Article 2 (right to life); Article 5 (right to liberty); Article 6 (right to a fair trial); Article 8 (right to respect for family life); Article 9 (freedom of religion and belief); Article 10 (freedom of expression).

It is necessary to show that there is a 'real risk' of a particular human right being breached for the ECHR to be engaged. Further, for each category of right, a particular threshold of harm or hurt must be met. The rights and freedoms protected by the ECHR can be categorised in three ways: absolute, limited and qualified rights.

Absolute rights include the right to life (Art 2), the right not to be subjected to torture or to inhuman or degrading treatment or punishment (Art 3), the right not to be held in slavery or servitude (Art 4), the right not to be punished by retrospective laws (Art 7) and the right not to be condemned to the death penalty or executed except in time of war (Protocol 13). There can be no opting out by a member state from an absolute right even in time of war or public emergency. The threshold for inhuman and degrading treatment in Article 3 immigration removal cases relying on medical conditions is extremely high and will only be reached in *truly exceptional cases* involving *extreme circumstances*.[26] The continuing development of Article 3 caselaw has made this a complex area of law where even the most compassionate cases can succeed or fail.

Limited rights, which are subject to exceptions or opt-outs in some circumstances, include the right to liberty and security (Art 5), the right to a fair trial (Art 6), the right to freedom of thought, conscience and religion (Art 9), the right to education (Art 2 of the First Protocol) and the right to enjoy Convention rights and freedoms without discrimination (Art 17). The threshold for a limited right to be breached in an immigration removal case is a *'flagrant breach'*.

Qualified rights must be balanced against, and may have to give way to other competing public interests – eg, immigration control and national law and order.[27] The principle of 'proportionality' has been developed by both Strasbourg and UK caselaw. However, in the majority of cases, a decision taken pursuant to the lawful operation of immigration control would be found to be 'proportionate'.[28] Qualified rights include the right to respect for private and family life (Art 8), to manifest one's religion and belief (Art 9(2)), to freedom of expression, peaceful assembly and movement (Arts 10 and 11). In Article 8 cases, involving a breach of family life, you would need to show that you have actually established family life and that your family life could not be maintained abroad. Often you also need to provide an explanation for why it is not possible to return to your own country to obtain an entry clearance for the purposes of coming back to the UK to pursue your family life here. Having established these factors, you are also required to show that that the claimed breach is *'truly exceptional'* for the ECHR to be engaged.[29]

If your removal from the UK would breach your human right(s) you may be granted either HP or DL. Home Office policy is generally to grant HP to those who need some sort of protection from harm by others whereas other cases, including those who have satisfied the Article 3 threshold on medical grounds, will be granted a more limited period of DL (see p67).

2. Asylum decisions and refugee status

If the Home Office decides that you are a refugee, then you must be granted leave to enter or remain in the UK as a refugee. The decision to recognise you as a refugee, or to refuse to recognise you, is not the same as the immigration decision which is subsequently made. For example, recognition as a refugee will usually lead to a grant of leave to remain, whereas refusal to recognise you as a refugee may lead to refusal of leave to enter or the setting of removal directions. The asylum decision on recognition as a refugee is one which is made by the Home Office in accordance with the EC Qualification Directive (p56).

A grant of refugee status

From 30 August 2005, a person recognised as a refugee is normally granted an initial five years' leave to remain. The previous policy was to grant indefinite leave to remain (ILR). During the limited five-year period your refugee status can be reviewed and removed, although this is unlikely to occur. A review may be triggered in two ways:
- if your own actions bring you within the scope of the 1951 Refugee Convention cessation clauses (Articles 1C(1)-(6) 1951 Refugee Convention) – eg, if you travelled back to your country of origin without a reasonable explanation; *or*
- if there is a 'significant or non-temporary' change in conditions in the country of origin or part of the country that places in doubt the continuing need for your protection.

One result of the review may be that you are expected to return to your country of origin. Normally there is no review at the end of the five-year period, but a review can be triggered if there is evidence of criminality or if you apply for settlement after your initial period of leave has expired (ie, you apply 'out of time'). If there is no review during or at the end of the five-year period, you are eligible to settle in the UK subject to passing an ESOL with citizenship course or a *Life in the UK* test (see p27). There are specified forms on which these applications must be made.

Once recognised as a refugee, an application may be made for family reunion with your pre-existing spouse and minor children who formed part of the family unit prior to your departure.[30] Your sponsor is not expected to meet the maintenance and accommodation requirements of the immigration rules. Under the New Asylum Model (see p58) there is a grant memorandum that the Home Office will keep on file in cases in which asylum is granted. This sets out a brief summary of the reasons why asylum has been granted. Current policy is that the memorandum will not automatically be disclosed to successful applicants but a request can be made for it.

At the time of writing there was no firm date for introducing section 12 of the Asylum and Immigration (Treatment of Claimants, etc) Act 2004 which abolishes the right of those recognised as refugees to claim backdated benefits. Consequently, those granted refugee status may continue to claim backdated benefits to the recorded date of their asylum claim.

Negative decisions

If the decision is negative, the Home Office may, depending on circumstances of the case, make one or more of the following immigration decisions:[31]
- refuse leave to enter and set directions for your removal (where you claimed asylum at port);[32]
- set directions for your removal as an illegal entrant (where you entered the UK unlawfully and subsequently claimed asylum);[33]
- set directions for your removal as an overstayer or as a person who has breached one or more of their other conditions of leave (where you entered lawfully but then claimed asylum having overstayed or breached your conditions of leave or obtained leave to *remain* by deception);[34]
- refuse to extend leave so as to grant leave to remain as a refugee and/or to curtail existing leave (where you make an in-country claim for asylum within the period of a separate leave, eg, as a visitor);
- issue a notice of intention to deport you (where you are liable to be deported because the Secretary of State has determined that your presence is not conducive to the public good);[35] *or*
- issue a deportation order (where you claimed asylum after notice of intention to deport has been issued or a court has recommended deportation as part of your sentence if you have been convicted of a criminal offence); *or*[36]
- refuse to revoke a deportation order (where you claimed asylum after a deportation order has already been made).[37]

The asylum refusal itself is set out in a 'reasons for refusal letter', which gives the substantive reasons why asylum has been refused. This is sent to you, together with one of the administrative immigration decisions referred to above. If the refusal is based on the fact that you are the responsibility of a third country, this will also be clear from the letter.

In addition, if an asylum application is refused, the caseworker also decides whether to **'certify'** the claim to asylum and the claim to remain on human rights grounds.[38]

3. Humanitarian protection and discretionary leave to remain

Before 1 April 2003

Advisers will continue to meet people who were granted exceptional leave to enter or remain before its abolition from 1 April 2003. There is a dwindling group of people who currently have this status, although there will continue to be those to whom it was granted at some point but for whom it has since lapsed. In addition, the term 'exceptional leave' is still in popular use.

Historically the immigration authorities have exercised their discretion to treat people more favourably that the immigration rules allow. Immigration advisers often talk of the Home Office's discretion to 'depart from' the immigration rules or to 'waive' the rules or 'act outside' the rules. Whenever applicants are treated more beneficially than the immigration rules allow, they can be said to be treated 'exceptionally'. Indeed, everyone who was not held to the letter of the immigration rules may be said to have been treated exceptionally and indeed may have been granted leave exceptionally, although this may not always be obvious from the format of the actual grant of leave. This type of leave is referred to by the Home Office as 'leave outside the rules'.[39]

However, a grant of 'exceptional leave to remain' (ELR) had a more limited meaning and application. It described the leave granted to asylum seekers who were not found to be refugees but the Home Office, for humanitarian or compassionate reasons, determined it would not be right to require them to return to the country from which they had come.

Those who, up until 2007, have spent four years with ELR will have an application for indefinite leave to remain (ILR) considered under the previous policy. Those who have spent less than four years on exceptional leave will have any application to extend their leave to remain considered under the new, stricter policy relating to humanitarian protection (HP).

From 1 April 2003

The Home Office abolished ELR with effect from 1 April 2003 and replaced it with HP or discretionary leave (DL). The 2003/04 Asylum Policy Instructions (APIs) stated that HP or DL may be granted for **up to** three years. However, further changes have been made to the term of grants and Home Office practice of 'active review' when an application for an extension or settlement is made. These changes are explained below according to the category of leave.

Humanitarian protection

HP is leave granted to a person who, if removed, would face a serious risk to life or person arising from the death penalty, unlawful killing or torture or inhuman or degrading treatment or punishment in the country of return. That is, while they do not satisfy the criteria laid down in Article 1(A)2 of the Refugee Convention, they would be at risk of treatment in violation of Articles 2 or 3 of the ECHR. Protection pursuant to Articles 2 and 3 used to be outside the immigration rules until the changes in the rules on 9 October 2006 following the implementation of the EC Qualification Directive (p56).

If you claimed asylum but were refused refugee status and granted HP, you should be issued with a 'full reasons for refusal of asylum' letter. The letter should also state why you are being granted HP and the date it expires.

From 30 August 2005, if you are granted HP you are also granted limited leave of five years, after which you can apply for settlement. Unlike with refugee status, however, if an application for settlement is submitted at the end of the five years of HP, there is an automatic review of whether there is a continuing protection need. There is also an English language and *Life in the UK* test. There are specified forms on which these applications must be made.

The previous policy, prior to 30 August 2005, was for a grant of three years after which there was an avenue to apply for settlement if the circumstances which gave rise to the need for protection continued to exist.

Previously, those with HP were not entitled to family reunion until they had been granted settlement (ILR) and could sponsor their family members. For those granted HP on or after 30 August 2005, similar family reunion provisions to those who have been granted refugee status apply. The 'principal' claimant can apply for family reunion with their pre-existing spouses and minor children who formed part of the family unit prior to the principal's departure. The sponsor is expected to meet the maintenance and accommodation requirements. At the time of writing the APIs were being rewritten to reflect these changes.

Even if you are able to establish that there is a real risk of a breach of your human rights, you are not granted HP if you fall within various 'exclusion criteria'. These criteria include those whose presence in the UK is considered not to be conducive to the public good (eg, having committed a serious crime) and/or they are considered a threat to security. Those who would have been granted HP but are subject to the exclusion criteria, are normally granted a limited period of DL (see below).

Further, where the risk of treatment in violation of Article 3 arises owing to a medical condition, HP is not given but you will be considered for DL.

Discretionary leave

The most common situations where DLR was granted were cases involving medical treatment and cases where family life rights would be breached. Also, a person who would be excluded from a grant of refugee leave under Article 1F(b) of the Refugee Convention or from HP under the exclusion criteria would qualify for a grant of DL if her/his removal would involve a breach of the ECHR.

In cases where a human rights claim has rested on the severity of a medical condition, even where you risk treatment in violation of Article 3, HP is not to be given but you could be considered for DL.[40] The IDIs (Chapter 1 paragraph 3.4) were amended in December 2006 to withdraw the Home Office health policy and so it is not currently clear whether DL will continue to be granted in health cases that do not meet the extremely narrow test set out in *N v SSHD* [2005] UKHL 31. In that case the claimant's appeal was rejected. She was suffering from AIDS and it was agreed that if she was removed she was likely to die within a year after a period of acute mental and physical suffering. The House of Lords decided that a human rights breach would only occur if the claimant was already dying or, in other exceptional circumstances such as where there is a complete absence of relevant medical treatment in the receiving country.[41]

Most other circumstances in which DL may be granted are Article 8 cases. The most common situations are where family rights would be breached by removal, unaccompanied minors for whom there are no adequate reception arrangements in their country of origin and where the individual circumstances are so compelling that it is considered appropriate to grant some form of leave, and also those who are covered by Home Office concessions – eg, carers.[42]

DL is granted for up to three years but can be granted for much shorter periods – eg, six months. An application to extend a period of DL must be made 'in-time' (ie, before the previous period of grant expires). Applications are considered in the light of circumstances prevailing at the time. A person will not become eligible to apply for settlement until they have completed six years of DL or, for those who are subject to the exclusion criteria, 10 years.

There are specified forms on which these applications must be made.

Unaccompanied asylum seeking children

In the case of unaccompanied asylum seeking children (UASCs), if their asylum claim is refused and there is no family to return to or adequate reception arrangements cannot be established, the period of DL to be granted depends upon the country of origin. In all cases, the grant of DL may be up to three years or until the child's 18th birthday, whichever is the shorter period. At 18 years old, if not eligible for settlement, their case becomes subject to 'active review' and their application dealt with as an adult and therefore not subject to the UASC non-returns policy.

Temporary protection

Temporary protection is a separate and specific category of leave.[43] Introduced as a category by EC Directive 2001/55/EC, temporary protection is granted only to individuals where they are covered by a declaration of the EU Council in recognition of a mass influx of displaced persons. There have been no such declarations since the Directive came into force.

Notes

1. The Refugee or Persons in Need of International Protection (Qualification) Regulations 2006 (No.2525) and statement of changes to the immigration rules (Cm 6918)
2. para 334 HC395; Art 1(A)(2) Geneva Convention on Refugees 1951
3. This is partly because one of the criteria for qualifying as a refugee is that the applicant is 'outside their country of nationality or former habitual residence' (Art 1A(2) 1951 Refugee Convention) although the IND does, in very rare cases, consider applications for asylum from abroad outside the immigration rules where the UK is the most appropriate country of refuge. Further, the House of Lords has decided in *European Roma Rights Centre v Immigration Officer at Prague Airport* [2004] UKHL 55, [2005] 2 WLR 1 that the Convention does not operate extra-territorially so as to oblige states to enable asylum claimants to travel to the UK.

1. Consideration of cases
4. s55(1) NIA 2002
5. s2 AI(ToC)A 2004
6. *Thet v DPP* [2006] EWHC 2701
7. s77-78 NIA 2002

8. s33 and Sch 3 AI(TC)A 2004
9. Sch 3 Part 2 AI(TC)A 2004
10. *Zeggiri v SSHD* [2002] ImmAR 42
11. Sch 3 Part 3 AI(TC)A 2004
12. see *Razgar* [2004] UKHL 27; Sch 3 para 10 AI(TC)A 2004
13. para 359 HC 395
14. para 358 HC 395
15. para 328 HC 395 under the criteria of the 1951 UN Convention
16. s142 NIAA 2002
17. paras 340-342 HC 395
18. Council Directive 2003/9/EC
19. Art 11(1) Council Directive 2003/9/EC
20. Art 11(2) Council Directive 2003/9/EC
21. Art 11(3) Council Directive 2003/9/EC
22. paras 360 and 361 HC 395
23. HRA 1998; para 2 HC 395 as amended by Cmnd 4851 from 2 October 2000
24. also see Sch1 Part 1 HRA 1998
25. *Chahal v UK* [1997] 23 EHRR 413
26. *D v UK* (1997) 224 EHHR 423; *N v SSHD* [2003] EWCA Civ 1165; *SSHD v R(Razgar)* [2004] UKHL 27, 17 June 2004
27. *Boultif v Switzerland* [2001] 33 EHRR 50 para 471

28 *R(Razgar) v SSHD* [2004] 2AC 368(20);
   SSHD v R(Razgar) [2004] UKHL 27, 17
   June 2004
29 *Razgar*, as above; *Ullah* [2004] UKHL 26;
   Huang v SSHD [2005] EWCA Civ 105;
   Mahmood [2001] 1 WLR 840 (CA)

2. Asylum decisions and refugee status
30 UNHCR Handbook Part 2; also dicta in
   Robinson v SSHD [1997] Imm AR 568,
   Brooke LJ at para 11
31 Immigration decisions listed in s82(2)
   NIAA 2002 are appealable (see Chapter
   6)
32 para 2A(8),(9) Sch 2 IA 1971
33 paras 8-10 Sch 2 IA 1971
34 s10 IAA 1999
35 s5(1) IA 1971
36 s5(1) IA 1971
37 s5(2) IA 1971
38 Sch 4 para 9 IAA 1999

3. Humanitarian protection and discretionary leave to remain
39 IDIs ch 1 s14 para 1.2
40 *D v United Kingdom* [1977] 24 EHRR 423
41 This reflects the Home Office
   interpretation of the majority decision in
   the Court of Appeal in *N v SSHD* [2-3]
   EWCA Civ 1369, [2004] 1 WLR 118,
   upheld by the House of Lords at [2005]
   UKHL 31
42 IDIs ch 17
43 s2 para 354 HC 395

6

Chapter 6
. . . .
Enforcement and appeals

This chapter provides a summary of the main problems people may face under immigration law if they wish to enter or remain in the UK but have had their application to do so refused by the immigration authorities, who then proceed to enforce their departure from the UK; and the rights of appeal which are available against negative immigration decisions. It covers:
1. Deportation, illegal entry and removal (below)
2. Refusals and appeals (p76)

Different legal provisions apply to European Economic Area citizens and their dependants (see Chapter 8).

1. Deportation, illegal entry and removal

If you are in the UK and you need leave to enter or remain here (see Chapter 3), but you cannot satisfy the immigration rules, then the immigration authorities have the power to enforce your departure. There are also possible criminal penalties if you are in breach of immigration control. Prosecution for criminal immigration offences is not frequent, save for the offence of entering or seeking to enter without a valid immigration document.[1] There have been many convictions for this offence since it was introduced in September 2004 but, following recent caselaw, convictions are likely to decline.[2] The immigration authorities have wide powers of detention to assist with regulating control and enforcement. Detention powers may be used against individuals, whether or not they are charged with any offence, either immigration or otherwise.

'**Deportation**' means sending people away from the UK under an order signed by the Secretary of State and forbidding their re-entry. Deportation proceedings are usually brought against those subject to immigration control who have leave to enter or remain in the UK but who have committed a criminal offence.

Another process of removal, called '**administrative removal**', is usually used for those who do not have leave to enter or remain or who have breached the conditions of their stay. Administrative removal is also the main means of removing '**illegal entrants**' (see p74).

The basic four methods of enforcing a person's departure from the UK are:

. . . .

- removal following refusal of entry (see below);
- deportation (see below);
- administrative removal (see p73); *and*
- removal of illegal entrants (see p74).

The form of 'enforcement' used depends on your immigration status.

Removal following refusal of entry

If you arrive in the UK and are refused leave to enter in whatever category you apply to come in (eg, as a visitor, student or refugee), the process by which you may be forced to leave the UK is known simply as '**removal**'. Removal does not have to take place immediately after you arrive in the UK. It may not be possible to make a decision on whether you should be granted leave to enter straight away and you may have a right of appeal before you can be removed. In refugee cases, the process can often take years before you may be removed. During the time you are waiting for, or appealing against, a decision to refuse to grant you leave to enter, you are not treated as having actually entered the UK for immigration purposes.[3] During this period you may either be granted temporary admission (this is a licence to be in the UK which may be granted subject to conditions as to work, address, etc – see p111) or detained.[4] This process, therefore, applies if you present yourself to the immigration officer when you arrive but are, either immediately or eventually, refused entry.

Deportation

British citizens or other Commonwealth citizens with the right of abode are exempt from deportation, save that there is a power to deprive certain persons of citizenship or the right of abode. This can now be exercised on grounds that it is conducive to the public good.[5] This enables deportation of nationals who were previously exempt. Other people generally exempt from deportation include:
- certain diplomats and their family members;[6]
- certain Commonwealth nationals and citizens of the Republic of Ireland who were ordinarily resident in the UK on 1 January 1973;[7] *and*
- those who become British citizens after the deportation process has commenced.[8]

There is a separate deportation process that applies to European Economic Area citizens and their dependants (see Chapter 8).
You can only be deported if you fall into one of the following groups:[9]
- the Secretary of State decides that your deportation is conducive to the public good;
- you have overstayed leave which was granted to you (see p49), and, before 2 October 2000, you made a valid application to the Secretary of State to

'regularise' your stay in the UK (the application must have been made setting out certain required information);[10]

- you have been convicted of an imprisonable offence and a criminal court makes a recommendation that you be deported; *or*
- you are a spouse, civil partner or child (under 18) of a person in any of the above categories who is to be deported.

It is up to the Home Office to prove that there are grounds to deport you. The immigration rules now state that where a person is liable to deportation, the presumption is that the public interest requires deportation. The rules go on to state that the Home Office will take into account all relevant factors known although it will only be in exceptional circumstances that the public interest in deportation will be outweighed.[11] (See p73 for the relevant factors that are also considered in administrative removal cases.)

If you are to be deported as a spouse, civil partner or child of someone who is to be deported, the Home Office must also consider:

- in the case of a spouse or civil partner, whether you are able to maintain and accommodate yourself;
- in the case of a child, the effect on your education and the practical arrangements for your care in the UK if your parents are deported.[12]

If you already have permission to stay indefinitely, acquired pursuant to an independent right, or were living apart from the person who is to be deported, your deportation would not normally be considered.[13]

Even where a court has recommended your deportation, the first step in the actual deportation process is usually for the Home Office to make a decision in principle to deport you. This is sometimes preceded by a notice of intention to deport being sent to you, which allows you to submit representations to the Home Office prior to a decision to deport being taken. If the Home Office decides to deport you, you must be informed in writing, normally on a standard letter called a 'notice of decision to deport'. There is a right of appeal (see p76), including where you are being deported following a recommendation by a criminal court, unless the Home Secretary also certifies the deportation on grounds of national security. In these cases an appeal right may be acquired by making a human rights or asylum challenge (see p78). The national security certificate may then be challenged by appeal to the Special Immigration Appeals Commission, as may any certificate that a human rights application is unfounded.[14]

If the appeal is lost, the Home Secretary can then sign a deportation order and force you to leave. If a decision to make a deportation order is made against you, it may be possible to avoid an actual deportation order being made by leaving the UK before this happens. The benefit of this is that you are not automatically excluded from re-entering the UK, but the general grounds for refusal may make it difficult for you to re-enter the UK in any event.[15] A deportation order is not valid until it has been properly served on you, which often takes place in person.

If you are deported, you cannot return unless the deportation order is revoked.[16] Usually you have to be outside the UK for at least three years before the Home Office will consider this. After the order has been revoked, you need to satisfy again the ordinary requirements of the immigration rules in order to re-enter.[17]

Administrative removal

You are liable to be administratively removed if:[18]
- you were allowed to enter or remain in the UK for a certain length of time and have overstayed your leave to enter or remain; *or*
- you have broken a condition of your leave – eg, you have worked when prohibited from doing so, or you have claimed a public funds benefit when you had a condition stating that you must maintain and accommodate yourself without recourse to public funds. After your leave has expired, there can no longer be any question of any conditions applying because the conditions can only be attached to the leave itself (although after leave has expired, you will become an overstayer); *or*
- you obtained leave to remain or tried to obtain leave to remain in the UK by deception;[19] *or*
- the Home Office considers that you have ceased to be a refugee and your indefinite leave to remain is revoked.[20] There is an appeal right against revocation and against the decision to take administrative removal; *or*
- you are the spouse, civil partner or the child (under 18) of a person who is to be deported.[21]

The Home Office may obtain evidence about breaching conditions from an employer (about working without permission) or from the DWP (about claiming benefits in breach of your conditions).

Unlike deportation, there is only one stage to administrative removal. You are usually removed after the immigration officer sets directions for your removal unless you have an in-country right of appeal on human rights or asylum grounds. It is important to note, however, that, before you can be removed under these powers, the Home Office must consider the following factions:
- age;
- length of residence in the UK;
- strength of connections with the UK;
- personal history, including character, conduct and employment record;
- domestic circumstances;
- the nature of any offence of which the person has been convicted;
- previous criminal record;

- compassionate circumstances;
- any representations received on your behalf.[22]

Detailed representations referring to these factors should, therefore, be made.

Illegal entry

The Secretary of State can decide to treat you as an illegal entrant if you:[23]
- avoid the immigration officers altogether (this is sometimes known as 'clandestine' entry – ie, arriving in the back of a lorry or in a sealed container and passing through controls without being examined by the immigration officer);
- enter while a deportation order is in force against you; *or*
- obtain entry by deceiving an immigration officer about your identity or your reasons for coming to the UK.

A person will sometimes have stamps on her/his passport which state that s/he has been granted leave to enter and will not understand how s/he can be an illegal entrant. The Home Office or the immigration service may say that s/he lied when applying for permission to enter. There is often no evidence to support the Home Office view, so it relies heavily on questioning people about their entry and using their answers against them. Those who use false passports or other identity documents (eg, EEA national travel documents) are also illegal entrants. You may also be an illegal entrant where, although you used no deception yourself, someone else told lies in order to secure your entry. This can happen in cases where family members or sponsors have made inaccurate statements to an immigration officer or an entry clearance officer.

If you are treated as an illegal entrant, you will be informed in writing. The only appeal rights that may be available are an asylum or human rights challenge.

In cases of removal after being refused leave to enter, administrative removal and illegal entry, the Home Office may try to act very quickly. It is therefore necessary for you or your advisers to act promptly in making representations. The Home Office may delay removing you while the case is being considered, particularly if your MP has agreed to take it up. You may also be able to apply for judicial review of the decision or it may become necessary to issue such proceedings to compel the Home Office to consider representations before any removal. In asylum and human rights cases, it may be argued that such representations constitute a fresh claim. Alternatively, you may have been advised that the prospects of successfully challenging removal are remote and there are better prospects for applying for entry clearance to return to the UK after your removal. If you are released on temporary admission while your case is considered, you will be told the terms and conditions of your release on Form IS 96.

Other enforcement procedures

There are various other procedures which may be invoked in order to enforce the departure of individuals in certain circumstances.

- European Union/EEA nationals may be removed from the UK if they cease to exercise free movement rights or if their removal is justified on grounds of public policy, public security or public health.[24]
- People who are members of the armed forces of various friendly states may be arrested, detained and removed from the UK if a request is made by the country concerned.[25]
- Certain people who are receiving in-patient treatment for mental illness may also be removed from the UK with the approval of a mental health review tribunal provided that proper arrangements have been made for their treatment and it is in the interests of the person to be removed.[26]
- People whose return is requested by foreign authorities in respect of criminal offences may be removed from the UK in a procedure known as 'extradition'. This is a large subject with rules of its own. It is not a common occurrence.[27]

Working unlawfully

Since 27 January 1997, it has been an offence for an employer to employ someone who is not permitted to work in the UK.[28] It is therefore currently unlawful for an employer to employ a person who:

- has not been granted leave to enter or remain in the UK; *or*
- has leave containing a condition prohibiting her/him from taking the particular job or whose leave is invalid; *or*
- has overstayed her/his leave.

It is not unlawful, however, for an employer to employ an asylum seeker who has been given written permission to work by the immigration authorities.

Employers are not legally liable if, before the employment started, they saw and kept a copy of certain specified documents relating to the employee. Such documents include an official document containing the person's national insurance number (eg, a P45), as well as passports and Home Office letters which indicate that the employee is lawfully able to work in the UK.[29] The offence only relates to people who started jobs from 27 January 1997.

When section 21 of the Immigration, Asylum and Nationality Act 2006 comes into force, an employer will only commit an offence if s/he knowingly employs a person who does not have permission to work. A civil offence, similar to the existing criminal offence, will come into force at the same time.

2. **Refusals and appeals**

If you apply to come to or remain in the UK, the immigration authorities may grant or refuse your application. If the Home Office considers that you satisfy the requirements of the immigration rules in the particular category in which you are applying, you should be granted permission to come or to stay here (see Chapter 3). If you do not fit into the rules but the Home Office believes there are good reasons, usually of a compassionate or family nature, to make an exception to the rules, you may be granted permission to enter or remain outside the rules. Otherwise, your application will be refused. Depending on the nature of an application and whether or not it was validly made while you had permission to be in the UK, there may be a formal right of appeal against a refusal. The immigration authorities can also make decisions, without any application being made to them, which affect people's immigration status and against which there may be a right of appeal.

When to appeal

There are rights to appeal against many immigration decisions and against most asylum refusals. When such decisions are made, you should be given:[30]
- notice of the decision and the reasons for it; *and*
- essential information concerning your rights of appeal – eg, the time limit for appealing and the place to which the notice of appeal should be sent.

However, it is worth bearing in mind that the immigration authorities do not always accurately advise people of their appeal rights.[31]

There are very strict time limits laid down in special procedure rules with regard to lodging appeals. These time limits are important because the right of appeal may be lost if the forms are not received in time. When you have been refused, therefore, and have a right of appeal, the first thing to check is the date of refusal. This is to ensure that any appeal is still in time. In order to ensure that there is proof that the forms have been sent back, they should be faxed or posted by recorded delivery to the Asylum and Immigration Tribunal (AIT). Appeal forms may also be served on the entry clearance officer in entry clearance cases (at the time of writing this actually leads to your appeal being listed by the appeal authority more quickly than if you serve it on the AIT itself) or on your custodian if you are in detention in the UK.[32]

It is always necessary to give full details of the reasons for the appeal.

If you are given a notice of refusal or directions for removal or a notice relating to deportation and, in particular if you want to appeal, you should immediately seek further specialist advice. The Immigration Advisory Service and the Refugee Legal Centre are funded by the Legal Services Commission to provide free appeal representation to those who are eligible; law centres and other specialist advice centres may be able to give free help, as can solicitors who have a contract to do immigration work under the Community Legal Service (see Appendix 1).

Immigration decisions which can be appealed

The Nationality, Immigration and Asylum Act 2002 (NIAA 2002) sets out the only types of immigration decision that can be appealed to the AIT[33] and the possible grounds of appeal.[34] The Act then goes on to remove certain appeal rights it may appear that you have – ie, mandatory refusals,[35] visitors and students on entry without entry clearance,[36] non-family visitors,[37] prospective and short-term students,[38] where the Secretary of State certifies that matters should have been raised in an earlier appeal or when an earlier one stop notice was issued,[39] where s/he certifies that national security is engaged (instead there is an appeal to the Special Immigration Appeals Commission – SIAC),[40] or s/he takes a decision in whole or in part on public good grounds.[41] The NIAA 2002 also provides for many types of immigration appeal to be conducted from abroad,[42] including asylum and human rights cases that have been certified by the Secretary of State as clearly unfounded.[43]

When it comes into force, the Immigration, Asylum and Nationality Act 2006 (IANA 2006) will withdraw appeal rights for all entry clearance appeals save for family visitors and 'dependants'. Any appeals based on human rights or race discrimination grounds will also be preserved.[44] It also removes rights of appeal from those seeking entry unless they hold an appropriate entry clearance, or seek to appeal on human rights or race discrimination grounds.[45] The IANA 2006 introduced an asylum appeal where asylum is withdrawn or revoked but leave is granted in another capacity (in effect from 31 August 2006).[46]

Outside the UK

As stated above, once IANA 2006 is in force there will only be a right of appeal for those coming to visit a family member (as defined in regulations), those applying as dependants, and for appeals raising issues of human rights or race discrimination. This means that, for example, spouses, civil partners and children will still have a right of appeal against a refusal of entry clearance, but work permit holders, students and working holidaymakers will not.

There will not be appeal rights from abroad for those without entry clearance who are refused leave to enter, again, save for where an appeal raises race relation or human rights issues.[47] Instead of appeal rights, it is intended to provide improved internal monitoring of refusals.

If you are removed from the UK as an illegal entrant or under an immigration officer's powers of administrative removal (see p73), you may appeal against the directions to remove you after you have already been removed, although not on human rights or asylum grounds.[48] You may also appeal from abroad against a decision to refuse to revoke a deportation order.[49]

You may also appeal from abroad (again after you have been removed) if you have made an asylum or human rights claim but the Home Office has certified the claim as clearly unfounded[50] or if the Home Office has certified the claim on third country grounds, in which case there maybe a limited human rights appeal from abroad.[51]

At the port

If you are refused entry at a British port, there may be a right of appeal. If you obtained entry clearance and are seeking leave to enter for the purpose specified in the entry clearance then you will have an appeal right and you may remain in the UK while the appeal is under consideration.[52] You may also appeal on the ground that your removal would breach the Refugee Convention or on human rights grounds[53] provided that the refusal is not certified. Additionally, you may appeal on race discrimination grounds.

After entry to the UK

If the Home Office refuses you permission to stay longer in the UK after you make an in-time application, there is a right of appeal against the decision if you no longer have leave as a result of the refusal[54] save if the decision is subject to a mandatory refusal (see p79). There is also an appeal right where you are refused asylum but granted limited leave of at least 12 months.[55] The latter is an asylum appeal only, commonly known as an 'upgrade appeal'. There is also an asylum appeal right where asylum is withdrawn but you have leave to remain in another capacity.[56]

When the Home Office makes a notice of a decision to make a deportation order against you there is a right of appeal,[57] unless the decision is certified for national security reasons in which case the appeal is to SIAC, although this is not necessarily an 'in-country' appeal.[58] While you are in the UK you may also appeal against an immigration decision as set out in s82 NIAA 2002 on the grounds that your removal would breach the 1951 Refugee Convention unless the refusal is certified on the basis of return to a safe third country or the claim is certified as clearly unfounded.[59]

Human rights appeals

There is a right of appeal for any person who alleges that an immigration decision as defined by s82 NIAA 2002 taken by the immigration authorities relating to her/his right to enter or remain in the UK is 'in breach of [her/his] human rights' or racially discriminates against her/him,[60] unless the refusal is certified on the basis of return to a safe third country or the claim is certified as clearly unfounded.[61] The appeal may be brought on these grounds alone or, alternatively, may be argued in the course of any other appeal.

A decision which is in breach of your human rights means a decision which is in contravention of your rights under the ECHR, incorporated into UK law by the

Human Rights Act 1998.[62] The most important rights affecting immigration decisions are the right to respect for private and family life, which may be infringed by immigration decisions causing separation between family members (Article 8), and the prohibition on subjecting people to torture or inhuman or degrading treatment or punishment (Article 3). This will be contravened if the Home Office proposes to send a you to another country where you will be subjected to that treatment (see p61 for the differences between Article 3 and the 1951 Refugee Convention).

Exclusions from appeals

Visitors and students

Visitors have no right of appeal against being refused entry clearance abroad[63] unless they are a 'family visitor'.[64] There are similarly limited rights of entry clearance appeals for students. Those accepted onto courses of six months or less, prospective students and dependants have no rights of appeal. Such visitors and students are also excluded from appeal rights if they are refused entry at a port and if they have no entry clearance for these purposes.[65] However, all visitors and students may appeal if the appeal raises an issue of human rights or racial discrimination. Only these latter appeal rights and the appeal right for family visitors will remain after s4 IANA 2006 comes into force.

Mandatory refusals

Subject to appeals on grounds of racial discrimination, human rights and asylum, when a refusal is mandatory there is no right of appeal against a decision refusing leave to enter or an extension of leave.[66] A mandatory refusal relates to people who:

- do not have a document specified as required under the immigration rules – ie, entry clearance, passport or other identity document, or work permit and, since 31 August 2006, a medical report or certificate;[67] *or*
- do not meet a requirement of the rules as to age, nationality or citizenship. For example, a working holidaymaker must be a Commonwealth national aged between 17 and 27. A 29-year-old Japanese national who applied for entry as a working holidaymaker would have no right of appeal against refusal; *or*
- apply to remain longer than permitted under the rules – eg, a visitor applying to stay longer than six months; *or*
- seek to enter or remain for a purpose other than one permitted by the rules.

When the Home Office refuses your application on these grounds, it will inform you in writing stating that the application has been refused, that there is no right of appeal and you should leave the country within 28 days. If you do not leave within that time, the Home Office may, if you have no other basis of stay, make a decision to administratively remove you.[68] Note that if you are already in the UK, your immigration status lapses as soon as you are served with the decision and you therefore become an overstayer. Where similar decisions are made by entry clearance officers abroad or immigration officers at the port, they should also issue you with a notice explaining the basis of the decision and that there is no right of appeal. It may be possible to contest these refusals by applying for judicial review.

Decisions based on national security grounds

You cannot appeal in the ordinary way against an immigration decision where the Secretary of State has determined that your exclusion from the UK is justified on grounds of national security. If a decision is made against which you would ordinarily have the right of appeal but for the fact that the decision was made on national security grounds, you can appeal instead to SIAC, which has a special and complicated procedure of its own.[69] Only human rights aspects of these appeals are held in-country, and even this can be denied if the Secretary of State certifies that your removal would not breach the European Human Rights Convention.[70]

Decisions and appeals under these procedures are not common.

One stop notices and the appeal process

A 'one stop notice' can be served by the immigration authorities or the Home Office at any point after an application for leave to enter or remain is made. You are required to return a statement of additional grounds setting out any other grounds for seeking leave to enter/remain not previously disclosed. These may include human rights grounds.[71] The AIT is then obliged to consider any such grounds at a future appeal.[72] The Secretary of State for the Home Department (SSHD) is entitled to certify the refusal of an application (ie, to deny an appeal right) if the matters raised in support of that application could have been disclosed in response to an earlier one stop notice.[73]

Since 4 April 2005 notices of appeal can be served on the AIT.[74] If you are appealing against an entry clearance refusal then the appeal notice may be served on the post abroad that issued the refusal, or if you are in detention in the UK on your custodian.[75] Unless you are subject to a fast track procedure, for which the rules are different,[76] the time limits for appealing are:

- 10 working days if your appeal is being made within the UK[77] but five working days if you are detained;[78]
- 28 days if you are overseas (although if the notice is being sent to you overseas, then you are not taken to have received it for 28 days and time begins at that point).[79]

If the appeal forms are served on the AIT, the AIT will send a copy to the Home Office or relevant entry clearance post who then serve the appeal documents on the Tribunal. The AIT will then fix a date for hearing the appeal. The main hearing centre is at Taylor House, Rosebery Avenue, Clerkenwell, London, but there are other hearing centres in London and throughout the country.

Appeals are now usually listed within two months. Appeals are first heard by a single immigration judge. The losing side then has the right to apply for a paper review, referred to as a reconsideration application, to the AIT on grounds of an error of law in the initial determination and a real possibility that the tribunal would decide the appeal differently.[80] This application must be made within five days if you are within the UK and within 28 days if you are abroad[81] (again with an additional 28 days for deemed service). If that application is unsuccessful then a further paper application for reconsideration can be made to the Administrative Court.[82] If that is also unsuccessful there is no right to an oral renewal of the application or any onward challenge to the Court of Appeal.

If a Senior Immigration Judge in the AIT or a Judge in the Administrative Court makes an Order for reconsideration then the appeal is listed for a reconsideration hearing, usually in front of a panel of immigration judges. An application for leave to appeal to the Court of Appeal can be made from such a reconsideration determination.[83]

Protection from removal while an appeal is pending

While you have an appeal pending, you may no longer have any leave to stay in the UK. However, you are generally protected from being removed from the UK provided the appeal is an in-country appeal.[84]

Protection from removal while an asylum or human rights claim is outstanding

In asylum cases, you cannot be removed from, or required to leave, the UK from when you make a claim for asylum until the Secretary of State gives you notice of the decision.[85] An exception to this is where, after the asylum claim, the Secretary of State issues a certificate to the effect that you may be sent to a safe third country which is a member state of the European Union or has been designated for such purpose by the Secretary of State. In such a case, you may be removed to the safe third country without a decision being reached on your asylum claim although you may be able to bring a human rights appeal.[86]

You are able to remain in the UK (pending appeal as above) following any refusal where the claim is not certified as clearly unfounded and you exercise an in time appeal right or the AIT has accepted an out of time appeal.

Notes

1. Deportation, illegal entry and removal

1 s2 AI(TC)A 2004
2 *See Thet v Director of Public Prosecutions* [2006] EWHC 2701 (Admin)
3 s11 IA 1971. However, for benefit purposes, *Szoma v DWP* [2005] UKHL 64 decided that those on temporary admission are 'lawfully present'.
4 Sch 2 para 21 IA 1971
5 ss56 and 57 IANA 2006
6 s8(3) IA 1971; I(EC)O 1972 (No.1610)
7 See s7 IA 1971
8 ss2(2) and 5(2) IA 1971
9 s3(5) and (6) IA 1971 (as amended by Sch 14 para 4(2) IAA 1999)
10 ss9 and 10(2) IAA 1999; Immigration (Regularisation Period for Overstayers) Regulations 2000
11 para 364 HC 395 as amended by HC 1337 with effect from 19.7.06
12 para 367 HC 395 as substituted
13 paras 365-366 HC 395 as substituted
14 ss97 and 97A NIAA 2002 as amended by s7 IANA 2006
15 para 320 HC395
16 s5(1) IA 1971
17 paras 390-392 HC 395
18 s10 IAA 1999
19 s3(5)(aa) IA 1971 as inserted by Sch 2 para 1(2) AIA 1996 but now contained in s10(1)(b) IAA 1999 and s74 NIAA 2002
20 s76(3) NIAA 2002
21 s10(1)(c) IAA 1999
22 para 395C HC 395 as inserted by para 67 HC 704
23 s33 and Sch 2 para 9 IA 1971
24 See I(EEA) Regs 2006
25 Visiting Forces Act 1952
26 s86 Mental Health Act 1983; IDIs ch 1 s8
27 For more about extradition, consult *Jones on Extradition and Mutual Assistance* (2001) Alun Jones QC, Sweet & Maxwell
28 s8 AIA 1996
29 Immigration (Restrictions on Employment) Order 2004

2. Refusals and appeals

30 paras 4-5 Immigration (Notices) Regulations 2003
31 See the various reports of the Independent Monitor on Entry Clearance, available at www.ukvisas.gov.uk
32 r6 AIT (P) Rules 2005
33 ss82 and 83 NIAA 2002
34 s84 NIAA 2002
35 s88 NIAA 2002
36 s89 NIAA 2002
37 s90 NIAA 2002
38 s91 NIAA 2002
39 s96 NIAA 2002
40 s97 NIAA 2002
41 s98 NIAA 2002
42 s92 NIAA 2002
43 s94 NIAA 2002
44 s88A NIAA 2002 as amended by s4 IANA 2006
45 s89 NIAA 2002 from 31.08.06
46 s83A NIAA 2002 as amended by s1 IANA 2006
47 s89 NIAA 2002 as amended by s6 IANA 2006
48 ss92 and 82(2)(g),(h) and (i) NIAA 2002
49 ss92 and 82 (2)(k) NIAA 2002
50 s94 NIAA 2002
51 s33 and Sch 3 AI(TC)A 2004
52 s92(3) NIAA 2002
53 s88(4) NIAA 2002
54 ss82(d) and (e) and 92(2) NIAA 2002
55 s83 NIAA 2002
56 s1 IANA 2006 from 31.8.06
57 ss82(1)and (2) and 92(2) and (4)(a) NIAA 2002
58 s97 NIAA 2002
59 s94 NIAA 2002
60 s84 (1)(b)and (c) NIAA 2002
61 ss92 and 94 NIAA 2002; s33 AI(ToC)A 2004
62 s6 HRA 1998
63 s89 NIAA 2002
64 s90 NIAA 2002. Note that 'family' visitor is fairly widely defined under reg2(2) of the Immigration Appeals (Family Visitor) (No.2) Regulations 2000
65 s89 NIAA 2002
66 s88 NIAA 2002
67 s5 IANA 2006
68 s10 IAA 1999

69 Special Immigration Appeals
    Commission Act 1997; Special
    Immigration Appeals Commission
    (Procedure) Rules 2003
70 s97A NIAA 2002 as amended by s7 IANA
    2006
71 s120 NIAA 2002
72 s85 (2) and (3) NIAA 2002
73 s96 NIAA 2002
74 r6(1) and (2) AIT(P) Rules 2005
75 r6(4) AIT(P) Rules 2005
76 In these cases an appeal notice must be
    lodged within two days, the Home
    Office appeal bundle served within the
    following two days, the appeal heard
    within two further days and the appeal
    decided within two days of the hearing:
    Asylum and Immigration Tribunal (Fast
    Track Procedure) Rules 2005. Appellants
    in fast track have two days to apply for a
    s103A review to the AIT and two days to
    renew that application to the
    Administrative Court: Asylum and
    Immigration (Fast Track Limits) Order
    2005.
77 r7(1)(b) AIT(P) Rules 2005
78 r7(1)(a) AIT(P) Rules 2005
79 r7(2) AIT(P) Rules 2005
80 s103A(2) NIAA 2002; Sch 2 para 30
    AI(ToC)A 2004
81 s103A(3) NIAA 2002
82 Sch 2 para 30(5) AI(TC)A 2004
83 ss103B and 103E NIAA 2002
84 s78 NIAA 2002
85 s77 NIAA 2002
86 Sch 3 Parts 2(4), 3(9) and 4(14) AI(TC)A
    2004

7

Chapter 7

Recourse to public funds under the immigration rules

This chapter covers:
1. The importance of the public funds requirements (below)
2. What are public funds (p86)
3. Recourse to public funds: the general tests (p87)
4. Applying the public funds tests (p90)
5. Sponsorship and undertakings (p94)

1. The importance of the public funds requirements

Requirements under the rules

In the majority of cases, in order to obtain entry clearance or leave under the immigration rules you will need to show that you and your dependants will be adequately maintained and accommodated without recourse to public funds (see p87). The Government's reason for the predominance of this requirement is to protect the taxpayer from those who are believed to be here to take advantage of the social security system or who may become a burden on it. The categories of leave to which these requirements are applied are set out in Appendices 4 and 5. The only categories in the rules to which these requirements do not apply are:
- visitors in transit;[1]
- non-British citizen children born in the UK to parents given leave to enter or remain;[2]
- refugees and their dependants;[3]
- a bereaved spouse of a person who was present and settled in the UK, but who died during the 24-month initial period of leave;[4]
- a bereaved unmarried partner of a person who was present and settled in the UK, but who died during the 24-month initial period of leave;[5]
- a spouse who is able to provide evidence that the relationship permanently broke down during the 12/24-initial month period due to domestic violence;[6]

Chapter 7: Recourse to public funds under the immigration rules
1. The importance of the public funds requirements

7

- EEA nationals and their family members[7] (save as a primary carer/relative[8]);
- discharged Gurkhas and foreign armed forces members and their dependants;[9]
- those seeking refugee family reunion;[10]
- those with humanitarian protection, discretionary leave and, usually, exceptional leave –the latter two categories are outside the rules (see below);
- those applying for leave on the basis of long residence.[11]

Returning residents (who had indefinite leave)[12] also do not have to satisfy these requirements, but they have to show that they did not receive assistance from public funds towards the cost of their previous departure from the UK.

If leave is granted outside the rules, it is usually not necessary to satisfy the maintenance and accommodation requirements. Whether the requirements need to be satisfied depends on the basis on which such leave is granted. If it is granted on a humanitarian basis instead of granting refugee status or if it is granted on human rights grounds under the European Convention on Human Rights, the maintenance and accommodation requirements are not applied. Where, however, the dependants of a person granted exceptional leave (the Home Office stopped granting this on 31 March 2003) are seeking family reunion, they are expected to meet the maintenance and accommodation requirements.

If you are not in any of the above groups, in order to obtain entry clearance, leave to enter or leave to remain, you have to show that you can satisfy the public funds requirements.

If you are not excluded from benefit entitlement under s115 of the Immigration and Asylum Act 1999 (ie, are not a 'person subject to control') then it is now clear (since an amendment to the rules on 15 March 2005) that you are not regarded as having recourse to public funds.[13] The Home Office has also indicated that it will not treat you as having had recourse to public funds if you claim benefit that you are eligible to under exemptions relating to the European Convention on Social and Medical Assistance or the Social Charter (see p380).[14]

Conditions of leave

Since 1 November 1996, being able to maintain and accommodate yourself and your dependants without recourse to public funds may be a condition attached to your limited leave.[15] If you do subsequently have recourse to public funds, this will be in breach of your conditions of leave. The possible consequences of this are severe (see Chapter 6), since you:

- are liable to administrative removal (see p73);[16]
- are liable to be prosecuted for committing a criminal offence;[17]
- may be refused entry clearance, leave to enter or leave to remain in the UK on any future application (see p49);[18]
- may have your leave curtailed (see p49).[19] This is an exceptional course only to be used where a person is likely to be a continuing and significant burden on public funds.[20]

7

Chapter 7: Recourse to public funds under the immigration rules
1. The importance of the public funds requirements

The Home Office has said that, in the case of spouses/partners applying for indefinite leave, that temporary recourse through no fault of the applicant should not, by itself, warrant a refusal.[21]

People who need to satisfy the public funds requirements under the rules are likely to have a public funds condition attached to any leave which they obtain. Even if no public funds condition was *actually* imposed on your leave but, nevertheless, you had to satisfy the public funds requirements under the rules to get leave, your application for further leave to remain could still be affected.[22]

A public funds condition can also be added to your existing leave by the Home Office.[23] There is no right of appeal, at present, against a decision to add a condition to your leave.

2. **What are public funds**

Not all benefits and services count as public funds for the purposes of immigration control and the immigration rules. For example, the National Health Service and education services are not public funds nor is incapacity benefit. Public funds are presently defined in the immigration rules as:[24]

- attendance allowance;[25]
- carer's allowance;[26]
- child benefit;[27]
- child tax credit;[28]
- council tax benefit;[29]
- disability living allowance;[30]
- housing benefit;[31]
- housing provided by local authorities – either under homelessness legislation or from the housing register;[32]
- income-based jobseeker's allowance;[33]
- income support;[34]
- pension credit;[35]
- severe disablement allowance;[36]
- social fund payments;[37]
- working tax credit.[38]

The list of public funds is exhaustive, which means that if a type of benefit does not appear in the list, it is not considered to be a 'public fund'. The Immigration Directorate Instructions (IDIs),[39] are out of date in reference to certain benefits.

3. **Recourse to public funds: the general tests**

The specific requirements for each category are set out in the immigration rules (see tables in Appendices 4 and 5). In interpreting the rules it is also useful to consider Home Office policy as stated in the Immigration Directorate Instructions[40] and as contained in comments made by Home Office ministers.

Adequate maintenance without recourse to public funds

There is no specific guidance in the immigration rules or in Home Office policy documents on how much income is sufficient to adequately maintain an applicant and her/his dependants. Determining adequate maintenance in any one case is, therefore, not a simple question of calculation. You should, however, try to work out your outgoings and income and regular commitments such as rent, bills, travel and tax, so that an approximate figure for disposable income is available.

If this figure is equivalent to what a person on income support (IS) receives, the Asylum and Immigration Tribunal takes the view that this amounts to adequate maintenance.[41] However, you must show that your income is genuinely equivalent to IS, bearing in mind that a person receiving IS may also receive other benefits, such as housing benefit, council tax benefit and free school meals. You therefore have to show that these other needs are also met, and that your disposable income after housing, council tax and so on is at least equivalent to IS levels.

You can, without breaching the public funds prohibition, be indirectly reliant upon the public funds claimed by a third party (see p89). It is not possible for you to rely upon the proceeds of illegal working (eg, working when not permitted by immigration law to work) or fraudulent activities for maintenance.

If the leave you seek would entitle you to work, then reliance for maintenance might be placed on income to be obtained from employment in the UK. Evidence of job offers or advertisements for suitable positions and evidence of formal skills and past employment history are important, and your English language ability, general resourcefulness and good character are also relevant. The expression of a mere hope of obtaining employment is unlikely to be sufficient.

It is not possible to provide a definitive list of the types of evidence that would assist you in demonstrating that the adequate maintenance requirement of the rules is satisfied, as everyone's personal situation is different. However, the following list may provide some ideas:

- Bank statements for at least the three months prior to making the application, preferably six months. This can be straightforward in some countries but very difficult in other countries. Alternative evidence is usually accepted where an explanation is provided for why bank statements cannot be obtained. Entry clearance officers sometimes contact the bank concerned to verify that the records are accurate, particularly at entry clearance posts with high refusal rates.

- Evidence of the origin of payments into the bank account. This may be as simple as wage or salary slips, but could be more complex for a self-employed or business person or for those with informal working arrangements. Entry clearance officers routinely query large payments into a bank account and may assume that an unexplained large payment is a loan specifically taken out for the purposes of obtaining entry clearance, to be repaid once entry clearance is obtained.
- Evidence of savings or other assets that can be converted into funds. This can be straightforward in the case of bank statements, share certificates or similar but can be more problematic in the case of business assets, land or livestock, for example. If the assets belong to another person, such as parents or a sponsor, it can be difficult to convince the immigration authorities that the person is willing to sell them should that become necessary to prevent you from becoming reliant on public funds in the future. If assets are sold prior to an application for entry clearance, evidence should be retained in order to explain the origin of the funds.

Adequate accommodation without recourse to public funds

In order to be adequate for your needs, the appellate authorities have adopted tests used in housing legislation – ie, the accommodation available must:[42]
- comply with the environmental health provisions so that it must not be 'statutorily unfit';
- be capable of accommodating the sponsor and the applicant(s) without overcrowding.

Overcrowding is decided in accordance with housing legislation.[43] Accommodation is overcrowded if two people, aged 10 or over, of opposite sexes (other than partners) have to sleep in the same room. This is known as the 'room standard'. The accommodation is also overcrowded if the number of people sleeping in the house is greater than that permitted by the housing legislation, having regard to the size of the accommodation. This is known as the 'space standard'. The housing legislation sets out two tests for measuring the space standard but, in practice, it is the following test that is used by the Home Office.[44] The number of people who are allowed to stay in the accommodation depends on the number of rooms available as set out in the table on p89. A room for this purpose must be 50 square feet or more. Living rooms count, but bathrooms, kitchens, etc do not. Children between one and 10 years old only count as half a person; children under one year do not count at all. The number of permitted persons to each room is as follows:[45]

Rooms	Permitted number of persons
1 room	2 persons
2 rooms	3 persons
3 rooms	5 persons
4 rooms	7 and a half persons
5 rooms	10 persons, with an additional 2 persons for each room in excess of 5

The provider of the accommodation, whether it is the sponsor (see p94), friend, relative or applicant, must have some form of interest in the property. They do not need to own the freehold or leasehold as long as they have a tenancy or a licence to occupy. As far as the common requirements of the rules are concerned, there is no objection to sharing communal facilities. The immigration rules relating to family members frequently state that the accommodation must be owned or occupied 'exclusively' by the sponsor for the use of the family. The Home Office has confirmed that this does not mean that accommodation cannot be shared, provided that part of it is for the exclusive use of the sponsor and her/his dependants. A separate bedroom for the exclusive use of the applicant and sponsor is sufficient to meet this requirement.[46]

In most immigration applications, as long as good evidence of the right to occupy the property is provided, such as a lease or tenancy agreement or a mortgage agreement, the immigration authorities will be satisfied by a letter or by oral evidence at interview that a property is as described – ie, that it possesses as many rooms as claimed and is occupied by as many people as claimed. However, in some cases, the immigration authorities may require proof, such as a report by a local council housing officer or a surveyor or property professional of some sort.

If you are making an application for which the accommodation has to be shown to be adequate, it may be wise to obtain this type of evidence before making the application. This is particularly so if you are applying for entry clearance at an entry clearance post with a high refusal rate and/or you are seeking to occupy a room in a property at which several other people (such as family members already based in the UK) already reside.

Additional recourse to public funds

In some cases, you may wish to rely on public funds claimed by another person. The immigration rules state that you are not to be regarded as having recourse to public funds merely because you are (or will be) reliant in whole or in part on public funds provided to your sponsor, unless, as a result of your presence in the UK, your sponsor is (or would be) entitled to increased additional public funds.[47]

The key question then is: will the admission of the applicant or extension of leave to remain granted to the applicant cause an extra demand upon public funds? The answer may not always be straightforward.

The Home Office has stated that where a partner who is subject to control claims working tax credit on behalf of her/his partner who is present and settled in the UK, this will not be considered as having recourse to public funds.[48] Immigration applications will also not be refused on public funds grounds in marriage cases where one partner is settled and the only benefit being claimed is child benefit.[49]

You can rely in part on the income from public funds of a settled spouse who already receives public funds. Care must be taken in making such an application, however. For example, if your sponsor is receiving disability living allowance (DLA) and there is good evidence to show that there is additional support available to her/him, such as from family members, which renders the income from DLA surplus to her/his ordinary requirements, the surplus income may be used to support you. In a case like this, the immigration authorities will closely consider whether there genuinely is additional support available to the sponsor and it will normally be assumed that the sponsor requires the whole of the DLA to which s/he is entitled.[50]

When the test has to be satisfied

Maintenance and accommodation can become an issue overseas when applications for entry clearances are made. The means to maintain and accommodate do not have to exist at the time the decision on the application is made, but only when the applicant expects to arrive in the UK.

It is only the circumstances appertaining at the time of the decision to refuse that can be taken into account in an appeal against a refusal.[51] The appeal authorities can take into account evidence that post-dates the decision, but only where this evidence casts light on what the situation really was at the time of the decision. Evidence of facts arising after the decision cannot therefore be taken into account on appeal.[52]

If the rules are satisfied, but only from a later date, this can form the basis of a request to an immigration judge to make a recommendation that entry clearance or leave be granted, which may assist when making a fresh application.

4. Applying the public funds tests

Are the requirements the same

Where maintenance and accommodation without recourse to public funds is a requirement of the rules, there are a number of ways in which the rules vary in relation to the different categories of applicant. There are three main ways in which the requirements appear to differ.

Resources that are not included

In many categories, the maintenance and accommodation requirements must be met not only without recourse to public funds but also without income from working or business activities in the UK or without working *except* in certain employments. This stipulation is added where the rules for leave in a particular category require that you do not intend to engage in any economic activity, or do not intend to engage in any economic activity other than that for which you have been granted leave (see below). Indeed, a condition is likely to be imposed upon the leave preventing you from doing any other economic activity. In this way the maintenance and accommodation requirements closely reflect the rules for granting leave in each category. The following are examples of these rules.

Writers, composers and artists

A writer, composer or artist[53] must show that s/he is able adequately to maintain and accommodate her/himself and any dependants without recourse to public funds from her/his own resources without working except as a writer, composer or as an artist.

Work permit holders, working holidaymakers and other employment schemes

The same pattern is not followed for each category. Work permit holders will always in the conditions of their leave be prohibited from taking employment other than that specified in their work permit, meaning that they are not permitted to rely on alternative employment to meet the maintenance and accommodation requirements.

The maintenance and accommodation requirements for a working holidaymaker[54] are not expressly qualified by the words 'without taking any employment other than that which is incidental to a holiday' – ie, the requirement in the working holidaymaker rules. However, if it is clear that, in order to maintain and accommodate her/himself and any dependants, an applicant would have to spend more than 50 per cent of her/his time in the UK in full-time employment then s/he would be likely to be refused admission. The ground for refusal, if s/he was not refused under the maintenance and accommodation rules, is the rule requiring applicants not to intend to take such employment. This would also apply to a teacher or language assistant under an approved scheme[55] or a person undertaking approved training or work experience.[56]

Students and visitors

Another example is the difference between the maintenance and accommodation requirements for students and visitors. Students must be able to meet the requirements without having to take account of any earnings from employment or business in the UK.[57] However, after entry to the UK students on courses of longer duration than six months automatically receive permission to do part-time work during term time (not more than 20 hours a week) or full-time vacation work.[58] Nevertheless, the immigration rules preclude income from this employment being taken into account in assessing maintenance and accommodation.

Some visitors to the UK transact business while here, although they are not allowed to produce goods or services or take employment.[59] The activities which 'business' visitors can engage in are limited but the immigration rules make no attempt to exclude any income derived in part from business transactions conducted while in the UK when considering whether a visitor can maintain and accommodate her/himself.[60]

Reliance on third-party support for maintenance and accommodation

The rules across the different categories also suggest that there may be differences about when it is permissible to rely on resources provided by a third party (see below). In some categories, the rules state that you must be 'able to meet' the costs of your maintenance and accommodation; in others it is necessary to show that you 'can and will' be maintained and accommodated; in others you must be 'able and willing' or have 'sufficient funds available' or 'resources available [to you]' to be so maintained and accommodated without recourse to public funds. (For the rules for the different categories of leave see Appendices 4 and 5.)

Again, the differences reflect the different purposes and nature of the leave being sought (see the following examples). The difference in the wording of the rules can be interpreted as simply describing the different scenarios for different applicants. An interpretation which denied entry, even where there was, in fact, likely to be no demand on public funds may, in family cases, be in breach of Article 8 of the European Convention on Human Rights. The most restrictive formulation of the rules, as far as preventing third-party support is concerned, is the way they are written for children, retired persons of independent means and persons intending to establish themselves in business (see below).

Visitors

Visitors should maintain and accommodate themselves:[61]
- out of resources available to them; *or*
- through the support of relatives or friends.

Clearly, it is reasonable to expect a short-term visitor to be maintained or accommodated over a limited period by a sponsoring relative or a friend.

Children

The immigration rules specifically require that a child be accommodated and maintained 'by the parent, parents or relative' s/he is seeking to join or remain with.[62] The rules were amended in 2000 in order to preclude third-party support following the case of *Arman Ali*.[63]

Fiancé(e)s, spouses and civil partners

There has been a difference of view in the appeal courts as to how the rules about fiancé(e)s and spouses and now civil partners should be interpreted – in particular, whether the wording of the relevant rules requires a couple to be self-supporting or will permit them to rely on third-party support. One leading commentator has referred to the fact that the rules are expressed in terms of the parties being able to 'maintain themselves and their dependants' but not necessarily be maintained 'by themselves'.[64] This view has been supported by several tribunal cases over the years[65] and has also been lent support by the High Court.[66] The other interpretation, which continues to find favour with some judges, is that third-party support is not permissible.[67] Pending a definitive resolution of this legal dispute, third-party support can be argued to be permissible, although in practice it may be more difficult to demonstrate that there will be *lasting* third-party support; this problem is about credibility and believability rather than the law, however.[68] So, in cases where the applicant is seeking indefinite leave to remain, the evidence of the lasting nature of third-party support needs to be particularly clear and cogent compared with when an applicant proposes to maintain and accommodate her/himself out of her/his own resources or those generated by her/his own work.[69]

Retired people of independent means

In order to obtain leave, retired people of independent means must have an income of £25,000 a year which is under their control and is disposable in the UK. They must also be able and willing to maintain and accommodate themselves and any dependants indefinitely in the UK:[70]

- from their own resources with no assistance from any other person; *and*
- without taking employment; *or*
- without having recourse to public funds.

People intending to establish themselves in business

People who wish to establish themselves in business have to show that their share of the profits from the business will be 'sufficient to maintain and accommodate' themselves and any dependants without recourse to public funds.[71]

Accommodation 'owned or occupied exclusively'

For certain permanent categories of leave – in particular, spouses, fiancé(e)s and civil partners – the maintenance and accommodation requirements specify that the accommodation must be owned or occupied exclusively by the parties (to a marriage/civil partnership), the sponsor, parent or relative. As discussed above, exclusive occupation does not mean occupation of the entire premises in which you reside. Provided the relevant person occupies a bedroom within those premises for themselves only, the remainder of the facilities on the premises (eg, kitchen, living room, toilet, bathroom, halls etc) can be shared with other people.[72]

---

5. **Sponsorship and undertakings**

The sponsor (usually a relative or friend) of any person seeking leave to enter or to remain in the UK may be asked to give a written undertaking to be responsible for that person's maintenance and accommodation for the period of leave granted and any further period of leave to remain that s/he may be granted while in the UK.[73] The rules are drafted very widely, so it is possible that such an undertaking could be required of a sponsor even if the requirements of the rules under which leave is sought do not specify that the applicant is maintained and accommodated without public funds. However, in practice, it is very unlikely that an undertaking would be required in such a case. Examples of cases where undertakings are often requested are:

- dependent relatives (although not for children under 16 years coming for settlement);
- students relying upon a private individual in the UK.

The Home Office has stated that it rarely asks for undertakings from spouses/fiancé(e)s or unmarried partners.[74] One reason for this is that people entering in these categories will normally be granted limited leave with a prohibition on claiming public funds condition attached, meaning that initially they will not generally be able to access public funds. Those admitted as dependent relatives are given indefinite leave immediately and so, unless an undertaking is entered into, they are not 'subject to immigration control' for benefits purposes and therefore entitled to claim benefits.

If the person sponsored subsequently claims benefit while in the UK, you may be asked to pay back any benefit which is claimed (see p195).[75] Court action may be initiated to enforce payment if it is not forthcoming. However, it has been government policy to do this only where the sponsor, although financially able, refuses to honour the undertaking without good reasons.[76] A person granted leave on the basis of a maintenance undertaking is not entitled to benefit even if the sponsor does not maintain her/him.

A person who has leave to enter or remain given as a result of a maintenance undertaking is included within the definition of a 'person subject to immigration control' and is excluded from claiming benefits on this basis.[77] There are, however, exceptions for those whose sponsor has died and those who have been in the UK for five years since the date of the undertaking or the date of entry (whichever is later – see p157).

Some sponsors voluntarily make declarations as to maintenance and accommodation without being asked to provide an undertaking. Because of the possible consequences, it is advisable not to make such declarations of sponsorship unless specifically asked to make such a promise.[78]

The immigration rules require the use of a specific form, the SET(F), for applications for certain family members.[79] Attached to this is a supplementary form which can be used for maintenance undertakings. A written statement that the sponsor will support the applicant, although not formally drafted, has also been held to be enforceable.[80] Equally, a formal declaration that the 'sponsor' was able and willing to maintain and accommodate has been held not to amount to an undertaking as it does not include a promise to support.[81] Note that where the sponsor refuses to give an undertaking to be responsible for an applicant's maintenance and accommodation in the UK after being requested to do so, the applicant is likely to be refused entry clearance or leave to enter or remain.[82]

Notes

1. **The importance of the public funds requirements**
   1 paras 47-50 HC 395
   2 paras 304-309 HC 395
   3 paras 327-352 HC 395
   4 para 287(b) HC 395 as inserted by para 31 HC 704 and amended by HC 538 and Cm 6339
   5 para 295M HC 395 as inserted by para 32 HC 704 and amended by Cm 6339
   6 para 289A HC 395 from 18.12.02
   7 paras 11-15 I(EEA) Regs 2006; paras 255-257b HC 395
   8 para 257c-d HC 395
   9 para 276E-AH HC 395
   10 paras 352A-352F HC 395
   11 paras 276A-D HC 395
   12 paras 18-20 HC 395
   13 para 6B HC 395
   14 IDI chap 1 s7
   15 s3(1) IA 1971 as amended by AIA 1996; para 8(ii) HC 395 as substituted by para 3 Comnd 3365 August 1996
   16 s10 IAA 1999
   17 s24(1)(b) IA 1971
   18 paras 320(11) and 322(3)(4) HC 395
   19 para 323 HC 395
   20 'Policy and Practice', *Immigration and Nationality Law and Practice*, January 1988, p102
   21 IDI chap 8 s1 Annex F para 8
   22 paras 322(4) and 323 HC395
   23 s3(3)(a) IA 1971

2. **What are public funds**
   24 para 6 HC 395
   25 Under Part III SSCBA 1992 or Part III SSCBA (Northern Ireland) 1992
   26 Part III of SSCBA 1992 (as amended)
   27 Under Part IX SSCBA 1992 or Part IX SSCBA (Northern Ireland) 1992; s10 AIA 1996
   28 Under Part 1 TCA 2002
   29 Under Part VII SSCBA 1992 or Part VII SSCBA (Northern Ireland) 1992
   30 Under Part III SSCBA 1992 or Part III SSCBA (Northern Ireland) 1992
   31 Under Part VII SSCBA 1992 or Part VII SSCBA (Northern Ireland) 1992
   32 Under Housing Act 1985 and Parts VI or VII Housing Act 1996, Parts I or II Housing (Scotland) Act 1987 or Part II Housing (Northern Ireland) Order 1988
   33 Under JSA 1995
   34 Under Part VII SSCBA 1992 or Part VII SSCBA (Northern Ireland) 1992
   35 Under SPCA 2002
   36 Under Part III SSCBA 1992 or Part III SSCBA (Northern Ireland) 1992
   37 Part VIII of SSCBA 1992
   38 Under Part 1 TCA 2002
   39 At chap 8 s1 annex F

3. Recourse to public funds: the general tests

40 IDI ch1 sVII and 8 sF
41 *KA and others (Pakistan)* [UKIAT] 00065, *Azem* (7863), *Uvovo* (00/TH/01450) and see *Begum* (Momotaz) (18699)
42 IDI chap 8 annex F
43 ss324-325 Housing Act 1985
44 IDI chap 8 s1 annex F para 6.3
45 s326 Housing Act 1985
46 IDI chap 8 annex F para 6; *Kasuji* [1988] Imm AR 587
47 para 6A HC 395
48 IDI chap 1 s7 para 5.1.3
49 IDI chap 1 s7 para 5
50 *Munibun Nisa v ECO, Islamabad* [2002] UKIAT 01369
51 s85(5)b NIAA 2002
52 *DR Morocco* [2005] UKIAT 00038

4. Applying the public funds tests

53 paras 232-239 HC 395
54 paras 95-100 HC 395
55 paras 110-115 HC 395
56 paras 116-121 HC 395
57 paras 57-62 HC 395
58 paras 57(v) and 58 HC 395
59 As a rule of thumb, business visitors may be paid from abroad to transact some forms of brief business in the UK but may not receive a salary or fee from a UK source. See IDI chap 2 s1 annex B para 5 for details
60 paras 40-46 HC 395
61 paras 40-46, 51-56 HC 395
62 paras 297(iv)-(v) and 298(iv)-(v) HC 395
63 *Arman Ali* [2001] INLR 89, [2000] Imm AR
64 See Jackson, *Immigration Law and Practice,* Sweet and Maxwell
65 *Hussain* (5990); *Azad* (5993); *Sadiq* (6017); *Saleem* (6017); *Akhtar* (7837); *Kaur* (12838); *Akhtar* (9903); *Khan* (6283); *Yousaf* (9190); *Njoku* (18520)
66 *ex parte Arman Ali per Collins J , Mahmood v ECO, Islamabad* [2002] UKIAT 018919
67 See *KA and others (Pakistan)* [2006] UKAIT 00065
68 IDI Ch8 s1 Annex F para 5.1 is unnecessarily restrictive in stating that in spouse cases only short-term third-party support in exceptional circumstances is acceptable.
69 *AK and others (Long term third party support) Bangladesh* [2006] UKIAT 00069
70 paras 263-270 HC 395

71 paras 201(ix) and 206(ix) HC 395
72 IDI ch8 annex F para 6.1

5. Sponsorship and undertakings

73 para 35 HC 395
74 IDI ch1 s7 annex Y para 2
75 para 35 HC 395; ss78, 105 and 106 SSAA 1992; SSAA (Northern Ireland) Act 1992
76 Parliamentary answer 29 January 1986 of Secretary of State for Social Services and letter 4 January 1991 from DSS to JCWI.
77 s115(9)(c) IAA
78 s115(10)
79 para 32 HC395
80 R(*Begum*) [2003] *The Times,* 4 December
81 *Ahmed v SSWP* [2005] EWCA Civ 535
82 paras 320(14) and 322(6) HC 395

Chapter 8

European Economic Area nationals

This chapter covers:
1. European Economic Area nationals' rights (below)
2. Family members of European Economic Area nationals (p99)
3. Permanent residence (p101)
4. Public funds (p102)
5. UK nationals as European Economic Area nationals (p102)
6. A8 nationals (p103)
7. A2 nationals (p103)
8. Exclusion and removal (p104)

There is a significant overlap between immigration and social security law in this area as a consequence of the introduction of the right of residence test to benefit entitlement on 1 May 2004. Chapter 24 provides details of the European Economic Area (EEA) law that relates to the right of residence.

For the sake of clarity, some of the information in Chapter 24 is repeated here. This chapter then goes on to provide information about immigration control relating to EEA nationals.

---

1. European Economic Area nationals' rights

The European Economic Area (EEA) is comprised of all European Union (EU) states plus Norway, Liechtenstein and Iceland. EU nationals are citizens of Austria, Belgium, Bulgaria, Cyprus, Czech Republic, Denmark, Estonia, Finland, France, Germany, Greece, Hungary, Ireland, Italy, Latvia, Lithuania, Luxembourg, Malta, Netherlands, Poland, Portugal, Romania, Slovenia, Slovakia, Spain, Sweden and the United Kingdom.

From 1 June 2002 Swiss nationals have the same rights as EEA nationals in the UK.[1]

The eight states, which joined the EU on 1 May 2004 (Czech Republic, Estonia, Hungary, Latvia, Lithuania, Poland, Slovakia and Slovenia) are referred to as the

A8 countries. A8 nationals have additional restrictions regarding access to employment. Since 1 January 2007, nationals of Romania and Bulgaria (the A2 countries) also possess some EEA rights but have even more restrictive rights of access to employment than A8 nationals (see p103).

EEA nationals and their family members have the right to enter the UK.[2] They also have the right to remain after the first three months in the UK to:[3]

- work or to seek work;
- establish a business;
- provide or receive services;
- live here as a pensioner or as a person of independent means;
- study.

These rights are known as the 'treaty rights' because they were established at the Treaty of Rome in 1957, the founding treaty of the European Economic Community, the forerunner of the EU. The purpose was to facilitate freedom of movement for workers, goods and services. The rights are therefore provided for by EC law which takes precedence over domestic law. This means that, if the UK interpretation falls short, it can be corrected by looking at the primary EC law.

The most recent major European legislation is Directive 2004/38/EC (known as the Citizens' Directive). This consolidates and replaces previous EU law on residence rights. This Directive was transposed into UK law in the Immigration (European Economic Area) Regulations 2006. This chapter provides some analysis of where the Regulations may fail fully to implement this and other Directives.

Right of admission

EU nationals and their family members seeking entry to exercise their treaty rights do not require leave to enter or remain in the UK.[4] EEA nationals have a right to be admitted on production of an identity card or passport. Non-EEA family members have a right to be admitted on production of a family permit or residence card. In the absence of these documents you must be given a reasonable period of time to produce the requisite document or some other relevant evidence of your nationality, relationship or entitlement.[5]

Initial right to reside

Although EEA nationals and their family members do not need leave to enter the country, their right to reside here after entering the UK is subject to some restrictions. They have an initial right to reside for three months so long as they do not become 'an unreasonable burden on the social assistance system' during that period (see p364).[6]

Thereafter, they have a right of residence while they are exercising their treaty rights or they are the family members of such EEA nationals or they have 'retained the right of residence'. These limited restrictions on residence are different from requiring leave to remain.

Qualified persons

EEA nationals who are exercising their treaty rights (known as 'qualified persons' in the regulations) have a right of residence.[7] Qualified persons are:
- jobseekers;
- workers (including certain former workers);[8]
- the self-employed;
- the self-sufficient;
- students.

There is further detail of the meaning of these terms in Chapter 24. Former workers include those who have worked and subsequently received jobseeker's allowance for up to six months. If employment or self-employment was for less then 12 months then after six months of subsequent unemployment it is necessary to show that the worker is actively seeking employment and has a genuine chance of being employed.[9] Former workers also include those temporarily unable to work though accident or illness and may include those who have embarked on vocational courses after becoming unemployed.

Qualified persons may apply to the Home Office for a **registration certificate** on Form EEA1. There is no fee for this application and the forms are not mandatory. The certificate will be issued for the length of the employment if this is between three and 12 months, otherwise it should normally be valid for five years. Registration certificates, for qualifying people, are automatically renewable. They are not to be regarded as periods of 'limited leave' in the way that other periods of limited leave prevent access to benefits and there are no conditions attached.[10]

---

2. Family members of European Economic Area nationals

The family members of European Economic Area (EEA) nationals may come to join them (although at present the EEA regulations create an obstacle to free movement of family members travelling from outside the EEA – see p100).

For **workers and self-employed people**[11] these include:
- spouses or civil partners (this includes separated spouses/partners);
- children under 21 of the EEA national and her/his spouse or civil partner;
- other children and grandchildren, if still dependent, of the EEA national and her/his spouse/partner;
- dependant ascendants of the EEA national and her/his spouse/partner.

Extended family relatives[12] who are dependants or members of the same household may also qualify. This includes:
- an unmarried partner in a durable relationship;
- relatives who were dependent or part of the same household before the EEA national arrived in the UK;
- seriously ill or disabled relatives requiring the personal care of the EEA national or her/his spouse/partner;
- dependant relatives who would qualify under the domestic immigration rules if the EEA national or spouse/partner was settled.[13]

In considering applications from extended family members the Home Office is required to facilitate entry, residence and undertake an extensive examination of the personal circumstances and justify any denial of entry or residence.[14] The Home Office has stated that part of this examination includes considering the extent to which an EEA national would be deterred from exercising her/his treaty rights by a refusal of the application of the extended family member.[15]

Eligible **family members of students** who remain in the UK for longer than three months are confined to:
- a spouse or civil partner;
- unmarried partner in a durable relationship;[16]
- dependant children of both parties;
- seriously ill or disabled relatives as above;[17]
- extended family members where it appears appropriate to the entry clearance officer to issue a family permit.[18] It could be argued that this should include dependant ascendants.[19]

An EEA student should also provide 'assurance' that her/his resources would exceed any entitlement to benefit for her/himself and her/his family members throughout his period of residence.[20]

The UK regulations do not fully incorporate all EC rights of residence. In particular a former worker who has children in education has a right of residence under Article 12 EC Regulation 1612/68 (see p355).

Family members, including extended family members, who are themselves EEA nationals can apply to the Home Office for a registration certificate on an EEA1 form in line with the EEA national who is a qualified person. Family members who are not EEA nationals can apply for **residence cards** on an EEA2 form.

If the non-EEA family member is abroad, s/he should apply for a family permit. There is a form on the UKvisas site, but again, it is not mandatory and the application is free of charge. If the non-EEA family member is not lawfully resident in an EEA state then according to the current EEA regulations it is additionally necessary to satisfy the requirements for a settlement entry clearance under the domestic immigration rules in order to qualify for a family permit.[21] At the time of writing this transposition of the Residence Directive is under challenge.

Family members who have retained the right of residence

Normally, if the EEA national with whom the family member resides leaves the UK or the family relationship is somehow terminated, the non-EEA national needs to leave the UK. As mentioned above, rights of residence are not affected by separation (rather than divorce) of a married couple or civil partners. However, in some additional circumstances family members can retain a right of residence in the UK. The category 'family members who have retained the right of residence'[22] includes:

- descendants of the EEA national or spouse/partner, provided they were attending an educational course in the UK when the qualified person died or left the UK;
- a person with the actual custody of a child in the above bullet point;
- family members who are working, self-employed or self-sufficient and had lived in the UK for a year before the death of the qualified person;
- divorced spouses or civil partners who are working, self-employed or self-sufficient and were living here when the relationship terminated and either:
  – had been married for three years and had lived in the UK for at least a year; *or*
  – have custody of the qualified person's child; *or*
  – have an access right that must take place in the UK; *or*
  – continued residence is 'warranted' – eg, because of domestic violence.

The Residence Directive does **not** include a requirement that the widowed or divorced spouse or partner be economically active as described above unless the family member wishes to apply for permanent residence. Under the Directive, the family member can therefore retain a right of residence even though s/he may have difficulty obtaining or renewing a registration certificate.

3. Permanent residence

After five years a qualified person (see p99) and her/his family members may become eligible for permanent residence.[23]

Family members who retain the right of residence for five years (as above) can apply for permanent residence themselves.

Family members who were residing with an European Economic Area (EEA) worker or a self-employed person who died are also eligible for permanent residence so long as the EEA national lived here for two years before s/he died or s/he died because of an accident at work or an occupational disease.

A worker or a self-employed person who has **'ceased activity'**[24] can apply for permanent residence. This is a worker or self-employed person who:

- is eligible for a pension or takes early retirement and worked here for a year and resided here for three years; *or*
- becomes permanently incapacitated and resided here for two years beforehand or the incapacity arises from an accident at work/occupational disease;
- was resident in the UK for three years and returns to her/his residence here at least once a week.

Family members of those who have ceased activity can also apply for permanent residence.

EEA nationals apply for permanent residence on an EEA3 form and non-EEA nationals apply for a permanent residence card[25] on an EEA4 form.

4. **Public funds**

European Economic Area (EEA) nationals and their family members are not subject to the public funds requirement save that as from 1 January 2005 the primary carer, parent or sibling of a self-sufficient EEA national child may be granted leave to enter/remain so long as s/he can be maintained and accommodated without recourse to public funds.[26]

Students and those who qualify as 'self-sufficient' will have difficulty obtaining or renewing registration cards if they claim public funds. This is the case even if they have been previously self-supporting for a period and would not be considered an 'unreasonable burden' (see p364). However, the Home Office accepts that students and the self-sufficient in these circumstances would retain a right to reside.[27]

5. **UK nationals as European Economic Area nationals**

There may be circumstances where UK nationals choose to rely on European Economic Area (EEA) rights instead of domestic immigration legislation. This is most frequently the case where a UK national seeks to bring family members to the UK from another EEA country as the EEA rules are less arduous.

A family member of a UK national with dual citizenship (ie, another EEA citizenship) may apply for a family permit. A UK national who is working or is self-employed in another EEA state with her/his spouse/civil partner, who is lawfully resident there, can also exercise rights as an EEA national.[28] However, the family member cannot subsequently apply under the immigration rules for 24 months' leave as a spouse/civil partner. Having entered with a family permit, s/he cannot qualify for permanent residence (or indefinite leave) except as a family member of an EEA national.

It is not necessary for a UK national in these circumstances to satisfy the relevant residence conditions required in order to be regarded as having 'ceased activity' (see p102).

6. **A8 nationals**

Although nationals from these eight countries (see p97) are now European Union nationals and may rely on European Community (EC) law, they do not have full EC rights. A8 nationals do not have complete freedom of movement. An A8 national may set up in business and having done so as a self-employed person has a right of residence. However, an A8 national who wants to take up employment has to comply with conditions under the **workers registration scheme**. Once this has been done the employee is treated as having a right to reside in the UK. A8 nationals do not acquire a right to reside while they are jobseekers.

A8 nationals are required to register their first 12 months of employment under the workers registration scheme.[29] This should be done within one month of taking up employment on a WRS form (a fee of £70 is payable). They obtain a registration certificate which relates to the specific employment and a registration card which relates to the worker. Changes in employment should be notified to the Home Office within a month and a new registration certificate will then be issued.

After 12 months' employment an A8 national is entitled to the same rights as other EEA nationals. The self-employed and the self-sufficient do not need to register, neither did those who were legally working for over a year on 3 April 2004 or those that had no condition on their leave on 30 April 2004 that prohibited employment.

Non-EEA family members of A8 nationals during the first 12 months of employment can apply for a residence stamp by completing form FMRS.

7. **A2 nationals**

Nationals of Romania and Bulgaria (known as A2 nationals) became European Union nationals on 1 January 2007. These nationals have severely limited access to the labour market (see p360) and are usually required to apply for **accession worker cards** (AWCs).[30] These are purple cards that authorise employment. A2 nationals enjoy other freedom of movement rights including rights to self-employment.

As with the provisions applicable to A8 nationals (see p103), certain A2 nationals are not required to apply for an AWC and can apply for a blue registration card on a BR1 form to provide evidence of their exemption if they:

- are in the UK and were entitled to work without restriction on 1 January 2007;
- were working lawfully in the UK on 1 January 2007, after they have completed 12 months in continuous employment;
- are providing services in the UK on behalf of an employer established in another European Economic Area (EEA) state;
- are family members of EEA nationals (from other member states) or spouses/ civil partners of British nationals or people with indefinite leave to remain.

Self-employed or self-sufficient A2 nationals do not need to register but may apply for yellow registration certificates on the BR1 form.

A2 nationals who are not exempt are only able to apply to the Home Office directly for an AWC if they are offered employment in one of 10 listed areas of employment (eg, as au pair placements or domestic workers). In addition, A2 nationals may work in the UK under the Seasonal Agricultural Workers Scheme or apply for an AWC having obtained a work permit or a letter of approval from an employer under the work permit scheme. The work permit scheme covers posts that require considerable experience and qualifications as well as low-skilled sector-based employment. This application is made on a BR3 form.

EEA family members of an A2 national with, or applying for, an AWC or yellow registration card apply on a BR4 form if they wish to work themselves. They will be issued with AWCs and are not limited in the type of work they can undertake but can only work for a named employer. Non-EEA family nationals apply for family residence stamps on a BR6 form and there are no restrictions endorsed in relation to employment.

A2 nationals can apply for a blue registration card instead on a BR3 form if they can establish that they satisfy the criteria of the Highly Skilled Migrants Programme (see p36) save that it is not necessary for A2 nationals to pass the English language requirement.

Students can also obtain yellow registration certificates as evidence of their entitlement to take part-time work.

8. **Exclusion and removal**

European Economic Area (EEA) nationals and their family members can be removed if they do not have or cease to have a right to reside.[31] They are not removed as an automatic consequence of having recourse to public funds.[32]

EEA nationals and their family members who have a right of residence can only be excluded or removed on grounds relating to public policy, public security or public health. If the person has permanent residence then there must be serious grounds.[33] The existence of previous criminal convictions does not justify deportation unless the personal conduct of the person represents a genuine, present and sufficiently serious threat affecting one of the fundamental interests of society.[34]

An EEA national who is a minor cannot be removed unless it is in her/his best interests or her/his removal is imperative on grounds of national security. Similarly an EEA national who has resided here for 10 years cannot be removed unless it is imperative on grounds of national security.[35]

Appeals

There is an appeal right in the UK for EEA nationals and their family members against decisions to remove and to issue a notice to deport and to refuse to issue, renew or revoke a residence certificate or card or a permanent registration certificate or card.[36] There is also an appeal right in the UK against a decision to refuse admission where the EEA national or family member holds a family permit, registration or residence card or can prove residence in the UK. Finally, there is also an appeal right in the UK on human rights and asylum grounds unless the refusal is certified as clearly unfounded.

There are out of country appeal rights against a decision to refuse to issue a family permit or refuse to revoke a deportation order.[37]

An appeal right can be denied where the EEA national does not produce an identity card or passport or where the family member does not produce a family permit or evidence that s/he is related as claimed.

An appeal to the AIT is denied if the Secretary of State for the Home Department certifies that a decision is taken on grounds of national security. In these circumstances the appeal is to the Special Immigration Appeals Commission.[38]

Notes

1. **European Economic Area nationals**
   1 The I(EEA) Regs 2006 apply to all EEA nationals and Swiss nationals. There is no distinction in the UK in the application of these regulations between EU nationals and non-EU nationals within the EEA.
   2 s7(1) IA 1988; reg 11 I(EEA) Regs 2006
   3 Reg 14 I(EEA) Regs 2006
   4 s7(1) IA 1988
   5 Reg 11 I(EEA) Regs 2006; Art 5 Directive 2004/38

   6 Reg 13 I(EEA) Regs 2006; Art 6 Directive 2004/38
   7 Reg 6 I(EEA) Regs 2006; Art 7 Directive 2004/38
   8 Reg 4 I(EEA) Regs 2006; Art 7 Directive 2004/38. The same regulation gives definitions of 'worker', 'self-employed', 'self sufficient' and 'student'.

9 Reg 6(2) I(EEA) Regs 2006; Art 7(3) Directive 2004/38; and see *Antonissen* 292/89 26.2.91. **NB** reg 6(2) only provides for former workers to retain their status where they have previously worked for 12 months and not less. The Home Office has accepted in correspondence with ILPA that, despite its wording, this regulation will be interpreted consistently with the Directive.
10 Reg 16 I(EEA) Regs 2006; Art 8 Directive 2004/38

2. **Family members of European Economic Area nationals**
11 Reg 7 I(EEA) Regs 2006; Art 2 Directive 2004/38
12 Reg 8 I(EEA) Regs 2006; Art 3 Directive 2004/38
13 Reg 12(1)I(EEA) Regs 2006
14 Art 3 Directive 2004/38
15 ECI ch 2 para 2.4
16 Reg 7(3) I(EEA) Regs 2006
17 Reg 7(3) I(EEA) Regs 2006
18 Regs 7(4) and 12(2) I(EEA) Regs 2006
19 Arts 3(2) and 7(4) Directive 2004/38
20 Reg 4(2) I(EEA) Regs 2006
21 Reg 12(1)(b) I(EEA)Regs 2006
22 Reg 10 I(EEA) Regs 2006; Arts 12-14 Directive 2004/38

3. **Permanent residence**
23 Reg 15 I(EA) Regs 2006; Arts 16-18 Directive 2004/38
24 Reg 5 I(EEA) Regs 2006; Art 17 Directive 2004/38
25 Reg 18 I(EEA) Regs 2006; Arts 19-20 Directive 2004/38

4. **Public funds**
26 para 257c HC 251 pursuant to *Chen* ECJ C-200/02
27 ECIs ch 12 para 1.3

5. **UK nationals as EEA nationals**
28 Reg 9 I(EEA) Regs 2006 following *Surinder Singh* [1992] 3 All ER 798.Following *Carpenter*, it may be possible for a UK national to claim an entitlement to exercise EEA rights where s/he has remained in the UK but provided services in the EU.

6. **A8 nationals**
29 The Accession (Immigration and Worker Registration) Regulations 2004 (SI No 3214); ECIs ch 7 s1

7. **A2 nationals**
30 The Accession (Immigration and Worker Authorisation) Regulations 2006 (SI No 3317); ECIs ch 7 s2

8. **Exclusion and removal**
31 Reg 19 (3) I(EEA) Regs 2006
32 Reg 19(4) I(EEA) Regs 2006
33 Reg 21(3) I(EEA) Regs 2006; Art 28(2) Directive 2004/38
34 Reg 21(5) I(EEA) Regs 2006; Art 27(2) Directive 2004/38
35 Reg 21(4) I(EEA) Regs 2006; Art 28(3) Directive 2004/38
36 Reg 26 I(EEA) Regs 2006and Arts 30 -31 Directive 2004/38
37 Reg 27 I(EEA) Regs 2006
38 Reg 29 I(EEA) Regs 2006

Chapter 9

Determining immigration status

This chapter covers:
1. British citizens and those with the right of abode in the UK (below)
2. Leave to enter (p108)
3. Leave to remain (p110)
4. Refugees, asylum seekers and those with humanitarian protection and discretionary leave (p110)
5. Enforced departure (p112)
6. Other endorsements on passports (p113)

The stamps referred to in this chapter can be found in Appendix 8 to this book. See also *JCWI Immigration, Nationality and Refugee Law Handbook* for more examples of stamps and endorsements in passports.

1. British citizens and those with the right of abode in the UK

Passports are one form of evidence of nationality. They are not the only form of evidence (many people do not possess passports, after all), and they cannot be considered definitive proof of a person's nationality as a passport may only be accurate at the time it was issued.

British citizens

People with passports issued before 1 January 1983, which describe them as a citizen of the United Kingdom and colonies (CUKC) (on page 1) with the right of abode (on page 5) are almost certainly British citizens. Their passports, if issued after 1 January 1983, would simply describe them as British citizens. If they have the right of abode, a statement to that effect is not endorsed on the passport. British overseas territories citizens (BOTCs – formerly British dependent citizens) became British citizens on 21 May 2002. Passports of BOTCs issued before May 2002 therefore do not accurately state their citizenship. Passports issued now are the uniform European Union passport format which are maroon in colour.

Other British nationals and Commonwealth citizens

If your passport was issued:

- before 1 January 1983 and you are a British overseas citizen (BOC), a British subject, etc (see p21), it should describe you as a CUKC (on page 1) but the statement of right of abode (on page 5) will be crossed out or there may be no such statement;
- after 1 January 1983, it should describe you as a BOC, British subject, etc on the same page as sets out your personal details.

If you are a Commonwealth citizen with the right of abode in the UK, any passport issued should have a stamp of 'certificate of patriality' if it was issued before 1 January 1983. Passports issued after this date should be endorsed with a 'certificate of entitlement to the right of abode' to demonstrate that you have the right of abode in the UK.[1] Certificates of entitlement to the right of abode are endorsed in the passport in the form of a sticker together with the stamp of the issuing post or the Home Office (Appendix 8, Figure 1).

For the granting of British citizenship to British overseas territories citizens and, British overseas citizens, see Chapter 2.

Citizenship by registration and naturalisation

If you have been granted citizenship after having applied to register or naturalise, the Home Office will issue a certificate of naturalisation or registration as evidence of citizenship. You can then apply to the Passport Agency for a British passport.

2. Leave to enter

As described on pp32-37, entry clearances (visas) now operate as leave to enter. These are referred to here as 'new style' entry clearances. The conditions to which the leave is subject are stated on the entry clearance sticker itself. If the entry clearance is to have effect as indefinite leave this is also stated on the entry clearance sticker.

New style entry clearances (issued for visits, airside and transit visas to visa nationals, stateless persons and refugees) have been in use since 2 October 2000. They are issued in the form of a green 'uniform format visa' (Appendix 8, Figure 2). All other new style entry clearances are red (Appendix 8, Figure 3). When you arrive with a new style entry clearance and the immigration officer admits you (for circumstances in which an immigration officer can refuse to admit a person with an entry clearance or other person who has leave when s/he arrives, see p37), the officer will probably simply place a rectangular date stamp, with the name of the port of entry, over the entry clearance (Appendix 8, Figure 4). This is known simply as a 'date stamp'.

Entry clearances state the purpose for which they are granted. However, where you arrive without an entry clearance and are granted leave to enter (because you are a non-visa national entering in a category for which an entry clearance is not needed) the endorsement which the immigration officer places in the passport does not state the purpose for which leave is granted. If limited leave is granted, the endorsement is a rectangular stamp which states the period for which leave is granted and what, if any, conditions are attached to the leave. The example shown (Appendix 8, Figure 5) is the kind of stamp usually issued to a visitor or a student on a short course (of six months or less). The visitor or student is prohibited from working and there is a condition prohibiting recourse to public funds. This means that s/he is a 'person subject to immigration control' for benefit purposes.

Dependants of refugees are granted family reunion entry clearance without any public funds restrictions and if they do not have passports these can be issued on GV3 documents (Appendix 8, Figure 6). The example at figure 6 shows an endorsement that reads 'VISA FAMILY REUNION – Sponsor'. The sponsor referred to is the relative with refugee status who the dependant is joining in the UK. The endorsement does not indicate that a maintenance undertaking has been given within the context of s115(9) IAA 1999 (see p94).

People returning to the UK who already have indefinite leave to enter, are simply given a date stamp if re-admitted with indefinite leave. Each of the stamps issued by an immigration officer to grant leave to a person who does not have an entry clearance is accompanied by the immigration officer's rectangular date stamp (see above).

Refusal of leave to enter

If you arrive in the UK with leave (either granted by an entry clearance, or because you are returning to the UK with leave which did not lapse (see p37), or if you have otherwise been granted leave before your actual arrival in the UK), and the immigration officer refuses to admit you, your leave is 'cancelled'. The immigration officer can endorse a large 'CANCELLED' stamp across the previous endorsement granting leave *or* will write the same endorsement across the stamp in either red or black ink.

Where you arrive without leave and are refused leave to enter, a date stamp with an ink cross through it is placed in your passport as shown (Appendix 8, Figure 7). You are also given a written notice of refusal of leave to enter with details of any rights of appeal.

3. **Leave to remain**

Leave to remain (ie, after you have already entered the UK), is granted by officials at the Home Office. Where limited leave is granted, the endorsement shows the length of the leave granted and any conditions attached to it. The leave is now endorsed on a residence permit (see Appendix 8, Figure 8). Previously, leave may have been endorsed on a vignette sticker or as in the example shown in Appendix 8 Figures 9 and 10, on a rectangular stamp accompanied by a pentagonal date stamp. In both cases the terms of the leave indicate that you are subject to immigration control because a public funds conditions is included. Where you do not have a passport, the leave, either limited or indefinite, is endorsed on an immigration document, similar to a letter but bearing a photograph of the holder. If you have indefinite leave and subsequently obtain a passport, you can complete a No Time Limit (NTL) form for which there is a fee and request that the indefinite leave be transferred to the passport.

When the Home Office grants indefinite leave to a person with a passport, the passport is endorsed with a residence permit as shown (Appendix 8, Figure 11).

Refusal of leave to remain

Where the Home Office refuses to grant leave to remain, it underlines the most recent grant of leave, or the date stamp accompanying it, to show the refusal. Where you do not have a grant of leave in your current passport to enable this to be done, the Home Office may write your Home Office reference number on the inside back cover of the passport and underline it. A '**Home Office reference number**' is given to anyone who has dealings with the Home Office (as opposed to the officials at the ports of entry) – eg, by applying to extend your leave after you have entered the UK. It is normally the first letter of your surname followed by six or seven numbers. You are also given a written notice of the refusal of leave to remain with details of any rights of appeal.

4. **Refugees, asylum seekers and those with humanitarian protection and discretionary leave**

Until early 2002, asylum seekers were issued with a 'standard acknowledgement letter' (SAL). '**SAL1**' was issued to those claiming asylum at the port and '**SAL2**' was issued to those who claimed asylum once they were already in the UK. Since 2002, the Home Office has issued the '**application registration card**' (ARC) for asylum applicants (Appendix 8, Figure 12). This contains details about the applicant, such as whether you have any dependants and whether you have permission to work.

Between July 1998 and 31 August 2005, when you were granted refugee status, you were granted indefinite leave. Since 31 August 2005, refugees have been granted five years' leave which is endorsed on an immigration document and may be subject to review. You are also issued with a standard letter providing information about refugee status (Appendix 8, Figures 13 and 14).

Before 31 March 2003, those who were refused asylum may have been granted exceptional leave, usually for four years, endorsed in a letter explaining that they have been refused asylum but granted exceptional leave instead. The letter explained the various rights and entitlements the person has as a result of her/his exceptional leave. Where leave is granted exceptionally other than after an asylum claim (see Chapter 5), this may be difficult to identify. You should have an endorsement granting leave in your passport or, if you do not have a passport, on a letter. Since 31 March 2003 humanitarian protection (HP) for five years, subject to active review, has been granted to those who fear intentional ill treatment or torture contrary to the protection afforded by the European Convention on Human Rights (see p65). If you are granted Article 3 protection on a different basis (eg, health grounds, although this is rare), are excluded from refugee status (eg, due to a serious crime) or are permitted to remain to maintain your Article 8 family or private life rights, you are granted discretionary leave (DL). In most cases (save for exclusion cases) DL is granted for three years (subject to active review – see p67). Your leave is endorsed in immigration documents and your status explained in a separate letter (Appendix 8, Figures 15 and 16).

Refugees may also be issued, on application to the Home Office, with a blue UN Refugee Convention travel document. The leave granted will be endorsed inside it.

Those with exceptional leave, HP or DL may obtain from the Home Office a 'certificate of identity'. These are brown in colour and the leave is endorsed inside. Some countries, however, refuse to accept them as valid for travel.

Policy on obtaining travel documents for those with exceptional leave, HP and DL has changed. Since 30 August 2005 there has been an entitlement to a travel document so long as you can show that you have unreasonably been refused a passport from your own national authorities. This latter requirement does not apply if you have been granted HP because the Home Office has accepted your fear of the relevant national authority. The Asylum Policy Instructions should be consulted for the latest position.

Temporary admission

Most asylum seekers do not have any leave when they claim asylum. While the asylum claim and appeal are being determined you are either detained or granted a licence to be in the UK. This licence is known as 'temporary admission'. Notice of temporary admission is usually given on Form IS96 as shown (Appendix 8, Figure 17). There are variants on temporary admission – eg, 'temporary release' if you have been detained and later released by the immigration authorities and 'restriction orders' if you would otherwise be detained on the basis that you are liable to deportation. Temporary admission is normally granted with conditions, which are stated on the form itself – eg, a restriction to reside at a particular address. Where you have been waiting for a decision from the Home Office on your asylum application for 12 months or more (very unusual at the time of writing unless the claim is a fresh claim), you can apply for your working restriction to be lifted.

Temporary admission is not only issued to asylum seekers, it can also be granted to anyone who needs leave to be in the UK but does not have it and is awaiting a decision on their application for leave or, in some cases, pending immigration enforcement action being taken against them.

Where you are liable to be detained and are released on bail by the Asylum and Immigration Tribunal, you will have forms stating the terms and conditions of your bail.

Because temporary admission is not leave, but is given to a person who needs leave, those granted temporary admission are 'persons subject to immigration control' for benefit purposes (see p155). They are also now considered to be 'lawfully present' for benefit purposes.

5. **Enforced departure**

Illegal entry and administrative removal

When the immigration authorities decide that you are liable to removal (and detention, although this power may not be exercised) as an illegal entrant or may be 'administratively removed' (see Chapter 6) from the UK, they give you a form explaining this (Appendix 8, Figure 18).

Deportation

Where you are subject to deportation you are first issued with a notice of intention to deport against which there is a right of appeal. If the appeal is unsuccessful, you can then be issued with a deportation order which states that the 'Secretary of State by this order requires the said [...NAME...] to leave and prohibits him/her from entering the United Kingdom so long as this order is in force'. The actual deportation order is usually served shortly before you are removed from the UK.

Removal

The final stage for enforcing your departure from the UK is the setting of removal directions (see p73). This is the case whether you are being forced to leave after having been:

- refused leave to enter at port;
- declared to be an illegal entrant;
- notified of your liability to be 'administratively removed'; *or*
- if you have had a deportation order made against you.

The form which states when and where you are to be removed by the carrier varies depending on the procedure which led to your removal. The form shown in Appendix 8, Figure 19 is the one given to notify a person refused asylum who has also been classed as an illegal entrant or as a person liable to be administratively removed, of the directions made for her/his removal (Appendix 8, Figure 19).

---

6. **Other endorsements on passports**

Embarkation from the UK

You may see a triangular stamp on a passport (Appendix 8, Figure 20). This stamp has not been issued since March 1998. It used to be issued to mark a person's departure from the UK, but passports are no longer routinely marked to show the date of embarkation from the UK.

New passports and endorsements

Where you have limited leave and obtain a new passport, you may obtain a stamp from the Home Office in the new passport which states that 'the holder has leave to enter/remain' and the date it was granted and the date on which it expires. The endorsement also contains a reference to a 'code' which indicates the conditions to which the leave is subject. If you have indefinite leave and obtain a new passport, you complete an No Time Limit (NTL) form and pay a fee to have the indefinite leave endorsed into the new passport by the Home Office with a stamp which states 'there is at present no time limit on the holder's stay in the UK'. When you enter a port with existing indefinite leave in an old passport but bearing a new one, the immigration officer will generally issue the ordinary 'given indefinite leave to enter the United Kingdom' stamp into the new passport.

Illegible passport stamps

If the stamp in your passport is either unclear or illegible, you are deemed to have been granted leave to enter for six months with a condition prohibiting you from taking employment.[2]

If you arrived in the UK before 10 July 1998 and were given an unclear or illegible stamp in your passport, you are deemed to have been given indefinite leave to enter the UK.[3]

If you require leave to enter the UK and no stamp is placed in your passport (because, for example, you were simply waved through by the immigration officer) through no fault of your own you may, nevertheless, be considered an 'illegal entrant'.[4]

Notes

1. **British citizens and those with the right of abode in the UK**
   1 Non-Commonwealth nationals can also apply for a certificate of entitlement to evidence their entitlement to the right of abode.

6. **Other endorsements on passports**
   2 Sch 2 para 6(1) IA 1971 as amended
   3 Sch 2 para 6(1) IA 1971 prior to amendment and as interpreted by the courts
   4 *Rehal v SSHD* [1989] Imm AR 576

Part 2

Immigration and benefits

Chapter 10

....

Immigration and benefits

This chapter covers:
1. Social security and immigration control (below)
2. Home Office links with benefits authorities (p118)
3. National insurance number requirement (p120)
4. National insurance contributions (p121)
5. Proving immigration status, age and relationships (p124)

---

1. **Social security and immigration control**

Social security rules and administration are a key part of government immigration policies. Over the past decade there have been significant legislative changes making access to most benefits for people from abroad extremely difficult. The main source of law governing immigration status and benefits is the Immigration and Asylum Act 1999 which came into force in April 2000.[1] However, the residence tests for certain benefits have also been made harsher with the effect that many people who are lawfully living in the UK are left without any form of support.

The exclusion of some of the most vulnerable people in our society from the social security and tax credit system is of considerable concern and has been criticised for causing widespread hardship and even attributed to the rise of racist attacks in the UK. The linking of entitlement to benefit to immigration status has also had consequences for benefit authorities who have had to take on the role of immigration officers, but who are not trained to do so. This inevitably leads to errors and confusion with people who are eligible for benefit being wrongly refused.

This policing role by benefit authorities has led to a fundamental clash of cultures. The basic purpose of benefits authorities and their staff is to ensure payment of benefits to members of the community who cannot support themselves or who require special support. Increasingly, immigration legislation seeks to exclude people from access to the welfare state even where the individual is severely disabled or where the family includes children or other vulnerable people.

2. **Home Office links with benefits authorities**

Benefits are administered by several different government bodies, some of which are divided into different agencies (see below). All of these have links with the Home Office which administers immigration control in the UK.

The benefits authorities

The main authority responsible for overall administration and policy work concerning social security benefits is the Department for Work and Pensions (DWP). Tax credits, child benefit, guardians allowance and national insurance contributions are dealt with by Her Majesty's Revenue and Customs (the Revenue).

The administration of housing benefit (HB) and council tax benefit (CTB) is carried out by local authorities.

Benefits authorities staff are expected to understand immigration law as well as the complicated benefits rules. In practice, their understanding is very limited because they have virtually no training or support in this area. They usually have to rely on internal guidance to make a decision about benefit entitlement but often this is insufficient to enable them to understand the complexity of immigration rules.

Even though the benefits rules which apply to migrants may be different from those for other people, benefits decisions are made in the same way and by the same authorities and staff, regardless of the immigration status of the claimant. All claimants have the same rights of review and appeal. For details of how decisions are taken and how to appeal, see CPAG's *Welfare Benefits and Tax Credits Handbook*.

Immigration checks by benefits authorities

All benefits authorities have links to the Home Office. The main purpose of the links is for benefits authorities to check whether your immigration status affects your rights to benefits.

Immigration checks are usually triggered if a benefits authority believes you may not be British. In the case of income support (IS) and income-based jobseeker's allowance (JSA) claimants, the claim form asks, 'Have you, your partner, or any of the children you are claiming for, come to live or returned to live in the UK in the last two years?' If you answer 'yes' you are asked for the nationality of any person who has come in the last two years, the date you last came, whether you came to work or live in the UK and details of any limits on your stay in the UK. Claim forms for other benefits have similar questions.

If you receive IS, income-based JSA or pension credit, a local authority dealing with a claim by you for HB/CTB should not make immigration checks.[2]

If you give your nationality as other than British, you are normally asked to show the DWP a passport or, for European Union/European Economic Area nationals, an identity card. The benefits authority may take your immigration status from your passport or from any letter sent to you by the Home Office. Otherwise, the benefits authority is likely to contact the Home Office to establish your immigration status. This may still be done even if your passport shows your status. If you have a British passport but are not a British citizen (eg, you are a British overseas citizen) the benefits authority may check or may treat you as a British citizen (see p19).

The Home Office Immigration Status Enquiry Unit is responsible for dealing with immigration status enquiries from benefits authorities. Enquiries are usually made by faxing an enquiry form[3] to the Unit which is then returned with the information completed. Sometimes enquiries are made by telephone. There are sometimes long delays in receiving information. For advice on proving your immigration status, see p124.

Links with entry clearance officers abroad

There are also links between the DWP Overseas Benefits Directorate and entry clearance officers (sometimes called visa officers – see p12) abroad. If you are a non-British citizen living abroad and you claim a retirement pension or bereavement benefit on the basis of your spouse's contributions, the Overseas Directorate may contact an entry clearance officer in your country to see whether you have ever been refused a UK visa. Extracts from the entry clearance officer's file may be sent to the DWP. If there was an appeal against the visa refusal, the entry clearance officer's explanatory statement for that appeal is usually passed to the DWP but other documents, including those which were sent in to support your visa request, may not be passed on. The entry clearance officer's papers are most important if the visa was refused because the entry clearance officer did not accept that you were married as claimed. The DWP may agree with the entry clearance officer and refuse benefit on the ground that, for example, you are not a widow. If this happens, you should appeal and get advice. The vast majority of visa refusals made in disputed relationship cases in the 1970s and early 1980s were wrong, as was proved by later DNA tests.[4]

Home Office use of benefits information

The Home Office uses its links with benefits authorities to check on immigrants and to locate those not here legally with whom it is has lost contact.
- If you are not here legally and the Home Office has lost contact with you, information from a benefits authority query may allow the Home Office to start or continue removal action against you (see Chapter 6).
- If you apply for further leave to remain in the UK, the Home Office application form asks whether you are receiving benefits, which count as public funds. If

you are applying for leave as the spouse or civil partner of a settled person, you are also asked whether your spouse/civil partner is receiving public funds. The Home Office does *not* normally refuse further leave just because your partner has claimed benefits to which s/he is entitled. However, a claim could lead the Home Office to decide that you cannot *adequately* support yourself without recourse to public funds (see p84).

3. National insurance number requirement

In order to claim most benefits it is necessary to satisfy the national insurance (NI) number requirement, known as the NINO requirement. You satisfy this requirement if you:

- provide an NI number together with evidence to show that the number is yours;
- provide evidence or information to enable your NI number to be traced; *or*
- apply for an NI number and provide sufficient information or evidence for one to be allocated.

If you do not satisfy the NINO requirement you are not eligible for benefit. This requirement applies both to you and any person for whom you are claiming benefit, but it does not apply to any child or young person that you may be claiming for. To apply for a NINO call the Jobcentre Plus NI number allocation service helpline on 0845 6000 643. An 'evidence of identity' interview will be arranged – an interpreter can be available if needed. They will ask you to bring sufficient documentary evidence, like a birth certificate, a passport or an identity card. If you have not got any official documents you still have to go to the interview. You might be able to prove your identity with the information you give at the interview. Regulations introduced in December 2006[5] require that a person whose immigration status places restrictions on employment must provide certain prescribed documents (eg, passport, identity card, birth certificate or immigrations status document). However, the legality of these regulations is in question. If you are affected by the new rules seek specialist independent advice.

The NINO requirement is particularly controversial. Despite apparently neutral criteria, the requirement appears to have had a disproportionate effect on black and minority ethnic claimants. This appears to be because, in practice, benefit authority staff often work to a set list of documents that may be produced as evidence of identity. However, many non-British claimants do not have these documents and therefore fall foul of the rule.

A further problem arises where couples have different immigration status. A person who is not a 'person subject to immigration control' (see p155) will find that s/he is refused benefit because her/his partner does not have and is unable to obtain a NINO. However, such an application of the law may well be incompatible with Article 8 of the European Convention on Human Rights (ECHR) (right to respect for family life) because the only way in which the settled person can obtain benefit is to separate from her/his partner. A number of legal challenges have been started on this point, but before any case has reached the courts the DWP has so far resolved the matter favourably towards the claimant.

National insurance numbers

Your NI record is kept under an NI number which looks like this: MN 42 56 93 D. This number is also used as a reference for tax and for contribution-based benefits. If you do not have or know your number, benefits authorities, employers and the Revenue are likely to want to check your immigration status.

NI numbers are allocated automatically to children shortly before their 16th birthday, but only if child benefit is being claimed for them. If child benefit was being claimed for you at that time, you should have an NI number. The number you are given is based on the child benefit reference number.

If you do not have an NI number, you can apply for one. Having an NI number is important because:
- an employer should accept it as showing that there is no bar under immigration law on you taking work;
- it means any contributions you or your employer make should be correctly allocated to your name;
- it means any contributions for which you are credited should be correctly allocated to your name;
- you can deal more easily with official bodies, such as the Revenue.

---

4. **National insurance contributions**

Many benefits are paid out of the national insurance (NI) fund, which is funded by social security contributions of employees, employers, the self-employed and other people who choose to make them. In this book we only cover the rules that particularly affect migrants.

There are six types or *classes* of contribution payable:[6]
- Class 1 – by employed earners and their employers;
- Class 1A – by employers of employed earners;
- Class 1B – by employers of employed earners;
- Class 2 – by self-employed earners;
- Class 3 – by voluntary contributors;
- Class 4 – by self-employed earners.

Contributions are collected and recorded by the Revenue. Contact with the Revenue may lead to information about you being passed to the Home Office (see p118).

For full details of the NI scheme and contribution conditions for benefits, see CPAG's *Welfare Benefits and Tax Credits Handbook*.

Residence and presence

If your earnings are high enough for you/your employer to have to pay contributions, those contributions only have to be paid if the residence and presence rules apply (see Chapter 11). If contributions are not compulsory, you can pay voluntary Class 2 or 3 contributions to help you meet the contribution conditions for benefits. If you wish to pay contributions while abroad, the application form is in DWP leaflet NI38.

Contributions paid in Northern Ireland or the Isle of Man count towards British benefits. You may also be able to use special rules if you have lived in another European Union/European Economic Area member state (see Part 4) or a country with which the UK has a reciprocal agreement (see Part 5) even if you are not a national of that country.

Class 1 contributions

You are liable for Class 1 contributions in any week in which you are:
- employed in Great Britain (GB):[7] *and*
  - either resident or present in GB; *or*
  - ordinarily resident in GB;[8]
  There is an exception to this rule if you are not ordinary resident in the UK, are employed by an overseas employer and normally work abroad.[9] You are only liable once you have been resident in the UK for one year. This also applies to some overseas students and apprentices;[10] *or*
- employed abroad, but only for the first year of that employment (after that you can voluntarily pay Class 3 contributions – see p123)[11] if:[12]
  - your employer has a place of business in GB; *and*
  - you were resident in GB before your employment started; *and*
  - you are ordinarily resident in GB.

Class 1A and 1B contributions

Class 1A contributions are paid by employers for certain benefits in kind such as the use of a company car. Class 1B contributions are paid by an employer who enters into a Pay As You Earn Settlement Agreement with the Revenue.

Class 2 contributions

You are liable for Class 2 contributions in any week in which you are self-employed in GB and either:[13]
- you are ordinarily resident in GB; *or*
- you have been resident in GB for at least 26 weeks in the last year.

You can voluntarily pay Class 2 contributions for any other week in which you are either employed or self-employed and present in GB.[14]

If you are self-employed abroad, you can voluntarily pay Class 2 contributions if you were employed or self-employed immediately before you left GB and:[15]
- you have been resident in GB for a continuous period of at least three years at some time before that; *and*
- you have paid sufficient GB contributions to give you a full contribution record for three past contribution years (for details see CPAG's *Welfare Benefits and Tax Credits Handbook*).

If you are a volunteer development worker employed abroad but ordinarily resident in GB, you can voluntarily pay Class 2 contributions.[16] These are paid at a special rate and (unlike normal Class 2 contributions) count for contribution-based jobseeker's allowance. They are only payable if the Revenue certifies that it would be consistent with the proper administration of the law to allow you to do so.

Class 3 contributions

Class 3 contributions are always voluntary. You can pay them:
- for any year during all of which you were resident in GB; other conditions apply where you have recently arrived in GB;[17] *or*
- for any year, during part of which you were outside the UK, if you meet the conditions for voluntary payment of Class 2 contributions (see p122), except that you do not need to have been employed or self-employed before you left GB;[18] *or*
- if you have previously been paying Class 1 contributions from abroad.

Class 4 contributions

You are liable for Class 4 contributions in any week in which you are resident in GB for income tax purposes.[19]

Credits and home responsibilities protection

You may be credited for Class 1 or 2 contributions in certain weeks, normally where you would satisfy the qualifying conditions for a benefit, including if you are incapable of work, or unemployed and actively seeking and available for work. Credits help meet the contribution conditions for benefits. The various types of credit each have their own residence conditions, usually linked to those for the equivalent benefit. For details of credits, see CPAG's *Welfare Benefits and Tax Credits Handbook*.

Making the most of your contribution record

Your benefits entitlement may depend upon your contribution record. In particular, your right to a state retirement pension and the amount of that pension is set by the number of contributions you have made. A small shortfall in your record may make a big difference to your benefits. A shortfall may, in some cases, be made up by voluntary contributions or by allocating to your name contributions already made.

If you have returned from abroad you should ask the Revenue Contributions Office for a copy of your contribution record. You can then check that contributions have been made while you were abroad. You may also be able to make up any shortfall in your record by voluntary contributions.

You may have used another person's number or a false number while in the UK because you did not wish to come to the attention of the Home Office. If you have since been given leave to remain in the UK, you should apply for an NI number in your own name. You may wish to ask the Contributions Office to transfer contributions allocated to the number you used in the past to the number issued in your name. This means that the contributions paid for your work will be allocated to you. You may need to provide evidence that the contributions were paid because of your work. However, you may have committed a criminal offence by using a number which was not allocated to you – eg, if you used that number to get work you may have committed the offence of obtaining property (your wages) by deception (pretending that the number was allocated to you). Because of this, you should take independent advice before asking the Contributions Office to transfer contributions to your name.

5. Proving immigration status, age and relationships

For most people, proving immigration status, identity, age and their relationships to others (eg, marriage or parentage) is straightforward. However, some people may have problems and migrants are most likely to be affected.

Immigration status

It is often difficult for people who have come from abroad to prove their immigration status. Often documents have been sent to the Home Office and you may not have documentation to show to the benefit authority. Equally, although the benefit authority may contact the Home Office for your details, it often does not bother to do so and even when it does Home Office staff often cannot locate a file. Even where documents are available (eg, a passport) these may not clearly indicate your immigration status. The absence of clear documentation means that benefit authority staff have to make decisions on your immigration status. However, with virtually no training in this area they are not equipped to do so.

Age

Your age, or the age of members of your family, may affect your rights to benefit, or the amount of benefit. This most commonly arises in claims for retirement pension, but the amount of other benefits (eg, income support) can also be affected.

The most common situation in which the benefits authorities dispute age is where you were born abroad in a place where dates of birth were not accurately recorded at that time.

Benefits authority officials are generally more willing than the Home Office to accept foreign records as accurate. If you have a birth certificate, it is usually accepted as proof of your birth date. Other evidence which can show your birth date includes:

- passport or identity card;
- school or health records;
- army records;
- statements from people who know you or your family;
- astrological charts made for a baby at the time of the birth.

You may be able to show your birth date by referring to the accepted birth dates of other relatives. For example, if you are recorded as the eldest child and your sister has been accepted as born on a date in 1937, you must have been born before that date.

Medical assessments are sometimes used as evidence of age. This involves a doctor examining you and guessing how old you are. Some doctors use X-rays as part of this assessment. In adults this method is only accurate to within a few years at best.

A common problem is conflicting evidence. Your birth date may have been wrongly recorded in your passport when it was issued – eg, because you gave the wrong date or because of an administrative error. Passports are commonly recorded as '1 January' where the exact date is unclear. The date in the passport may then have been used in many other official documents. It may be difficult to persuade the benefits authorities that all these dates are wrong. You should explain that all these dates come from one document, so the only real evidence for the date is the passport. If there is other evidence showing that date is not right, the passport is not conclusive evidence.

While each piece of evidence has to be considered, the oldest documents may be more reliable, since they were made nearer to the time of the events to which they refer.

If there is no documentary evidence, the benefits authorities should accept your own statements unless they are contradictory or improbable.

Your birth date may be given in the document(s) as a year or a month rather than an actual date. If this applies, the DWP assumes your birth date is the date least favourable to you. If you claim retirement pension, this is the last day of the year/month. However, this date should then be used for all other benefit decisions, even if that is more favourable to you.

If a benefits authority refuses to accept your evidence about your age and so refuses benefit or pays it at a lower rate, you should appeal and take independent advice.

Marriages, divorces and civil partnerships

You may need to show that you are/were married or in a civil partnership. This is most likely to apply to claims for bereavement benefits. It may also apply where there is a question of the validity of the marriage or civil partnership.

A marriage or civil partnership certificate is the best evidence. However, if one is not available, other evidence can count. Your own statement that you were married or had a civil partnership should be enough. This is because, unlike your date of birth, you can be expected to remember that you were married or had a civil partner and who your spouse/civil partner was. If there is contradictory evidence, or if you are claiming benefit as an appointee for a person whose mental state prevents them from making such a statement or for a person who has died, you may need to show by other ways that there was a marriage or civil partnership.

The most important of these is the cohabitation presumption. If a couple live together as if they were husband and wife or civil partners, it is presumed that they are married to each other or in a civil partnership, unless there is clear contradictory evidence to which the benefits authority can point.[20] This presumption is even stronger where there are children of the couple.

Parentage

In rare cases you may need to show that you are (or your late spouse or civil partner was) the parent of a child. This could apply where child benefit is claimed for a child by you and one or more other people, none of whom is living with the child. In this situation, a parent has priority over other claimants.[21] It may also arise if you are refused widowed parent's allowance (or awarded it at a reduced rate) because it is disputed that your child or children are children of your late spouse.[22]

DNA testing may be able accurately to establish whether the person is/was the parent of the child concerned. If this is not possible, the parent may be able to use the presumption of legitimacy. If the child was conceived by or born to a married woman, there is a legal presumption that her husband is the father.[23] If you were married to the mother, you are presumed to be the father. In the case of widowed parent's allowance, your late husband is therefore presumed to be the father of any child conceived or born during the marriage. The presumption applies even if the child was born after the wedding but obviously conceived before.[24] The presumption can be overridden by evidence that the husband was not the father.[25] For the benefits authorities to do this, there must be evidence that shows the child was probably not legitimate.[26] If you are the claimed father but the mother was married to another man, he, rather than you, is presumed to be the father.

If the mother was not married at the time of conception or birth, there is no presumption.

Notes

1. **Social security and immigration control**
   1 In particular, s115 IAA 1999. For the rules before that date, see the 2nd edition of this *Handbook*.

2. **Home Office links with benefits authorities**
   2 HB/CTB Circular A1/96 para 4
   3 The DWP uses a DCI 100 form.
   4 See Dummett and Nicol, *Subjects, Citizens, Aliens and Others*, Weidenfeld & Nicholson, 1990, p233

4. **National insurance contributions**
   5 Reg 2 Social Security (National Insurance Numbers) Amendment Regulations 2006; Sch Parts I and II Immigration (Restrictions on Employment) Order 2004
   6 s1(2) SSCBA 1992
   7 s2(1)(a) SSCBA 1992
   8 Reg 119(1)(a) SS(Con) Regs
   9 Reg 145(2) SS(Con) Regs
   10 Reg 145(3) SS(Con) Regs
   11 Reg 146(2)(b) SS(Con) Regs
   12 Reg 146 SS(Con) Regs
   13 s2(1)(b) SSCBA 1992; reg 145(1)(d) SS(Con) Regs
   14 Reg 145(1)(c) SS(Con) Regs
   15 Reg 147 SS(Con) Regs
   16 Regs 149-154 SS(Con) Regs
   17 Reg 145(1)(e) SS(Con) Regs
   18 Reg 147 SS(Con) Regs
   19 Reg 91 SS(Con) Regs

5. **Proving immigration status, age and relationships**
   20 *Re Taylor* [1961] WLR 9, CA. For more cases see Keane, *The Modern Law of Evidence*, Butterworths
   21 Sch 10 SSCBA 1992
   22 s39A(3) SSCBA 1992
   23 See Keane (note 20)
   24 *The Poulet Peerage Case* [1903] AC 395. In Scotland, s5(1)(a) Law Reform (Parent and Child) (Scotland) Act 1986
   25 For possible sources of evidence, see Keane (note 20).
   26 s26 FLRA 1969; *S v S* [1972] AC 24 at 41. In Scotland, s5(4) Law Reform (Parent and Child) (Scotland) Act 1986

Chapter 11

Presence and residence tests

This chapter covers:
1. Presence and absence (p129)
2. Ordinary residence (p129)
3. Habitual residence (p132)
4. Right to reside (p137)

There are various types of residence conditions for benefits. In the past many benefits had a simple presence test and some benefits required the claimant to be 'ordinarily resident'. Presence, absence and ordinary residence are quite straightforward.

However, more recently far more complex residence tests have been introduced by way of the habitual residence test in 1994 and the right to reside test in 2004.

Benefit rules are usually precise, even if they are complicated but the right to reside and habitual residence tests are simple but very vague. They need judgement and weighing up of many different factors. Two different decision makers can legally reach different opinions about the residence of a particular person.

Guidance to benefits staff states that a decision must be made on all the facts, but sets out certain factors which may be relevant. Because staff are used to applying precise rules, they tend to change these factors into checklists. This often leads to far too much weight being given to certain factors and to decisions which are obviously wrong from a common sense point of view.

Example
One tribunal decision[1] concerned a British citizen born abroad who lived and worked in the UK for two years and who then made an overseas visit of one month to her estranged husband who was very ill. The tribunal decided that on her return she was not habitually resident in the UK because her husband and children lived abroad and she was unlikely to be able to afford ever to bring them to the UK, even if they were permitted to enter, and she may have owned property abroad. That decision was clearly wrong on any understanding of habitual residence. The length of time the claimant had lived here, renting her own flat with her own permanent job (from which she had been made redundant), meant she became habitually resident, regardless of the whereabouts of her family and property or her prospects of finding work. Her visit abroad did not break that

residence. The tribunal went wrong because it focused on her family ties and prospects of employment.

1. Presence and absence

Presence means physical presence. Great Britain (GB) is Wales, Scotland, England and adjacent islands (but not the Isle of Man or Channel Islands).[2] The United Kingdom (UK) is GB and Northern Ireland.[3]

The UK includes UK territorial waters and GB includes UK territorial waters adjacent to GB.[4] Territorial waters are those within 12 miles of the shore,[5] except off Dover and near the Isle of Man where they stop mid-point to France/Isle of Man.[6] This means that if you travel to GB by boat, you become present when the boat enters these adjacent territorial waters. If you travel to GB by plane, you become present when the plane lands.

If you have to be **present** in GB to be entitled to a benefit, you must show that you were in GB from midnight to midnight.[7] If a benefits authority wants to disqualify you from benefit because you were absent from GB, it must show you were absent throughout that day. This means that on the day you leave GB and the day you arrive in GB you count as neither present nor absent.

2. Ordinary residence

You must be ordinarily resident in Great Britain (GB) to be entitled to:
- attendance allowance;[8]
- carer's allowance;[9]
- child benefit;[10]
- child tax credit;[11]
- disability living allowance;[12]
- incapacity benefit for incapacity in youth;[13]
- Category D retirement pension;[14]
- working tax credit.[15]

There is no definition in the benefits regulations of ordinary residence. This means that 'ordinary residence' is given its ordinary and natural meaning.[16] The most important case on ordinary residence is *Shah*.[17] In that case the House of Lords decided that ordinary residence means:[18]

'a person's abode in a particular place or country which he has adopted voluntarily and for settled purposes as part of the regular order of his life for the time being, whether of short or long duration.'

It should usually be clear whether residence is voluntary or for a settled purpose.[19] The caselaw on ordinary residence shows that:

- ordinary residence can start on arrival in GB, or it can start before (see below);
- a person in GB for a temporary purpose can be ordinarily resident in GB (see below);
- a person who lives in GB but has no fixed abode can be ordinarily resident;[20]
- ordinary residence can continue during absences from GB, but leaving to settle abroad will normally end ordinary residence (see below);
- a person who spends most of the time (or even almost all of the time) outside GB can be ordinarily resident;[21]
- a person can be ordinarily resident in more than one place or country;[22]
- ordinary residence is different from the concept of 'domicile'.[23]

Special rules apply to children (see p132) and other people whose place of residence is beyond their control (see p131).

Ordinary residence on arrival

Ordinary residence can begin immediately on arrival in GB.[24] In a family law case, a man who separated from his wife in one country (where he had lived and worked for three years) and went to live at his parent's house in another, was found to become immediately ordinarily resident there.[25] The Court of Appeal said that, where there is evidence that the person intends to make a place her/his home for an indefinite period, s/he is ordinarily resident when s/he arrives there. In another case, a court decided that a woman returning from Australia after some months there had never lost her ordinary residence in England, but, if she had, she became ordinarily resident again when the boat embarked from Australia.[26] The students in *Shah* had to show that they were ordinarily resident within a few weeks of first arriving in the UK, but it was not argued that they could not be ordinarily resident because they had only just come to GB.[27]

Temporary purpose

To be ordinarily resident in GB you do not have to intend or be able to live here permanently. The purpose can be for a limited period and Lord Scarman said that 'education, business or profession, employment, health, family, or merely love of the place spring to mind as common reasons for a choice of regular abode'.[28] You may have several different reasons for a single stay – eg, to visit relatives, get medical advice, attend religious ceremonies and sort out personal affairs.[29]

The reason must be a settled one. This does not mean that the reason has to be long-standing,[30] but there must be evidence of it. In most of the cases on ordinary residence, the court was looking back to see whether a person had been ordinarily resident months or years before.[31] This is much easier than deciding whether a person has recently become ordinarily resident. There is no minimum period of residence before you are ordinarily resident. If, for example, you have arrived in the UK and started work, the benefits authorities should consider how long you are likely to reside in the UK. If you intend to live here for the time being, the benefits authorities should accept your intention as sufficient, unless it is clearly unlikely that you are going to be able to stay. The benefits authorities should not make a deep examination of your long-term intentions.[32] The type of accommodation you occupy may be relevant.[33]

Absence from the UK

If you are ordinarily resident in GB, you can lose that status if you go abroad. This depends upon:
- why you go abroad;
- how long you stay abroad;
- what connections you keep with GB – eg, accommodation, furniture and other possessions.[34]

If you decide to move abroad for the foreseeable future, then you will normally stop being ordinarily resident in GB on the day you leave.[35] A possible exception to this is where your plans are clearly impractical and you return to GB very quickly.

If your absence abroad is part of your normal pattern of life, your ordinary residence in GB will not be affected.[36] This applies even if you are out of GB for most of the year.[37] For example, if you spend each summer in GB but all winter abroad, you may be ordinarily resident in GB.

If your absence abroad is extraordinary or temporary, and you intend to return to GB, your ordinary residence will not be affected.[38] A British woman who spent 15 months in Germany with her husband over a period of three years kept her ordinary residence in England. She had always intended to return here.[39]

However, if you are away from GB for a long time and do not keep strong connections with GB you may lose your ordinary residence, even if you intend to return. A citizen of the UK and colonies (see p20) lived in the UK for over four years, and then returned to Kenya for two years and five months because her business here failed, and there was a business opportunity in Kenya. She intended to make enough money to support herself on her return to the UK. Her parents and parents-in-law remained in the UK. She was found to have lost her ordinary residence during her absence.[40]

Involuntary residence

A person who is held in a place against her/his will may not become ordinarily resident. These cases are very rare. Examples given by the courts are kidnap victims and being stranded on a desert island.[41] The courts have recognised that circumstances which limit or remove a person's choice, may not stop them from being ordinarily resident where they reside.[42] A woman who became mentally ill on a visit to England and remained in an asylum until she died over 50 years later, was ordinarily resident in GB by the time she died, even though she never decided to stay here.[43] Deportation to GB does not prevent you becoming ordinarily resident here.[44] The issue is whether the person's residence is part of their settled purpose. If you have decided to live in GB, it does not matter that you have made that decision because you have been deported here.

Children

If you are a child or young person, ordinary residence is decided using the same rules as for adults.[45]

The only benefit for children under 16 with an ordinary residence test is disability living allowance. The residence of a child aged under 16 is usually decided by her/his parent(s) or person(s) with parental responsibility (or in Scotland, parental rights and responsibilities). Therefore, if the child lives with that person, the child will usually have the same ordinary residence as that person.[46] So, a child joining a parent or other person with parental responsibility may become ordinarily resident almost immediately.[47] If there is only one person with parental responsibility, the child has the same ordinary residence as that person.[48]

Where there are two such people who live apart, one of them should get the consent of the other to a change of residence of the child, otherwise the child may be treated as abducted. A child who is abducted is considered still to have the same ordinary residence as the person(s) with parental responsibility.[49] Agreement to a change of residence may be assumed if the other person takes no action.[50]

---

3. Habitual residence

The **habitual residence test** (HRT) was introduced on 1 August 1994 and affects entitlement to income support (IS), income-based jobseeker's allowance (JSA), pension credit (PC), housing benefit (HB) and council tax benefit (CTB). In order to qualify for one of these benefits you must be 'habitually resident' in the '**common travel area**' (CTA) which is comprised of the UK, Ireland, the Channel Islands and the Isle of Man. The way in which the test operates for each benefit is slightly different but the outcome is the same. If you are not habitually resident in the CTA, you are not entitled to IS, income-based JSA, PC, HB or CTB.[51]

If you fail the test you are classed as a '**person from abroad**' for IS,[52] income-based JSA,[53] HB[54] and CTB.[55] This is a social security definition and can apply to British citizens. The effect of this is to give an applicable amount of 'nil' for IS and income-based JSA, to treat you as not liable for rent or council tax for HB and CTB and to treat you as not meeting the presence test for PC.[56]

The test is both complex and subjective and since 1 May 2004 the test has been amended to include a further condition. You are deemed not to be habitually resident unless you have right of residence.

You are deemed not to be a 'person from abroad' if you:[57]

- are an employed or self employed person (worker) for the purposes of EC Directive 2004/38;
- are a former worker who has retained worker status;
- are a refugee;
- have exceptional leave or humanitarian protection;
- are not a person subject to immigration control under section 115 of the Immigration and Asylum Act, and you are in the UK as a result of deportation, expulsion or other removal by compulsion of law from another country to the UK;
- left Montserrat after 1 November 1995 because of volcanic eruption;
- for HB and CTB, you are deemed to satisfy the HRT if you are in receipt of IS or income-based JSA.[58]

The meaning of habitual residence

A person must be habitually resident in the CTA (see p132) and must be **resident for an appreciable period of time**.[59] The length of the appreciable period depends on your case but may be short (eg, a month).[60] However, there is no fixed minimum period.[61] Therefore, it might be a matter of days. It can include visits to prepare for settled residence made before that residence is actually taken up.[62] There are some situations when no appreciable period may be necessary:

- where you have been habitually resident in the UK in the past, even though the length of your absence means that the previous habitual residence has come to an end. This exception originates from a comment made in a House of Lords case that 'there may indeed be special cases where a person concerned is not coming here for the first time but is resuming an habitual residence previously had'.[63] The DWP often uses this exception in favour of UK citizens returning after a long period living in one of the former colonies;
- where you can take advantage of EC law (see p136).

The factors that are relevant to deciding whether you are habitually resident include:[64]

- bringing possessions;
- doing everything necessary to establish residence before coming;
- having a right of abode (see p5);
- bringing or seeking to bring family;
- ties with the UK.

To be habitually resident you must be seen to be making a home here, but it does not have to be your only home or a permanent one.[65] So a long-standing intention to move abroad (eg, when debts are paid) does not prevent a person from being habitually resident.[66]

You can be seen to be making a home here even though you have very few or no resources. For example, approaching housing associations and trying to find work help to show that you are making a home here.

The practicality or 'viability' of your arrangements for residence might be relevant to deciding whether you are resident and the length of the appreciable period.[67] A person who has no money to support her/himself in GB but who intends to stay is likely to be resident here for the foreseeable future because s/he cannot afford to go anywhere else. So a person with no income will have a short appreciable period. Lack of viability can only make it more difficult to show habitual residence if it means that you are likely to leave the UK soon. However, EEA nationals in this situation may fail the right to reside test (see p139).

Events after the benefit claim or decision may show that your intention was always to reside in the UK.[68] For example, if you are refused income-based JSA because the DWP does not accept you have a settled intention to stay in the UK, the fact that you are still here by the time of the appeal hearing may help to show that you always intended to stay. Even if you are not currently habitually resident the decision maker should consider whether you will shortly become habitually resident and decide your claim in advance.[69]

The decision about whether or not you are habitually resident has to be made on the 'balance of probabilities'. If the probabilities in favour of each answer are exactly equal, the decision should be that you *are* habitually resident. This is because the benefits authority has to show that you are *not* habitually resident.[70]

There is now a considerable amount of caselaw both from the commissioners and higher courts which have sought to define the term and lay down guidance on the interpretation of 'habitual residence'. These decisions form binding caselaw and should be relied on rather than any guidance.

The House of Lords[71] confirmed that, 'It seems to me plain that as a matter of ordinary language a person is not habitually resident in any country unless he has take up residence and lived there for a period . . . it is a question of fact to be decided on the date where the determination has to be made on the circumstances of each case whether and when that habitual residence has been established. . . the requisite period is not a fixed period. It may be longer where there are doubts. It may be short.'

In another case[72] the ECJ considered whether EC law allowed some EEA nationals to override the HRT. The claimant had returned to the UK after working in France but was denied benefit under the HRT because he did not have an appreciable period of residence, in addition to settled intention. The ECJ considered EC Regulation 1408/71 under which IS is listed as a special non-contributory benefit, and held that 'completion of an appreciable period of residence' could not be imposed as a requirement for benefit, in addition to an intention to reside, in the case of a person covered by EC Regulation 1408/71 (see below).

The ECJ has previously considered the meaning of habitual residence for the purposes of EC Regulation 1408/71.[73] The Court held that habitual residence corresponds with where the habitual centre of interests is situated. Account should be taken of the:

- length and continuity of residence before the person moved;
- length and purpose of absence;
- nature of the occupation found in the other member state; *and*
- intention of the person concerned as it appears from all the circumstances.

There are numerous commissioners' decisions on habitual residence. In one case the commissioner[74] made the following points:

- The burden of proof in habitual residence cases lies with the decision maker not the claimant.
- You must be resident for an appreciable period of time before you can be treated as habitually resident.
- What counts as an appreciable period depends on the facts of each case. There is no minimum period before you acquire habitual residence.
- The current home need not be the only home nor need it be intended to be a permanent one, but it must be a genuine home for the time being.
- Once you have acquired habitual residence that status is not lost if you go abroad for a temporary purpose.

In another case[75] the Commissioner confirms that:

- What constitutes an appreciable period depends on the circumstances of the particular case.
- In general the period lies between one and three months and that cogent reasons would need to be given by a tribunal supporting a decision in which a significantly longer period had been required.
- Whether the residence is viable is a factor that is relevant to the test but must be given appropriate weight and not overemphasised.
- The danger of overemphasising viability is that the only claimants who can establish habitual residence will be those who have sufficient access to funds not to need the benefit and that cannot be right as the habitual residence test is a test of entitlement, not a bar to it.

The effect of all of this caselaw is that people may be affected by the HRT and in some cases excluded from benefit for a short period.

Dealing with the habitual residence test

You will normally be interviewed. You should explain the steps you have taken to make the UK your home. You should provide any documents which will help your case – eg, registration with local doctor; school/college enrolment; evidence of looking for work; letters from relatives and friends settled in the UK.

The DWP and local authorities often do not apply the HRT properly or even consistently. In practice, the test usually means that you are denied benefits at first, but not indefinitely. Local offices may have a rule of thumb, such as three or six months, after which a person will pass the test. Applying such a blanket policy is unlawful and therefore should be challenged either by judicial review or by bringing a complaint. Practice varies between and within offices, so even if you fail the test at one office, you could pass it at another. However, once you are accepted as habitually resident, you are very unlikely to fail the test at a later date, even if your benefit claim stops or you change benefit offices.

Because establishing an appreciable period of residence is only a matter of time, if you fail the test, you should make further claims at regular intervals. You should appeal against every refusal, but the tribunal which hears that appeal will only be able to consider whether you were habitually resident on or before the DWP decision. Some DWP offices tell claimants the appreciable period for them to be accepted as habitually resident. If this applies, you should reclaim when you have been resident for that period but still appeal the earlier refusal.

Habitual residence under European Community law

Under the EC co-ordination rules (see p295), you are entitled to receive any 'special non-contributory benefits', which include IS, in the EU member state in which you reside, so long as you qualify for it under that country's social security scheme.[76] For this purpose, 'residence' means 'habitual residence'.[77] This phrase has a slightly different meaning in EC law than UK law. If you come under the co-ordination rules, you are entitled to have the question of your habitual residence for IS, income-based JSA or PC purposes dealt with under EC law rather than UK law.

Habitual residence in EC law is not defined. The caselaw of the ECJ[78] explains what habitual residence means, but (except for *Swaddling* – see below) only in the situation where a person wishes to claim an unemployment benefit in a country other than the one where s/he last worked.[79] The ECJ decided that, because this is a special situation, there must be a very restrictive approach to who can qualify. For that reason we consider that the caselaw on this special provision is not useful guidance on habitual residence in other situations under UK or EC law.

Unlike UK law, EC law does *not* always require an 'appreciable period' for habitual residence.[80] This only applies to you if you can rely on the EC co-ordination rule (see p295). This is most likely to apply if you are returning to the UK, but it might apply in other cases. In the case of *Swaddling* the ECJ said 'the length of residence cannot be regarded as an intrinsic element of the concept of [habitual] residence'.[81] This has been explained in a commissioner's decision[82] as meaning that it is not essential under EC law that the residence should have lasted for any particular length of time, but the length of residence remains a factor to be considered. So, in some cases where other factors point in favour of you being considered habitually resident, this can be so from the date of your arrival in the UK.

EC law may allow your residence in another EEA country to count towards any appreciable period of residence under UK law.[83]

4. Right to reside

In response to the accession of eight new member states to the European Union (EU) on 1 May 2004, a complex residence test was introduced for certain social security benefits and child tax credit (CTC). Claimants now have to have a right of residence in the UK in order to qualify for:

- child benefit;
- CTC;
- council tax benefit (CTB);
- housing benefit (HB);
- income-based jobseekers allowance (JSA);
- income support (IS);
- pension credit (PC).

For child benefit and CTC the test is part of the existing presence test. For the other benefits listed, the requirement to reside forms part of the habitual residence test.

How the test operates

Income support, income-based jobseeker's allowance, pension credit, housing benefit and council tax benefit

In order to qualify for these benefits you must be habitually resident in the common travel area (CTA – see p132). You are deemed not to be habitually resident unless you have a right of residence in the CTA. The habitual residence test (HRT) therefore now involves a two-stage test comprised both of the original HRT and the new right to reside test.

The rules differ very slightly for **JSA** in that a workseeker can be treated as having a right to reside whereas for IS, PC, HB and CTB a workseeker does not. However, if you are a workseeker and you claim income-based JSA, you can be passported onto HB and CTB.

For **IS, PC, HB and CTB** you are a 'person from abroad' if you are not habitually resident in the CTA (see p132).

However, you cannot satisfy the test if you do not have a right of residence. You are treated as not having a right of residence if you are:[84]

- an EU national who is not economically active and are in the UK during the first three months of your stay;
- a workseeker.

The deeming of EU nationals not to have a right of residence during the first three months of stay is not at odds with the rights in EC law.[85] Member states are under no obligation to confer entitlement to social assistance during the first three months of residence, or indeed for any longer period where the person remains economically inactive.

For **income-based JSA** the rules are the same apart from the fact if you are signing-on for JSA you are treated as having a right to reside. This reflects the rights contained in Article 39 of the EC Treaty which allows free movement for those in search of work as well as workers.

Child benefit and child tax credit

For child benefit and CTC the right to reside is linked to the presence test. You need to be present in order to be entitled to benefit. Regulations[86] provide that a person shall be treated as not being present in GB where a claim is made after 1 May 2004 and that person does not have the right to reside in GB for child benefit and the UK for CTC. There are no exempted groups for these benefits.

Who has a right to reside

Whether or not you have a right to reside is a matter of law and fact and is dependent upon your immigration status and nationality.

This makes the right to reside test a very complex area because a person's status is not always apparent and in order to make accurate decisions it is essential to have at least a basic understanding of both UK immigration law and of EC law.

You have a right to reside if you:
- are a British citizen or have the right of abode;
- have leave to remain in the UK under UK immigration rules;
- have a right to reside under EC law.

British citizens and others with a right of abode

British citizens have a right of abode and do not need leave to enter or remain in the UK. They are free to live in and to come and to go from the UK. They therefore have a right of residence in the UK by virtue of their nationality.

There are some Commonwealth citizens who also have a right of abode even though they are not British citizens. This applies if, before 1 January 1983, they were Commonwealth citizens who had a parent born in the UK or women who were married to a person with a right of abode.

Leave to remain under UK immigration rules

Irish citizens have a right of residence under UK law.

A person with temporary leave to remain under UK immigration rules (eg, as a spouse or visitor) has a right of residence, albeit temporary, but people in this group are not affected by the new rules because they are already largely excluded from entitlement to benefit under separate rules.

Refugees have a right of residence under UK immigration rules.

The position of asylum seekers is more complicated. They are allowed to remain in the UK while their asylum application is determined but this does not necessarily give them a right of residence. However, asylum seekers are largely excluded from benefits under separate rules and therefore are unlikely to be affected by the right to reside test.

EEA nationals

The group most likely to experience difficulties with the new rules are EU nationals, apart from Irish citizens. This is also the area where there is likely to be a high error rate in decision-making because a person's right to reside under EC law can be a complex matter to determine. EEA nationals only have a right of residence in certain circumstances. Generally this means that they must have worked in the UK or be exercising some other EC right. A8 and A2 nationals in particular are subject to some restrictions in terms of their right to reside. For full details of an EEA nationals right to reside, see Chapters 8 and 24.

Notes

1 R(IS) 6/96

1. Presence and absence
2 Union With Scotland Act 1706; Sch 2 para 5(a) IntA 1978
3 Sch1 IntA 1978, definition of 'UK'; R(S) 5/85
4 s172 SSCBA 1992; s35(1) JSA 1995, definition of 'GB'
5 s1 Territorial Sea Act 1987
6 Territorial Sea (Limits) Order 1989 SI No.482
7 R(S) 1/66

2. Ordinary residence
8 Reg 2(1)(a)(i) AA Regs
9 Reg 9(1)(a) SS(ICA) Regs
10 Reg 23 CB Regs

11 Reg 3(1) TC(R) Regs
12 Reg 2(1)(a)(i) DLA Regs
13 Reg 16 SS(IB) Regs
14 Reg 10(b) SS(WB&RP) Regs
15 Reg 3(1) TC(R) Regs
16 R(M) 1/85
17 *R v Barnet LBC ex parte Shah aka Akbarali v Brent LBC* [1983] 2 AC 309; [1983] 2 WLR 16; [19830 1 All ER 226; [1983] 127 SJ 36; [1983] 81 LGR 305; [1983] 133 New LJ; HL, Lord Scarman at p343H
18 *Shah* p343H
19 *Shah* p344G
20 *Levene v Inland Revenue Commissioners* [1928] AC 217, HL
21 *Levene; Inland Revenue Commissioners v Lysaght* [1928] AC 234, HL

22 eg, Lysaght was found to be ordinarily resident in England even though he was clearly also ordinarily resident in the Irish Free State.

23 *Shah* p345E-H (see note 17)

24 R(F) 1/62

25 *Macrae v Macrae* [1949] P 397; [1949] 2 All ER 34; 93 SJ 449; 47 LGR 437, CA (the countries were Scotland and England which are separate for family law purposes). In R(IS) 6/96 para 27 the commissioner doubts the correctness of *Macrae* because he considers it used a test very close to the 'real home' test rejected in *Shah*. He does not seem to have heard any argument about this: *Macrae* was cited in *Shah* and was not one of the cases mentioned there as wrong: pp342-43.

26 *Lewis v Lewis* [1956] 1 WLR 200; [1956] 1 All ER 375; 100 SJ 134, HC

27 The facts are in the Court of Appeal's judgment: *R v Barnet LBC ex parte Shah* [1982] QB 688 at p717E; [1982] 2 WLR 474; [1982] 1 All ER 698; [1982] 80 LGR 571

28 *Shah* p344C-D (see note 17). In R(F) 1/62 education was the purpose.

29 *Levene* (see note 20)

30 eg, Macrae's decision to move to Scotland was made shortly before he went.

31 eg, *Shah* (see note 17)

32 *Shah* p344G (see note 17)

33 R(F) 1/82; R(F) 1/62; R(P) 1/62; R(P) 4/54

34 R(F) 1/62; R(M) 1/85

35 *Hopkins v Hopkins* [1951] P 116; *R v Hussain* (1971) 56 Crim App R 165, CA; *R v IAT ex parte Ng* [1986] Imm AR 23, QBD

36 *Shah* (see note 17); CG/204/1949; *R v IAT ex parte Siggins* [1985] Imm AR 14, QBD

37 *Levene* (see note 20); *Lysaght* (see note 21)

38 *Shah* p342D (see note 17)

39 *Stransky v Stransky* [1954] 3 WLR 123; [1954] 2 All ER 536

40 *Haria* [1986] Imm AR 165, IAT

41 *Shah* (see note 17)

42 *Lysaght* (see note 21)

43 In *Re Mackenzie* [1941] 1 Chancery Reports 69

44 *Gout v Cimitian* [1922] 1 AC 105, PC: deportation of an Ottoman subject from Egypt did not stop him becoming ordinarily resident in Cyprus.

45 *Re A (A Minor) (Abduction: Child's Objections)* [1994] 2 FLR 126: on habitual residence, but also applies to ordinary residence.

46 *Re M (Minors) (Residence Order: Jurisdiction)* [1993] 1 FLR 495, CA: on habitual residence, but also applies to ordinary residence.

47 *Re M (Minors) (Residence Order: Jurisdiction)* [1993] 1 FLR 495, per Hoffman LJ: on habitual residence, but also applies to ordinary residence.

48 *Re J (A Minor) (Abduction: Custody Rights)* [1990] 2 AC 562 at 578

49 *Re M (Minors: Residence Order: Jurisdiction)* [1993] 1 FLR 495

50 *Re A (A Minor) (Abduction: Acquiescence)* [1992] 2 FLR 14: on habitual residence, but also applies to ordinary residence.

3. Habitual residence

51 Reg 21(3) IS Regs 'person from abroad'; reg 85(4) JSA Regs 'person from abroad'; reg 2 SPC Regs; reg 10 HB Regs; reg 7 CTB Regs

52 Reg 21AA IS Regs

53 Reg 85A JSA Regs

54 Reg 10 HB Regs

55 Reg 7 CTB Regs

56 Reg 2 SPC Regs

57 Reg 21AA IS Regs; reg 85A JSA Regs; reg 2 SPC Regs; reg 10 HB Regs; reg 7 CTB Regs

58 Reg 10 HB Regs; reg 7(4)(k) CTB Regs

59 *Nessa v Chief Adjudication Officer* [1999] 1 WLR 1937; [1999] 4 All ER 677; [1999] 2 FLR 1116, HL

60 *Re F (A Minor) (Child Abduction)* [1994] FLR 548, CA, cited in *Nessa v Chief Adjudication Officer* [1999] 1 WLR 1937, HL; R(IS) 2/00

61 R(IS) 2/00 para 24; *Cameron v Cameron* [1996] SLT 306

62 R(IS) 2/00 para 26

63 R(IS) 2/00 (House of Lords decision)

64 R(IS) 2/00

65 CR(IS) 6/96 para 19

66 *M v M (Abduction: England & Scotland)* [1997] 2 FLR 263, CA

67 R(IS) 6/96 paras 28-30; R(IS) 2/00 para 28

68 R(IS) 2/00 para 30

69 *Secretary of State for Work and Pensions v Bhakta* [2006] EWCA Civ 65

70 R(IS) 6/96 para 15

71 *Nessa v the Chief Adjudication Officer*, 21 October 1999, HL

72 *Swaddling* (Case C-90/97, 25.2.99) ECJ

73 *Di Paolo* Case C-76/76
74 R(IS) 6/96
75 CIS/4474/2003
76 Art 10A(1) EC Reg 1408/71
77 Art 1(h) EC Reg 1408/71
78 R(U) 7/85; R(U) 8/88 and the cases listed
    in that case
79 Under Art 71(1)(b)(ii) EC Reg 1408/71
80 Case C-90/97 *Swaddling* [1999] 2 CMLR
    2679; [1999] 2 FLR 185
81 para 30
82 R(IS) 3/00 para 16
83 Under Art 10a(2) EC Reg 1408/71. This
    argument was mentioned but not
    resolved in R(IS) 3/00.

4. The right to reside test
84 Reg 21AA (2) IS Regs; reg 7(3) CTB Regs;
    reg 10(3) HB Regs; reg 2(2) SPC Regs
85 Art 24(2) EC Residence Directive 2004/
    38
86 Reg 21 CB Regs; reg 3 TC(R) Regs

Chapter 12

Special rules for family members

This chapter covers the special rules which apply to:
1. Families with different immigration statuses (below)
2. Couples where one partner is abroad (p143)
3. Families where a dependent adult is abroad (p149)
4. Families where a child is abroad (p149)
5. Children born in the UK without the right of abode (p151)

For the rules where the whole family is abroad, see Part 3. For the rules relating to families with rights under EC law, see Part 4.

There are special rules to stop you losing benefit if you move between Great Britain and Northern Ireland.[1] You may also be able to use special rules if you have lived in another European Economic Area member state (see Part 4) or a country with which the UK has a reciprocal agreement (see Part 5) even if you are not a national of that country.

1. Families with different immigration statuses

Sometimes members of the same family may have different immigration statuses. For example, a husband may be a British citizen or have indefinite leave to remain while his wife has limited leave to remain as a spouse. Couples with different statuses often have difficulties with benefit claims. One of the couple may be eligible for benefit but they may have difficulty convincing the benefit authorities that they are eligible and in particular that they satisfy the national insurance number requirement (see p120). A major consideration is often whether or not a claim will jeopardise the immigration position of the partner who wishes to settle in the UK. Where a couple are refugees one of the couple may have been granted leave to remain or full refugee status while their partner awaits a decision on their asylum claim and therefore remains an asylum seeker. Some benefits have rules which deal with this type of situation. For example, the income support and income-based jobseeker's allowance rules allow a couple with 'mixed' immigration statuses to claim benefit at the single person's rate. Pension credit has a similar rule but treats the person as not being a member of your household.[2] In order to establish the benefit position for couples and families in this situation you should check the individual chapter for that immigration status in this book.

2. **Couples where one partner is abroad**

If you are in Great Britain (GB) but your partner (see p144) is abroad, your benefit entitlement may be affected. For example, if your partner is working full time while abroad, you may be refused income support (IS)/income-based jobseeker's allowance (JSA) (see p144).

If you are entitled to maternity allowance, incapacity benefit, a retirement pension, or carer's allowance, you may get an increase for your spouse, even though s/he is abroad. For the rules on increases for adult dependants other than spouses, see p149.[3]

Household

Under the rules for:
- IS;[4]
- income-based JSA;[5]
- pension credit (PC);[6]
- housing benefit (HB);[7]
- council tax benefit (CTB),[8]

a person can only count as your partner if you share the same household.

This applies if you are a 'couple'.[9] A **'household'** is something abstract, not something physical like a home. It is made up of either a single person or a group of people held together by social ties.[10] A person cannot be a member of two households at the same time.[11] A person can be temporarily absent from the home but still be a member of the household.[12] If it is not obvious whether people share a household, the important factors are:
- whether they share the same physical space – eg, a house, flat or room(s) in a hostel;
- whether they carry out chores for the benefit of all of them – eg, cooking, shopping, cleaning.

Each benefit has special rules allowing certain temporary absences of one partner from other members of the family to be ignored when considering whether there is a common household. These special rules do not override *all* the normal rules above about what is a household.[13] This means that, even if the temporary absence is ignored, your general situation may have changed enough for your partner no longer to be in your household. This is most likely to apply if your partner is now a member of a different household abroad.

Income support/income-based jobseeker's allowance

If a person who is abroad counts as your partner for IS/income-based JSA (see below) then:

- if your partner is in full-time employment (see CPAG's *Welfare Benefits and Tax Credits Handbook*) you are *not* entitled to IS/income-based JSA.[14] This applies even if your partner is employed abroad and her/his earnings are very low in British terms or cannot be exchanged for pounds sterling;
- your partner's income and capital are taken into account as if they were your income or capital.[15] There are special rules about calculating capital abroad (see CPAG's *Welfare Benefits and Tax Credits Handbook*);
- your applicable amount (see pxii) includes an amount for your partner, but only in certain cases and then only for up to eight weeks (see p146);
- you lose any entitlement to family premium at the lone parent rate (which applies to some pre-6 April 1998 claimants, see CPAG's *Welfare Benefits and Tax Credits Handbook*).[16]

If a person abroad counts as your partner, these rules mean that you may be paid less IS/income-based JSA than if s/he were living with you, or none at all. If this applies you can use the following rules to argue that the person should not count as your partner. If you receive income from that person while s/he does not count as your partner, that counts as maintenance and so might be disregarded as your income (see CPAG's *Welfare Benefits and Tax Credits Handbook*). If these rules would mean that you do not have enough to live on, then that may breach the European Convention on Human Rights.[17] However, the Human Rights Act 1998 requires tribunals and courts, if possible, to interpret the law to avoid such a breach.[18] By interpreting 'partner' (see below) to apply to a couple who cannot practically live together at the moment, such a breach can usually be avoided.

When does a person count as your partner

A person can count as your partner even though you are not married or in a civil partnership. In practice, if your partner is abroad and you are not married or in a civil partnership, the DWP does not usually treat you as a couple for benefit purposes (but see p146 for when you may want to argue against this decision).

A person only counts as your partner if you are members of the same household (see p143). Some absences of your partner are ignored when considering whether you remain members of the same household. These rules do not apply if you have never actually shared a household with your partner.[19] For PC a person is treated as not being your partner if they are a 'person subject to immigration control' (see p155) or they are not habitually resident[20] (see p132).

Example

Rifat marries Amjad in Pakistan. They have a week-long honeymoon. Rifat then returns to her home in the UK. Amjad intends to apply for a visa to join her in the UK. He works full time but earns the equivalent of £10 a week. Rifat loses her job and has to claim income-based JSA. The honeymoon was too short to count as sharing a household. Because they have never shared a household, the rules about ignoring temporary absences do not apply and Amjad does not count as Rifat's partner.

Temporary absences from other family members

If you are the claimant and your partner is temporarily living away from you (for the meaning of temporary, see p247), that absence is ignored when considering whether you share a household with your partner *unless*:[21]

- your partner and/or you do not intend to resume living with each other.[22] You may intend to resume living with each other, but your intentions may depend upon something beyond your control, such as getting a visa or a job. If this applies, you may be able to argue that your intention does not count because it depends on these things;[23]
- your absence from each other is likely to exceed 52 weeks, but not if:
  - there are exceptional circumstances. The rules give an example of your partner having no control over the length of the absence, which would include delays caused by immigration controls; *and*
  - the absence is unlikely to be substantially more than 52 weeks;
- your partner is detained in custody serving a sentence imposed by a court pending trial or sentence.

These rules can apply where your partner is abroad. If your partner is the claimant, see p164.

Your partner's absence is from *you*, not from the family home, so these rules can apply even if your partner has never lived in your current home.[24] The length of the absence is worked out from when it started to when it is likely to finish. If circumstances change so that the likely total absence gets longer (or shorter) – eg, a family member falls ill – then the absence may become too long (or short enough) to count as temporary under these rules.

Example

Rifat joins Amjad in Pakistan for three months. She then returns home to the UK but, because of sickness, claims IS. Amjad applies for a visa to come to the UK. Because his absence from Rifat is likely substantially to exceed 52 weeks, she is treated as a single person and is entitled to IS. Three months later, Amjad is refused a visa on maintenance and accommodation grounds and he appeals. One year later he wins his appeal and a visa is issued. Before he can travel to the UK his mother falls ill and he stays in Pakistan to care for her. Her illness is only expected to last a short time so Amjad expects to travel to the UK within a month. However, because his total absence from Rifat is now substantially more than 52 weeks, he is not treated as her partner even though the absence is expected to end soon.

If a couple is separated because one partner has to apply for a visa to come to the UK, there may be delay:
- to meet the immigration rules before applying for a visa, for example:
  - trying to get a job (or a job offer for the partner) so that the maintenance and accommodation rules are met;
  - waiting for recognition as a refugee, or for four years' exceptional leave to remain, or for indefinite leave to remain;
- waiting for a decision on a visa application – this often takes months;
- waiting for an appeal against a visa refusal – this usually takes at least six months from bringing the appeal until a visa is issued, if successful, and would often take at least a year.

The likely length of your separation depends upon how likely you are to be refused a visa. Refusal rates are high in African and Asian countries. If the absence is likely substantially to exceed 52 weeks, your absence from each other does not count as temporary (see p145).

Getting income support/income-based jobseeker's allowance for a partner abroad

If your partner is temporarily absent from GB but you are in GB, then for the first four weeks (or eight weeks if your partner is taking a child or young person abroad for treatment under the rules described on p250):
- your applicable amount continues to include any amounts for your partner;[25] *and*
- your partner counts as a member of your household, so her/his income and capital is taken into account in the usual way.[26]

This does not apply if your partner counts as a 'person subject to immigration control' (see p155).

If your partner stops meeting the temporary absence rules, or is absent for more than four/eight weeks, your applicable amount is reduced to that for a single person, even though any income or capital of your partner still counts as your income.[27] You may then want to argue that s/he no longer counts as your partner (see p144).

Pension credit

The rules for PC largely mirror those for IS (see p144). The major difference is that if your partner is categorised as a 'person subject to immigration control' s/he is treated as not being a member of your household. Consequently her/his income or work does not affect your claim for benefit.

Housing benefit and council tax benefit

Claimant on income support/income-based jobseeker's allowance

If you are being paid IS, income-based JSA or PC your partner's absence does not affect the amount of your HB, and only affects CTB in exceptional circumstances (see below). This is because you are treated as having no income or capital, so you are entitled to maximum HB/CTB regardless of whether your applicable amount is for a single person or a couple.[28] The local authority dealing with your HB/CTB claim should not make enquiries about your partner's absence.

Claimant not on income support, income-based jobseeker's allowance or pension credit

If you are *not* being paid IS/income-based JSA/PC the HB/CTB rules about who counts as your partner and temporary absences are the same as for IS (see p144), except:[29]

- there are no special rules for partners;
- for CTB, there are no rules setting out the exceptions to the general rule that a temporary absence is ignored. However, absences which are likely to be more than 52 weeks may not count as temporary anyway. In practice, local authorities deal with CTB in the same way as HB.

If a person abroad counts as your partner under these rules then:

- your partner's income and capital is taken into account as if they were your income and capital.[30] There are special rules about calculating capital abroad (see CPAG's *Welfare Benefits and Tax Credits Handbook*);
- your applicable amount includes an amount for your partner;[31]
- you lose any entitlement to family premium at the lone parent rate (which applies to some pre-6 April 1998 claimants, see CPAG's *Welfare Benefits and Tax Credits Handbook*);[32] *and*
- for HB, your partner's absence does not affect the fact that you normally occupy your accommodation as your home.[33]

These rules mean that your HB/CTB is usually the same as if your partner is living with you. This is different from the IS/income-based JSA/PC rules, under which you may be often worse off.

If a person abroad does *not* count as your partner, your applicable amount is for a single person, not a couple, so your HB/CTB may be paid at a lower rate.

In very unusual cases the person abroad may still be liable for current council tax, even though s/he no longer counts as your partner under CTB rules.[34] This is because the rules about council tax liability are different from those for CTB entitlement. If this happens, your CTB is calculated on the basis of your 'share' (ie, half the council tax) even though you are legally liable to pay all the council tax.[35] If this applies, the local authority can top up your CTB to the amount of your liability. You should ask it to do this and also try to get your partner's name removed from the list of liable people. For more details, see CPAG's *Council Tax Handbook*.

For more information about HB/CTB temporary absences, see p253.

Tax credits

If your partner is in another European Economic Area (EEA) member state, different rules may apply (see p334).

For child tax credit and working tax credit, if your partner goes abroad other than for a temporary absence for the allowed period you must make a fresh claim as a single person. The allowed periods are:[36]

- the first eight weeks of any temporary absence;
- the first 12 weeks of any period when you are temporarily absent from the UK if that absence is in connection with certain illnesses or death within the family.

Spouse/civil partner increase for contributory benefits and disability benefits

You may be entitled to an increase for your spouse/civil partner (see CPAG's *Welfare Benefits and Tax Credits Handbook*) if you are entitled to:

- incapacity benefit;
- carer's allowance;
- maternity allowance;
- Category A or C retirement pension.

This increase is still payable while your spouse/civil partner is abroad, if you are residing together.[37] You are treated as residing together during any temporary period (see p145) apart from each other.[38] Even if you both intend to be permanently absent from GB, as long as your absence from each other is only temporary, the increase for your spouse is not affected.[39]

Any separation only because one (or both) spouses is an in-patient in a hospital or similar institution does not count as separation under this rule, even if it may be permanent.[40]

There are special rules if your spouse is in another EEA member state (see Part 4) or you are a national of Algeria, Morocco, Tunisia or Turkey (see p381).[41]

3. Families where a dependent adult is abroad

You may be entitled to an increase for a dependent adult who is looking after a child for whom you are responsible (for spouses see p143). You can get an increase (see CPAG's *Welfare Benefits and Tax Credits Handbook*) if you are entitled to:
- incapacity benefit;
- carer's allowance;
- maternity allowance;
- Category A or C retirement pension.

This increase is still payable while the adult is abroad, but only if you are residing together outside Great Britain (GB) and you are not disqualified from receiving the benefit because of any absence from GB.[42] You are treated as residing together during any temporary absence (see p145) from each other.[43] Even if you both intend to be permanently absent from GB, as long as your absence from each other is only temporary, the increase is not affected.[44]

There are special rules if the adult is in another European Economic Area member state (see Part 4) or you are a national of Algeria, Morocco, Tunisia or Turkey (see p381).[45]

4. Families where a child is abroad

Some benefits are paid at a higher rate if you are responsible for a child. If that child goes abroad, your benefit entitlement may be affected.

Income support, income-based jobseeker's allowance and pension credit

For claims made before 6 April 2004 your income support (IS), income-based jobseeker's allowance (JSA) or pension credit (PC) applicable amount may include an amount for each child for whom you are responsible.[46] This only applies to a child who is in your household (see p143).[47] You also get a family premium which may be paid at the lone parent rate (for certain pre-6 April 1998 claimants – see CPAG's *Welfare Benefits and Tax Credits Handbook*).

When considering whether the child remains a member of the household, only the following temporary absences (see p145) of a child from your household are ignored:
- up to eight weeks' absence from the UK if you and/or your partner meet the temporary absence rules for IS/income-based JSA due to treatment of a child abroad for a medical condition (see p250);[48] *otherwise*
- up to four weeks' absence from the UK.[49]

If you claimed either IS or income-based JSA after the child went abroad and you were not entitled to the other benefit immediately before claiming, these periods run from the date of claim.[50] If the child is abroad for longer than these periods, your IS/income-based JSA is worked out ignoring the child.

However, if your child has gone to live in another European Economic Area member state, see Part 4.

Housing benefit and council tax benefit

If you are being paid IS/income-based JSA a child's absence from the UK does not affect the amount of your housing benefit (HB)/council tax benefit (CTB). If you are not being paid IS/income-based JSA, then you may lose money if a child is treated as not being in your household. The following rules apply.

Your HB/CTB applicable amount includes an amount for each child for whom you are responsible.[51] This only applies to a child who is in your household (see p143).[52]

For HB/CTB, temporary absences (see p145) from your household of a child are ignored when considering whether the child remains a member of the household. For HB, the exceptions to this rule are if:[53]

- the child and/or you do not intend to resume living with each other;
- your absence from each other is likely to exceed 52 weeks, unless:
  - there are exceptional circumstances. The rules give an example of you having no control over the length of the absence; *and*
  - the absence is unlikely to be substantially more than 52 weeks.

For CTB, there are no rules setting out the exceptions to the general rule that a temporary absence is ignored. However, absences which are likely to be more than 52 weeks may not count as temporary anyway. In practice, local authorities are likely to deal with CTB in the same way as HB.

Child benefit and guardian's allowance

For the rules which apply when a child is abroad, see p170.

Child tax credit

You are only entitled to child tax credit (CTC) if you or your partner is responsible for a child or young person.[54] The child does not have to be present or ordinarily resident in the UK, only the claimant.[55] You are responsible for a child under the CTC rules if the child is normally living with you.

5. Children born in the UK without the right of abode

Since 1 January 1983 not all children born in the UK are British citizens by birth (see p25). The child may have the nationality of her/his parents but have no immigration status in the UK. S/he is not an overstayer nor an illegal entrant, even if her/his parents were at the time of the birth. A deportation order can be made against the child if the parent(s) are to be deported or removed. The child may have a right to register as a British citizen (see p28).

The benefit rules which apply where a child does not have leave are covered below. A child may reach the age of 16 without an application for citizenship having been made and wish to apply for benefits in her/his own right. This is very unlikely, so it is not deal with here. Such a person should seek expert immigration advice.

Benefit rules for children with no right of abode

For almost all benefits the status of a child is irrelevant. The only differences are as follows.

Income support/income-based jobseeker's allowance

The child's status only affects entitlement where the claimant's partner is a 'person subject to immigration control' (PSIC – see p155) and it does not matter where:

- both members of the couple are PSICs; *or*
- neither member of the couple is a PSIC.

In particular, if both the couple are PSICs any entitlement to urgent cases payments of income support is not affected.

Where the claimant is not a PSIC but the partner is, the claimant's applicable amount does not include an amount for a child who is a PSIC.

A child born in the UK without the right of abode who has not been given leave to remain is a PSIC. That is because the child's immigration status is clear: s/he requires leave to enter or remain in the UK but does not have that leave.

Housing benefit/council tax benefit

The status of the child is irrelevant.

Notes

1 Reg 2 and Sch 1 SS(NIRA) Regs

2. **Couples where one partner is abroad**
2 Reg 5(1)(h) SPC Regs
3 Reg 2 IS Gen Regs
4 Reg 1 IS Regs
5 Reg 1 JSA Regs
6 Reg 1 SPC Regs
7 Reg 2 HB Regs
8 Reg 2 CTB Regs
9 s137 SSCBA 1992 'couple'; R(SB) 17/81
10 *Santos v Santos* [1972] 2 WLR 889; [1972] 2 All ER 246, CA
11 R(SB) 8/85
12 R(SB) 4/83
13 CIS/671/1992
14 s124(1)(c) SSCBA 1992; s3(1)(e) JSA 1995
15 s136(1) SSCBA 1992; s13(2) JSA 1995
16 Sch 2 para 3 IS Regs; Sch 1 para 4 JSA Regs
17 Denial of benefits of last resort to a person in GB on the ground of income or work abroad which cannot provide support for them here may breach Art 8 ECHR (private and family life and home). Art 14 (discrimination) may also be relevant.
18 s3 HRA 1998
19 The rules say 'resume living with': reg 16(2) IS Regs; reg 78(1) JSA Regs
20 Reg 5 SPC Regs
21 Reg 16(1)-(3) IS Regs; reg 78(1)-(3) JSA Regs. Only the rules relevant to partners abroad are dealt with here.
22 Reg 16(2)(a) IS Regs; reg 78(2)(a) JSA Regs. Either person's lack of intention counts because the rules refer to the 'person who is living away from the other members of his family' and each partner is living away from the other.
23 See CIS/508/1992 and CIS/484/1993 on a similarly worded IS housing costs rule: now Sch 3 para 3(10) IS Regs
24 Reg 16(1) IS Regs; reg 78(1) JSA Regs. Compare with the pre-4 October 1993 version of reg 16(1) which refers to absence from the home.
25 Reg 21(1) and Sch 7 paras 11 and 11A IS Regs; reg 85(1) and Sch 5 paras 10 and 11 JSA Regs
26 Reg 16(1) IS Regs; reg 78(1) JSA Regs

27 Reg 21(1) and Sch 7 paras 11 and 11A IS Regs; reg 85(1) and Sch 5 paras 10 and 11 JSA Regs
28 Sch 5 para 4 and Sch 6 para 5 HB Regs; Sch 4 para 4 and Sch 5 para 5 CTB Regs
29 Reg 21(1) and (2) HB Regs; reg 11(1) CTB Regs
30 s136(1) SSCBA 1992
31 Reg 22(a) and Sch 3 para 1 HB Regs; reg 12(a) and Sch 1 para 1 CTB Regs. These apply because you still count as a couple.
32 Sch 3 para 3 HB Regs; Sch 1 para 3 CTB Regs
33 para A3.16 GM
34 These comments do not apply to arrears.
35 Reg 51(3) CTB Regs: reg 51(4) will no longer apply. Every resident of a dwelling is jointly and severally (ie, collectively and individually) liable to pay all the council tax. If there are two or more people liable for council tax on your accommodation, your CTB will be worked out on the basis that the total liability is divided equally between them.
36 Reg 4 TC(R) Regs
37 Reg 13 SSB(PA) Regs disapplying s113 SSCBA 1992
38 Reg 2(4) SSB(PRT) Regs made under s122(3) SSCBA 1992
39 CSS/18/1988
40 Reg 2(2) SSB(PRT) Regs
41 CS/15000/1996

3. **Families where a dependent adult is abroad**
42 Regs 10(2)(c) and (3) and 12 and Sch 2 para 7(b)(iv) SSB(Dep) Regs; reg 14 SS(IB-ID) Regs. The general disqualification in s113 SSCBA 1992 does not apply to adult dependant increases.
43 Reg 2(4) SSB(PRT) Regs made under s122(3) SSCBA 1992
44 CSS/18/1988
45 CS/15000/1996

4. **Families where a child is abroad**

46 Reg 17(b) IS Regs; reg 83(b) JSA Regs
47 s137(1) SSCBA 1992 'family' (b) and (c);
    s35(1) JSA 1995 'family' (b) and (c)
48 Reg 16(5)(aa) IS Regs; reg 78(5)(b) JSA
    Regs
49 Reg 16(5)(a) IS Regs; reg 78(5)(a) JSA
    Regs
50 Reg 16(5)(a)(i) and (aa)(i) and (5A) IS
    Regs; reg 78(5)(a)(i) and (b)(i) and (6)
    JSA Regs
51 Reg 22(b) HB Regs; reg 12(b) CTB Regs
52 s137(1) (b) and (c) SSCBA 1992 'family'
53 Reg 21(1)-(3) HB Regs. Only the rules
    relevant to partners abroad are dealt
    with here.
54 Reg 3 CTC Regs
55 s3(3) TCA 2002; reg 3 TC(R) Regs

13

Chapter 13

Immigration status and benefit entitlement

This chapter provides an overview of how your immigration status affects your entitlement to benefit. It covers:
1. Immigration status and benefit entitlement (below)
2. Non-means-tested benefits (p156)
3. Means-tested benefits (p157)
4. Tax credits (p159)
5. Urgent cases payments (p160)

1. Immigration status and benefit entitlement

It is important, before making a claim for benefit, to know your immigration status. This is not only because this can determine your right to social security benefits but also because a claim for benefit can affect your right to remain in the UK. If you are unsure about your immigration status you should seek specialist advice.

Most people, apart from British citizens, are subject to immigration control. This means that you cannot freely enter the UK, but will be subject to scrutiny by the immigration authorities. The degree of control varies according to your nationality, for example, European Economic Area (EEA) nationals do not need leave to enter or remain and therefore enjoy much greater freedom to enter by virtue of European Community law. If you are subject to immigration control you require leave, or permission, to enter or remain. Such leave can be:
- limited leave to enter or remain;
- indefinite leave to enter or remain;
- leave outside the rules which can include exceptional leave to enter or remain, discretionary leave or humanitarian protection.

If you have limited leave you are only permitted to remain in the UK for a limited period of time. Certain conditions are frequently attached to a grant of limited leave – eg, a restriction may be made on your working or claiming benefits. If you breach these conditions you may put your right to remain in the UK at risk. For more information, see Chapter 4.

The interrelationship between immigration and social security law is extremely complex and your immigration status may not always be clear. There are close links between the benefit authorities and the Home Office (see Chapter 10). Making a claim for benefit could alert the immigration authorities to the fact that you are here unlawfully, or that you have broken your conditions of entry by claiming 'public funds'. It is vitally important, therefore, to get specialist independent advice before claiming if you are unsure about your position. You can get advice from your local law centre, citizens advice bureau or another advice agency which deals with immigration problems. If you are a community legal services contract holder (in any branch of law) you can also get specialist advice from the Joint Council for the Welfare of Immigrants (JCWI) or the Immigration Advisory Service. If you are a refugee or asylum seeker, you can contact the Refugee Council (see Appendix 1).

Person subject to immigration control

You are not eligible for most benefits if you are a '**person subject to immigration control**' (PSIC). This phrase has a special meaning for benefit purposes.

You are a PSIC if you are not an EEA national and:

- you require leave to enter or remain but do not have it;
- you have leave to enter or remain with a public funds restriction (see p84);
- you have leave to enter or remain and are the subject of a formal undertaking (see p94);
- you are appealing a decision about your immigration status.

Even if you fall within the above definition, regulations nevertheless treat certain people from abroad as not being PSICs. The exemptions vary according to the benefit involved (see below), and there remain some transitional regulations that provide entitlement to some claimants.

Benefits which are affected by immigration status[1]

Attendance allowance	Incapacity benefit for incapacity in youth[2]
Carer's allowance	Income-based jobseeker's allowance
Child benefit	Income support
Child tax credit	Pension credit
Council tax benefit	Severe disablement allowance
Disability living allowance	Social fund payments
Housing benefit	Working tax credit

Who is not a 'person subject to immigration control'

You are *not* a PSIC and therefore cannot be excluded on grounds of immigration status if you are:

- a British citizen;
- a person with right of abode/certificate of partiality (see p21);
- a British national with right of re-admission;
- an EEA national;
- a refugee;
- a person with exceptional leave to enter or remain;
- a person with indefinite leave to enter or remain (but not if you are the subject of a formal undertaking – see p94).

There are some people who come within the general definition of a PSIC who are nevertheless eligible for some benefits. For details about who can qualify, see below for non-contributory non-means-tested benefits, p159 for tax credits, p157 for means-tested benefits and p160 for urgent cases payments of income support and income-based jobseeker's allowance.

Public funds

Most people admitted to the UK with limited leave, such as spouses or visitors, are given limited leave to stay here on condition that they do not have recourse to 'public funds'. If you have recourse to public funds in breach of your permission to stay (your 'leave conditions') you could be liable to deportation, refusal of further leave and prosecution. See Chapter 7 for more information.

---

2. Non-means-tested benefits

Contributory benefits

Your immigration status does not, by itself, prevent you from getting contributory benefits, but in practice you may have paid insufficient national insurance contributions to be entitled. Moreover, to qualify for contributory benefits you will normally have had to have worked in the UK.

Non-contributory benefits

You should be aware of your immigration status before claiming non-contributory benefits (ie, attendance allowance (AA), carer's allowance (CA), child benefit and disability living allowance (DLA)) because these are public funds (see p84). A claim could have serious consequences on your immigration status. Incapacity benefit for incapacity in youth is not listed as a public funds benefit but some people subject to immigration control are excluded from access to it.

Attendance allowance, child benefit, disability living allowance, carer's allowance and incapacity benefit for incapacity in youth

You are not excluded from getting these benefits by your immigration status if:[3]

- you come within one of the groups on p156;
- you are a person with indefinite leave to remain and you are subject to a formal undertaking (see p94);
- you are a family member of a European Economic Area national regardless of your nationality or whether or not your partner is a 'worker'. This includes family members of British citizens (see p7);
- you, or if you are living with them a member of your family, are *lawfully working* in Great Britain and are a citizen of a state with which the European Community has an agreement concerning equal treatment in social security. This applies to citizens of Algeria, Morocco, Tunisia and Turkey (see p381). The DWP often argues that an asylum seeker cannot be *lawfully working*. However, a commissioner has held that an asylum seeker who had worked in the UK was able to fulfil the condition of 'lawfully working' and therefore held that he was eligible for benefit;[4]
- in the case of AA/DLA and child benefit you are covered by a reciprocal arrangement;
- you are protected by the transitional rules relating to asylum seekers (see p222) and others with limited leave.

3. **Means-tested benefits**

You should be aware of your immigration status before claiming means-tested benefits. These are 'public funds' and claiming could affect your right to stay or chance of getting indefinite leave to stay (see p84).

Income support, income-based jobseeker's allowance, housing benefit, council tax benefit, pension credit and the social fund

You are not excluded from getting these benefits by your immigration status if:[5]

- you come within one of the groups listed on p156;
- you are a national of a country that has ratified the European Convention on Social and Medical Assistance or the Council of Europe Social Charter (1961) (this includes all European Economic Area (EEA) countries, Croatia, Macedonia and Turkey) and you are lawfully present. These rights do not stem from European Community (EC) law and consequently do not override any 'public funds' restriction attached to your stay. Therefore, any claim for benefit could affect your right to remain in the UK. However, it is current Home Office policy normally not to consider that a person has had recourse to public funds if s/he has evidence from the DWP to show that s/he was eligible for benefit under these agreements.[6] This provision clearly protects those with limited leave,

such as students or visitors, but the position is less clear when it concerns asylum seekers. The House of Lords has held that an asylum seeker with temporary admission is lawfully present and consequently is able to access benefit under these agreements.[7]

- you are a family member of an EEA national who is economically active (see p7);
- you have indefinite leave and are the subject of a formal undertaking that was given five or more years ago and you have been in the UK for five years or more (see p94);
- you are the subject of a formal undertaking given within the past five years but the person who gave the undertaking has died;
- you have limited leave and there is a 'public funds' restriction attached to your stay and your funds from abroad are disrupted. (Note: this does not apply to tax credits);
- you are an asylum seeker who has transitional protection (see p222). In some cases this can include the separated partner or grown-up children of the asylum seeker. (Note: this does not apply to tax credits).

If you qualify for benefit it is usually paid at the normal rate. However, if you qualify for income support (IS) or income-based jobseeker's allowance (JSA) on the basis that funds from abroad are disrupted, your sponsor has died or because you are an asylum seeker with transitional protection, you receive benefit at the urgent cases rate (see p160).

For the social fund, you are also exempt from the restriction if you are *lawfully working* in Great Britain and are a national of Algeria, Morocco, Tunisia or Turkey.

Couples and families

The following rules apply where one or more members of your family are 'persons subject to immigration control' (PSIC).

- If you claim any of the listed means-tested benefits as a PSIC, you are not entitled to any benefit for yourself or for any members of your family, unless you come under one of the exemptions (see p156).
- If your partner is not a PSIC but you are, s/he can claim IS/JSA under the normal rules but does not receive any benefit for you or any other family member who is a PSIC. Full housing costs are payable.[8] You are still treated as a couple, so your joint resources are taken into account. For pension credit the rules are slightly different in that although a single person rate will be paid to couples with different immigration statuses you are not treated as a couple in terms of joint resources. HB and CTB rules do not allow for payment to be made as a single claimant so a claim could cause potential problems if the PSIC is subject to the 'no recourse to public funds' restriction.
- Couples where both partners are not PSICs and lone parents who are not PSICs, can claim IS for children who are.[9] But claimants who are 'subject to

immigration control' cannot claim benefit for children even if the children are *not* 'subject to immigration control'.

- Foreign fiancé(e)s, spouses and civil partners who are admitted for settlement on the condition that they can maintain and accommodate themselves, count as PSIC's, and are not entitled to any of the listed benefits until they are granted indefinite leave to remain in the UK.
- A person can qualify for JSA without having to satisfy the joint-claims rules if her/his partner is a PSIC.

4. **Tax credits**

For both working tax credit (WTC) and child tax credit (CTC) you are *exempt* from the 'person subject to immigration control' definition if:[10]

- you are subject to a maintenance undertaking but the person who sponsored you has died or you have been resident in the UK for a period of at least five years from the date of the undertaking or the date you arrived whichever is later; *or*
- you have limited leave with a public funds restriction and you are temporarily without funds because money from abroad has been disrupted and there is a reasonable expectation that your funds will resume.

For CTC only there is a further exemption if:

- you are lawfully working in Great Britain and are a citizen of a state with which the European Community has an agreement concerning equal treatment in social security (this applies to Algeria, Morocco, Tunisia and Turkey).

For WTC only there is a further exemption if:

- you are lawfully present in the UK and are a national of a state which has ratified the European Convention on Social and Medical Assistance or a state which has ratified the Council of Europe Social Charter of 1961 and who is lawfully present in the UK. (This includes all European Economic Area countries, Croatia and Turkey.)

Couples and families

For tax credits, where a couple have different immigration statuses, one of which allows the person to claim, the claim is determined as though both members of the couple are not subject to immigration control.[11] This means that a claim can be made. Changes to the immigration rules from March 2005 mean that a person who is entitled to benefit under social security law will not be regarded as having recourse to public funds.[12] Therefore a couple with different immigration statuses will not put their immigration position at risk by making a claim for tax credits.

5. **Urgent cases payments**

Urgent cases payments are payments of income support (IS) and income-based jobseeker's allowance (JSA) at a reduced rate. Certain people who are excluded from ordinary rate benefit because of their immigration status may be eligible for an urgent cases payment. However, since April 2000 when most asylum seekers were excluded from access to benefits there are far fewer recipients of urgent cases payments.

If you are not entitled to normal rate IS or income-based JSA because you are classed as a 'person subject to immigration control' (PSIC – see p155) you may be entitled to urgent cases payments if:
- you have 'limited leave' to remain in the UK on the condition that you do not have recourse to 'public funds' (see p84) but you are temporarily without money; *and*
  - you have supported yourself without recourse to public funds during your limited leave; *and*
  - you are temporarily without funds because remittances from abroad have been disrupted; *and*
  - there is a reasonable expectation that your supply of funds will be resumed; *or*[13]
- you have been in the UK subject to a sponsorship undertaking for less than five years and your sponsor has died (see p94); *or*
- you are an asylum seeker entitled to benefit under transitional protection rules (see p222).

There is no equivalent of urgent cases payments for pension credit (PC). A PSIC who qualifies for PC receives it at the full rate.

How to claim

There is no special procedure for claiming urgent cases payments. You claim IS or income-based JSA in the normal way. You do not have to make a separate claim for an urgent cases payment. In practice, you may need to request the urgent cases payment and should not rely on the DWP to decide automatically whether you are entitled.

Amount of the payment

Urgent cases payments of IS and income-based JSA are paid at a reduced rate. Your applicable amount (see glossary of terms at the beginning of this book) is:
- a personal allowance for you and possibly your partner. This is paid at 90 per cent of the personal allowance that would have been paid had you qualified for benefit in the normal way; *plus*
- premiums and housing costs.

Income

All of your income counts, but the following is ignored:[14]
- any tariff income from capital. However, as all capital is taken into account this concession is of very little assistance;
- any arrears of urgent cases payments of IS or income-based JSA;
- concessionary urgent cases payments of IS or income-based JSA;
- any housing benefit (HB) and/or council tax benefit;
- any payment made to compensate you for the loss of entitlement to HB;
- social fund payments;
- any payment from any of the Macfarlane Trusts, the Eileen Trust, the Fund or the Independent Living Funds;
- payments made by people with haemophilia to their partners or children out of money originally provided by one of the Macfarlane Trusts. If the person with haemophilia has no partner or children, payments made to a parent, step-parent or guardian are also disregarded, but only for two years. These payments are also disregarded if the person with haemophilia dies and the money is paid out of the estate;
- payments arising from the Macfarlane Trusts which are paid by a person to a partner who has haemophilia, or to their child(ren).

Certain income is treated as capital if you get IS under the normal rules. However, if you apply for an urgent cases payment the following capital is treated as income:[15]
- any lump sum paid to you not more than once a year for your work as a part-time firefighter, part-time member of a lifeboat crew, auxiliary coastguard or member of the Territorial Army;
- any refund of income tax;
- holiday pay which is not payable until more than four weeks after your job ended;
- any irregular charitable or voluntary payment.

Capital

Your capital is calculated in the usual way, but the usual disregards do not apply to urgent cases payments. Any capital taken into account affects your urgent cases payment, not just that over the capital limit. However, arrears of urgent cases payments are disregarded.

Notes

1. **Immigration status and benefit entitlement**
   1 s115 IAA 1999
   2 Reg 16 SS(IB) Regs

2. **Non-means-tested benefits**
   3 s115(9) IAA 1999; regs 2, 12 and Sch
   Part II SS(IA)CA Regs; reg 16(1)(b) Social
   Security (Incapacity Benefit)
   Miscellaneous Amendments Regulations
   2000 No.3120
   4 CFC/2613/1997 (*25/00)

3. **Means-tested benefits**
   5 s115(9) IAA 1999; regs 2 and 12 and
   Sch Part I SS(IA)CA Regs
   6 This statement was made in a letter to
   UKOSA on 5 December 2000
   7 *Szoma v Secretary of State for Work and
   Pensions* reported as R(IS) 2/06
   8 Sch 7 para 16A IS Regs
   9 Regs 21(3), 70, 71 and Sch 7 para 16A IS
   Regs

4. **Tax credits**
   10 Reg 3(1) TC(I) Regs
   11 Reg 3(2) TC(I) Regs
   12 para 6B HC 395

5. **Urgent cases payments**
   13 Reg 2 SS(IA)CA Regs
   14 Reg 72(1) IS Regs; reg 149(1) JSA Regs
   15 Reg 72(1)(c) IS Regs; regs 149(1)(c) and
   110(1)-(3) and (9) JSA Regs

Chapter 14

British citizens and others with the right of abode

This chapter contains the benefit rules that affect British citizens and those with the right of abode in the UK. It covers:
1. Income support (p164)
2. Income-based jobseeker's allowance (p166)
3. Pension credit (p167)
4. Housing benefit and council tax benefit (p167)
5. Tax credits (p168)
6. Child benefit and guardian's allowance (p170)
7. Contribution-based benefits (p173)
8. Retirement pensions and bereavement benefits (p175)
9. Maternity allowance (p178)
10. Industrial injuries benefits (p178)
11. Disability benefits (p181)
12. Statutory sick pay and statutory maternity, paternity and adoption pay (p184)
13. The social fund (p185)

Introduction

British citizens and others with a right of abode generally have rights to access all social security benefits and tax credits. The hurdles for this group are residence tests and in particular the habitual residence test. The right to reside test does not impact on British citizens or those with a right of abode as both have a right of residence.

Who has the right of abode

Nearly everyone who has the right of abode in the UK is a British citizen. All British citizens have the right of abode, but most of those who hold some other form of British nationality do not. Some Commonwealth citizens, including people who hold another British nationality, also have the right of abode, but it has not been possible to gain the right of abode since 1983 without also being a British citizen. Commonwealth citizens who had the right of abode then still have it, but since the beginning of 1983 the only way to obtain the right of abode is by becoming a British citizen. For full details of British citizenship and the right of abode, see Chapter 2.

If you are a British citizen or have the right of abode for other reasons:
* you are not a 'person subject to immigration control' (see p155);
* you do not need leave to enter or remain in the UK;
* you are exempt from deportation; *and*
* any leave you were given, and any conditions attached to it, has no effect once you become a British citizen.

The right of abode is a 'stronger' status than indefinite leave to remain. The only real limitation as far as benefit entitlement is concerned is that as a British citizen you may still have to satisfy certain residence and presence tests for some benefits (see Chapter 11).

1. Income support

General rules

You are only entitled to income support (IS) if:
* you are in Great Britain (GB)[1] (see p129), or temporarily absent from GB[2] (see p247); *and*
* *either* you are actually habitually resident (see p132) in the UK, Ireland, the Channel Islands or the Isle of Man *or* deemed to be habitually resident (see below); *and*
* you have a right to reside in the UK (see p137). However, all British citizens and those with a right of abode have a right of residence in the UK.

For the rules about the amount of IS if one or more members of your family are 'persons subject to immigration control' (PISC), see p155.

The habitual residence test

For full details of the habitual residence test (HRT), see p132. If you fail the HRT you are referred to as a 'person from abroad'. This applies even if you are a British citizen. You are not entitled to benefit, even at the urgent cases rate, but you may be able to get help from a local authority under the National Assistance Act 1948 or under legislation for the support of children.[3] You should claim benefit again within a few weeks, and be prepared to appeal against a refusal of benefit.

A household or family abroad

If your partner is living abroad and you once lived with her/him abroad this could affect your entitlement here (see p143). If you are treated as being part of a household abroad even though you are living here, you may not be entitled to benefit. This depends on whether your partner is working or has income that would affect any claim for benefit you might make. If your partner is not likely to join you within 52 weeks you do not count as a couple anyway, so any earnings your partner has, or whether s/he is in full-time work are not relevant. If your partner is away for slightly longer than 52 weeks and the reason for the extended absence is outside her/his control then you continue to be treated as a couple (see p143-143). If your partner is temporarily away from this country, see p145.

The amount of benefit you get may be affected even if you are not counted as part of a household abroad. You may also get less benefit if your child is abroad (see p149). If you are not treated as responsible for your child because the child is abroad, you may need to qualify for IS on different grounds if you originally qualified as a lone parent. If you do not qualify for IS you may need to claim income-based jobseeker's allowance instead – you must be available for and actively seeking work. See CPAG's *Welfare Benefits and Tax Credits Handbook* for the rules on who can receive IS.

If a member of your family is a 'person subject to immigration control'

General rules

You may be entitled to a benefit because of your immigration status but if you are claiming a means-tested benefit which includes an applicable amount for other people in your family then problems may arise in relation to public funds. See Chapter 7 for the treatment of public funds in immigration law. The calculation of how much benefit is payable, and whether a PSIC's needs are included, vary according to the means-tested benefit concerned. It may therefore not be enough to know whether *you* are entitled. You also need to know whether a claim for benefit by you will mean that your spouse/civil partner or dependent children are having 'recourse to public funds' through you. A person with a 'no recourse to public funds' condition may find her/his status in jeopardy or s/he may be refused indefinite leave when s/he applies for it if s/he has failed to keep to her/his conditions in this way. Breaching a condition of stay is also a criminal offence, although the Home Office does not seem to prosecute anyone for receiving benefits.

Even if there is no recourse to public funds there is a second question to answer. *Is it desirable that you claim a public funds benefit?* A list of the benefits included in the public funds conditions can be found on p86. If you are admitted to the UK on condition that you have no recourse to public funds then it is because another person has said that you can be accommodated and maintained without recourse to public funds. A claim for benefit is an indication that you are not able to maintain yourself, let alone your partner or children, and therefore calls into question any previous commitment you may have given that you would do so. In the case of a spouse joining a partner here, no formal 'undertaking' (see p94) will have been given, but there is an assumption in the immigration rules that the couple will maintain each other. A claim for benefit which calls into question your ability to maintain the other person could mean that the other person's application for indefinite leave to remain is initially refused. This does not mean that you should never claim if your partner is still on a time limit. There may be circumstances where it is necessary (eg, unexpected illness or accident), but you should consider carefully, and take independent advice if possible.

How your income support is affected

You do not get benefit for a spouse who is a PSIC, unless s/he is in one of the exempt categories (see p156). See p155 for the rules on who is counted as a PSIC for IS.

For Home Office purposes it may not be desirable to claim unless you are financially desperate and cannot get financial support from another source because getting benefit indicates that you cannot maintain yourself, let alone your partner or children (see above and Chapter 7). You should seek further independent advice.

If you have worked in the European Economic Area and therefore exercised Treaty rights of free movement, your partner may have a right to join you in the UK, regardless of her/his nationality or country of origin. This applies if you are a 'worker' for the purposes of EC Regulation 1612/68 (see p348), or a 'qualified person' under British law.[4] If this is the case you can claim benefit for your partner and children immediately and the question of recourse to public funds does not arise. If your partner or child is an overstayer or does not have permission to be here you should get immigration advice before claiming IS even for yourself.

If your partner is an asylum seeker s/he may be receiving support from the National Asylum Support Service (see Part 6). This will not affect your benefit claim for yourself. If s/he came to GB before 2 April 2000 and claimed asylum before that date s/he may be exempt from the PSIC rules.

---

2. Income-based jobseeker's allowance

For contribution-based jobseeker's allowance (JSA), see p173.

The income-based JSA rules about who is a 'person subject to immigration control' (PSIC) are the same as for income support (IS) (see p164).[5] For the rules about the amount of income-based JSA if one or more members of your family are a PSIC, see Chapter 13.

Some couples are required to make a joint claim for income-based JSA (see CPAG's *Welfare Benefits and Tax Credits Handbook*). Certain couples are not required to make a joint claim – eg, if they have children. If your partner is a PSIC you qualify for income-based JSA paid at the single rate even if your partner does not make the claim with you, provided you satisfy the means test, are not entitled to IS and meet the conditions for getting JSA apart from making the joint claim. If you have a child, even if that child is a PSIC, you are exempt from satisfying the conditions for joint-claim JSA.

Remember that you have to be able to take employment as a condition of getting JSA. European Economic Area nationals and Commonwealth citizens with the right of abode have a right to take employment.

3. **Pension credit**

The rules for pension credit (PC) to some extent mirror those for income support (IS) and income-based jobseeker's allowance (JSA). You are entitled to PC if:
- you are present in Great Britain (GB) (see p129); *and*
- you satisfy the habitual residence test or are exempt from the test (see p132); *and*
- you have a right to reside (all British citizens and those with a right of abode have a right to reside).

You can be treated as satisfying the presence test for certain temporary absences (see p247).

If your partner has a different immigration status to you then the rules are similar to that of IS. You can claim for yourself but not your partner if s/he is a person subject to immigration control. However, under PC rules such a couple are not treated as being members of the same household and therefore your partner's resources are not taken into account.

4. **Housing benefit and council tax benefit**

You are entitled to housing benefit (HB) or council tax benefit (CTB) if:
- you are in Great Britain (GB) (see p129), or only absent temporarily; *and*
- either you satisfy the habitual residence test (see p132) or you are exempt, or you are being paid income support (IS) or income-based jobseeker's allowance (JSA);[6] *and*
- you have a right to reside[7] (all British Citizens and those with a right of abode have a right of residence); *and*
  - for HB, you have accommodation in GB which you normally occupy as your home (which may apply during a temporary absence – see p247);[8] *or*
  - for CTB, you are liable to pay council tax for accommodation in which you reside (see p254);[9] *and*
- you are not part of a household abroad (see p168).

Household or family members abroad

This may affect your entitlement or reduce the amount of benefit you get. Broadly, the rules are the same as for IS except that if you are receiving IS or income-based JSA you are entitled to the *maximum* HB and CTB anyway.

If your partner is living abroad, your entitlement here could be affected (see under IS on p164).

If your partner is abroad, but you do not count as part of her/his household (see p143), then your HB or CTB is calculated on the basis of the members of the family who are living here. If the partner abroad is temporarily absent s/he may be treated as being here for the purposes of calculating benefit (see p147). If you are getting IS or income-based JSA, the absence of your partner abroad does not affect your HB and only affects your CTB in exceptional circumstances (see p147).

The amount of benefit you get may be affected if you have a child abroad (see p149), but only if you are *not* already receiving IS or income-based JSA, because these benefits give you maximum HB or CTB.

If a member of your family is a 'person subject to immigration control'

For the general position see under IS, on p165. However, the rules for claiming HB and CTB where a member of the family is a 'person subject to immigration control' (PSIC) are different to those for IS and income-based JSA. The fact that a member of the family is a PSIC will make no difference to your HB if you are getting IS or income-based JSA, but see below for special considerations.

Your HB or CTB is calculated taking into account all the members of the family, regardless of their immigration status. If one or more of your family members is a PSIC and is here with a condition that s/he has no recourse to public funds, your claim for HB or CTB could affect her/his right to stay. This is because her/his presence in the household will increase the amount of HB and CTB payable (see p165 under IS). This problem does not arise, however, if you are already getting IS or income-based JSA as you will already be getting maximum HB and CTB and there is therefore no question of additional public funds being paid out because the PSIC members of the family are now included in your claim.

The second question (see p165) about the desirability of making a claim is still an issue.

If your partner is an overstayer or does not have permission to be here you should get independent immigration advice before making a claim for benefit.

5. Tax credits

Child tax credit (CTC) and working tax credit (WTC) are administered by the Revenue. For details of entitlement and amounts payable, see CPAG's *Welfare Benefits and Tax Credits Handbook*.

General rules

To be entitled to CTC you must:[10]
- not be a person subject to immigration control (PSIC);
- be present and ordinarily resident in the UK (see p129). You can be treated as present and ordinarily resident in the UK in some circumstances (see below);
- satisfy the right to reside test (see p137).

CTC can be claimed by either member of the couple, as long as you (or your partner) are responsible for at least one child, even though that child does not need to be present or ordinarily resident in Great Britain (GB) when you claim.[11] However, the child(ren) must normally live with you or your partner in the UK and you or your partner must have the main responsibility for them.

To be entitled to WTC you must:[12]
- not be a PSIC;
- be present and ordinarily resident in the UK.

Temporary absence

It is possible to be treated as present and ordinarily resident for CTC and WTC during temporary absences abroad. If you remain ordinarily resident in the UK and your absence is unlikely to exceed 52 weeks, tax credits continue to be paid during:[13]
- the first eight weeks of any temporary absence;
- the first 12 weeks of any period when you are temporarily absent from the UK if that absence (or any extension to that period of absence) is in connection with:
  - the treatment of an illness or disability of you, your partner, a child for whom you are responsible, or another relative of either you or your partner; or
  - the death of your partner, a child for whom you are responsible, or another relative of you or your partner.

The following are exempt from the presence test:[14]
- a Crown servant posted overseas who immediately prior to being posted abroad was:
  - ordinarily resident in the UK; or
  - in the UK in connection with that posting; or
- the partner of a Crown servant posted overseas who has accompanied their partner to a country of posting or is temporarily accompanying them for one of the reasons set out above.

Partner abroad

If your partner is abroad for longer than the period allowed s/he is no longer ordinarily resident. If you have remained in the UK you or your partner must terminate the claim. This is because a claim for tax credits by a couple is a joint claim. To make a joint claim you must both be treated as being in the UK. The person who remains in the UK can make a fresh single claim if s/he meets the conditions for getting WTC or CTC. If you fail to notify the Revenue that one of the couple has gone abroad they may be overpaid tax credits. For further details of joint claims, see CPAG's *Welfare Benefits and Tax Credits Handbook*.

If a member of your family is a 'person subject to immigration control'

As a British citizen or Commonwealth citizen with the right of abode you are entitled to CTC, and the nationality and immigration status of your partner and children makes no difference to eligibility. If one member of a couple would fail the immigration test the other partner should claim. Where one member of the couple is subject to immigration control but the other is a British Citizen both members of the couple will be treated as though they are not PSICs.

Although CTC and WTC are listed in the immigration rules as 'public funds', they should not be treated by the Home Office as 'recourse to public funds' for immigration purposes where one of the couple is British or has a right of abode.[15] For information on public funds and the immigration rules, see Chapter 7.

6. **Child benefit and guardian's allowance**

Child benefit

Residence

You are only entitled to child benefit for a child if:[16]

* you are in Great Britain (GB) (claimant presence rule); *and*
* the child is in GB (child presence rule); *and*
* you and the child are ordinarily resident; *and*
* you have a right to reside (see p137).

There are exceptions to these rules and there are special rules for people working overseas, including civil servants and serving members of the armed forces.

There are special rules to stop you losing benefit if you move between GB and Northern Ireland.[17] You may also be able to use special rules if you have lived in another European Union (EU) or European Economic Area (EEA) member state (see Part 4) or a country with which the UK has a reciprocal agreement (see Chapter 25), even if you are not a national of that country.

A member of the household abroad

If you often go abroad and may lose entitlement to child benefit under these rules, you should consider whether there is another person who could make a claim instead – eg, if your partner does not often go abroad, s/he could claim. For the rules on who can claim, see CPAG's *Welfare Benefits and Tax Credits Handbook*.

Residence conditions for the claimant

You are treated as not present and, therefore, not eligible for child benefit if:

- you are not ordinarily resident in GB;
- you do not have a right to reside in the UK and your claim for child benefit was made after 1 May 2004;
- you are out of the country for longer than the permitted periods.

You satisfy the presence test if you are:[18]

- a Crown servant, or a partner of a Crown servant, posted overseas and immediately prior to your posting abroad you were:
  - ordinarily resident in the UK; *or*
  - in the UK in connection with that posting; *or*
- in the UK as a result of you having been deported or legally removed from another country.[19]

If you remain ordinarily resident in the UK and your absence is unlikely, from the start of the absence, to exceed 52 weeks, child benefit continues to be paid during:[20]

- the first eight weeks of any temporary absence; *or*
- the first 12 weeks of any period when you are temporarily absent from the UK if that absence, or any extension to that period of absence is in connection with:
  - the treatment of an illness or disability of you, your partner, a child for whom you are responsible, or another relative of either you or your partner; *or*
  - the death of your partner, a child for whom you are responsible, or another relative of you or your partner.

Generally in order to claim child benefit the child for whom you are claiming must be present in the UK. However, a child will be treated as present if her/his absence abroad is temporary, during:

- the first 12 weeks of any period of absence; *or*
- any period during which s/he is absent for the specific purpose of being treated for an illness or physical or mental disability which commenced before her/his absence began; *or*
- any period when s/he is in Northern Ireland;
- any period during which s/he is absent only because:
  - s/he is receiving full-time education at a recognised educational establishment in another EEA member state (including A8 and A2 States or in Switzerland); *or*

– s/he is engaged in an educational exchange or visit made with the written approval of the recognised educational establishment which s/he normally attends.

If the child is born outside the UK during a period in which the mother is treated as present in the UK, the child is also treated as present.[21]

If a member of your family is a 'person subject to immigration control'

The immigration status of the child for whom you claim is irrelevant. If you are responsible for a child and another person has been refused child benefit for that child because of her/his immigration status, you should claim child benefit instead. For details see CPAG's *Welfare Benefits and Tax Credits Handbook*.

Guardian's allowance

General rules

Guardian's allowance is paid to a person entitled to child benefit for a child who is not her/his child where both of the child's parents are dead, or, in some situations, where only one parent is dead (for details of these situations, see CPAG's *Welfare Benefits and Tax Credits Handbook*).[22] The nationality and immigration status of the child is irrelevant. The rules above for child benefit must be met and there is a further condition that at least one of the child's parents must have been born in the UK or have, at some time after reaching the age of 16, spent a total of 52 weeks in any two-year period in the UK.[23]

If you are not ordinarily resident (see p129) in GB, or you cease to be ordinarily resident in GB, then the amount of guardian's allowance paid for any day you are absent is frozen. The allowance will be paid at the rate paid when you stopped being ordinarily resident, or the rate at which it was first paid, if that was later.[24]

If one parent is dead, guardian's allowance can be paid while the other parent is in prison.[25] Only serving prisoners (and those detained in hospital by order of a court because of mental illness) are treated as being 'in prison' under the guardian's allowance rules.[26] A person serving a sentence of two years or more in a prison abroad counts as a person 'in prison'. Anyone detained under administrative detention, however, is not counted as being 'in prison' for this purpose.

When a child is adopted, the adoptive parents usually take on the full legal status of parents, and are treated as such under guardian's allowance rules. This rule applies only to adoptions carried out in the UK, or to foreign adoptions recognised under British law.[27] This means that you can only get guardian's allowance if the adoptive parents are both dead or, in certain situations, if one is dead.[28] An overseas adoption that is not recognised under British law does not have this effect. An unrecognised adoption will not confer full legal parentage,

Chapter 14: British citizens and others with the right of abode
7. Contribution-based jobseeker's allowance and incapacity benefit

14

and if both (or, in certain situations, one) of the child's natural parents are dead, the unofficial adoptive parents may be entitled to guardian's allowance.

7. Contribution-based jobseeker's allowance and incapacity benefit

Contribution-based jobseeker's allowance

General rules

It is not a condition of entitlement to contribution-based jobseeker's allowance (JSA) that you hold a particular immigration status. You simply need to qualify according to the normal contribution rules. Entitlement to contribution-based JSA depends on having worked and paid national insurance contributions, or had contributions credited, in the two complete tax years before the calendar year in which you make your claim (see CPAG's *Welfare Benefits and Tax Credits Handbook* for details). There are no conditions about residence in Great Britain (GB), but the need to have paid contributions means you must have been present for long enough to qualify. You must be 'capable of work',[29] and show that you are 'available for work'[30] and 'actively seeking work'[31] by signing on. In certain circumstances you may be treated as available for work even though in fact you are not (see CPAG's *Welfare Benefits and Tax Credits Handbook*).[32]

Residence rules

Because you must also meet the contribution conditions (see CPAG's *Welfare Benefits and Tax Credits Handbook*), you are unlikely to qualify unless you have lived and worked in the UK for several years or unless you can use a reciprocal agreement (see p375).

There are special rules to stop you losing benefit if you move between GB and Northern Ireland.[33] You may also be able to use special rules if you have lived in another European Union or European Economic Area member state (see Part 4) or a country with which the UK has a reciprocal agreement (see Part 5), even if you are not a national of that country.

It is also possible to receive contribution-based JSA during a temporary absence from this country if the reason is that:
- you are taking a child or young person who is a member of your family for medical treatment – benefit is payable for up to eight weeks;
- you are attending a job interview (you will need to tell the employment officer in advance) – benefit is payable for one week;
- you receive a pensioner or disability premium for your partner, and you are both away from GB – benefit is payable for up to four weeks.

If you qualify for a top-up allowance of income-based JSA because of your financial circumstances, this is not covered by the contribution rules, so that unlike contribution-based JSA it is affected by a dispute about your immigration status.

If a member of your family is a 'person subject to immigration control'

Contribution-based JSA is paid only to the applicant for up to six months. There are no additions for dependants. This means it will make no difference to your entitlement to contribution-based JSA if you have family members who are 'persons subject to immigration control' (PSIC). This rule does not apply to any income-based JSA you may expect to receive as a top-up allowance.

Incapacity benefit

General rules

Incapacity benefit (IB) can be paid whether or not you are still employed, and your entitlement is not affected by any savings you may have. If you are working and become sick you usually claim statutory sick pay (see p184) for up to 28 weeks, and may become eligible for IB after that. You can make a claim before the 28-week period is complete if it seems likely that you will not be able to return to work at the end of that time. Some young people may qualify for IB without needing to have worked (see CPAG's *Welfare Benefits and Tax Credits Handbook* for details of entitlement).

You are only entitled to IB if you are:[34]

- present in GB (see p129); *or*
- treated as present in GB (see below).

Residence rules

You may also be entitled for a maximum of 26 weeks while you are temporarily absent from GB (see Part 3).[35] There is no definition of when an absence is 'temporary', except that a permanent absence, or staying away for an indefinite period, does not count.[36] All the circumstances of the absence must be taken into account, but an absence of over 12 months is usually not treated as temporary unless there are exceptional reasons.[37]

If your absence is not 'temporary' you cannot receive IB during the absence. You will also need to satisfy the contribution conditions on your return, which you may not be able to do if you have been away from GB for a long period (see CPAG's *Welfare Benefits and Tax Credits Handbook* for details).

You are treated as in GB while you are absent if the reason for the absence is that you are a mariner or an offshore worker.[38]

8. Retirement pensions and bereavement benefits

These benefits are Category A, B and D retirement pensions, bereavement payment, widowed parent's allowance, and bereavement allowance.

Retirement pensions

Residence rules

If you are present in Great Britain (GB) these benefits are calculated in the normal way, even if you are not ordinarily resident (see p129) in GB.[39]

There are no residence conditions imposed on the first claim for these benefits except for Category D pension.

Because you (or your late spouse or civil partner in the case of bereavement benefits) must meet the contribution conditions (see CPAG's *Welfare Benefits and Tax Credits Handbook*), you are unlikely to qualify unless you have (or your late spouse/civil partner had) lived in the UK for several years or you are able to make use of a reciprocal agreement (see Part 5).

You may wish to 'de-retire' to increase the amount of your pension (see CPAG's *Welfare Benefits and Tax Credits Handbook*). You can only do this if you are ordinarily resident (see p129) in GB.[40]

There are special rules to stop you losing benefit if you move between GB and Northern Ireland.[41] You may also be able to use special rules if you have lived in another European Union/European Economic Area member state (see Part 4) or a country with which the UK has a reciprocal agreement (see Part 5), even if you are not a national of that country.

Household or family abroad

If you are not ordinarily resident (see p129) in GB, then the amount of benefit (except a lump-sum bereavement payment) paid for any day you are absent from GB is normally frozen, unless you are residing in some countries with which there is a reciprocal agreement (see Part 5). It is frozen at the rate paid when you stopped being ordinarily resident, or at the rate it was first paid, if that was later (except Category A and B pension for certain claimants – see below).[42] Freezing also applies to additional state pension and any graduated retirement benefit.[43]

Your frozen benefit may be paid at a higher rate than it would be under current rules if it was frozen before 7 August 1991.[44] These old rules are not covered in this book.

There are special rules (see below) for certain benefits.

Category A and B pensions

If your entitlement to part or all of a Category A or B pension depends on your spouse/civil partner or former spouse/civil partner's national insurance (NI) contributions, your annual up-rating of that pension is not frozen if your spouse/ civil partner or former spouse/civil partner whose contributions are used is ordinarily resident (see p129) in GB on the day before the date of that up-rating.[45]

You are still entitled to annual up-rating of your Category B pension even while you are not ordinarily resident in GB if:[46]

- the spouse/civil partner on whose contributions the Category B pension is based has died or you are divorced from her/him; *and*
- you have married or entered into a civil partnership again; *and*
- your new spouse/civil partner was not entitled to a Category A pension before the up-rating date; *and*
  - *either* you were still married or in a civil partnership on the day before the up-rating date; *or*
  - you married or entered into a civil partnership with her/him on or after that date.

Category D pension

You are only entitled to a Category D pension if:[47]

- you were resident in GB for at least 10 years in any continuous period of 20 years ending on or after your 80th birthday; *and*
- you were ordinarily resident (see p129) in GB on:
  - *either* your 80th birthday; *or*
  - the later date on which you claimed Category D pension.

Age addition

You are only entitled to an age addition for any day you are absent from GB, if either:[48]

- you are ordinarily resident (see p129) in GB; *or*
- you were entitled to an age addition before you stopped being ordinarily resident in GB; *or*
- you are entitled to an increased rate of any category of retirement pension under a reciprocal agreement (see Part 5).

If a member of your family is a 'person subject to immigration control'

For adult increases, see Chapter 12.

Retirement pensions are not within the list of benefits restricted by immigration status (see p155), so it should make no difference to your eligibility for an addition if any dependant is a 'person subject to immigration control' (PSIC). Similarly, receipt of a retirement pension can be treated as income under the immigration rules, in the same way as earnings, and does not count as recourse to public funds.

Bereavement benefits

General rules

Payment of the three bereavement benefits depends on whether your late spouse/ civil partner satisfied the contribution conditions (see CPAG's *Welfare Benefits and Tax Credits Handbook* for details), although you may qualify if s/he died as the result of an industrial disease or an accident at work, even if the contribution conditions are not met. Bereavement benefits can be paid whether or not you are working, and any savings you have are not taken into account. Some people who claim bereavement allowance or widowed parent's allowance may have to attend a work-focused interview (see CPAG's *Welfare Benefits and Tax Credits Handbook*).

Bereavement payment

You are only entitled to this lump-sum payment if either:[49]
- you were in GB at the time of your spouse/civil partner's death; *or*
- your spouse/civil partner was in GB at the time of her/his death; *or*
- you returned to GB within four weeks of your spouse/civil partner's death.

The payment is made at a single, once only rate, with no additions for any dependants, so if you have family members who are PSICs this does not affect your entitlement.

Bereavement allowance

This can be paid for up to 52 weeks. You must have been aged at least 45 but still under pension age by the date of death of your spouse/civil partner. Your entitlement will end if you re-marry or enter into a civil partnership during the year.

No additions are paid for any dependants.

Widowed parent's allowance

As the name suggests, this benefit is paid only to people who have the care of children, or to women who are pregnant at the time of their spouse/civil partner's death. It is paid instead of bereavement allowance, and the two allowances cannot be paid together. Payment is not limited to a 52-week period. In order to qualify you must be responsible for a 'qualifying child', who must be:[50]
- living with you; *or*
- maintained by you, at least to the value of the child addition to widowed parent's allowance plus the amount of child benefit; *and either*
- the child of you and your late spouse/civil partner; *or*
- a child for whom you or your late spouse/civil partner were receiving child benefit at the time of death; *or*
- a child for whom you were receiving child benefit at the time of death and you were residing with your late spouse/civil partner at that time.

This means that the only dependants taken into account for the purposes of widowed parent's allowance are qualifying children, and the conditions of qualification are the same as for child benefit (see p170). Immigration status is not taken into account in any other circumstance, and receipt of widowed parent's allowance cannot count as recourse to public funds for immigration purposes.

9. Maternity allowance

General rules

Eligibility for maternity allowance (MA) does not depend on your national insurance (NI) contribution record, but you must have been working, either as an employee or a self-employed person, for a period before the expected birth, and earning at least a minimum, threshold amount. Maternity allowance can be paid as a flat-rate allowance, with additions, or it can be paid at a variable rate, if your earnings have been too low to pay NI contributions. For details of the general conditions of entitlement and of dependants' additions that can be paid with MA, see CPAG's *Welfare Benefits and Tax Credits Handbook*.

Residence rules

There are no residence conditions for entitlement to MA, but the requirement to have been working and earning in the UK for a period of time means you are unlikely to qualify if you have not been resident.

If a member of your family is a 'person subject to immigration control'

Maternity allowance is not a benefit included in the list of benefits restricted because of a person's immigration status, and an addition can be paid for a dependant whether or not s/he counts as a 'person subject to immigration control'. Receiving MA does not count as recourse to public funds for the purposes of the immigration rules, so can be relied on, if necessary, in order to show an adequate income for a family reunion claim, either before entry or on application to the Home Office.

10. Industrial injuries benefits

The benefits covered are disablement benefit, reduced earnings allowance, retirement allowance, constant attendance allowance and exceptionally severe disablement allowance.

General rules

You are entitled to an industrial injuries benefit *for an accident* only if that accident 'arises out of and in the course of' an employed earner's employment (see CPAG's *Welfare Benefits and Tax Credits Handbook* for these rules).

You are entitled to an industrial injuries benefit *for a disease* only if that disease is 'prescribed in relation to' an employed earner's employment (see CPAG's *Welfare Benefits and Tax Credits Handbook* for these rules).

Residence rules

To qualify for benefit as the result of an accident at work you must have been in Great Britain (GB) (which includes adjacent UK territorial waters – see p129)[51] when the accident happened.[52] And to qualify for benefit because of a disease you must have been engaged in GB in the employment which caused that disease (even if you have also been engaged outside GB in that employment).[53]

There are exceptions to these rules[54] for various categories of worker, as follows. You can qualify for benefit in respect of an accident which happens or a disease which is contracted outside GB while you are:

- employed as a mariner or airman or airwoman;[55]
- employed as an apprentice pilot on board a ship or vessel;[56]
- on board an aircraft on a test flight starting in GB in the course of your employment.[57]

In these cases there are also more generous rules for defining when accidents arise out of and in the course of your employment, and for complying with time limits under benefit rules.[58]

You can qualify for benefit if, since 1986, an accident happens or you contract a disease outside GB[59] while you are paying GB national insurance contributions, either at Class 1 rate or at Class 2 rate as a volunteer development worker.

Benefit is not payable until you return to GB after the accident or contracting the disease.

You can qualify for benefit if you count as an offshore worker when an accident happens or you contract a disease. This applies in two situations. The first is where the accident happens or the disease is contracted while you are in an area where the UK exercises sovereign rights over the exploitation of the natural resources of the seabed or travelling between that area and GB.[60] The seabed is where you:

- are employed on a rig or boat at sea in connection with exploring or exploiting the seabed, subsoil or natural oil or gas in an area over which a European Union (EU) state or Norway exercises sovereign rights over the exploitation of the natural resources of the seabed but which was outside any country's territorial seas; *and*

- sustained the accident or contracted the disease in an area over which the sovereign rights are exercised or travelling between that area and an EU state (including the UK) or Norway.[61]

In the second case, your employment also counts as employed earner's employment only if:[62]
- had it been in GB, it would have been employed earner's employment; *and*
- you are ordinarily resident (see p129) in GB; *and*
- you were resident (see p129) in GB immediately before the employment began; *and*
- your employer has a place of business in GB.

If you sustain an accident or contract a disease while in the territory of an EU member state, the accident or disease is treated as if it happened (or arose) in GB.[63]
    You do *not* qualify for an industrial injuries benefit if you are:[64]
- a member of visiting armed forces; *or*
- a civilian employed by visiting armed forces, except if you are ordinarily resident (see p129) in the UK; *or*
- employed as a member of certain international organisations, *unless*:
    – there is liability for Class 1 national insurance contributions (see CPAG's *Welfare Benefits and Tax Credits Handbook*); *and*
    – you are ordinarily resident (see p129) in the UK.

If the ordinary residence exceptions do not apply to you, you are treated as not being in 'employed earner's employment'.
    If you qualify under the rules above you do not have to be present or resident in GB to be entitled to disablement benefit or retirement allowance.[65] They are up-rated annually regardless of where you live.
    You are not entitled to reduced earnings allowance (REA), constant attendance allowance or exceptionally severe disablement allowance unless you are *either*:[66]
- present in GB; *or*
- temporarily absent from GB (see p131).

For REA, you count as present in GB while you are employed as a mariner or airman or airwoman.[67] This benefit ended for new claims in 1990, but it is still possible to make a claim for REA now if you suffered an accident at work or the onset of an industrial disease before then (see CPAG's *Welfare Benefits and Tax Credits Handbook* for details).
    For decisions on entitlement to constant attendance allowance and exceptionally severe disablement allowance there is no right of appeal to a tribunal, and any challenge must be in the High Court.[68]

There are special rules to stop you losing benefit if you move between GB and Northern Ireland.[69] You may also be able to use special rules if you have lived in another EU or European Economic Area member state (see Part 4) or a country with which the UK has a reciprocal agreement (see Part 5), even if you are not a national of that country. There are also rules enabling you to retain benefits while working as an offshore worker.[70]

If a member of your family is a 'person subject to immigration control'

None of the industrial injuries benefits is included in the list of benefits restricted because of a person's immigration status. It is not a condition of entitlement to these benefits that you should not be a 'person subject to immigration control'. None of them have any additional allowances for dependants, except that some people who have been receiving disablement benefit since before 1987 may receive a supplement (see CPAG's *Welfare Benefits and Tax Credits Handbook*).

Receipt of one of these benefits does not count as recourse to public funds for the purpose of the immigration rules.

11. **Disability benefits**

These are disability living allowance (DLA), attendance allowance (AA) and carer's allowance (CA). Severe disablement allowance, which was previously grouped together with these benefits, ended for new claims from 6 April 2001, and is now only paid to people who were entitled to it before that date (for details see CPAG's *Welfare Benefits and Tax Credits Handbook*).

There are special rules to stop you losing benefit if you move between Great Britain (GB) and Northern Ireland.[71] You may also be able to use special rules if you have lived in another European Union or European Economic Area (EEA) member state (see Part 4) or a country with which the UK has a reciprocal agreement (see Part 5), even if you are not a national of that country.

Disability living allowance and attendance allowance

General rules

Disability living allowance is payable to people who are under the age of 65 when they claim, and who satisfy the tests for residence and disability. It is in two parts, a care component and a mobility component. The care component is intended for people whose disability means that they need supervision or attention in their daily life, and is paid at one of three rates, higher, middle or lower, depending on the needs. The mobility component has a separate test, intended for people who cannot walk out of doors, or cannot do so without help. It is paid either at a higher or lower rate. DLA is a non-contributory benefit, and eligibility does not depend on a record of contributions or of employment, but a claimant must show that s/he has satisfied the disability condition for at least three months before the date of the claim.[72] For details of the conditions of entitlement, and rates of payment, see CPAG's *Welfare Benefits and Tax Credits Handbook.*

AA can be paid to claimants who are over the age of 65. The disability conditions are similar to those for DLA, but there is no mobility component with AA. It is payable either at a higher or lower rate, and claimants must have satisfied the disability conditions for at least six months before the date of claim. For details of the conditions of entitlement, and rates of payment, see CPAG's *Welfare Benefits and Tax Credits Handbook.*

Residence rules

You are not entitled to DLA or AA for a day, unless on that day:[73]
* you are ordinarily resident (see p129) in Great Britain (GB); *and*
* you are present in GB (but see also below); *and*
* you have been present in GB for a total of at least 26 weeks in the last 52 weeks.

You are treated as present in GB for these rules, including the 26-week rule, if you are abroad only because:[74]
* you are a serving member of the armed forces; *or*
* you live with a serving member of the armed forces and are the spouse, civil partner, son, daughter, step-son, step-daughter, father, father-in-law, step-father, mother, mother-in-law or step-mother of that person; *or*
* you are a mariner or airman or airwoman;[75] *or*
* you are an offshore worker.[76]

You may also be treated as present in GB during a temporary absence (see p130). This may help you meet the 26-week presence rule.

If you are terminally ill, the 26-week presence rule is waived.[77]

For children aged less than six months, the 26-week period is reduced to 13 weeks.[78] Because presence does not start until birth,[79] a child born in GB must be 13 weeks old before being entitled to DLA, unless s/he is terminally ill, in which case the 13-week period is waived. If DLA entitlement begins before a child is six months old, the period of 26 weeks continues to be reduced to 13 weeks until the child's first birthday.[80]

There is an extra residence condition if any of your earnings or your spouse's earnings are exempt from UK income tax because of a double taxation treaty or exemption for foreign officials. This is most likely to affect you if you are (or your spouse is) a member of a foreign armed service or in exempt employment as a diplomat or a member of a foreign mission. This also applies to a child aged under 16 who is the daughter, step-daughter, son or step-son of a person receiving UK tax-free earnings. If this applies, the person receiving the tax-free earnings must have been actually present in GB for a total of 156 weeks in the four years before starting to receive tax-free earnings.[81] For this rule, you are not treated as present during any absence, but you may be able to use the special European Community rules (see Part 4). This rule is not waived if you are terminally ill.

Carer's allowance

General rules

CA can be claimed by people who are engaged in 'regular and substantial' care for someone who receives higher or middle rate DLA, AA or a constant attendance allowance in respect of industrial or war disablement. As a non-contributory benefit there is no test of contributions or employment record, but there is an immigration condition (see below).

Residence rules

The rules for CA are the same as those for DLA and AA (see p182) except that:[82]
- the 26-week rule is not waived if the disabled person is terminally ill;
- people who receive (or whose spouse/civil partner or parents receive) UK tax exempt earnings are not treated differently;
- the detailed rules about temporary absence are different.

For adult increases, see Chapter 12.

If a member of your family is a 'person subject to immigration control'

There are no dependant additions payable with DLA or AA, but where the person with the disability is a child, benefit can be claimed on her/his behalf by a parent or guardian. An addition can be paid with CA for the claimant's partner, although her/his income is taken into account.

DLA, AA and CA all count as public funds for the purposes of the immigration rules.[83] It is a condition of entitlement that the claimant is not a 'person subject to immigration control' (PSIC), so if you are a British or Commonwealth citizen with the right of abode you cannot make a claim for DLA on behalf of a child who joins you in the UK from abroad, nor are you entitled to an addition of CA for a dependant, until that person has ceased to be a PSIC (see p155 for details). If you do so, it is likely to affect the immigration status of your partner and any children. The DWP may pass information about you to the Home Office (see Chapter 10). Similarly, if you are in need of care from a member of your family who is a PSIC, it is not possible for that person to make a claim for CA until after the immigration restrictions have ended. On the other hand it should not matter if you qualify for a care component of either DLA or AA because of assistance given to you by a PSIC. That is benefit money to which you are personally entitled, and could be claimed by you whether or not that person was in the UK. The Home Office cannot take it into account when it considers an application to stay on behalf of that person under the immigration rules.[84]

If your partner or any child is covered by Chapters 18 of this book is a national of a country outside the EEA and is abroad you should seek specialist independent advice before claiming or renewing a claim.

12. **Statutory sick pay and statutory maternity, paternity and adoption pay**

General rules

See CPAG's *Welfare Benefits and Tax Credits Handbook* for details of entitlement to and payment of these benefits.

Residence rules

The rules on entitlement for these benefits concentrate more on whether you count as an employee in this country rather than whether you are physically present here. You only count as an employee if you are:
* an employed earner for Great Britain (GB) national insurance (NI) purposes (even if you work outside GB);[85] *or*
* you are employed in a European Economic Area (EEA) member state (including A8 or A2 states prior to and after accession) other than the UK and if that employment was in GB you would be an employee under the relevant benefit rules and the UK is the appropriate country under European Community rules (see p302);[86] *or*
* an offshore worker;[87] *or*
* a mariner (but see below);[88] *or*
* for statutory sick pay (SSP) only, an airman or airwoman (but see below).[89]

Only mariners or airmen and airwomen who meet certain rules count as employees.[90] These are not dealt with here.

You can satisfy the test of continuous employment for statutory maternity pay (SMP) purposes if:[91]
* you were employed in another EU country in any week in the 26 weeks before the 15th week before your expected week of childbirth (see CPAG's *Welfare Benefits and Tax Credits Handbook*); *and*
* you were employed in GB by the same employer in that 15th week.

Your entitlement to SSP, SMP, statutory paternity pay (SPP) and statutory adoption pay (SAP) is not affected by any absence from GB, but you can only receive SSP while you remain an employee.[92]

Your employer is not required to pay you SSP, SMP, SPP or SAP if:[93]

- your employer is not required by law to pay employer's Class 1 NI contributions (even if those contributions are in fact made) because at the time they become payable your employer is:[94]
  - not resident or present in GB; *nor*
  - has a place of business in GB; *or*
- because of an international treaty or convention your employer is exempt from the Social Security Acts or those Acts are not enforceable against your employer.

In some cases the rules require notice to be given about SSP or SMP, either by you to your employer, or by your employer to you. If you are in one of the circumstances where notice is required but it cannot be given because you are outside the UK, you (or your employer) are treated as having complied with the rules if the notice is given as soon as is reasonably practicable.[95] For details of when notice must be given see CPAG's *Welfare Benefits and Tax Credits Handbook*.

If a member of your family is a 'person subject to immigration control'

There are no additions payable with these benefits for dependants and none of these benefits are included in the list of payments restricted because of immigration status.[96] This means that they cannot be taken into account by the immigration authorities when they are dealing with applications to enter or stay in the UK.

13. **The social fund**

The social fund is run by the DWP and is in two parts: regulated and discretionary. Decisions concerning the regulated social fund can be appealed to a tribunal in the same way as decisions about income support (IS), but there is a separate review and appeal system for discretionary social fund decisions. For a full description of the fund, see CPAG's *Welfare Benefits and Tax Credits Handbook*.

Regulated social fund

General rules

There are four types of payments within the regulated social fund: maternity expenses, funeral expenses, cold weather payments and winter fuel payments.[97]

You are entitled to a **Sure Start maternity grant** if, at the date you claim, you or your partner is entitled to IS or income-based jobseeker's allowance (JSA) (including urgent cases rate), pension credit (PC), child tax credit (CTC) at an amount higher than the family element or working tax credit (WTC) where a disability or severe disability element is included in the award.[98]

You are entitled to a **funeral expenses payment** if, at the date you claim, you or your partner is entitled to IS or income-based JSA (including urgent cases rate and hardship payments), housing benefit, council tax benefit, PC, CTC at an amount higher than the family element and WTC where a disability or severe disability element is included in the award.[99]

The funeral (ie, the burial or cremation) must take place in the UK or (if you can claim rights under European Community (EC) law) another European Economic Area (EEA) state.[100] This rule is not unlawful under British rules against racial discrimination.[101] However, it may contravene the Human Rights Act 1998. If you are refused a payment because the funeral took place outside the UK, you should appeal and seek advice.

The deceased must have been ordinarily resident (see p129) in the UK at the time of death.[102] This only applies to claims made after 6 April 1997. This rule may breach EC law.

You are not entitled to a **cold weather payment** unless, on a day within the cold weather period, you are entitled to IS or income-based JSA (including urgent cases rate) and this includes one of the pensioner or disability premiums or you are responsible for a child under 5 or you are getting CTC which includes a disability or severe disability element.[103] Cold weather payments are normally paid without the need for a separate claim.[104]

To qualify for a **winter fuel payment** you must be aged over 60 and ordinarily resident in Great Britain (GB), but you do not have to be entitled to, or receiving, any other benefits.[105] For conditions of entitlement, and rules for people in certain kinds of accommodation, see CPAG's *Welfare Benefits and Tax Credits Handbook*. A 'person subject to immigration control' (PSIC) is not entitled to winter fuel payments. If you are already entitled to a winter fuel payment you can continue to receive future payments even if you go to live in another EEA state.[106]

Discretionary social fund

General rules

There are three types of payment: community care grants, budgeting loans and crisis loans.

You cannot be given a **community care grant** unless, when you apply, you are in receipt of IS, income-based JSA (including urgent cases rate) or PC with one exception.[107] This means that, while there are no residence or presence conditions in the community care grant rules, you must meet the residence or presence rules for IS or income-based JSA (see pp164 or 166).

The exception is when:[108]

- the grant is to help you establish yourself in the community following a stay in institutional or residential care; *and*
- your discharge from that care is planned to be within six weeks; *and*
- you are likely to receive IS or income-based JSA upon that discharge.

If you are within this exception you do not need to show you are entitled to IS or income-based JSA in order to qualify, so you do not need to meet the residence or presence rules for either of those benefits when you apply. However, you must show that you are likely to meet those rules (and the other IS or income-based JSA rules) after you are discharged. The place providing your care does not have to be in the UK. This means that if you are being cared for abroad but intend to return to GB on your discharge, you may be considered for a grant.

This type of grant can only be paid to 'establish' a person in the community. For these purposes it has been decided that 'the community' refers to GB, so to be eligible a person must intend to live in GB.[109]

You cannot be given a **budgeting loan** unless, when you apply, you are being paid IS, income-based JSA (including urgent cases rate) or PC.[110] This means that, while there are no residence or presence conditions in the budgeting loan rules, you must meet the residence or presence rules for IS or income-based JSA (see pp164 and 166).

You do not need to be receiving any benefits to be given a **crisis loan.**

If you are not entitled to IS or income-based JSA because you are a 'person from abroad' (or would not be entitled if you claimed) you can only be given a crisis loan if you meet certain rules. You count as a 'person from abroad' if you are not habitually resident in the UK, Ireland, the Channel Islands or the Isle of Man and are not exempt (see p132).

The loan must be:[111]

- to meet expenses to alleviate the consequences of a disaster; *and*
- the only way to prevent serious damage or serious risk to your health or safety or to that of a member of your family.

A crisis loan is made if the DWP considers that you are likely to be able to repay it.[112] The overall maximum loan is £1,000.[113] The maximum loan for living expenses is 75 per cent of the IS personal allowance for you and your partner plus the full allowance for each child.

There is no definition of 'disaster'. If you have been refused IS because the DWP has decided that you are not habitually resident, you could argue that this refusal is a 'disaster' in the ordinary meaning of that word. You should explain why the refusal is disastrous for you and your family, and the serious damage/risk that the refusal causes.

You will also need to explain how you would repay the loan. Since it is only a matter of time before you are treated as habitually resident and awarded benefit, you will then be able to repay the loan.

If you are refused a loan, you should apply for a review of that refusal and seek specialist advice.

Residence rules

There are no residence or presence conditions for the claimant in the rules covering these payments, but because you must be in receipt of certain qualifying benefits to get a payment you must meet the residence or presence rules for one of those benefits.

Payments from the discretionary social fund can only be paid to meet needs that occur in the UK.[114] That should not exclude a need that occurs in the UK because of expenditure abroad – eg, a need for a budgeting loan because you spent money helping relatives abroad. It is the place of the need that matters, not the ultimate reason for that need. This rule may breach EC law (see p305).

If a member of your family is a 'person subject to immigration control'

The social fund rules do not generally provide for allowances in the same way as other benefits, so there are no specific rules concerning amounts for dependants, except for crisis loans. There may be difficulties in an application for a crisis loan for any partner or children who are PSICs, but as it is the claimant's needs as a whole that are considered you should argue that your own needs are greater because of your responsibilities for your family. If you need to receive a crisis loan it should not be taken into account by the Home Office when it deals with an application for your family members because it will only have been a loan, to be repaid, so there will have been no extra payment of any benefit because of their presence.[115]

In assessing other social fund payments it is likely that the only needs taken into account will be those of the person or family member for whom benefit is being paid. However, if the need is for a funeral expense, it should not matter if the deceased person was a PSIC, and no benefit was being paid for her/him, so long as the DWP accepts that it is reasonable for you to have to meet the expense rather than someone else.

Notes

1. **Income support**
   1 s124(1) SSCBA 1992
   2 s137(2)(b) SSCBA 1992; reg 4 IS Regs
   3 s21 National Assistance Act 1948; s7 Children Act 1989
   4 Reg 5 I(EEA) Regs

2. **Income-based jobseekers allowance**
   5 s115(9) IAA 1999; reg 2 SS(IA)CA Regs; reg 85(4) JSA Regs

4. Housing benefit and council tax benefit
6 Reg 10(4) and (5) HB Regs; reg 7(4) and (5) CTB Regs
7 Reg 10(5) HB Regs; reg 7(3) CTB Regs
8 s130(1)(a) SSCBA 1992; reg 7 HB Regs
9 s131(3)(a) SSCBA 1992

5. Tax credits
10 Reg 3(1) TC(Imm) Regs
11 s115(9) IAA 1999; s3(3) TCA 2002
12 s115(9) IAA 1999; reg 3 TC(R) Regs
13 Reg 4 TC(R) Regs
14 Reg 3(2) TC(R) Regs
15 Reg 3 TC(Imm) Regs

6. Child benefit and guardian's allowance
16 s146(2) and (3) SSCBA 1992
17 Reg 2 and Sch 1 SS(NIRA) Regs
18 Reg 30 and 31 CB Regs
19 Reg 21 CB Regs
20 Reg 24 CB Regs
21 Reg 21 CB Regs
22 s77 SSCBA 1992
23 Reg 9 SS(GA) Regs
24 Reg 5(3)(f) SSB(PA) Regs. See also s113(1) SSCBA 1992; reg 4(1) SSB(PA) Regs
25 s77(2)(c) and (8)(b) SSCBA 1992; reg 5 SS(GA) Regs
26 Reg 5 SS(GA) Regs
27 s77(8)(a) SSCBA 1992; reg 2 SS(GA) Regs. The reference in reg 2 to s4(3) Adoption Act 1968 is (because of s17(2)(a) IntA 1978), a reference to ss38(1)(d) and (e) and 72(1) and (2) Adoption Act 1976. The Adoption (Scotland) Act 1978 uses the same definition as under English law: ss38(1)(d) and 65(1) and (2).
28 Except where the adoptive parents were entitled to guardian's allowance immediately before adoption: s77(11) SSCBA 1992.

7. Contribution-based JSA and incapacity benefit
29 s1(2)(f) JSA 1995
30 ss1(2)(a) and 6(1) JSA 1995
31 ss1(2)(c) and 7 JSA 1995
32 Reg 14 JSA Regs
33 Reg 2 and Sch 1 SS(NIRA) Regs
34 s113(1) SSCBA 1992; s1(2)(i) JSA 1995
35 Regs 2 and 11 SSB(PA) Regs
36 R(S) 1/85

37 See generally *CAO v Ahmed* 16 March 1994, CA
38 SS(MB) Regs

8. Retirement pensions and bereavement benefits
39 The disqualification under s113(1) SSCBA 1992 only applies on a day of absence from GB.
40 Reg 6 SSB(PA) Regs
41 Reg 2 and Sch 1 SS(NIRA) Regs
42 Regs 4(3) and (4) and 5(3)-(6) SSB(PA) Regs
43 Regs 4(4) and 5(3)(c) SSB(PA) Regs
44 Reg 5(8) and Sch to SSB(PA) Regs
45 Reg 5(3)(a) and (aa), (5) and (6) SSB(PA) Regs. These only disqualify where the husband/former partner is not ordinarily resident in GB.
46 Reg 5(7) SSB(PA) Regs
47 Reg 10 SS(WB&RP) Regs
48 Reg 8(1) SSB(PA) Regs
49 Reg 4(2B) SSB(PA) Regs
50 ss39A(3), 81(2) and (3) SSCBA 1992

10. Industrial injuries benefits
51 s172(a) SSCBA 1992
52 s94(5) SSCBA 1992
53 s109(1) SSCBA 1992; reg 14 SS(IIPD) Regs
54 ss109(2)(a), 117, 119 and 120 SSCBA 1992
55 Reg 2(1) SS(IIMB) Regs; reg 2(1) SS(IIAB) Regs. For 'mariner' and 'airman' see regs 4-7 and Sch 2 SS(EEEIIP) Regs
56 Reg 2(2) SS(IIMB) Regs
57 Reg 2(2) SS(IIAB) Regs
58 Regs 3, 4, 6 and 8 SS(IIMB) Regs; regs 3 and 6 SS(IIAB) Regs
59 Reg 10C(5) and (6) SSB(PA) Regs
60 Regs 11(3) SSB(PA) Regs
61 Reg 10C(2)(a) SSB(PA) Regs
62 Reg 10C(2A) SSB(PA) Regs
63 Reg 10C(2)(b) SSB(PA) Regs
64 Reg 3 and Sch 1 Part II paras 3 and 4 SS(EEEIIP) Regs
65 Reg 9(3) and (7) SSB(PA) Regs
66 s113(1) SSCBA 1992; reg 9(4) and (5) SSB(PA) Regs
67 Reg 5(b) SS(IIMB) Regs; reg 4(b) SS(IIAB) Regs. For 'mariner' and 'airman' see regs 4-7 and Sch 2 SS(EEEIIP) Regs
68 Sch 2 para 14 SS(SDA) Regs
69 Reg 2 and Sch 1 SS(NIRA) Regs
70 Reg 11(2) and (2A) SSB(PA) Regs

11. Disability benefits
71 Reg 2 and Sch 1 SS(NIRA) Regs
72 ss72 and 73 SSCBA 1992

73 Reg 2(1)(b) SS(AA) Regs; reg 2(1)(b) SS(DLA) Regs
74 Reg 2(2) SS(AA) Regs; reg 2(2) SS(DLA) Regs
75 Regs 112 and 118 SS(Con) Regs
76 s120 SSCBA 1992; reg 114 SS(Con) Regs
77 Reg 2(3) SS(AA) Regs; reg 2(4) SS(DLA) Regs
78 Reg 2(5) SS(DLA) Regs
79 R(A) 1/94
80 Reg 2(6) SS(DLA) Regs
81 Reg 2(1)(b) SS(AA) Regs; reg 2(1)(b) SS(DLA) Regs
82 Reg 9 SS(ICA) Regs
83 s115(1) IAA 1999
84 para 6 HC 395 as amended in October 2001, definition of 'public funds'

12. Statutory sick pay and statutory maternity, paternity and adoption pay
85 **SSP** ss151(1) and 163(1) SSCBA 1992 'employee'
   SMP ss164(1) and 171(1) SSCBA 1992 'employee'
   SPP ss171ZA(1) and 171ZJ(2) SSCBA 1992 'employee'
   SAP ss171ZL(1) and 171ZS(2) SSCBA 1992 'employee'
86 Reg 5 SSP(MAPA) Regs; reg 2 SMP(PAM) Regs; reg 3 SPPSAP(PAM) Regs
87 Regs 4 and 8 SSP(MAPA) Regs; reg 8 SMP(PAM) Regs; reg 9 SPPSAP(PAM) Regs; s120 SSCBA 1992; reg 76 SS(Con) Regs
88 Reg 6 SSP(MAPA) Regs; reg 7 SMP(PAM) Regs; reg 8 SPPSAP(PAM) Regs; reg 81 SS(Con) Regs
89 Reg 7 SSP(MAPA) Regs
90 Regs 6 and 7 SSP(MAPA) Regs; reg 7 SMP(PAM) Regs; reg 8 SPPSAP(PAM) Regs
91 Reg 5 SMP(PAM) Regs
92 These rules changed on 6 April 1996 (SSP) and 18 August 1996 (SMP). Before that, entitlement normally ended when you were absent from the EU: reg 10(1) SSP(MAPA) Regs, reg 9(1) SMP(PAM) Regs before amendment.
93 Reg 16(2) SSP Regs; reg 17(3) SMP Regs; reg 32 SPPSAP(G) Regs
94 Reg 145(1)(b) SS(Con) Regs
95 Reg 14 SSP(MAPA) Regs; reg 6 SMP(PAM) Regs; reg 7 SPPSAP(PAM) Regs
96 s115(1) IAA 1999

13. The social fund
97 s138(1)(a) and (2) SSCBA 1992
98 Reg 5(1)(a) SFM&FE Regs
99 Reg 7(1)(a) SFM&FE Regs. See CPAG's *Welfare Benefits and Tax Credits Handbook* for possible limits on CTB route.
100 Reg 7(1)(b) SFM&FE Regs
101 *Nessa v CAO* [1999] 4 All ER 677
102 Reg 7(1)(c) SFM&FE Regs as amended by reg 5 Social Fund and Claims and Payments (Miscellaneous Amendments) Regulations 1997 S1 No.792
103 Reg 1A SFCWP Regs
104 SS(C&P) Regs still apply to cold weather payments (regs 4 and 2(2)(b)), but the particular rules and time limit have been revoked (reg 15A and Sch 4 para 9A).
105 Reg 2 SFWFP Regs
106 Art 10 EC Reg 1408/71
107 SF Dir 25(a)
108 SF Dir 4(a)(i) and 25(b)
109 *R v SFI, ex parte Amina Mohammed*, *Times*, 25 November 1992
110 SF Dir 8(1)(a)
111 SF Dirs 3(1)(a) and 16(b)
112 SF Dir 22
113 SF Dir 18
114 SF Dirs 2, 23(1)(a) and 29
115 para 6 HC 395

Chapter 15

Indefinite leave to remain

This chapter covers the benefit rules that affect people with indefinite leave to remain in the UK. The benefits covered are:

1. Income support (p194)
2. Income-based jobseeker's allowance (p196)
3. Pension credit (p196)
4. Housing benefit and council tax benefit (p197)
5. Child benefit and guardian's allowance (p197)
6. Tax credits (p198)
7. Contribution-based jobseeker's allowance and incapacity benefit (p198)
8. Retirement pensions and bereavement benefits (p198)
9. Industrial injuries benefits (p198)
10. Disability benefits (p198)
11. Statutory sick pay, statutory maternity, paternity and adoption pay and maternity allowance (p199)
12. The social fund (p199)

Generally people with indefinite leave to remain are not excluded from entitlement to social security benefits. The only two exceptions to this are in respect of income support, income-based jobseeker's allowance, pension credit, housing benefit and council tax benefit where the person with indefinite leave:

- is subject to a formal sponsorship undertaking (see p192); *or*
- fails the habitual residence test (see p132).

What is indefinite leave to remain

You have indefinite leave to remain if you have been given permission ('leave') to be in the UK with no time limit on your right to stay. This is also referred to in immigration law as 'settled' status.[1] It is sometimes known unofficially as 'permanent residence'. Once you acquire this status you will only lose it if a deportation order is made against you on criminal or security grounds, or if you remain outside the UK for a continuous period of more than two years. Adults aged 18-65 who apply on or after 2 April 2007 for indefinite leave to remain in the UK, will normally need to demonstrate knowledge of language and of 'life in the UK' as well as meeting the usual requirements for settlement. For full details, see Chapter 2.

Acquiring British citizenship

If you become a British citizen you no longer have leave to remain because you are no longer subject to immigration control. Remember, however, that British nationals who are not British citizens can have indefinite leave to remain. If you become a British citizen, the most important changes in your rights to benefits are:

- the sponsored immigrant rule cannot apply (see below); *and*
- you can use European Community (EC) rules on benefits (see Part 4).

European Economic Area nationals and indefinite leave

The immigration rules allow a European Economic Area (EEA) national to obtain indefinite leave to remain, although there is no requirement to do so, and most do not. This does not apply, of course, if you are a British citizen because British citizens are not subject to immigration control. If you are an EEA national with indefinite leave, you can use either the rules for people with indefinite leave or the rules for EEA nationals (see Part 4), whichever one is more favourable.

Indefinite leave with a sponsorship undertaking

Some people have indefinite leave to remain but only as a result of an undertaking having been made by another person (usually a relative) to maintain and accommodate them (see p94). A sponsorship undertaking can affect entitlement to certain benefits although this is only the case where the sponsorship undertaking is made in pursuance of the immigration rules; a voluntary commitment to maintain another person does not count as a sponsorship undertaking.

A written undertaking

Sometimes a person has been sponsored to come to the UK and the sponsor has confirmed their willingness to support the person by providing bank statements or pay slips. Application forms for entry clearance ask for this. These informal arrangements help an applicant to get a visa or the required leave. However, once the requirement to grant the application is met there are no further checks to ensure compliance. This type of informal sponsorship has no bearing on a person's entitlement to benefit. Only a formal undertaking should count, because otherwise it is not 'given in pursuance of the immigration rules' as the benefit rules require. Any other type of informal sponsorship or promise, even one in writing, does not count.

When an application for leave to remain or for entry clearance is made for an elderly parent, a child aged between 16 and 18, or another, more distant relative, the Home Office or entry clearance officer dealing with the application may request a written undertaking. An undertaking will not usually be required for a spouse or for younger children. Applications on behalf of people who are already in the UK will be made on one of the Home Office's standard forms, usually the

SET(F) form, although children may be included with the other parent on Form FLR(M). The SET(F) contains a section with a written undertaking, and though the use of this part of the form is voluntary, the Home Office will usually expect it to be completed. If it has not been, or if children have been included on another form, there will be no written undertaking for the purpose of the rules unless the Home Office specifically requests that an undertaking is made. That may be done by sending a separate form, currently a RON 112. The forms in use for entry clearance (the visa application forms) do not include an undertaking, and unless the entry clearance officer requests a formal undertaking on a RON 112 form there will be no undertaking for the purpose of the benefit rules. An undertaking will usually be expected to be given by the relative whom the applicant is to join.

The benefits authorities are sometimes unclear as to who is a sponsored immigrant under benefit rules. Even where the Home Office has told the DWP that an undertaking has not been signed, claimants have sometimes been treated as sponsored immigrants. The main confusion lies with a failure to recognise the difference between sponsorship arrangements with formal undertakings and those with an informal sponsorship. For benefit purposes you can only be treated as a sponsored immigrant if the DWP can show that a formal undertaking has been given. If it cannot obtain the written undertaking on a SET(F) or RON 112 from the Home Office, or the RON 112 from the entry clearance officer, you should not be treated as a sponsored immigrant, and should not be refused benefit.

Public funds

A person with indefinite leave is not affected by the public funds restrictions (see p84). A public funds restriction is a condition attached to a persons leave and no conditions can be attached to indefinite leave. A formal undertaking given by a sponsor is not a condition attached to leave.

When you stop being a sponsored immigrant for benefit purposes

You cease to be a sponsored immigrant when:
- you have been resident in the UK for five years;
- you become a British citizen;
- you acquire an EC right to reside in the UK because you become a family member of an EEA national.

Once you stop being a sponsored immigrant under the benefit rules, the ordinary rules on entitlement apply. Special rules apply if your sponsor dies within the first five years (see p194).

1. Income support

You are entitled to income support (IS) if:

- you are in Great Britain (GB)[2] (see p129) or temporarily absent from GB[3] (see p131); *and*
- you are habitually resident in the UK, Ireland, the Channel Islands or the Isle of Man (see p132), or you are exempt from the habitual residence test (see p132); *and*
- you are not a 'sponsored immigrant'; *or*
- you are a 'sponsored immigrant' but your sponsor has died.

Your entitlement might also be affected if you are a member of a household that includes a person living abroad.

In practice, if everyone for whom you are claiming has been present in the UK for the two years before you sign the IS claim form, the DWP will normally assume that you meet those rules. This is because the claim form asks if the claimant, partner or children being claimed for have come to live or returned to live in the UK in the last two years. However, even if you answer 'no' to this question, the DWP might ask you extra questions about your immigration history, particularly if you have recently been paid IS or income-based jobseeker's allowance (JSA) at the urgent cases rate (see p160).

Sponsored immigrants and income support

You are only a sponsored immigrant for IS if you have been admitted to the UK or allowed to stay here because another person (known as your 'sponsor') gave a written undertaking under the immigration rules[4] to be responsible for your maintenance and accommodation in the UK.[5]

If this does not apply, you are not a sponsored immigrant and you are entitled to IS in the same way as any other person with indefinite leave to remain. If you are treated as a sponsored immigrant you should appeal and take independent advice.

If you are a sponsored immigrant you are not entitled to IS (or income-based JSA, pension credit, housing benefit or council tax benefit), unless one of the exceptions below applies:[6]

- you have been resident in the UK for five years or more since the date you entered the UK or the date of the undertaking, whichever is later; *or*
- you have been resident in the UK for less than five years but your sponsor has died.

If you are a sponsored immigrant under the benefit rules and the sponsor who gave the undertaking has died, you are entitled to IS at the urgent cases rate.[7] If more than one sponsor gave an undertaking (this would be exceptional, but is provided for), each of them must have died for this to apply to you. To work out the urgent cases rate, see Chapter 13.

If the sponsored immigrant rule stops applying to you (eg, you have been resident for five years) you get ordinary rate IS.

If you are a sponsored immigrant, you should consider whether your partner, if you have one, should claim instead. For details of the rules dealing with the situation when a member of your family is a sponsored immigrant, see Chapter 12.

Five years' residence

Residence does not have to be continuous. Once you have been allowed to enter or stay on an undertaking, you remain a 'person subject to immigration control' (see p155), but you stop being a sponsored immigrant for benefit purposes when you have been resident (see p129) in the UK for five years.[8] This does not have to be continuous residence. The DWP is instructed to work out the length of your residence starting with the date you first entered the UK or if it was later, the date of the undertaking.[9] The rule is that you must be resident not present, so time abroad may count for your period of residence in the UK (see p130). If the DWP decides that, because your absences abroad do not count as periods of residency, you are still a sponsored immigrant even though five years have passed since you first entered, you should seek independent advice.

If you are given indefinite leave on an undertaking and you later travel abroad you continue to be subject to the undertaking. The Court of Appeal has held that on re-entry the original commitment of the sponsor continues to apply.[10]

Sponsor's liability to maintain and recovery of income support

Since 1980, the DWP has had the power to recover any IS paid to a sponsored immigrant from the person who gave the sponsorship.[11] Recovery is through the magistrates' court (in Scotland, sheriff's court). There is also a power to prosecute for failure to maintain the claimant.[12] The DWP has used the threat of court action to persuade sponsors to provide some financial support to the claimant concerned. If the sponsor could not support the claimant, the DWP usually took no further steps. Court action has apparently been rare, and is not likely to be considered where the sponsor is in receipt of benefits.

The definition of sponsored immigrant for the purpose of the rules on liability to maintain (see p94) is different from that for the claimant's benefit entitlement. Under the liability to maintain rules, a sponsored immigrant is a person for whom a sponsorship undertaking has been given after 22 May 1980.[13] There is no five-year rule, so there is no cut-off point, and a sponsor would, in theory at least, remain liable indefinitely.

These powers (or the threat of them) may still be used against sponsors of claimants on IS, especially where the claimant has transitional protection. If the DWP approaches you about an undertaking you have made, you should consider seeking independent advice. A liability to maintain should not delay an award of IS to which the claimant is entitled. Nor can any IS which is paid be recovered from the claimant.

The habitual residence test

The second way in which people who are settled or have indefinite leave to remain can be refused IS is by the habitual residence test (HRT). This usually happens because the person with indefinite leave to remain has been abroad for a period of time. The rules for the HRT and people with indefinite leave to remain are broadly the same as for British citizens (see p164). However a person with indefinite leave to remain may be more likely to be affected by the test – eg, because they have family or friends living abroad and may, therefore, travel abroad more frequently than a British citizen. In some cases people with indefinite leave to remain have been taken abroad as children and only return to the UK when they are adults. In such cases they will have great difficulty in establishing habitual residence immediately on arrival, but they may be able to show that they are habitually resident after a very short period.

From 1 May 2004, in order to satisfy the HRT the person must also have a right to reside. However, a person with indefinite leave to remain has a right of residence under UK immigration rules (see p139).[14]

Whether or not a person is habitually resident is a complex issue. This is primarily because there is no statutory definition of the term and consequently this has led to a considerable amount of caselaw on the point. For full details of the test, see Chapter 11.

2. Income-based jobseeker's allowance

For contribution-based jobseeker's allowance (JSA), see p198.

The rules for income-based JSA in respect of people with indefinite leave to remain are the same as for income support (IS) (see p194).

The rules about liability to maintain (see p195) apply to income-based JSA as they do to IS, except that the DWP cannot recover from the sponsor any JSA paid to the claimant.[15]

3. Pension credit

The rules for pension credit (PC) for people with indefinite leave to remain largely mirror those for income support. The main difference is that a person who is a sponsored immigrant where the sponsor has died is entitled to full PC rather than payment at the urgent cases rate.

4. **Housing benefit and council tax benefit**

Generally the housing benefit (HB) and council tax benefit (CTB) rules for people with indefinite leave to remain are the same as those for income support (IS) but there are some differences.

In respect of the habitual residence test (HRT), if you are being paid IS (including urgent cases rate) or income-based jobseeker's allowance (JSA) you are not a 'person from abroad' (see p132) for HB or CTB.[16] The local authority that deals with your HB or CTB claim should not make enquiries about your immigration status or habitual residence.[17] If you are not being paid IS or income-based JSA the following rules apply.

You are only entitled to HB or CTB if:
- for HB, you have accommodation in Great Britain which you normally occupy as your home (which may apply during a temporary absence – see p253)[18] or, for CTB, you are liable to pay council tax for accommodation in which you reside (see p254);[19] *and*
- you are not a sponsored immigrant (see below); *and*
- you are either habitually resident in the UK, Ireland, the Channel Islands or the Isle of Man, or treated as not being a 'person from abroad' for the purposes of the HRT (see p132).

If you do not meet these rules, you are not entitled to HB or CTB

The rules for sponsored immigrants are the same as those for IS (see p194), except that there is no urgent cases rate of payment, so if your sponsor has died you are entitled to HB or CTB at the normal rate.

The liability to maintain and recovery rules (see p195) do not apply to HB or CTB.

If you claim HB or CTB soon after you are given leave under an immigration rule requiring there to be no recourse to public funds, there is a theoretical risk to your immigration status (see p84).

If your partner or children have immigration leave on condition that they will be maintained without recourse to public funds, your HB or CTB claim may affect their immigration status (see p84).

5. **Child benefit and guardian's allowance**

The rules for child benefit and guardian's allowance are the same as those for British citizens (see p170). Sponsorship agreements do not affect entitlement to these benefits.

6. **Tax credits**

The rules for both child tax credit (CTC) and working tax credit (WTC) are the same as those for British citizens (see p168) apart from where you are the subject of a formal undertaking (see p94). Even if you are subject to an undertaking you are eligible for CTC or WTC if:[20]

- your sponsor has died; *or*
- the sponsorship was given more than five years ago.

7. **Contribution-based jobseeker's allowance and incapacity benefit**

The rules for contribution-based jobseeker's allowance and incapacity benefit are the same as those for British citizens (see p173). People with indefinite leave, even if they are sponsored immigrants, are not excluded from access.

8. **Retirement pensions and bereavement benefits**

The rules for Category A, B and D retirement pensions, bereavement payment, widowed parent's allowance and bereavement allowance are the same as those for British citizens (see p175). If you are not entitled to a full pension because part of your working life (or your spouse's or civil partner's working life) was spent abroad you may be able to use European Community rules (see Part 4) or a reciprocal agreement (Part 5) to increase your pension.

9. **Industrial injuries benefits**

The rules for disablement benefit, reduced earnings allowance, retirement allowance, constant attendance allowance and exceptionally severe disablement allowance are the same as those for British citizens (see p178). Sponsorship agreements do not affect entitlement to these benefits.

10. **Disability benefits**

The rules for attendance allowance (AA), disability living allowance (DLA), carer's allowance (CA) and non-contributory incapacity benefit are the same as those for British citizens (see p181).

DLA, AA and CA are counted as public funds for the purposes of the immigration rules.[21] However, because with indefinite leave there are no conditions to be broken, claiming these benefits should not affect your right to stay in the UK.

Sponsored immigrants remain 'persons subject to immigration control',[22] but they are exempted[23] from the usual ban on claiming these benefits.

11. Statutory sick pay, statutory maternity, paternity and adoption pay and maternity allowance

The rules for statutory sick pay, statutory maternity pay, statutory paternity pay, statutory adoption pay and maternity allowance are the same as for British citizens (see p184). Sponsorship agreements do not affect entitlement to these benefits.

12. The social fund

The social fund rules are the same as those for British citizens (see p185).

If a crisis loan is made to you and you are a sponsored immigrant under the liability to maintain rules (see p94) the DWP can recover the amount of that crisis loan from your sponsor.[24] Social fund guidance states that this will only be done if you are not entitled to income support (IS): if you are entitled to IS the loan will be recovered from you in the usual way. This might arise after you have been here five years because there is no time limit on the effect of an undertaking for the purposes of liability to maintain, although there is for the benefit entitlement rules. For recovery of crisis loans, see CPAG's *Welfare Benefits and Tax Credits Handbook*.

Notes

1 s33(2A) IA 1971

1. Income support
2 s124(1) SSCBA 1992
3 s137(2)(b) SSCBA 1992; reg 4 IS Regs
4 para 35 HC 395
5 s119(9) and (10) IAA
6 s115 IAA 1999; reg 2 and Sch Part 1
   SS(IA)CA Regs
7 Sch Part 1 para 2 SS(IA)CA Regs; reg
   70(2A) IS Regs
8 Sch Part I para 3 SS(IA)CA Regs
9 para 071896 DMG
10 *Mohammed Aziz Shah v Secretary of State*
   for Social Security [2002] EWCA CIV 285
11 s106 SSAA 1992
12 s105 SSAA 1992
13 ss78(6)(c) and 105(3) SSAA 1992

2. Income-based jobseeker's allowance
14 IA 1971
15 ss78(6)(c) and 105 SSAA 1992 as
   amended by s41(4) and Sch 2 paras 51
   and 53 JSA 1995. s106 SSAA 1992
   which gives the power to recover IS
   from a sponsor, was not amended to
   cover income-based JSA. **NB** This does
   not mean the benefit can be recovered
   from the claimant instead.

4. Housing benefit and council tax
benefit
16 Reg 10(2) HB Regs; reg 7(2) CTB regs
17 HB/CTB Circular A1/96 para 4
18 s130(1)(a) SSCBA 1992; reg 7(1) and
   (2) HB Regs; reg 7(1) and (2) HB(SPC)
   Regs
19 s131(3)(a) SSCBA 1992
20 Reg 3 TC(Imm) Regs 2003
21 para 6(b) HC 395 'public funds'
22 s115(9) IAA 1999
23 Sch Part II para 4 SS(IA)CA Regs

12. The social fund
24 s78(3)(c) and (6)(c) SSAA 1992

Chapter 16

Refugees

The benefits covered in this chapter are:
1. Income support (p202)
2. Income-based jobseeker's allowance (p204)
3. Pension credit (p204)
4. Housing benefit and council tax benefit (p205)
5. Child benefit and guardian's allowance (p205)
6. Tax credits (p205)
7. Contribution-based jobseeker's allowance and incapacity benefit (p206)
8. Retirement pensions and bereavement benefits (p206)
9. Industrial injuries benefits (p206)
10. Disability benefits (p206)
11. Statutory sick pay, statutory maternity, paternity and adoption pay and maternity allowance (p206)
12. The social fund (p207)

This chapter deals with refugees. Benefit rules often give equal treatment to refugees, and this is in line with the 1951 Refugee Convention, which obliges the UK authorities to provide refugees who are here lawfully with 'the same treatment with respect to public relief and assistance as is accorded to their nationals'.[1]

For the rules applying to the dependants of refugees who do not themselves have asylum, see the chapter relevant to their status. Dependants of a person who has been recognised in the UK as a refugee should be given indefinite leave to remain on the same terms as that person, and are exempt from the 'no recourse to public funds' requirements set out in the immigration rules (see p84).

Who is a refugee

A refugee is a person who is outside the country of her/his nationality because of a well-founded fear of persecution for reasons of race, religion, nationality, membership of a particular social group or political opinion.[2] Caselaw has established that you are a refugee from the moment that you meet this definition, not from the date that the Home Office recognised that status.[3] However, social security law and the DWP make a clear distinction between asylum seekers and refugees.

Until July 1997, when a person was recognised as a refugee s/he would be granted asylum for a four-year period, and could apply for indefinite leave at the end of that time. From July 1998 to August 2005 the Home Office practice was to grant indefinite leave at once, as soon as the decision has been made to approve a person's asylum claim. From 30 August 2005 refugees have been granted five years' leave which is subject to 'active review'. This means that refugee status may be withdrawn or revoked and leave curtailed if there has been a significant and non-temporary change in the conditions of the relevant country or the refugee's own actions justify this. If refugee status has been acquired by deception or if the refugee commits a serious criminal offence or her/his presence is not considered to be conducive to the public good refugee, status can also be withdrawn.

1. **Income support**

If you are a recognised refugee the rules for income support (IS) are generally the same as those for British citizens. Recognised refugees do not fall within the definition of 'persons subject to immigration control',[4] and are exempt from the habitual residence test. You are entitled to ordinary rate IS but only if you satisfy the general conditions of entitlement (see p164).[5] You are entitled to IS if:

- you come within one of the groups of people eligible for IS (see CPAG's *Welfare Benefits and Tax Credits Handbook* for full details of the groups that can qualify for IS);
- you are in Great Britain (GB)[6] (see p129) or temporarily absent from GB[7] (see p130);
- you satisfy the means test for IS.

Your entitlement might be affected if you are considered to be part of the same household as a person living abroad.

There is a special rule for IS entitlement,[8] allowing a refugee to receive benefit for up to nine months if:

- you are on a course of study for more than 15 hours a week in order to learn English;
- you are studying in order to improve your chances of finding work later;
- you begin the course within 12 months of arriving in the UK.

Backdating income support after recognition as a refugee

If you have been recognised by the Home Office as a refugee, you may be entitled to backdated IS for the period before you were recognised. The Government has introduced legislation to withdraw the backdating provision for refugees even though this is in breach of international law.[9] In place of the backdating will be a system of loans.

The rules differ according to when you made your claim for asylum and whether or not you were receiving any urgent cases payments.

The important date here is the date of the application for asylum, not the date of the Home Office decision to recognise you as a refugee.

Applications made after 3 April 2000

If you applied for asylum after 3 April 2000 and you are subsequently granted refugee status you will be entitled to the full, ordinary rate of IS backdated to the date on which the Secretary of State recorded your application as having been made,[10] whether to an immigration officer or in person at the Home Office. The normal rules on backdating do not apply and there is no three-month limit on arrears.[11] There is, therefore, scope for substantial backdating.

There is no difference, in these cases, between people who applied on arrival at a port or after entry to the UK. Nor is there any difference between those who are recognised straight away, and those who are first refused and only succeed after making an appeal against the Home Office decision. If you are one of a couple, and both of you have been recognised as refugees, you can choose which of you should make the claim.[12]

You are entitled to be paid the difference between the amount you would have been entitled to receive if you had been assessed as eligible for IS throughout, less any income and the value of any support you have received under the asylum support scheme.[13] For this purpose it will make no difference whether all or part of that support was provided under the interim arrangements by local authorities[14] or under the National Asylum Support Service (see Part 6).

Applied for asylum prior to 3 April 2000 and not entitled to income support

If you applied for asylum before 3 April 2000 but have been recognised as a refugee since that date you are entitled to use the transitional arrangements.[15] These entitle you to a backdated payment of IS at the urgent cases rate,[16] rather than the ordinary rate.

If you were refused IS (or did not claim) for a period between your asylum claim and the date you were recognised as a refugee by the Home Office, you can claim a backdated payment within 28 days of receiving the Home Office written notification that you have been recognised as a refugee.[17] This time limit cannot generally be extended. Your claim is treated as made on the date you applied for asylum or on the date you ceased to be entitled to benefit. Any IS already paid to you or your partner for that period is offset against any extra IS to which you are entitled.

You may have been paid contribution-based jobseeker's allowance (JSA), but still lost out because this was less than urgent cases IS. If this applies, you cannot claim urgent cases IS for any period when you received contribution-based JSA.[18] This only applies to the JSA claimant so, if your partner has been recognised as a refugee and did not receive contribution-based JSA, s/he should make the claim for backdated IS instead. Your contribution-based JSA will be treated as income, so your partner will get the difference between that and urgent cases rate. If this is not possible you should ask the DWP to make an extra-statutory payment of the difference between contribution-based JSA and urgent cases IS.

Applied for asylum prior to 3 April 2000 and in receipt of income support

If you fall within this category the backdating provisions are unlikely to help. This is because if you claimed asylum prior to 3 April 2000 the backdating provisions only allow backdating at the urgent cases rate. If you have received IS at the urgent cases rate the DWP will argue that you have not lost out and there are no arrears to be paid. It may be possible to argue that the DWP should award an *ex gratia* payment to cover the difference between the urgent cases rate and the full rate of benefit. The argument is that caselaw has established that a refugee is a refugee from the point that s/he claims asylum not from the date that s/he is recognised as a refugee by the Home Secretary.[19] Refugees are entitled to full benefit under UK social security rules and a claimant should not be penalised because of the delay by the Home Office in processing her/his asylum application.

2. Income-based jobseeker's allowance

For contribution-based jobseeker's allowance (JSA), see p206.

Refugees are not 'persons subject to immigration control' and are exempt from the habitual residence test and are, therefore, eligible for income-based JSA if they meet the general conditions of entitlement.[20] The rules are largely the same as those for British citizens (see p166). Before April 2000 the rules applying to income-based JSA were also the same as for income support, in distinguishing between asylum seekers who were eligible for benefit and those who were excluded. There are no special backdating provisions for refugees for income-based JSA.

3. Pension credit

The rules for pension credit (PC) are the same as for British citizens. There are no special rules for backdating. However, if you are recognised as a refugee it may be possible to claim backdated payments of PC for up to 12 months under the general backdating rules for PC.[21]

4. Housing benefit and council tax benefit

The rules of entitlement for housing benefit (HB) and council tax benefit (CTB) are largely the same as those for British citizens. If you are a recognised refugee you are not a 'person subject to immigration control' and you are exempt from the habitual residence test (see p132).[22]

Consequently you are eligible for both HB and CTB if you meet the general rules for those benefits.

Backdating housing benefit and council tax benefit after recognition as a refugee

If you have been recognised by the Home Office as a refugee, you may be entitled to backdated HB or CTB for the period before you were recognised. You must make a claim within 28 days of receiving notification of your refugee status.[23] The claim for backdated benefit should be made to the local authority where you are now living. That local authority then has to determine HB/CTB throughout the period in question even if you were living in a different authority's area. However, you are only eligible for a backdated payment if you were liable for rent and/or council tax.[24]

5. Child benefit and guardian's allowance

If you are a recognised refugee, the rules for child benefit and guardian's allowance are the same as those for British citizens (see p170). It is possible to get backdated payments of child benefit and guardian's allowance to the date that asylum was claimed if you are recognised as a refugee. A claim must be made within three months of receiving notification of refugee status.[25]

6. Tax credits

If you are a recognised refugee, the rules for child tax credit (CTC) and working tax credit are the same as those for British citizens (see p168).

Backdating tax credits after recognition as a refugee

If you are a recognised refugee it is possible to backdate CTC to the date that the claim for asylum was made. The claim must be made within three months of being notified that refugee status has been granted.[26]

7. Contribution-based jobseeker's allowance and incapacity benefit

If you are a recognised refugee, the rules for contribution-based jobseeker's allowance and incapacity benefit are the same as for British citizens (see p173).

8. Retirement pensions and bereavement benefits

If you are a recognised refugee, the rules for Category A, B and D retirement pensions, bereavement payment, widowed parent's allowance and bereavement allowance are the same as those for British citizens (see p175). If you are not entitled to a full pension because part of your working life (or your spouse's or civil partner's working life) was spent abroad you may be able to use European Community rules (see Part 4) or a reciprocal agreement (Part 5) to increase your pension.

9. Industrial injuries benefits

If you are a recognised refugee, the rules for disablement benefit, reduced earnings allowance, retirement allowance, constant attendance allowance and exceptionally severe disablement allowance are the same as those for British citizens (see p178).

10. Disability benefits

If you are a recognised refugee, the rules for disability living allowance, attendance allowance and carer's allowance are the same as those for British citizens (see p181).

11. Statutory sick pay, statutory maternity, paternity and adoption pay and maternity allowance

If you are a recognised refugee, the rules for statutory sick pay, statutory maternity pay, statutory paternity pay, statutory adoption pay and maternity allowance are the same as those for British citizens (see pp178 and 184).

12. **The social fund**

There is no special treatment for recognised refugees in the social fund rules. The rules are the same as those for British citizens (see p185).

Notes

1 Art 23 Convention Relating to the Status of Refugees 1951 (Geneva)
2 Art 1A(2) 1951 Refugee Convention. Similar rules apply to refugees who are stateless.
3 CIS/564/1994 paras 19-24 and 39; *Khaboka v SSHD* [1993] Imm AR 484

1. **Income support**
4 s115(9) IAA 1999
5 s124(1) SSCBA 1992
6 s124(1) SSCBA 1992
7 s137(2)(b) SSCBA 1992; reg 4 IS Regs
8 Sch 1B para 18 IS Regs
9 s12 AI(TC)A 2004
10 Reg 21ZB(3) IS Regs
11 Reg 6(4D) SS(C&P) Regs
12 Reg 4(3C) SS(C&P) Regs
13 Reg 21ZB(3) IS Regs
14 Sch 9 IAA 1999
15 Reg 12(1) SS(IA)CA Regs
16 Reg 21ZA(2) IS Regs
17 Reg 21ZA(2) and (3) IS Regs
18 s124(1)(f) SSCBA 1992
19 *Khaboka v Home Secretary* [1993] Imm AR 484 at 489

2. **Income-based jobseeker's allowance**
20 s115 IAA 1999; reg 85(4) JSA Regs

3. **Pension credit**
21 Sch 4 SS(C&P) Regs

4. **Housing benefit and council tax benefit**
22 Sch 4 paras 2 and 3 HBCTB(CP) Regs
23 Sch 4 para 1 HBCTB(CP) Regs
24 Sch 4 paras 2 and 3 HBCTB(CP) Regs
25 Reg 6 CBGA(A) Regs
26 Reg 3 TC(Imm) Regs

Chapter 17

Leave outside the rules

The benefits covered in this chapter are:
1. Income support (p210)
2. Income-based jobseeker's allowance (p210)
3. Pension credit (p211)
4. Housing benefit and council tax benefit (p211)
5. Child benefit and guardian's allowance (p211)
6. Tax credits (p211)
7. Contribution-based jobseeker's allowance and incapacity benefit (p211)
8. Retirement pensions and bereavement benefits (p212)
9. Industrial injuries benefits (p212)
10. Disability benefits (p212)
11. Statutory sick pay, statutory maternity, paternity and adoption pay and maternity allowance (p213)
12. The social fund (p213)

This chapter deals with benefits for people who have **leave outside the immigration rules**. The immigration rules generally dictate who can qualify for leave and what sort of leave a person will be given. If the Home Office decided an applicant did not qualify for leave within the normal immigration rules but nonetheless gave leave this was called 'exceptional' because it is outside the normal immigration rules. A person could be given **exceptional leave to enter or remain** (ELE or ELR). Exceptional leave to remain was until 1 April 2003 largely granted to asylum seekers where the Home Office considered that the person was deserving of protection but did not fall within the strict definition of the Refugee Convention. From 1 April 2003 the Home Office introduced two new types of leave outside the rules for asylum seekers: **humanitarian protection** (HP) and **discretionary leave** (DL).

HP is granted is generally granted for five years but it is subject to 'active review' of circumstances. HP can be revoked if you return to your country of origin or commit an offence.

DL is granted for a period of between six months and three years and such leave is also subject to active review (see Chapter 4).

For benefit purposes people with ELR, ELE, HP or DL are all treated in the same way.

If you have ELR, ELE, HP or DL you are generally put in the same position as a British citizen claiming benefit. You are not a 'person subject to immigration control' (PSIC) if you have leave outside the rules unless you have a public funds restriction attached to your stay.

You are not, however, given the same rights as those granted refugee status. Firstly, you are not able to rely on European Community law in the way that refugees may.[1] Another advantage that refugees have is that they may claim income support while studying but those with ELR, ELE, HP or DL cannot.[2] Another major difference is that if you are granted refugee status you may put in a backdated claim for certain benefits to the date that you claimed asylum. This can amount to several years' worth of benefit. However, this backdating provision only applies to refugees.[3]

If you apply for further leave (of any kind) before your leave outside the rules runs out, your leave is automatically extended until a decision is made on that application, by a process of statutory leave.[4] If the application is refused, your leave continues for as long as you have a right to appeal against that decision. For details, see Chapter 7.[5]

Normally, leave outside the rules is given with recourse to public funds but occasionally a person with this type of leave will have a public funds restriction attached to her/his stay. If your leave was given on the understanding that you would not have recourse to public funds, you can be treated as a PSIC for certain benefits and a claim for any public funds benefit could affect your immigration position.

For example, you are given leave to remain as an artist even though you entered on a student visa. Because the Home Office waived the rule that you should have an artist visa, you may be able to argue that you have exceptional leave. However, even though your leave is exceptional, it has been given on the understanding that you would maintain and accommodate yourself without recourse to public funds (unless that condition has also been waived). A benefit claim could lead to a refusal to extend leave, or your current leave could be taken away, on the ground that your leave was obtained by deception.

Showing that you have leave outside the rules

If you have limited ELR, HP or DL as a failed asylum seeker, the Home Office will have written to you stating that the Secretary of State has decided to grant leave outside the rules. This letter (see Chapter 9) should be good enough evidence of your immigration status to satisfy the benefits authorities.

If you have ELR, HP or DL as the dependant of a failed asylum seeker you may not have such a letter. The benefits authorities should accept your claim if you can show your relative's letter and show that your leave was granted in line with that of your relative.

Problems can arise when you have applied to renew or vary your immigration leave, and then need to make or renew a claim to benefits. While your papers are under consideration by the Home Office you will not have proof of your current status, but you will be protected by the arrangements for statutory leave, which means that the conditions of your permission to stay continue, until the Home Office makes a new decision. You should be able to satisfy the benefits authorities of this by producing evidence of your most recent grant of leave and of the date you applied for further leave.

The benefits authorities are often unclear about leave outside the rules. They can confuse it with 'indefinite leave to remain'. This is sometimes made worse by taking advice from Home Office staff who are rarely aware of all the different Home Office policies and practices about giving leave.

1. **Income support**

Generally people with leave outside the rules are not excluded from income support (IS)[6] and the rules of entitlement are broadly the same as for British citizens (see p164). You are not a 'person subject to immigration control' unless you have a public funds restriction attached to your stay.[7] In order to be eligible for IS you must meet the general conditions for IS. This means that you must come within one of the categories that are able to claim IS (eg, as a lone parent) and you must meet the income and capital rules. See CPAG's *Welfare Benefits and Tax Credits Handbook* for full details of the IS rules.

If you are an asylum seeker who is eligible for the urgent cases rate of IS (see p160) and you are subsequently granted humanitarian protection or discretionary leave, you are no longer eligible for urgent cases payments and must meet the general conditions for entitlement to benefit. Unless you come within one of the groups eligible for IS you must sign on and claim income-based jobseeker's allowance rather than IS.

If you have leave outside the rules, you are treated as being exempt from the habitual residence and right to reside tests.[8]

2. **Income-based jobseeker's allowance**

For contribution-based jobseeker's allowance (JSA), see p166.

Income-based JSA rules about who is a 'person subject to immigration control' are the same as those for income support (IS) (see above).[9] If you have leave outside the rules you are not excluded from benefit as long as you meet the general conditions of entitlement, unless you have a public funds restriction attached to your stay. The test for habitual residence[10] is also applied in the same way as for IS.

3. Pension credit

The rules for pension credit are the same as those for British citizens. You are not a 'person subject to immigration control' and you are not excluded from benefit as long as you meet the general conditions of entitlement. You are also not a person from abroad for the purposes of the habitual residence or right to reside tests.

4. Housing benefit and council tax benefit

If you have leave outside the rules you are generally not excluded from benefit as long as you meet the general conditions of entitlement. You are not a 'person subject to immigration control' for housing benefit (HB) or council tax benefit (CTB) unless you have a public funds restriction attached to your stay, and people with exceptional leave are specifically exempt from the habitual residence test.

If you are in receipt of income support or income-based jobseeker's allowance the local authority dealing with your HB or CTB claim should not make enquiries about your immigration status or habitual residence.[11]

5. Child benefit and guardian's allowance

The rules for child benefit and guardian's allowance are broadly the same as those for British citizens (see p170). A person with leave outside the rules has a right of residence under UK immigration rules so therefore should not be excluded from child benefit under the right to reside test (see p137).

6. Tax credits

The rules for child tax credit (CTC) and working tax credit are similar to those for British citizens (see p168). A person with leave outside the rules has a right to reside under UK immigration rules and therefore should not be refused CTC under the right to reside test.

7. Contribution-based jobseeker's allowance and incapacity benefit

The rules for contribution-based jobseeker's allowance (JSA) and incapacity benefit are the same as those for British citizens (see p173). There are no immigration conditions for these benefits. The habitual residence rules only apply to income-based JSA.[12]

8. **Retirement pensions and bereavement benefits**

The rules for Category A, B and D retirement pensions, bereavement payment, widowed parent's allowance and bereavement allowance are the same as those for British citizens (see p175). If you are not entitled to a full pension because part of your working life was spent abroad you may be able to rely on European Community (EC) law (see Part 4) or a reciprocal agreement (see Chapter 28) to increase your pension. If you have leave outside the rules you cannot rely on EC law to aggregate periods of insurance unless your spouse or civil partner is a European Economic Area national.

9. **Industrial injuries benefits**

The rules for disablement benefit, reduced earnings allowance, retirement allowance, constant attendance allowance and exceptionally severe disablement allowance are the same as those for British citizens (see p178). These benefits do not have any immigration tests.

10. **Disability benefits**

The rules for disability living allowance (DLA), attendance allowance (AA), carer's allowance (CA) and severe disablement allowance are broadly the same as those for British citizens (see p181).

For how long is benefit awarded

Where a medical condition is permanent, awards of DLA and AA are often made for life. DWP guidance suggests that people with limited leave outside the rules should not get life awards.

When you have been granted humanitarian protection or discretionary leave under the policy for asylum seekers whose applications are rejected, or under the European Convention on Human Rights, you become eligible to apply for benefit. DWP guidance states that any award of DLA, AA or CA should be limited to the date your current immigration leave is due to run out.[13] If your award is limited in this manner, you will need to claim that benefit again at the end of the award, and again show that you meet all the benefit conditions, including those about disability. This places you in a worse position than a British citizen who would have been given an indefinite award (or one longer than your period of leave), especially since her/his benefit can only be withdrawn if the DWP shows that the disability conditions are no longer satisfied.

11. Statutory sick pay, statutory maternity, paternity and adoption pay and maternity allowance

The rules for statutory sick pay, statutory maternity, paternity and adoption pay and maternity allowance are the same as for British citizens (see p184). There are no immigration conditions to these benefits and they are not public funds.

12. The social fund

There is no special treatment for people with leave outside the rules in the social fund rules. The rules are the same as those for British citizens (see p185). You are not a 'person subject to immigration control' (see p155) unless you have a public funds restriction attached to your stay, in which case you are not eligible for benefit.

Notes

1 Refugees and stateless persons can rely on EC Reg 1408/71 in order to aggregate contributions, satisfy residence requirements, export certain benefits and override discriminatory provisions within the benefit rules. However this only applies to refugees and stateless persons who have moved within the EEA.
2 Sch 1B para 18 IS Regs
3 Such claims must be made within 28 days of notification of refugee status: reg 21ZB IS Regs
4 s3C IA 1971 as amended in 2000 by s3 IAA 1999
5 s115(9)(d) and Sch 4 para 17 IAA 1999

1. **Income support**
   6 s115(9) IAA 1999
   7 s115(9)(b) IAA 1999
   8 Reg 21(3)(c) IS Regs 'person from abroad'

2. **Income-based JSA**
   9 s115(9) IAA 1999
   10 Reg 85(4)(c) JSA Regs 'person from abroad'

3. **HB and CTB**
   11 HB/CTB Circular A1/96 para 4

7. **Contribution-based JSA and incapacity benefit**
12 JSA Regs: the amount of contribution-based JSA is set by reg 79 and not reg 83 which refers to the 'persons from abroad' rule in reg 85(4).

10. **Disability benefits**
13 Memo AOG Vol 2/40 para 3

Chapter 18

Limited leave to remain, no leave to remain and asylum seekers

This chapter covers the rights of people who have limited leave or no leave to remain in the UK under the immigration rules or who are asylum seekers. The benefits covered in this chapter are:

1. Income support (p221)
2. Income-based jobseeker's allowance (p227)
3. Pension credit (p231)
4. Housing benefit and council tax benefit (p231)
5. Child benefit and guardian's allowance (p232)
6. Tax credits (p234)
7. Contribution based jobseeker's allowance and incapacity benefit (p236)
8. Retirement pensions and bereavement benefits (p237)
9. Industrial injuries benefits (p237)
10. Disability benefits (p238)
11. Statutory sick pay, statutory maternity, paternity and adoption pay and maternity allowance (p239)
12. The social fund (p239)

What is limited leave

In general, if you have limited leave, you are only entitled to benefit if you have no public funds condition attached to your leave or you are able to rely on European Community law. If you have limited leave and a public funds restriction attached, you are excluded from entitlement to most means-tested and non-contributory benefits. Rules differ according to the benefit involved.

You have limited leave to remain if you are in the UK and your right to stay here is subject to a time limit:

- as a condition placed on your visa or entry clearance;
- by an immigration officer on arrival in the UK; *or*
- by the Home Office if your leave to remain has been varied or extended.

Your limited leave may be shown by an entry clearance sticker, by a stamp in your passport or by a letter issued by the Home Office (see Chapter 9). In most cases, a person with limited leave is also subject to a condition or requirement that s/he does not have recourse to public funds. If you have limited leave which is not subject to a public funds condition you are not excluded from any benefits provided you satisfy the normal rules of entitlement. If the benefit is dependent on contributions or being in work you must not be debarred from taking employment as a condition of stay.

Temporary admission or temporary release do *not* count as leave to remain. Both are given by way of a standard immigration service form indicating that the holder remains liable to detention. If you are in the UK because you have temporary admission or temporary release you do not have limited leave to remain and the provisions set out in this chapter do not apply to you.

In this chapter, limited leave includes statutory leave for the purpose of an application to the Home Office.[1] Even if your original leave has expired, you still have limited leave to remain if you applied for an extension of leave before or on the date it was due to expire. This leave continues until the Home Office grants your application, or, if it is refused, until the time allowed for bringing an appeal against that decision has expired. If the application is granted and you are given further leave, the new leave, and any conditions attached to it, is effective from the date it is given. Any conditions of your original leave continue to apply as long as you have statutory leave,[2] since this period is treated simply as an automatic extension of your original period of leave.

If your application for an extension was made after the date your leave expired, then you are an overstayer and do not have leave to remain. See p218 for details of the provisions that apply.

If the time limit on your leave to remain has been removed in writing, you have indefinite leave to remain (see Chapter 15). Any other condition on your permission to be here also ends when the time limit ceases. The only restrictions on your right to benefit concern sponsorship undertakings (see p94) and habitual residence (see p132).

If you are a European Union (EU) or European Economic Area (EEA) national you are very unlikely to have limited leave to remain. This is because EU or EEA nationals arriving in the UK normally have a direct right to enter the UK and do not need leave to enter or remain,[3] so immigration officers do not give EU or EEA nationals leave to enter.[4] Since June 2002 the rights of free movement have been extended to Swiss nationals

Some EEA nationals have been issued with residence permits, but these merely record a right they already have, and do not amount to a grant of permission by the Home Office. EEA nationals and members of their families can apply for and may be granted indefinite leave to remain under the immigration rules,[5] but they are not required to do so. For the rules concerning EU and EEA nationals, see Part 4.

Your leave to enter or remain does not end when you leave the UK, unless it was granted for a period of six months or less. This is the result of a change in the law in 2000.[6] Any leave to enter or remain in the UK for longer than six months, whether given abroad by an entry clearance officer, or by an immigration officer on arrival in the UK, or at the Home Office as an extension or variation of stay by the Secretary of State, continues in force while you are abroad.[7] This includes indefinite leave to remain (see Chapter 15). So long as you return to the UK before the expiry of that period of leave you do not require fresh leave.

Who does not have leave to remain

Not all of those who are here without leave are in the country illegally; many are here with the express permission of the immigration authorities. You may be in the UK without leave to remain if you:

- have leave to remain until a deportation order is made (see p220);
- have been given temporary admission by an immigration officer (see below);
- have been granted bail, either by a chief immigration officer or by the Asylum and Immigration Tribunal;
- had permission to be in the UK, but have remained here in breach of the time limit (overstayer – see p218);
- made an unsuccessful application for asylum, and have remained in the UK after the case was completed;
- have lost your immigration appeal, but remain in the UK while you try for a judicial review or while the Home Office considers representations about your case;
- have entered the UK without obtaining leave to enter (see p220).

Temporary admission

If temporary admission has been given, you have permission to be in the UK outside the immigration rules. However, although you have permission to be here you do not have any type of leave to remain. Temporary admission is most commonly given to asylum seekers who are awaiting an asylum application decision. If you apply for asylum at the port of entry or enter illegally and then ask for asylum you can be detained or given temporary admission.

If you have already been refused entry you are only likely to be admitted to the UK, whether on temporary admission or on bail, if your application was made under the 1951 Refugee Convention or the European Convention on Human Rights (see p61).

You also have a right to remain here for your hearing against refusal of entry if you arrived with a valid visa (or other entry clearance), or if you were returning after a short absence and still have leave to remain. In these circumstances you are considered to be in the same position as someone who has remained here and applied to vary the terms of leave to remain. An immigration officer will have suspended your leave to enter or to remain when the decision to refuse you entry was made, but your permission is still effective for the purpose of your appeal. The Immigration Acts give you the right to remain on the conditions set out in your leave to remain or on the entry clearance sticker in your passport.

Someone with temporary admission has never had leave to enter the UK. However, as long as you comply with the terms of your temporary admission or bail (see below) you are in the UK legally. You are not an overstayer, nor are you subject to a deportation order, nor are you an illegal entrant.

If you are given leave, your immigration status changes and you should see the chapter relevant to your status. If you are refused leave, the rules covered by this chapter continue to apply to you until *either*:

- you are given leave to enter by an immigration officer; *or*
- you leave the UK.

If an immigration officer decides that you are an illegal entrant, then different rules apply (see below).

If you break the terms of your temporary admission or bail, or escape from immigration detention, an immigration officer may decide that you are an 'absconder', and that you should be treated as an illegal entrant. If this happens, different rules apply (see p220).

If you are not given temporary admission, but the Home Office is investigating whether you are a British citizen or have the right of abode, it may inform the DWP of this situation, although this is unlikely. If the DWP is aware that you are being investigated, you may be treated as a 'person subject to immigration control' (PSIC – see p155). If this happens, you can argue that you are not restricted because you are free from immigration control, as a person with the right of abode who does not require leave.

Overstayers

You are an overstayer if you had limited leave to enter or remain in the UK, but have remained in the UK beyond the date that leave expired, without applying for or being granted any other permission.

You become an overstayer on the day after your leave runs out. However, if you applied for leave to remain before your leave runs out, you may still have limited leave to remain, even if there is no stamp in your passport. This is a special form of statutory leave.

Overstayers can be removed from the UK without the need for deportation proceedings, but you are able to appeal against that decision under the 1951 Refugee Convention or the Human Rights Act 1998 before you are removed. The only exception to this rule might arise where you already had an opportunity to appeal under these provisions and cannot show any relevant change of circumstances in the meantime.[8] Before a decision is made on whether to order removal, you can be detained by the police. This is usually only for long enough for an immigration officer to conduct an interview, after which the officer will decide whether to temporarily release or detain you.

Overstaying your leave is a criminal offence,[9] although prosecutions are rare.

Former asylum seekers

If you have had an application for asylum in the UK refused, you generally have a right of appeal against that decision while you remain in the country. Unless you win your appeal, and are granted asylum, that right will eventually run out. If you did not keep in touch with the immigration authorities at the time of the decision you might have lost the right to appeal, or, if you failed to turn up for the hearing, your case may have been rejected.

You have a right to remain as long as the appeal process continues. If your appeal is heard and dismissed, that right ends. The point at which your right of appeal and the right it gives you to stay here ends, depends on the circumstances of your case:

- if the appeal was 'certified', the immigration laws give you a right to appeal once to an adjudicator;
- if it was not, you may be able to appeal again to the Asylum and Immigration Tribunal (AIT);
- if you were not given permission to appeal to the AIT, you only have the right to bring a further challenge by judicial review in the High Court;
- if you had a full hearing to the AIT, you can apply for permission to appeal against its decision to the Court of Appeal.

Staying on here does not always mean that you have made your stay illegal because you may not have committed any offence under the immigration laws, but it will always mean that you are liable to be detained.

Former asylum seekers in this situation are not be entitled to benefits.

Applications to remain outside of the immigration rules

Some people may be present in the UK while they try to persuade the Home Office to allow them to stay, even though they do not have any rights to stay under the immigration rules and have no right of appeal against a decision by the Home Office. This may happen because you have never had a right of appeal in this country; if you had no claim to asylum; if you never made an application to stay longer; or – in some circumstances – if you were unable to meet one of the special requirements of the immigration rules because of your age or nationality or because you did not have the correct papers. In the last case your only option to stay on is outside the appeals system. Similarly, if you had a right of appeal under the Immigration Acts but it has now run out, any further application to stay has to be made outside the framework of the immigration rules and the appeals system.

This can take two forms. You may make written representations to stay, often on compassionate grounds, either directly to the Home Office, or perhaps through a Member of Parliament. But if a decision has been taken that you should leave, and you no longer have a right of appeal, your only option is to challenge that decision by an application for judicial review. This does not count as an appeal, since it is not provided for under the immigration laws but under general rules of public or administrative law. In either of these cases you are very unlikely to be here unlawfully, in the sense that you are not committing any offence under immigration law while you wait for the result of your application, even if you have previously overstayed or entered the UK illegally.

Deportation order made while in UK with leave

A deportation order is a way of removing you from the UK and prohibiting your re-entry, if you have leave to remain. You are most likely to be deported if you commit a criminal offence and it is considered sufficiently serious. People who have the right of abode and Commonwealth citizens who have been settled here since before 1973 cannot be deported. Anyone else can, but the greater your ties to this country and the less serious the offence, the less likely you are to be deported.

A deportation order has the effect of ending your leave from the date it is signed. If you have leave to remain, a decision to make a deportation order (this is different from the deportation order itself) does not affect your benefit entitlement. For details about deportation orders and when they can be made, see Chapter 6.

If you do not appeal the decision to deport or you lose your appeal and a deportation order is made, a restriction order may be made. You cannot be given temporary admission or bail.

Once a deportation order is signed, removal directions (see p71) are usually made straight away or as soon as your whereabouts are known to the Home Office. If you are not going to be removed immediately, the Home Office will normally notify you in writing that your removal has been deferred.

Illegal entrants

You are only an illegal entrant for benefit purposes if an immigration officer has notified you in writing that you are an illegal entrant.[10]

You remain an illegal entrant until you are given leave to enter or remain in the UK, or you are removed. If you lose benefit because of an immigration officer's decision that you are an illegal entrant and the High Court or Court of Appeal overrules that decision,[11] you may be able to argue that the benefit decision was wrong because it relied on an invalid decision. Seek expert advice if this applies you.

Until an immigration officer decides that you are an illegal entrant, you are not one for benefit purposes, even if you obviously entered the UK illegally. Until

an immigration officer decides that you are an illegal entrant, the following rules apply:
- *either* you were given leave to enter the UK – eg, as a visitor; *or*
- you entered the UK without leave. This may be because:
  - you were not seen by an immigration officer – eg, you were hidden in a lorry; *or*
  - you presented a travel document which the immigration officer did not stamp – eg, a passport issued to a British citizen or EU or EEA national.

If you were given leave, that leave counts under the benefit rules until it runs out, at which point, if you are still here and have not applied for an extension of stay, you become an 'overstayer' (see p218). If that leave carried a condition that you should not have 'recourse to public funds' (see p84) you are a 'person subject to immigration control' (PSIC – see p155),[12] but if it does not, you are not. If you have not been given leave to enter by an immigration officer you are a PSIC if the law required you to have leave.[13] Any leave to enter given to you ends on the date of a decision by an immigration officer that you are an illegal entrant.[14]

1. **Income support**

Most people with limited leave, no leave or asylum seekers are not entitled to income support (IS) because of the rules concerning 'persons subject to immigration control' (PSIC).

A 'person subject to immigration control'

You are a PSIC if:[15]
- you need leave to be in the UK but have not been given it (see Chapters 3 and 4); *or*
- your leave was given under an immigration rule which requires no recourse to public funds (see p84); *or*
- you are a sponsored immigrant (see p94); *or*
- you only have leave to remain in the UK because you are awaiting an appeal under the immigration rules (see p81).

This definition would apply to a person with limited leave and a public funds restriction as well as to most people who do not have leave to remain and asylum seekers. However, some people who fall within one of these categories can qualify for benefit. There are two types of IS that you may be entitled to:
- **ordinary rate IS**, if you satisfy the general conditions for entitlement and are within one of the groups who can claim IS such as a lone parent, pensioner or because of incapacity for work; *or*

• **urgent cases IS**, paid at a lower rate than ordinary IS. The rules on income and capital are different to ordinary rate IS.

In order to qualify you must fall within one of the groups below that are exempt from the definition of PSIC as well as satisfying the following general conditions:
• being in Great Britain (GB) or only temporarily absent from GB;
• satisfying, or exempt from, the habitual residence test (see p132);
• satisfying all the other general conditions of entitlement to IS.

Your entitlement might also be affected if you are considered to be part of the same household as a person living abroad.

Qualifying for income support with limited leave

• You are from a country that has ratified the European Social Charter of 1961 or the European Convention on Social and Medical Assistance and are lawfully present. (This applies to all European Economic Area (EEA) countries, Croatia, Macedonia and Turkey.) IS is paid at the ordinary rate. For details on the meaning of 'lawful presence', see p129.
• You have been given limited leave as a sponsored immigrant (see p94) and your sponsor has died. Payment is at the urgent cases rate.
• You are a student or other person whose funding from abroad is temporarily interrupted and there is a reasonable expectation that your funds will be resumed. Payment is at the urgent cases rate and is for a maximum for 42 days (whether in one or more spells) within a period of leave.
• You are an asylum seeker with a right to benefit under the transitional rules (see below). Payment is at the urgent cases rate.
• You are lawfully employed and are a national (or a family member of a national) of Algeria, Morocco, Tunisia or Turkey. This is because there are European Community (EC) agreements with these countries, which provide for equal treatment within social security. Benefit is paid at the ordinary rate (see p221).[16]

Even if you are not a PSIC you do not qualify for IS if you fail the habitual residence or right to reside tests (HRT) (see Chapter 11).

Transitional protection rules for asylum seekers

The benefit rules were changed in 1996 and again in 2000 to largely exclude asylum seekers from access to benefits. However, some asylum seekers were entitled to transitional protection. The numbers to whom this applies are now dwindling but there may still be a small group to whom it applies.[17] You remain entitled to benefit from 3 April 2000 if you were an asylum seeker and:
• you applied for asylum on arrival on any date up to and including 2 April 2000;
  or

- you were in receipt of benefits before the changes to the benefit rules in 1996; *or*
- you are a national of one of the 'upheaval countries' (Sierra Leone and the Democratic Republic of Congo) who applied for asylum in the UK within three months of the declaration.

No recourse to public funds

You are a PSIC for IS purposes if your leave was given under an immigration rule requiring you not to have recourse to public funds (see below) and none of the exceptions to that rule apply (see p84).[18]

When deciding whether your permission counts as leave subject to a condition that you do not have recourse to public funds, it is the type of leave that was given that matters, not what the Home Office or the DWP says about the status later.

Limited leave given to adults normally requires there to be no recourse to public funds. The most important exception is family members of a recognised refugee who are given leave in line with that person, and are not made subject to a 'no recourse' condition. This may not apply if the refugee had already had indefinite leave for a long period by the time the family member is granted leave, as the Home Office may then treat the application as one made under the immigration rules. The family member could then be treated in the same way as a person applying to join a UK resident, without the advantages usually given to refugees. If you are applying for family reunion and you believe you should qualify as a refugee, seek advice about your family's status in the UK.

For full details of exceptions, see p84. If your permission to be in the UK comes within one of the exceptions, your limited leave does not make you a PSIC. This remains the case if you apply for an extension before this leave runs out. However, you still need to pass the HRT (see p132).

Even if you are not a PSIC, claiming IS may still affect your immigration status (see p154). In particular, if the leave stamp states that you must not have recourse to public funds you will break the terms of your leave and commit a criminal offence even if that condition ought not to have been attached to your category of permission.[19] If this condition has been attached, you may want to ask the Home Office to remove it, but you should seek expert advice before making such a request.

Sponsored immigrants

Most of the people who have this status have indefinite leave to remain (see Chapter 15), but some young people between the ages of 16 and 18, and most of the small number of people admitted under the immigration rules as 'other relatives' (that is, to join a relative other than a spouse, parent or child), may be admitted with limited leave and are only permitted to join parents or other relatives if their sponsors have signed undertakings.

Waiting for an immigration appeal

When you have been given leave to enter or remain in the UK and then you apply in time to vary or extend that stay there is, in most cases, a right of appeal against refusal of that application. If you lodge an appeal you have the right to remain in the UK to attend the hearing of that appeal. This also applies if you lodge an appeal against a refusal of leave to enter the UK at a time when you held a valid visa or still had a period of leave to remain. These provisions of immigration law were introduced during 2000. In these cases your right to stay is a form of statutory leave,[20] but it is not like the statutory leave you have while you are waiting for the Home Office to make a decision on an application made while you have leave to remain. While you wait for the Home Office to decide, any conditions attached to your previous leave, apart from the time limit, continue to apply. This means that if your leave was not subject to a 'no recourse to public funds condition', so that you were able to claim certain benefits, you remain entitled while you wait for a decision.

While you wait for an appeal, on the other hand, that entitlement does not apply, because the Home Office has taken a decision to end your leave. You still have leave to be here as long as the appeal is treated as pending, but no entitlement[21] to IS or any of the restricted benefits (see p84), unless you can show that one of the exceptions set out in the regulations[22] applies. The regulations specifically exclude from entitlement asylum seekers with transitional protection because transitional protection ends when the Home Office decides to refuse you asylum, and is not extended to cover an appeal.[23]

Temporary disruption of funds

If you are a PSIC with limited leave subject to a recourse to public funds condition, you are entitled to urgent cases IS if:[24]

- you were expecting to be sent money from abroad but those remittances have been temporarily disrupted; *and*
- there is a reasonable expectation that money will be sent in the future; *and*
- since you were last given leave to remain in the UK you have supported yourself without receiving public funds (see p84) except where those public funds were paid because of this rule.

The maximum period during which IS can be paid under this rule is 42 days in any one period of leave.[25] This does not have to be a continuous claim, but could, for example, be for seven separate weeks. The exact effect of the wording of this rule is uncertain. Most of the people who can make use of it are in the UK as overseas students. Before the changes were introduced in 2000 they would generally be given leave for one year at a time, and then have to apply for extensions. A period of leave would run from the last grant of leave to remain (or leave to enter if this was your first period since entering the UK), and end with the grant of the next period of leave to remain. Leave would also end when you travelled out of the common travel area (CTA – see p132). Students are now generally given a period of leave to cover the whole of their intended studies, and any leave to enter or remain of more than six months duration does not end when travelling out of the CTA.

The benefit rule still refers to 'any one period . . . including any period as extended'. But leave is not generally now 'extended', because students and others coming for a period of time are usually given a single period of leave, and it continues throughout that time, without the need to get further periods of leave on return to the UK. And if as a student you have only one period of leave to cover the whole of your stay, it is unclear how you can, in most cases, have supported yourself during one period of leave in order to claim an urgent cases payment in another period. Still, the rule is there, and seems intended to cover situations similar to those in which it applied before 2000.

Examples of the kinds of situations when this rule may apply are:

- a disruption to the banking system in your home country; *or*
- a collapse in exchange rates which means that your sponsor abroad cannot immediately buy hard currency; *or*
- if your sponsor abroad has unexpected financial difficulties.

You can only use this rule if you were expecting to receive money from abroad, so if your only sponsor or potential sponsor is in the UK you cannot use this rule if her/his support stops. However, the rule does not say that the money which you expect to receive in the future also has to be from abroad, so you could qualify because a person in the UK will give you financial support in the future.

Home Office policy is that reliance on public funds for a short period through no fault of the person concerned will not be used to refuse further leave.[26] However, even a claim for IS for a short period may mean that the Home Office will look much more closely at any application for an extension of leave and, in particular, your ability to support yourself.

Habitual residence test

To claim IS you must satisfy the habitual residence test (HRT – see p132).[27] This is because you are deemed by the DWP to be a 'person from abroad' irrespective of your nationality or immigration status. This applies even if your leave to remain is not subject to a 'no recourse to public funds' condition or a sponsorship undertaking. It is not necessary to be here for an indefinite period in order to be habitually resident.

The HRT only applies to the IS claimant[28] and not to a partner or child(ren) for whom IS is being claimed. If you might fail the HRT but your partner is more likely to pass, s/he could claim instead, although there may be disadvantages to this (see CPAG's *Welfare Benefits and Tax Credits Handbook*).

Right to reside test

To claim IS you must have a right to reside (see p137). This is a complex test as you may have a right to reside as a result of your nationality, under UK immigration rules or under EC law. If you do not have a right to reside you are treated as failing the HRT for IS and thus defined as a person from abroad for social security purposes (see p154).

Foreign spouses and civil partners

The question of whether it is wise for a person to claim benefit often arises in the context of those who have been joined from abroad by a foreign spouse or civil partner. The spouse or civil partner is allowed to work but has limited leave with a public funds condition attached to her/his stay.

In these circumstances the person with limited leave is generally not entitled to claim benefits because s/he is a PSIC but the partner who s/he has joined can claim benefit. IS, income-based JSA and PC allow the amount of benefit to be reduced so that payment is made only for the person who is free from immigration control or settled.[29] Other benefits, however, do not make this provision. The problem, therefore, is that the partner with limited leave could have recourse to public funds *indirectly*. If as a result of making that claim the partner who is eligible for benefit receives more benefit than s/he would have done if the PSIC had not been present in the household then there is 'additional recourse to public funds' (see p89 for more details).

If the spouse from abroad is joining a person who is an EEA national or a British citizen who is able to rely on EC rights these rules may not apply (see Part 4 on the rights of EEA nationals).

Foreign fiancé(e)s

The same problems apply as for spouses (see above). See p93 for details about immigration rules and foreign fiancé(e)s.

Spouse/civil partner abroad

The same rules apply as for British citizens if you have been living with your spouse or civil partner abroad before you came to the UK (see p164).

Other people in your family with a different status

If your partner has a more favourable immigration status s/he should claim instead. Check the chapter that deals with that person's status. If you count as a PSIC for IS, and do not come under any of the exemptions, your partner is unable to include you in her/his applicable amount unless s/he is getting IS paid at the urgent cases rate (see p160).

Chapter 18 : Limited leave to remain, no leave to remain and asylum seekers
2. Income-based jobseeker's allowance

18

Effect of claiming public funds on immigration status

IS is treated as public funds under the immigration rules.[30] If you have claimed asylum, then claiming any public funds is very unlikely to affect your immigration position. In other situations, whether or not you are a PSIC for IS purposes, claiming public funds may mean that:

- the Home Office may refuse you further leave to remain, if that leave would require 'no recourse to public funds'. Even though short periods of reliance on public funds should not lead to refusal of further leave, it may affect the Home Office's attitude towards you. For example, if you claim public funds during your one year's leave as the spouse of a person settled in the UK, at the end of that year you may be given a further year's leave before indefinite leave is considered, instead of immediate indefinite leave;
- if your leave was given after 1 November 1996 and the stamp states that you must not have recourse to public funds, you break the terms of your leave and commit a criminal offence by claiming IS. Any action is very unlikely, especially if your claim is covered by the Home Office policy.[31]

Because of these problems, you should weigh up the risks and advantages of claiming.

If you are one of a couple and your partner does not have limited leave s/he may claim benefit and be paid at the single person rate. For IS no payment can be made for you if you are a PSIC (unless you come under one of the exemptions) and therefore there is no recourse to public funds if your partner claims. However, it may not be wise for that person to claim because it could demonstrate that s/he could not maintain you, and your immigration position could be affected. To claim benefit implies that you cannot maintain yourself, let alone your partner. This could affect the application for indefinite leave made by a foreign spouse, as it would be clear that contrary to the claimant's statement to the Home Office s/he could not maintain her/him.

---

2. **Income-based jobseeker's allowance**

For the rules concerning contribution-based jobseeker's allowance (JSA), see p236.

It is difficult for people with limited leave or no leave to remain to meet the normal rules for income-based JSA, so you should always check to see if you may be entitled to income support (IS) instead (see p221).

Most asylum seekers are not allowed to work and therefore would also have difficulty meting the general rules of entitlement.

Income-based JSA counts as public funds under the immigration rules.[32] The possible effects of claiming income-based JSA on your immigration position are the same as those for IS (see p221).

18

Chapter 18 : Limited leave to remain, no leave to remain and asylum seekers
2. Income-based jobseeker's allowance

The rules about who is a 'person subject to immigration control' (PSIC) or 'person from abroad' are the same as for IS (see p221).[33] If you are a PSIC you are not entitled to income-based JSA unless you can fit within one of the exemptions of the PSIC definitions.

Qualifying for income-based jobseeker's allowance with limited leave

- You are an asylum seeker with transitional protection (see p222). Payment is at the urgent cases rate. It is easier to claim IS instead as there is no requirement to satisfy the labour market conditions for getting the urgent cases payment of IS.
- You are a national of a country that has ratified the 1961 European Social Charter or the European Convention on Social and Medical Assistance and you are lawfully present. See p129 for details of lawful presence. (This applies to all European Economic Area countries including Swiss nationals, Croatia, Macedonia and Turkey.) IS is paid at the ordinary rate.
- You have been sponsored (see p94) but your sponsor has died. The urgent cases rate is payable.
- Your funding is temporarily disrupted and there is a reasonable expectation that it will be reinstated. Benefit is paid at the urgent cases rate. In general it is easier to claim IS rather than income-based JSA as there is no condition to be available for work in order to qualify for an urgent cases payment of IS. See temporary disruption of funds above.
- You are lawfully employed and are a national (or a family member of a national) of Algeria, Morocco, Tunisia or Turkey. This is because the European Community (EC) has agreements with these countries, which provide for equal treatment within social security. These rights have not been incorporated into UK law for income-based JSA and therefore the DWP may not accept that there is entitlement. However, the agreements apply to benefits that provide for 'unemployment' and there is developing caselaw that income-based JSA is a benefit for 'unemployment' in EC terms (see p381 for further details of these association agreements).[34]

If you are not a PSIC, your entitlement to income-based JSA depends on whether or not your leave has a prohibition or restriction on employment (an employment condition).

Leave with an employment condition

Your limited leave may have a prohibition or restriction on working. This may have been superseded by the Home Office.

If you have a prohibition or restriction on working which has not been superseded, you cannot meet the usual JSA condition that you are immediately able to work as an employed earner.[35] This means that you can only be entitled to JSA if:

- you are treated as available for work. This is very unlikely to be useful for people with an employment condition; *or*
- you are entitled to hardship payments (see p230). This is different from urgent cases rate.

Who has leave with an employment condition

Conditions of your immigration leave can only be imposed in writing, except in specified circumstances.[36] If you do not have a written employment condition as part of your current leave (or your last leave, if the permission you have now is statutory leave while you wait for a Home Office decision on whether to grant an extension, then there is no employment condition on your stay. This applies even if an employment condition is normally imposed with the type of leave that you have. The only exceptions to these rules are if:

- you were given an unreadable leave stamp by an immigration officer. If this applies, you are treated as having been given leave to enter for six months with a prohibition on taking employment (see below);[37] *or*
- you entered the UK as a member of a tour group or other party, and the terms of your entry were given in writing to the person leading the group;[38] *or*
- you entered the UK from another part of the common travel area (see p132) without being given written leave. If this applies, you may be treated as having been given limited leave to enter for a limited period with a prohibition on taking employment.[39]

There are two types of employment condition:

- prohibition – the stamp reads 'employment prohibited' or 'condition that holder does not enter employment paid or unpaid'. This is usually imposed on visitors (including visitors in transit) and prospective students (see Chapter 9); *and*
- restriction – the stamp reads 'condition that holder does not enter or change employment paid or unpaid without the consent of the Secretary of State for Employment'. There are two groups affected:
  - people who have a work permit or permit for training and work experience who have permission to work in the job referred to in the permit; *and*
  - students, au pairs, seasonal workers, working holidaymakers and others (see Chapter 9). Seasonal workers are restricted to a particular short-term job; the others are generally treated as having been given the necessary consent without having to apply for permission to take a particular job.

A person who is here without a restriction on taking employment may qualify for income-based JSA. However, most people who are in the UK with limited leave and who are allowed to work are subject to a public funds condition.

18

Chapter 18 : Limited leave to remain, no leave to remain and asylum seekers
2. Income-based jobseeker's allowance

Note that a hardship payment is a payment of income-based JSA. See CPAG's *Welfare Benefits and Tax Credits Handbook* for who can get one and in what circumstances.

Leave with no employment condition

The most important types of leave with no condition on employment are:
- spouse/civil partner of a person settled in the UK;
- spouse/civil partner of a person with limited leave (eg, of a student, if the period of study is long enough, or of a work permit holder);
- private servant in a diplomatic household; *and*
- Commonwealth citizen with UK ancestry.

For full details of the types of leave with no conditions on employment, see p49.

If you are not a PSIC (see p155) and your leave has no condition on employment, you are entitled to income-based JSA as long as you meet the normal rules for entitlement. The most important of these are that you:[40]
- are not in full-time employment (ie, not working 16 hours or more a week);
- are available for and actively seeking employment; *and*
- have made a jobseeker's agreement.

For full details of these and the other rules, see CPAG's *Welfare Benefits and Tax Credits Handbook*.

Claiming JSA may break the conditions of your immigration leave and have other effects on your immigration status (see p85).

Hardship payments

Hardship payments of JSA are different from urgent cases income-based JSA. If you are entitled to a hardship payment, you do not have to be available for and actively seeking work or have signed a jobseeker's agreement.[41] This means that someone who has limited leave with an employment condition, but who is not a PSIC, can be entitled to a hardship payment of JSA. For details of hardship payments and how to claim them, see CPAG's *Welfare Benefits and Tax Credits Handbook*.

Habitual residence

The rules are the same as for IS (see p225).

Right to reside

The rules are the same as for IS (see p226)

Spouse/civil partner abroad

The rules are the same as for IS (see p226).

Chapter 18 : Limited leave to remain, no leave to remain and asylum seekers
4. Housing benefit and council tax benefit

18

Partner here with a different status

The rules are the same as for IS (see p226). Note that there are special rules for certain couples without children who claim income-based JSA. Such couples are usually required to claim 'joint-claim JSA' (see CPAG's *Welfare Benefits and Tax Credits Handbook*) as a condition of getting an award of income-based JSA. The rules recognise that this is not possible in the case of a partner who is a PSIC and excluded from benefit and simply restates under the joint-claim rules that benefit is paid at the single person rate to the person who can claim.

Recourse to public funds

The rules are the same as for IS (see p227).

3. Pension credit

The rules for pension credit are largely the same as for income support. However, one key difference is that where one member of a couple is a 'person subject to immigration control' (PISC) and the other is not, the PISC is treated as not being a member of the household.

4. Housing benefit and council tax benefit

Most people with limited leave are not eligible for housing benefit (HB) or council tax benefit (CTB) as they are likely to be a 'person subject to immigration control' (PSIC) because they have a public funds restriction attached to their stay. The HB and CTB rules are very like the income support (IS) rules, but with some differences. There is no urgent cases rate for HB or CTB; the categories of people covered by urgent cases rate get normal HB and/or CTB.

If you are being paid IS or income-based jobseeker's allowance (JSA) the local authority dealing with your HB or CTB claim should not make enquiries about your immigration status or habitual residence.[42] If you are not being paid IS or income-based JSA the following rules apply.

You are only entitled to HB or CTB if:

- you are not a PSIC unless you come under any of the exemptions (see p232); *and*
- for HB, you have accommodation in Great Britain, which you normally occupy as your home (which can include temporary absences – see p253),[43] or for CTB, you are liable to pay council tax for accommodation in which you reside (see p254).[44]

If you do not meet these rules, you are not entitled to HB or CTB.

18

Chapter 18 : Limited leave to remain, no leave to remain and asylum seekers
4. Housing benefit and council tax benefit

HB and CTB are public funds under the immigration rules.[45] The possible effects of claiming HB or CTB on your immigration position are the same as those for IS (see p227).

Persons subject to immigration control

The rules about who is a PSIC are the same as for IS (see p221). The exemptions from the definition are also the same as for IS apart from the fact that you cannot rely on European Community association agreements for either HB or CTB.

Habitual residence test

Even if you are not a PSIC you do not qualify for HB or CTB if you fail the habitual residence test (HRT). The rules on the HRT for HB and CTB are the same as for IS (see p225).

Spouse/civil partner abroad

The rules are the same as for IS (see p226).

Partner here with different status

The rules for HB and CTB are different from those for IS and income-based JSA as there is no provision within the regulations requiring the claim to be assessed only at the single person's rate. Both benefits are assessed at the couple rate.

Recourse to public funds

As there is no provision to pay at a lower rate for couples with different immigration statuses any claim for benefit may mean that the spouse/civil partner has had indirect recourse to public funds and her/his immigration position may be put at risk.

5. Child benefit and guardian's allowance

Child benefit counts as public funds under the immigration rules.[46] If your leave requires you to have no recourse to public funds (see Chapter 7), claiming or receiving child benefit can affect your immigration position (see p85). Guardian's allowance does not count as public funds, but cannot be paid without a current award of child benefit (see p172).

Child benefit

People with limited leave are generally excluded from entitlement to child benefit if they have a public funds restriction attached to their stay. They are therefore

Chapter 18 : Limited leave to remain, no leave to remain and asylum seekers
5. Child benefit and guardian's allowance

18

defined as 'persons subject to immigration control' (PSIC) and ineligible for benefit. However, there are exemptions.

If you are exempt or have transitional protection, you must still meet the other residence rules to be entitled to child benefit (see p234).

General rules

You qualify if:
- you are responsible for a child or paying a contribution towards the cost of the child (see Chapter 12);
- you and your child both satisfy the presence test (see below);
- you satisfy the immigration status test (see below);
- you are liable to pay UK income tax.

The rules are the same as for British nationals (see p170).

Immigration status test

If you are a PSIC you are excluded from entitlement to child benefit.[47] However, there are many exemptions to this rule. A number of people are entitled to child benefit despite being here with limited leave and some people can still claim as a result of transitional rules introduced in 1996 when immigration status first became a factor limiting access to child benefit.

Exemptions from the immigration condition

You are exempt from the PSIC rules if:
- you are the family member of a European Union or European Economic Area national, including a British citizen. This certainly includes a partner and probably also includes adult children, parents and other relatives (see p297). This means that the parent of a British citizen child is entitled to claim child benefit for any child, even if the child is subject to immigration conditions;
- you have leave given to you after another person gave a written sponsorship undertaking (see p94);
- you are a national, or a family member of (and living with) a national, of Algeria, Morocco, Tunisia or Turkey and that national is lawfully working in Great Britain.[48] 'Lawfully working' is not defined in the benefit rules. We consider that you are working lawfully if your work is not in breach of a condition attached to your leave to remain. The Revenue is likely to take the view that working while you have temporary admission is not enough, even if you have been given permission to work. This should be challenged;[49]
- in the past you have lived in a country to which a reciprocal agreement about child benefit applies (see p380). This can apply regardless of your nationality;
- you are entitled to child benefit because of transitional rules. This applies if you were being paid child benefit on 6 October 1996. Transitional protection continues until the award of child benefit is revised or superseded. If you have

18

Chapter 18 : Limited leave to remain, no leave to remain and asylum seekers
5. Child benefit and guardian's allowance

subsequent children you remain eligible for child benefit for your existing child(ren) as this does not constitute grounds for a revision or supersession.

If you are a PSIC and there is another person who could claim child benefit, it is advisable for the other person to make the claim.

Child's status is different

The child normally takes the status of the parents (see p24). Where there are parents of different status and the child is here with limited leave and subject to a public funds condition, a claim for child benefit would be recourse to public funds. It is probably unwise to claim unless the child comes within one of the above groups who are exempt from the PSIC rules.

Transitional protection for pre-1996 claimants

If you were in receipt of child benefit on 6 October 1996 you retain entitlement until the claim is revised or superseded by a decision maker. This can only be done if there are grounds for a revision or supersession – eg, a relevant change of circumstances. If you were in receipt of child benefit on 6 October 1996 and you claim child benefit for another child after that date (eg, following the birth of the child or the arrival of a child to join the household), the existing claim for child benefit should not be revised or superseded. Entitlement to that child benefit should continue to be paid. This is because the claim for 'additional child benefit' is in fact a new and separate claim for benefit.[50]

Guardian's allowance

The rules are the same as for British citizens (see p172). There is no immigration test but you are not entitled to guardian's allowance unless you are entitled to child benefit.[51]

6. **Tax credits**

Most people with limited leave do not qualify for child tax credit (CTC) or working tax credit (WTC) because 'persons subject to immigration control' (PSIC) are excluded from entitlement. Furthermore, WTC is linked to work and people with limited leave are likely to have a condition preventing them working while in the UK. There are some important exceptions.

General rules

To be entitled to CTC you must:
- not be a PSIC;[52]

- be present and ordinarily resident in the UK.[53] You can be treated as present and ordinarily resident in the UK in some circumstances;
- satisfy the right to reside test (see p137).

CTC can be claimed by either member of the couple, as long as you (or your partner) are responsible for at least one child or qualifying young person, even though that child does not need to be present or ordinarily resident in Great Britain when you claim.[54]

To be entitled to **WTC** you must:
- not be a PISC;[55]
- be present and ordinarily resident in the UK.

Temporary absence

It is possible to be treated as present and ordinarily resident for CTC and WTC during temporary absences abroad. If you remain ordinarily resident in the UK and your absence is unlikely to exceed 52 weeks, tax credits continue to be paid during:[56]
- the first eight weeks of any temporary absence;
- the first 12 weeks of any period when you are temporarily absent from the UK if that absence (or any extension to that period of absence) is in connection with:
  - the treatment of an illness or disability of you, your partner, a child for whom you are responsible, or another relative of either you or your partner; *or*
  - the death of your partner, a child for whom you are responsible, or another relative of you or your partner.

The following are exempt from the presence test:
- a Crown servant posted overseas; *and*
  - who immediately prior to being posted abroad was ordinarily resident in the UK; *or*
  - immediately prior to being posted abroad was in the UK in connection with that posting; *or*
- the partner of a Crown servant posted overseas who has accompanied her/his partner to a country of posting or is temporarily accompanying them for one of the reasons set out above.

Spouse or civil partner abroad

If you or your spouse or civil partner are abroad for longer than the period allowed or you are no longer ordinarily resident but you have remained in the UK, you or your partner must terminate the claim. This is because a claim for tax credits by a couple is a joint claim. To make a joint claim you must both be treated as being in the UK. The person who remains in the UK can make a fresh single claim if s/he meets the conditions for getting CTC or WTC. If you fail to notify the Revenue that one of the couple has gone abroad you may be overpaid tax credits. For further details of joint claims, see CPAG's *Welfare Benefits and Tax Credits Handbook*.

If a member of your family is not a 'person subject to immigration control'

If your partner is not a PSIC (eg, a British citizen), has settled status, is an EEA national or Commonwealth citizen with the right of abode, s/he is entitled to tax credits for you both subject to satisfying the normal rules of entitlement. Where one member of the couple is subject to immigration control but the other is not, you are both treated as though you are not PSICs.

Recourse to public funds

CTC and WTC are listed as 'public funds' under the immigration rules.

7. Contribution-based jobseeker's allowance and incapacity benefit

A claim for contribution-based jobseeker's allowance (JSA) or incapacity benefit (IB) may lead to the Home Office being told that you have been working. If you have worked in breach of your immigration conditions, there is a risk of prosecution for that breach.[57]

You cannot be excluded from contribution-based JSA and IB on grounds of immigration status nor do they count as public funds.[58] However, to be entitled to these benefits you must have paid sufficient national insurance contributions and/or have sufficient credits (see CPAG's *Welfare Benefits and Tax Credits Handbook* for full details). This means that you must have been employed. Some people with limited leave have the right to take employment (see p228) and they may be able to qualify for these benefits, but only if they have been in Great Britain for a period of approximately two years, during which time they have been able to work and been credited with contributions. For details of the contribution conditions, see CPAG's *Welfare Benefits and Tax Credits Handbook*. Even if you had permission to work, a claim may cause problems if the Home Office is informed. Any request for further leave may be looked at more closely to see if you can support yourself without recourse to public funds. If you were a student when you worked, the Home Office may check that your work was only vacation or part-time work. If it was not, further leave as a student could be refused.

Note that IB can be paid on a non-contributory basis.

Dependency additions

- **Contribution-based JSA** – there are no dependency additions paid.
- **IB** – dependency additions are payable for adults. For details of when these can be paid, see CPAG's *Welfare Benefits and Tax Credits Handbook*. A person with limited leave subject to a public funds condition may be an adult dependant. Your spouse or civil partner can claim an addition for you regardless of your immigration status.

8. Retirement pensions and bereavement benefits

The rules for Category A, B and D retirement pensions, bereavement payment, widowed parent's allowance and bereavement allowance are the same as those for British citizens (see p175). There are no special rules if you have limited leave.

These benefits are not treated as public funds for the purposes of the immigration rules.[59] However, to be entitled to these benefits you (or your spouse/civil partner) must have paid national insurance contributions (for details, see CPAG's *Welfare Benefits and Tax Credits Handbook*). If this means that you have worked in the UK, a claim may affect your immigration status, in the same way as a claim for contribution-based jobseeker's allowance or incapacity benefit (see p236).

You may be a dependant of a person claiming one of these benefits. Your spouse/partner may be entitled to claim the adult dependency addition for you.[60]

9. Industrial injuries benefits

The rules for disablement benefit, reduced earnings allowance, retirement allowance, constant attendance allowance and exceptionally severe disablement allowance are the same as for British citizens (see p178). There are no special rules if you have limited leave.

These benefits are not treated as public funds under the immigration rules.[61] However, to be entitled to these benefits you must normally have worked in the UK. This means a claim may affect your immigration status, in the same way as a claim for contribution-based jobseeker's allowance or incapacity benefit (see p236).

10. **Disability benefits**

These benefits are disability living allowance (DLA), attendance allowance (AA) and carer's allowance (CA). Anyone who is a 'person subject to immigration control' (PSIC) under the benefit rules is excluded. The definition of a PSIC is the same as for income support (IS) (see p221). However, there are some exceptions to this rule and some people have transitional protection dating back to 1996.

Even if you are exempt or have transitional protection, you must still meet the other residence rules for these benefits.

DLA, AA and CA are treated as public funds under the immigration rules.[62] If your leave requires you to have no recourse to public funds (see p84), claiming or receiving these benefits can affect your immigration position, in the same way as a claim for IS (see p223).

Exemptions from immigration condition

You are exempt from the immigration condition for DLA, AA, and CA if:[63]

- you are the family member of a European Union or European Economic Area (EEA) national (including Swiss nationals). This applies whatever the nationality or immigration status of the family member. Furthermore, there is no necessity for the EEA national to be a 'worker'. The exemption applies simply because of nationality including a British citizen. This exemption clearly includes a partner and children but in many cases also includes adult children, parents and other relatives (see p297);
- you are a national of Algeria, Morocco, Tunisia or Turkey and you are lawfully working (see p233) in Great Britain (GB);[64]
- you are a family member (see p297) of a person who is:
  - a national of Algeria, Morocco, Tunisia or Turkey and lawfully working (see p233) in GB; *and*
  - you are living with that person;[65]
- you are a 'sponsored immigrant' who has been given leave to remain in the UK after your sponsor made a written undertaking (see p94);[66] *or*
- for DLA and AA, in the past you have lived in the Isle of Man, Jersey or Guernsey (or, for AA only, Norway) and a reciprocal agreement about DLA or AA applies to you (see Chapter 25). This can apply regardless of your nationality.

Transitional protection for pre-February 1996 claimants

If none of the above exceptions apply, but you were being paid one of these benefits before 5 February 1996, the immigration condition does not apply to you for that benefit until that award is revised or superseded by a decision maker.[67]

The Court of Appeal ruled that transitional protection should end with the period of an award, and cannot be renewed by another claim after that. The

House of Lords has upheld the Court of Appeal's ruling.[68] Therefore, if there is a gap in claim or at the end of a time-limited award, transitional protection ends. Transitional protection also ends when a revision or supersession is carried out.

A request for a higher rate of one of the components of DLA or AA allows a revision or supersession to be carried out, and this will end your transitional protection. If you do ask for a revision or supersession and you are not exempt, you will lose all that benefit.

If you are claiming and you are not a family member of an EEA national or of a refugee then you may need to consider whether it is wise to claim. Under the immigration rules DLA, AA and CA are defined as public funds (see p86).

Residence test

You have to satisfy a residence and past presence test. The rules are the same as for British citizens (see p182).

11. Statutory sick pay, statutory maternity, paternity and adoption pay and maternity allowance

The rules for statutory sick pay, statutory maternity pay, statutory paternity pay, statutory adoption pay and maternity allowance (MA) are the same as those for British citizens (see p184). There are no special rules for people with limited leave. However, these benefits are only paid to people who have worked and if you have limited leave you may not be in a position to take up work. They are not public funds under the immigration rules.[69]

All these benefits apart from MA are social security benefits where responsibility for the administration and payment has been devolved to employers. These benefits are not listed as public funds. They are payable based on your past work record.

12. The social fund

Most people with limited leave are not eligible for social fund payments. This is because 'persons subject to immigration control' (PSICs) are excluded from entitlement. However, there are some exemptions.

People not excluded from social fund payments[70]

- You are from a country that has ratified the European Social Charter of 1961 or the European Convention on Social and Medical Assistance and are lawfully present. This applies to all European Economic Area (EEA) countries, Croatia, Macedonia and Turkey. For details on the meaning of 'lawful presence', see p129.

- You have been given limited leave as a sponsored immigrant (see p94).
- You are a student or other person whose funding from abroad is temporarily interrupted and there is a reasonable expectation that your supply of funds will be resumed.
- You are an asylum seeker with a right to benefit under the transitional rules (see p203).
- You are lawfully employed and are a national or a family member of a national (and are living with her/him) of Algeria, Morocco, Tunisia or Turkey.
- You are a family member of a European Union or EEA national. This applies whatever the nationality or immigration status of the family member. Furthermore there is no necessity for the EEA national to be a 'worker'. The exemption applies simply because of nationality including a British citizen. This exemption certainly includes a partner and children, but in many cases also includes adult children, parents and other relatives (see p297).

General rules

If you fall within one of the above exemptions you may be able to get a social fund payment if you also satisfy the general conditions of entitlement. See p185 for details of the main conditions for entitlement and different types of payment from the social fund.

You cannot get a budgeting loan or a community care grant from the discretionary social fund unless you are in receipt of, or about to be in receipt of, a means-tested benefit. This is referred to as a qualifying benefit. You must also be in receipt of a qualifying benefit in order to receive a maternity or funeral payment and cold weather payments. These rules mean that if you are not entitled to these benefits because of your immigration status, you cannot be given a social fund payment. You do not have to be in receipt of a means-tested benefit to qualify for a crisis loan or a winter fuel payment. However, any loans from the social fund have to be repaid and therefore you must be seen to have income and the possibility of being able to repay before an award can be made.

Residence rules

The residence conditions for the regulated social fund are the same as for British citizens (see p185). There are no specific residence conditions for the discretionary social fund, but if you are a 'person from abroad' under the income support or income-based jobseeker's allowance rules then a crisis loan can only be awarded in order to alleviate the consequences of a disaster.[71] A 'person from abroad' is a person who has failed the habitual residence test and is not the same as a PSIC.

Notes

1 s3C IA 1971
2 This is a new provision of law, amended in 1999.
3 s7 IA 1988
4 See also reg 14 I(EEA) Regs
5 para 255 HC 395
6 ss3A and 3B IA 1971; I(LER)O
7 Art 13 I(LER)O
8 s73 IAA 1999
9 s24(1)(b) IA 1971
10 Only immigration officers make illegal entry decisions. Adjudicators and the Immigration Appeal Tribunal have no power to decide that a person is an illegal entrant: *Khawaja v SSHD* [1984] AC 74; [1983] 1 All ER 765.
11 By quashing it.
12 s115(9)(b) IAA 1999
13 s115(9)(a) IAA 1999
14 *Khawaja*. Any statutory leave also ends.

1. Income support
15 s115(9) IAA 1999
16 The EC association agreements all differ but are largely based on the rights contained in EC Reg 1408/71. The agreements provide equal treatment in social security. The term social security has the meaning laid down in EC Reg 1408/71 which since June 1992 includes IS. See Chapter 25 for further details of the agreements.
17 As the numbers this applies to are likely to be quite small the rules are mentioned only briefly. For further details see the 3rd edition of this book.
18 s115(9) IAA 1999
19 s24(1)(b)(ii) IA 1971
20 Sch 4 para 17 IAA 1999
21 s115(9)(d) IAA 1999
22 Reg 2 SS(IA)CA Regs
23 Reg 12(5) SS(IA)CA Regs
24 Sch Part I para 1 SS(IA)CA Regs; reg 70(2A) IS Regs
25 Reg 71(2) IS Regs
26 Letter from Home Office Minister David Waddington to Max Madden MP in December 1985.
27 Reg 21(3) IS Regs 'person from abroad': habitual residence
28 Reg 21(3) IS Regs 'person from abroad': habitual residence
29 Sch 7 para 16A IS Regs; Sch 5 para 13A JSA Regs; reg 5 (1)(h) SPC Regs
30 para 6(c) HC 395 'public funds'
31 s24(1)(b)(ii) IA 1971

2. Income-based JSA
32 para 6(c) HC 395 'public funds'
33 s115 IAA 1999; reg 85(4) JSA Regs 'person from abroad'
34 In *Hockenjos v Secretary of State for Social Security* [2001] EWCA Civ 624 it was held that JSA came within the scope of EC Directive 79/7.
35 ss1(2)(a) and 6(1) JSA 1995
36 s4(1) IA 1971
37 Sch 2 para 6 to IA 1971. This only applies to people whose examination began on or after 10 July 1988. A person whose examination began before that has indefinite leave. For details, see *Macdonald*, pp66-69.
38 Art 9 I(LER)O. This is likely only to be used to grant entry to visitors anyway, and so can be expected to mean that all those who enter in this way are prohibited from working.
39 s9(4)-(6) IA 1971. For details see *Macdonald*, pp158-59.
40 s1(2) JSA 1995
41 Reg 141(4) JSA Regs
42 HB/CTB Circular A1/96 para 4
43 s130(1)(a) SSCBA 1992; reg 7 HB Regs
44 s131(3)(a) SSCBA 1992
45 para 6(c) HC 395 'public funds'

5. Child benefit and guardian's allowance
46 s115(1) IAA 1999; and see also para 6(b) HC 395) 'public funds'
47 S115(9) IAA 99
48 Sch Part II para 2 SS(IA)CA Regs. This exemption is included because of the UK's obligations under EC agreements with these countries.

49 In R(FC) 1/01 a commissioner held that a Turkish asylum seeker who was working as a minicab driver would have been able to rely on the Turkish Association Agreement to claim family credit even if UK rules had excluded him from entitlement. In EC law both family credit and child benefit are 'family benefits' therefore the caselaw has equal application to child benefit.

50 CF/1015/1995

51 s77(1)(a) SSCBA 1992

6. Tax credits

52 s15(9) IAA 1999

53 s56 TCA 2002; reg 3 TC(R) Regs

54 Reg 3 TC(R) Regs

55 s115(9) IAA 1999; reg 3 TC(R) Regs

56 Reg 4 TC(R) Regs

57 s24(1)(b)(ii) IA 1971. Any prosecution must be brought within six months of the last breach of conditions: s127 Magistrates Court Act 1980

58 s115(1) IAA 1999; and see also para 6(c) HC 395

8. Retirement pensions and bereavement benefits

59 s115(1) IAA 1999; see also para 6(c) HC 395

60 s83A SSCBA 92

9. Industrial injuries benefits

61 s115(1) IAA 1999; see also para 6(c) HC 395

10. Disability benefits

62 s115(1) IAA 1999; see also para 6(d) HC 395

63 Sch Part 11 to SS(IA)CA Regs

64 This exemption is included because of the UK's obligations under EC agreements with these countries (see Chapter 25).

65 Sch Part II para 3 to SS(IA)CA Regs

66 Sch Part II para 4 to SS(IA)CA Regs

67 Reg 12(10) SS(IA)CA Regs

68 M (a child) v Secretary of State for Social Security [2001] UKHL 35

11. SSP, SMP, SPP, SAP and MA

69 para 6(c) HC 395 'public funds'

12. Social fund

70 Sch Part ISS(IA)CA Regs

71 SF Dir 16(b)

Part 3

Going abroad

Chapter 19
Entitlement to benefit when going abroad

This chapter deals with the effect of going abroad on your entitlement to benefits.

1. Introduction (p246)
2. Considerations which affect benefit entitlement (p246)
3. Temporary absence (p247)
4. Income support (p249)
5. Income-based jobseeker's allowance (p251)
6. Housing benefit and council tax benefit (p253)
7. Pension credit (p255)
8. The social fund (p256)
9. Tax credits (p259)
10. Contribution-based jobseeker's allowance and incapacity benefit (p260)
11. Child benefit and guardians allowance (p262)
12. Retirement pensions (p263)
13. Bereavement benefits (p265)
14. Industrial injuries benefits (p265)
15. Disability benefits (p267)
16. Statutory sick pay and statutory maternity, paternity and adoption pay (p269)
17. Maternity allowance (p269)
18. Premiums and absence abroad (p270)

This chapter does not help you to determine if you are entitled to benefit in the first place. It deals with the *effect* of going abroad on your entitlement to benefits. For details of entitlement to benefits, see CPAG's *Welfare Benefits and Tax Credits Handbook*. To determine your immigration status, see Part 1 of this book. For the effect of your immigration status on your right to claim benefit, see Part 2.

1. **Introduction**

The rules concerning who may come to and go from the UK, the conditions that apply to them, and the procedures applied are explained in Part 1 of this book. Those rules are part of immigration law, and apply to the UK as a whole. There are no significant differences depending on which part of the UK you live in or return to. Most benefit rules, on the other hand, are set within Great Britain (GB), with slightly different arrangements for Northern Ireland.[1] The differences are largely administrative, and most benefits are extended to cover Northern Ireland by various Acts and regulations.[2] This Part deals with the main scheme of benefits, and follows the regulations in referring to GB. Most of these provisions can be applied to Northern Ireland in a similar way, but if you live in Northern Ireland you should take further advice on how, if at all, the differences in administration affect your entitlements.

2. **Considerations which affect benefit entitlement**

There are two main considerations which may affect your benefit entitlement if you travel:

- **the standard rules for Great Britain (GB) and Northern Ireland** which determine the effect of your absence on entitlement to the various benefits. There are important distinctions to be made depending on whether your absence is considered to be only 'temporary' or not (see p247);
- **the reciprocal agreements** existing between the UK Government and other governments under which you may qualify for benefits while abroad (see Part 5).

If you are travelling to or from a European Economic Area (EEA) member state and you are:

- a citizen of the European Union (EU) – ie, a national of one of the member states of the EU (see p97); *or*
- a citizen of one of the additional EEA states (see p97); *or*
- a Swiss national (see p97); *or*
- a member of the family of an EU or EEA citizen; *or*
- a national of one of the countries outside the EEA which has concluded an association agreement with the EU,

you may be entitled to certain benefit payments by virtue of European rules.

Benefit may be payable on account of being insured under the social security scheme of the other state while you are in the UK, or because you are covered under the UK schemes, or by combining cover under the two schemes. Certain benefits payable to you in the UK can continue to be paid while in the other country. Arrangements under the association agreements are essentially a special class of reciprocal agreements, covered by European Community law, rather than bilateral accords between two governments. All of these rights are covered in detail in Part 4.

In describing the effects of going abroad on your benefit entitlement, this *Handbook* uses a number of phrases which carry specific legal meaning, and which need to be defined. These include:

- presence;
- absence;
- temporary absence;
- permanent absence;
- residence;
- right to reside;
- habitual residence; *and*
- ordinary residence.

Generally speaking, the meaning given to these phrases is easy enough to grasp, but in law they require a precise rather than a general meaning because you can be entitled to or refused benefit depending on whether your circumstances fall one side or the other of a dividing line. Some of these are defined in Chapter 11. For the meaning of temporary and permanent absence, see below. For the meaning of habitual residence, see p132. For the meaning of right to reside, see p137.

3. **Temporary absence**

The term 'temporary absence' is important in determining whether you remain entitled to particular benefits when you go abroad.

For many benefits, the fact that your absence abroad is temporary is a precondition for retaining entitlement, but for certain benefits there are also additional requirements that relate primarily to the purpose and length of time you are away. For certain benefits, absences from Great Britain (GB) – temporary or otherwise – are of very little importance.

What is temporary absence

'Temporary absence' is not defined in the legislation and there are no clear rules determining whether your absence will be treated as being temporary. The only guidance available is the caselaw of the courts and the social security commissioners, which sets out the factors the DWP must consider in determining whether the absence is temporary. It also provides examples of situations that will lead to a finding that your absence is not temporary. Every absence is unique and distinct, and accordingly, your case will be given individual consideration, so it is important that you provide full details of:

- why you wish to go abroad;
- how long you intend to be abroad; *and*
- what you intend to do while you are abroad.

Each of these considerations needs to be taken into account, and it is your responsibility to demonstrate that your absence is a temporary one.[3]

The three most important factors in determining whether your absence is temporary are:[4]

- your intention for going abroad;
- the length of your absence; *and*
- the purpose of your absence.

Intention will always be an important factor but will never, on its own, be conclusive.[5] For example, a person may wish to return but find there are obstacles, such as an unexpected change in family responsibilities, which prevent her/him from returning for the foreseeable future. This may mean that her/his absence ceases to be temporary, despite intentions to the contrary.

Example

Momin returns to visit his family in Bangladesh for a three-month period. While he is there his father has an accident, and dies, leaving his disabled mother alone. As the only child of the family without other immediate dependants it falls on Momin to care for his mother until suitable long-term arrangements can be made. There are no nursing homes or similar institutions to care for his mother, and by the time he returns to the UK it is more than two years since he left.

There is no set period for a temporary or non-temporary absence, although commissioners have tended to treat a period of 12 months or more as demonstrating a non-temporary absence.[6] There is no reason in principle why an absence of several years cannot still be considered temporary, but the circumstances would need to be exceptional.[7] The number and lengths of other absences (past and intended) may also be taken into account in determining whether the immediate absence is temporary.[8]

If the purpose of the trip abroad is obviously temporary (eg, for a holiday or to visit friends or relatives or for a particular course of treatment) and you buy a return ticket, then your absence will be viewed as temporary.

The nature of an absence can change over time. If an absence, after the factors mentioned above have been considered, is found to be temporary at the beginning of the period, that does not mean that it will always remain temporary.[9]

If circumstances change while you are abroad (eg, you go abroad for one reason and decide to stay abroad for a different purpose) then your absence may in time come to be regarded as no longer temporary.

Example
Zeinab receives incapacity benefit (IB), housing benefit (HB) and council tax benefit (CTB). When she travels to visit family she leaves her council flat, and the absence is accepted as temporary by both the DWP and the local authority. Two months later she writes to say she intends to stay four months longer, as she is receiving medical treatment which is helping her. This is accepted as still temporary, and benefit continues to be paid. After six months her IB stops, as she has received the maximum payment of 26 weeks' benefit. A further two months later she writes again to say her new partner has work locally and she intends to remain there with him for a year or more before returning to the UK. Both the DWP and the local authority decide that her absence is no longer temporary, and payments of HB and CTB are stopped.

Where the rules for the different benefits refer to 'temporary absence' and 'temporarily absent', note that the absence is often qualified by other specific conditions which vary from benefit to benefit. For some benefits, you must 'intend' to return to GB within a specific period and for others you must 'intend' the absence to be temporary as well as it actually being temporary. In many cases, these differences should not affect the outcome.

Finally, it is important to note that in calculating the period over which you are temporarily absent from the UK, the day you leave and the day you return are counted as days in the UK.[10] This is a general rule which will apply unless the regulations dealing with a particular benefit specify otherwise.

4. Income support

To be entitled to income support (IS) you must be present in Great Britain (GB).[11] If you have become entitled to IS while in GB, during a temporary absence you may remain entitled for a period of either four or eight weeks. It is not necessary for any IS payments to be *received* prior to any temporary absence, but you must have claimed and satisfied the conditions of entitlement.

Regardless of the other reasons for your absence from GB, you only remain entitled to IS if:[12]
- you leave temporarily; *and*
- the period of your absence is unlikely to exceed 52 weeks; *and*
- you continue to satisfy all other conditions of entitlement to IS (ie, you do not work, you remain incapable of work, etc).

Housing benefit and council tax benefit may continue to be paid in addition to any IS you are paid during such an absence (see p253).

You will remain entitled for a period of eight weeks if you satisfy the above three requirements *and*:[13]

- you are accompanying abroad a child or young person who is a member of your family solely in order for that person to be treated for a disease or physical or mental disablement; *and*
- those arrangements relate to treatment outside GB which is provided by or under the supervision of an appropriately qualified person while you are abroad.

You will remain entitled for a period of four weeks if you satisfy the above three requirements *and*:[14]

- the reason you are exempt from the requirement to be available for work is *not* one of the following:
  - you are incapable of work – but see below for qualification for benefit when you are incapable of work;
  - you are in education;
  - you are involved in a trade dispute or are within a period of 15 days of returning to work following a trade dispute;
  - you are a 'person subject to immigration control' who is entitled to urgent cases payments of IS (see p160 – but in these cases you are unlikely to be allowed to travel and then return to continue with your asylum application);
  - you are appealing against a decision that you are not incapable of work; *or*
- you are incapable of work and the only reason you are absent from GB is to get treatment related to your incapacity from an appropriately qualified person; *or*
- you are in Northern Ireland; *or*
- you have a partner who is also absent from GB and who is entitled to a pensioner, enhanced pensioner, higher pensioner, disability or severe disability premium. It is only necessary for you to be entitled to the premium. It is not necessary for you to be being paid it; *or*
- on the day you leave GB you have been incapable of work for a period of:
  - 196 days (28 weeks) if you are either terminally ill or you are entitled to the highest rate of the care component of disability living allowance; *or*
  - 364 days in any other case.

Breaks in periods of incapacity of eight weeks or less are disregarded in both instances.

Habitual residence and right to reside

If you go abroad for a lengthy period you may lose your habitual residence and, for non-UK EEA nationals, the right to reside. For further details, see Chapter 11.

5. **Income-based jobseeker's allowance**

To be entitled to income-based jobseeker's allowance (JSA) you must be present in Great Britain (GB).[15] If you have become entitled to income-based JSA while in GB, during a temporary absence you may be treated as still in GB and therefore remain entitled for a period of up to one, four or eight weeks, provided that your absence is unlikely to exceed 52 weeks.[16] It is necessary that you satisfy all the other conditions of entitlement for income-based JSA,[17] the most important of which is that you are available for and actively seeking employment. Unless you go to Northern Ireland (in which case you may remain entitled for up to four weeks), there are certain other conditions you need to satisfy in order to be treated as present in GB[18] and these overlap with the circumstances in which you can be treated as available for and actively seeking work despite your absence (see below).

Available for and actively seeking employment

To get income-based JSA you must be available for and actively seeking employment.[19] You could cease to satisfy these conditions if you go abroad. However, when you go abroad you will still be treated as available for and actively seeking employment for:[20]

- **a maximum of one week** if you are temporarily absent from GB to attend a job interview (but you must notify an employment officer of your absence);[21] *or*
- **a maximum of four weeks** if you are part of a couple and you are getting the pensioner, enhanced pensioner, higher pensioner, disability or severe disability premium for your partner and both you *and* your partner are absent from GB; *or*
- **a maximum of eight weeks** if you take your child abroad for medical treatment by an appropriately qualified person;[22] *or*
- **a maximum of three months** if your absence is within another European Economic Area state (see Part 4).

In addition, in order to be treated as actively seeking work in any of these circumstances you (and in the case of the second condition, your partner) must be absent from GB for at least three days for each week you wish to be treated as available for work.[23] In all cases, in order to remain entitled to benefit, the temporary absence must be unlikely to exceed 52 weeks.[24]

Even if you satisfy the above requirement, you are not treated as still present in GB unless:

- if you are going abroad in order to attend an interview, you are:[25]
  - not actually absent from GB for more than seven continuous days; *and*
  - able to demonstrate to your employment officer on your return that you attended the interview;

- if you are taking your child abroad for medical treatment, the treatment is:[26]
  - for a disease or physical or mental disablement;
  - performed outside GB;
  - performed while you are temporarily absent from GB and is by or under the supervision of a suitably qualified person.

You are also treated as available for and actively seeking employment where someone else is abroad if you are:[27]

- part of a couple and you are looking after your child while your partner is temporarily absent from the UK;
- temporarily looking after a child on a full-time basis because the person who normally looks after the child is ill, temporarily absent from the home or is looking after another family member who is ill.

Entitlement is for a maximum of eight weeks in both cases. In addition, you must look after the child at least three days in every week you wish to be treated as actively seeking employment.[28]

People in receipt of a training allowance

People in receipt of certain training allowances but not receiving training can get income-based JSA without being available for or actively seeking employment and do not require a jobseeker's agreement.[29] In these circumstances, you can still get JSA for four weeks if you are temporarily absent from GB and entitled to a training allowance, without having to show that your absence is unlikely to exceed 52 weeks.[30]

Holidays from jobseeking

You can take a holiday from jobseeking and still remain entitled to JSA. You may spend a maximum of two weeks in any one 12-month period (not calendar years) not actively seeking work and living away from home.[31] You must:

- tell your employment officer about your holiday – in writing, if requested; *and*
- fill out a holiday form so you can be contacted if employment becomes available.

Although you are exempt from *looking* for work during this period, you still have to be *available* and willing to return to start work during the holiday. In practice, therefore, absences abroad during this period are unlikely to be allowed.

Housing costs

During your four- or eight-week temporary absence from GB you remain entitled to any housing costs paid as part of income support[32] or income-based JSA,[33] provided:

- your home is not let or sub-let to anyone else;

- you intend to return to live in it;
- the period of your absence is unlikely to exceed 13 weeks.

If you do not go abroad but:
- are absent from your home; *and*
- satisfy the above conditions; *and*
- continue to be entitled to some income-based JSA,

you remain entitled to your housing costs for a period of 13 weeks. In certain circumstances you may remain entitled to your housing costs for a period of 52 weeks.[34] See CPAG's *Welfare Benefits and Tax Credits Handbook* for details of these circumstances. The rules are similar to those for housing benefit and council tax benefit (see below).

Habitual residence and right to reside

If you go abroad for a lengthy period you may lose your habitual residence and, for non-UK EEA nationals, the right to reside. For further details see Chapter 11.

6. **Housing benefit and council tax benefit**

For the basic rules about who can get housing benefit (HB) and council tax benefit (CTB), see CPAG's *Welfare Benefits and Tax Credits Handbook*

Housing benefit

During a temporary absence abroad you can remain entitled to HB for a period of either 13 or 52 weeks.

You remain entitled to HB for the first 13 weeks of any period of temporary absence from your home provided that:[35]
- you intend to return to occupy the dwelling as your home; *and*
- the property is not let or sub-let while you are away; *and*
- you are unlikely to be away for more than 13 weeks; *and*
- you meet the other conditions of entitlement to benefit.

You remain entitled to HB for the first 52 weeks of any period of temporary absence from your home provided:[36]
- you intend to return to occupy the dwelling as your home; *and*
- the property is not let or sub-let while you are away; *and*
- you are unlikely to be absent from the property for longer than 52 weeks (although, under exceptional circumstances, you may be permitted to extend the period for which you remain away by a short amount, which DWP guidance interprets as meaning a maximum of a further three months); *and*
- you fall into one of the following categories:[37]
  - you are sick and in hospital; *or*

- you or your partner or child are undergoing medically approved treatment or convalescence in the UK or abroad; *or*
- you are on a training course in the UK or abroad approved by or on behalf of a government department, a local authority, any Secretary of State, Scottish Enterprise or Highlands and Enterprise or operated on their behalf by a local authority;[38] *or*
- you are caring for someone who is sick in the UK or abroad and the care you are providing is medically approved; *or*
- you are caring for a child whose parent or guardian is temporarily absent from her/his home because s/he is receiving medical treatment; *or*
- you are receiving medically approved care not in residential accommodation in the UK or abroad; *or*
- you are a student eligible for HB – see CPAG's *Welfare Benefits and Tax Credits Handbook; or*
- you left your home as a result of fear of violence and you are not entitled to HB for the accommodation you now occupy.[39]

In determining whether you intend to return home, account will be taken of whether you have left your personal belongings in the dwelling.[40]

With both durations of HB entitlement during a temporary absence the entitlement period begins on the first day that you are absent from the home[41] and the period of temporary absence begins again each time you leave, even if you only return for a very brief period.[42] However, you will not necessarily remain entitled by returning to your home for short periods and leaving again. You are only entitled to HB/CTB to help you pay for accommodation which you and your family (if any) *normally* occupy as your home.[43] If you have another home abroad which you or members of your family also occupy,[44] then your absences from the UK could affect your entitlement to benefit if your absences are long enough or regular enough to mean that your 'main' home ceases to be in the UK. However, you will not lose benefit on these grounds if members or your family normally occupy a home abroad, but are not part of your household.[45]

Council tax benefit

To be able to claim CTB you must first be liable to pay council tax for the accommodation in which you live.[46] If your main home is abroad you may avoid liability for the council tax altogether.[47] This carries a risk, though, since demonstrating that your main home is abroad would adversely affect your HB entitlement (see p253), and could have a negative effect on other benefits you may wish to claim.

If you are temporarily absent from GB you can continue to get CTB for a period of either 13 weeks or 52 weeks. The rules are almost the same as for HB (see p253).[48] You may also avoid liability for the council tax itself by showing that your dwelling is exempt.[49] Absences abroad may mean this is the case where the property is left unoccupied. The following are the most likely circumstances where this would apply:

- the property will be substantially unfurnished for a period of less than six months;
- the previous resident is receiving personal care other than in a hospital or home;
- the previous resident is providing someone else with personal care;
- the property is substantially unfurnished and requires or is undergoing major repairs or structural alterations to make it habitable;
- such major repairs or alterations have only been completed within the past six months.

For more details see CPAG's *Council Tax Handbook*.

Habitual residence and right to reside

If you go abroad for a lengthy period you may lose your habitual residence and, for non-UK EEA nationals, the right to reside. For further details, see Chapter 11.

7. Pension credit

To be entitled to pension credit (PC) you must be present in Great Britain (GB).[50]

Regulations allow for entitlement to continue during periods of temporary absence and set out situations in which a person can be treated as being present or not present in GB. In order to satisfy the presence test you must be habitually resident and have a right to reside (see Chapter 11).

You can be treated as satisfying the presence test for PC during certain temporary absences.[51] These are:

- **for a period of four weeks** if the absence is unlikely to exceed 52 weeks and while absent from GB you continue to satisfy the other conditions of entitlement to PC;
- **for a period of eight weeks** if the period of absences in unlikely to exceed 52 weeks and you continue to satisfy the other conditions of entitlement to PC and you are accompanying a young person solely in connection with arrangements for her/his treatment of a disease or bodily or mental disablement and those arrangements relate to treatment:
  - outside GB;
  - during the period in which you are temporarily absent from GB;
  - by, or under supervision of, a person appropriately qualified to carry out that treatment.

If you or your partner are receiving treatment in a hospital or other institution outside GB and the treatment is being provided under certain NHS provisions you can be treated as being present in GB for as long as the treatment continues.[52] However, this only applies if you satisfied the conditions for entitlement to PC immediately before you or your partner left GB. This does not apply in Scotland.[53] A person is treated as not being a member of the same household as you if s/he is living away from you and:[54]

- s/he does not intend to resume living with you; *or*
- her/his absence is likely to exceed 52 weeks.

Habitual residence and right to reside

On your return to GB you may have to show that you satisfy the habitual residence test (see p132) and if you are an EEA national (other than British or Irish) you will have to show that you have a right to reside (see p137).

8. The social fund

The social fund is divided into two parts:

- **the regulated social fund** from which benefits are payable:
  - Sure Start maternity grants;
  - cold weather payments;
  - funeral expenses; *and*
  - winter fuel payments;
- **the discretionary social fund** from which there are three types of payment:
  - budgeting loans;
  - community care grants; *and*
  - crisis loans.

For details of when you are entitled to payments from the social fund, see CPAG's *Welfare Benefits and Tax Credits Handbook*.

Regulated social fund

Maternity and funeral expenses

You are entitled to a **Sure Start maternity grant** if:

- you or your partner have been awarded one of the following qualifying benefits:[55]
  - income support (IS);
  - income-based jobseeker's allowance (JSA);
  - pension credit (PC);
  - working tax credit (WTC) which includes the disability or severe disability element;

- child tax credit (CTC) paid at a rate which exceeds the family element;
- one of the following applies:[56]
  - you or a member of your family are pregnant or have given birth in the last three months (including stillbirth after 24 weeks of pregnancy[57]);
  - you or your partner have adopted a child who is less than 12 months old;
  - you and your spouse/civil partner have a parental order allowing you to have a child by a surrogate mother;
- you have received health and welfare advice from a health professional relating to your baby or your maternal health.[58]

See CPAG's *Welfare Benefits and Tax Credits Handbook* for more details. Entitlement to a maternity grant during any absence from the UK is subject to the same rules as those for other benefits.

You qualify for **funeral expenses payments** if:
- you or your partner have been awarded one of the following qualifying benefits:[59]
  - IS;
  - income-based JSA;
  - PC;
  - housing benefit;
  - council tax benefit;
  - WTC which includes the disability or severe disability element;
  - CTC paid at a rate which exceeds the family element;
- you or your partner are treated as responsible for the funeral expenses (see CPAG's *Welfare Benefits and Tax Credits Handbook*);[60]
- the funeral takes place in the UK (but see below);[61]
- the deceased was ordinarily resident in the UK when s/he died.[62]

If you are treated as a worker for the purposes of European Community law (see p348) the rules concerning ordinary residence and the place of funeral are both extended to the European Economic Area (EEA) and Switzerland.[63]

You can get a funeral payment for a funeral that takes place in any member state of the EEA if you are a worker or a family member of a worker who has died. This also applies to people who are economically active other than being in employment – eg, who are self-employed or self-supporting. See Part 4 for full details of the rights of EU nationals.

There are no special rules concerning temporary absence, but since you or your partner must be in receipt of one of the qualifying benefits on the date of claim, payment is governed by the same rules as those benefits.

Cold weather payments

Cold weather payments are payable if, on at least one of the days during the qualifying week of cold weather, you have been awarded PC or, in some cases, IS or JSA.[64] See CPAG's *Welfare Benefits and Tax Credits Handbook* for more details.

You must be ordinarily resident in GB, but otherwise the presence and residence tests for the regulated social fund are dictated by the presence and residence conditions attached to the various means-tested benefits identified above. You should refer to the section in this chapter dealing with the relevant benefit to identify the effect of absences from GB on your entitlement to benefits from the regulated social fund.

Winter fuel payments

Winter fuel payments are available to anyone aged 60 or over to help towards the cost of fuel bills. The only condition apart from age is that you are ordinarily resident in GB in the qualifying week,[65] a week which is set by the DWP and announced in advance of winter. Eligibility does not depend on receiving any other benefits. For special conditions applying to people in certain kinds of accommodation, see CPAG's *Welfare Benefits and Tax Credits Handbook*. Temporary absence does not affect your entitlement as long as you remain ordinarily resident (see p129). You do not usually need to make a claim if you have received a winter fuel payment before, but if this is the first year in which you become entitled to a payment, or if you have been away from GB for long enough to have lost your entitlement in the meantime, you should contact your local office to make a claim. Claims can also be made for any of the past three years, if you have not received payment when you believe you should have been entitled. You are also entitled to claim a backdated payment if at the time of the qualifying week you were a 'person subject to immigration control' (see p155) but have since been granted leave, usually by recognition as a refugee, which covers the relevant week.[66]

Discretionary social fund

Payments from the discretionary social fund can only be paid to meet needs which occur in the UK.[67] It is only necessary, therefore, to show that you are in the UK for a sufficient period to allow your particular need to be established here.

Budgeting loans

In order to get a budgeting loan, you need to be receiving IS, income-based JSA or PC when the decision is made on your application and you or your partner must have been receiving that qualifying benefit for 26 weeks before that date.[68] It is likely, however, that if it is your partner who is the claimant, then your partner must also apply for the loan, and you would not qualify independently.[69] You should in any case check the rules relating to absence for the qualifying benefit – see p249 for IS or p251 for income-based JSA.

Community care grants

You can get a community care grant if, when you make your application, you are receiving IS, income-based JSA or PC.[70]

If you have been staying in institutional or residential care, and it is likely that you will receive IS, income-based JSA or PC when discharged, you should also be able to receive a grant. This is a long-standing concession, which applies to those 're-establishing' themselves in the community.[71] A claim should be made within six weeks of the date you expect to be discharged. The High Court has decided that in these cases the 'community' refers only to GB, so you can only claim successfully on this basis if you lived in GB before the time you made your application.[72] If your claim is made in any other circumstances, and providing you are in receipt of a qualifying benefit, there is no other presence or residence test to satisfy.

Crisis loans

You do not need to be entitled to or receiving any other benefit in order to get a crisis loan. The qualifying criteria are not restricted.[73] 'Persons subject to immigration control' (see p155) who are not entitled to IS, income-based JSA or PC are excluded from claiming a crisis loan, unless this is the only way of alleviating the consequences of a disaster.[74] Even in this situation, it will be necessary to show the social fund officer that you are able to repay the loan.[75]

9. **Tax credits**

To claim tax credits you must be present in the UK at the time of your claim and you must be 'ordinarily resident' in the UK. It is also a condition for child tax credit (CTC) that you have a right to reside (see p137).

It is possible to be treated as present and ordinarily resident during some temporary absences. If you remain ordinarily resident and your absence is unlikely to exceed 52 weeks tax credits continue to be paid during:[76]
- the first eight weeks of any temporary absence;
- the first 12 weeks of any period when you are temporarily absent from the UK if that absence (or any extension to that period of absence) is in connection with:
  - the treatment of an illness or disability of you, your partner, a child for whom you are responsible or another relative of either you or your partner; or
  - the death of your partner, a child for whom you are responsible or another relative of you or your partner.

This means that you not only continue to satisfy the residence conditions for entitlement to tax credits during the period of an award, but you could also make a fresh or renewal claim while abroad (but see p260 if you are a member of a couple). If you spend longer abroad than certain permitted periods you may no longer satisfy the residence conditions for your tax credits.

Crown servants[77] are exempt from the presence test if immediately prior to their posting they were ordinarily resident in the UK or were in the UK in connection with the posting; or are the partner of a crown servant and were accompanying her/him on the posting.

Couples

If you are a member of a couple and you are not entitled to tax credits while abroad or you have exceeded the permitted period for payment while you are abroad, your partner has to make a claim in her/his own right. If one of the couple fails to report that one of them has been temporarily absent for longer than the permitted period and does not terminate the couple claim, the couple may be overpaid as a result and be subject to a penalty.

The new claim is calculated on the basis of your past income, not that of your partner.

10. **Contribution-based jobseeker's allowance and incapacity benefit**

For details of the presence and residence conditions for contribution-based jobseeker's allowance (JSA) and incapacity benefit (IB), see Chapter 11.

Contribution-based jobseeker's allowance

The rules relating to absences for contribution-based JSA are the same as for income-based JSA (see p251).[78]

However, like other contributory benefits, you need to satisfy the contribution conditions[79] which means that you are unlikely to qualify unless you have lived and worked in the UK for several years. For the contribution conditions, see CPAG's *Welfare Benefits and Tax Credits Handbook*.

For contribution-based JSA, you are still treated as present in Great Britain (GB) if you are outside GB because you are an offshore worker[80] *or* because you are a mariner and you are left outside GB, provided you report to a consular officer or chief officer of customs within 14 days or as soon as reasonably practicable.[81] For what counts as an offshore worker for these purposes, see p179. If you fall into one of these categories, you remain entitled to benefit despite your absence from GB provided you fulfil all the other entitlement conditions.

In order to allow you to look for work elsewhere in the European Economic Area (EEA), you can receive contribution-based JSA for a period of up to three months, paid to you in another EEA country (see p329).[82]

European Community (EC) law can help you to satisfy the national insurance contributions for contributory JSA. Contributions paid in other EEA states including A8 and A2 states prior to accession can be taken into account to help

Chapter 19 : Entitlement to benefit when going abroad
10. Contribution-based jobseeker's allowance and incapacity benefit

19

you qualify for contributory JSA – eg, if you have worked in the UK for a few weeks but have previously worked in Poland you can aggregate the contributions paid in Poland in order to meet the conditions for contributory JSA.

Incapacity benefit

If you are temporarily absent (see p247) from GB then you can remain entitled to IB. Unless you are receiving either attendance allowance (AA) or disability living allowance or you are a member of the family of a serving member of the forces and are temporarily absent because you are living with that person,[83] then you can only remain entitled to benefit for the first 26 weeks of any such absence[84] and unless either of these conditions applies to you, the Secretary of State must certify that it would be consistent with the proper administration of the benefits scheme for you to qualify for benefit despite your absence.[85]

You *also* need to satisfy one of the following conditions:[86]

- you are going abroad for treatment for an incapacity which began before you go abroad. This must be the reason why you go abroad. You cannot simply decide to receive such treatment while you are abroad.[87] The treatment itself must be carried out by some other person[88] and must usually be of a medical nature: convalescence or a trip abroad for a change in environment will not qualify;[89] *or*
- your incapacity is the result of an industrial injury[90] (see CPAG's *Welfare Benefits and Tax Credits Handbook*) and you go abroad in order to receive treatment which is appropriate to that injury; *or*
- at the time you go abroad you have been continuously incapable of work for six months and you remain continuously incapable of work for the time that you are abroad and claiming benefit. In this case it is not necessary for your absence to be for the purpose of receiving treatment.

You can also get benefit for the whole of the period of the temporary absence if one of the above three conditions applies to you and you have been continuously absent from GB since 8 March 1994.[91]

You are also treated as present in GB and entitled to benefit if you are outside GB because you are an offshore worker[92] *or* because you are a mariner.[93] For what counts as an offshore worker for these purposes, see p179. If you fall into this category then you remain entitled to benefit despite your absence from GB provided you fulfil all other entitlement conditions.

You can rely on EC law in the same way as for JSA in terms of aggregating national insurance contributions. Under EC law IB can be exported to another EEA member state (see p316).

11. **Child benefit and guardian's allowance**

Child benefit

To claim child benefit you and the child for whom you are claiming must be present in the UK, be ordinarily resident and, since 1 May 2004, have a right of residence (see p137).[94]

You are treated as not present if:

- you are not ordinarily resident in GB;[95]
- you do not have a right to reside in the UK;[96]
- you are out of the country for longer than the permitted periods.[97]

If you remain ordinarily resident in the UK and your absence is unlikely, from the start of the absence, to exceed 52 weeks, child benefit continues to be paid:[98]

- **during the first eight weeks** of any temporary absence; or
- **during the first 12 weeks** of any period when you are temporarily absent from the UK if that absence, or any extension to that period of absence, is in connection with:
  - the treatment of an illness or disability of you, your partner, a child for whom you are responsible, or another relative of either you or your partner; or
  - the death of your partner, a child for whom you are responsible, or another relative of you or your partner.

The child for whom you are claiming must in general also be present in the UK. However, a child will be treated as present if her/his absence abroad is temporary, during:[99]

- the first 12 weeks of any period of absence; or
- any period during which the child is absent for the specific purpose of being treated for an illness or physical or mental disability which commenced before her/his absence began; or
- any period during which the child is absent only because:[100]
  - s/he is receiving full time education at a recognised educational establishment in another EEA member state (including A2 and A8) states or in Switzerland; or
  - s/he is engaged in an educational exchange or visit made with the written approval of the recognised educational establishment which s/he normally attends.

If the child is born outside the UK during a period in which the mother is treated as present in the UK, the child is also treated as present.

Guardian's allowance

To be entitled to guardian's allowance you must be entitled to child benefit and the above rules apply. Guardian's allowance can continue to be paid while you are absent from GB, but it will not be uprated during any absence.[101]

A further condition of entitlement to guardian's allowance is that at least one of the child's parents must have been born in the UK or have, at some time after reaching the age of 16, spent a total of 52 weeks in any two-year period in the UK.[102]

12. **Retirement pensions**

For the presence and residence requirements of retirement pensions and for further entitlement details, see p175. There are residence requirements for Category D retirement pensions.

Both Category A and B retirement pensions are contributory benefits. Category A pensions depend on either your own or your spouse's or civil partner's contribution record. For the contribution conditions, see CPAG's *Welfare Benefits and Tax Credits Handbook*. There are no residence or presence rules for either category, but you are unlikely to qualify unless you or your late spouse/civil partner lived and worked in Great Britain (GB) for several years. Special rules apply if you have worked for all or part of your working life in other European Economic Area countries, allowing you to add together periods of insurance under the schemes of the different countries in which you have worked (see p306). It is possible to qualify for a reduced rate Category A or B pension where insufficient national insurance contributions have been paid to satisfy the contribution conditions in full. Reduced rate pensions are frequently paid to people who have arrived in GB part way through their working lives, and to people who have spent periods of their working lives abroad and not paid sufficient contributions to maintain their pension entitlement. In certain cases where people have worked abroad, contribution records from the two countries can either be aggregated to build up an entitlement to a pension based on the combined totals, or part pensions from both countries can be paid – for details see p320.

If you are relying on your spouse/civil partner's contribution record, you may be entitled to a pension even if you have never worked in or been to the UK and you still remain abroad. You can also claim a retirement pension based on your own or your spouse/civil partner's contributions even if you are not living in GB when you reach pensionable age.

Example

When Muhith came to work in the UK he always intended only to stay a few years to earn enough to support his family at home. His wife Sumena never travelled here. The years passed, the family came to depend on Muhith's UK earnings, and he never found work back home. Some years before he reached pensionable age he became ill and returned home, where he later suffered a heart attack and died. Sumena can claim a retirement pension based on his contribution record as soon as the age conditions are met.

Category D pensions are for people aged over 80 years. You must satisfy the following residence and presence requirements:[103]

- you were resident in GB for at least 10 years in any continuous period of 20 years ending on or after your 80th birthday; *and*
- you were ordinarily resident in GB on:
  - your 80th birthday; *or*
  - a later date on which you claimed Category D pension.

A Category D pension is generally worth less than a Category A or B pension. The pensions 'overlap', which means that if you will be entitled to a Category A or B pension, the above residence and presence conditions are not important. Absences from GB during the 20-year period prior to your 80th birthday could, therefore, affect your entitlement to benefit, as could absences around the time of your 80th birthday or the date of your claim. If you wish to spend time abroad or live abroad after you are 80 then it is important to carefully plan such absences because you will be unlikely to qualify for any other benefit which you will be able to claim while you are abroad. Dependants' additions are not paid with a Category D pension.

After establishing entitlement to any retirement pension, you continue to be entitled to it regardless of any absences from GB.[104] However, absences abroad can still have an effect on the *amount* of benefit you receive. If you spend a sufficient amount of time abroad so that you cease to be ordinarily resident (see p129) in GB, the amount of benefit you receive is frozen for any day on which you are absent. This means that benefit for those days will be paid at the rate when you stopped being ordinarily resident or the rate at which it was first paid if that was later.[105] Your benefit is not up-rated along with everyone else's benefit. These rules do not apply in countries with which the UK has reciprocal agreements allowing for continued up-rating of pensions payments (see p379). The difference between these two groups of countries is not a breach of the Human Rights Act 1998.[106]

However, you are still entitled to an up-rated benefit, even if you are not ordinarily resident, if your entitlement is based on the contributions of your spouse/civil partner and s/he is ordinarily resident in GB on the day before the benefit is up-rated.[107]

In all of these cases you are entitled to the up-rated amount of benefit again after your return to GB *provided* you are once again ordinarily resident. You should therefore try to time any permanent retirement abroad so that you can take the maximum benefit with you.

You are only entitled to the age addition of 25p payable with your pension when you are 80 for any day you are absent from GB if you:[108]
- are ordinarily resident in GB; *or*
- were entitled to the age addition before you stopped being ordinarily resident in GB; *or*
- are entitled to an increased rate of any category of retirement pension under a reciprocal agreement (see Chapter 25).

13. **Bereavement benefits**

Bereavement benefits comprise bereavement payment, widowed parent's allowance and bereavement allowance (see p177).

The only presence and residence conditions that apply to these benefits are those which relate to bereavement payment.[109] These are:
- you or your late spouse/civil partner were in Great Britain (GB) at the time of her/his death; *or*
- you returned to GB within four weeks of your late spouse/civil partner's death; *or*
- you meet the contribution conditions for widowed parent's allowance or bereavement allowance.

Absences from GB are only significant for people who wish to claim the lump-sum bereavement payment who, if they or their spouse/civil partner were not in GB at the time of her/his death, have to come to GB within four weeks of the death in order to claim the payment.

It is therefore important for widows/widowers whose late spouse/civil partner has worked and paid national insurance contributions in GB, but who themselves are living abroad, to check their benefit entitlement. The time limit for claiming bereavement benefits is three months[110] and this can be extended when the bereaved person was unaware of her/his spouse/civil partner's death.[111] Therefore, it is always worth checking for these benefits. Once entitlement to bereavement benefits has been established, the rules governing entitlement to benefit while abroad are as for retirement pension (see p263).

14. **Industrial injuries benefits**

The relevant benefits are disablement benefit, reduced earnings allowance, retirement allowance, constant attendance allowance and exceptionally severe disablement allowance.

You are only entitled to these benefits if you:

- have an accident which 'arises out of and in the course of' employed earner's employment or a disease which is 'prescribed in relation to' employed earner's employment[112] – for details, see CPAG's *Welfare Benefits and Tax Credits Handbook*. An employed earner is defined as a person employed in Great Britain (GB);[113] *and*
- were in GB when the accident happened[114] or engaged in GB in the employment which caused the accident or disease.

For details about when you may be treated as being in or employed in GB, when your accident or disease may be treated as if it arose in GB, and when your employment may count as employed earner's employment (including mariners, airmen and women, volunteer development workers, and offshore workers) see p179.

To get **disablement benefit** or **retirement allowance** you do not have to satisfy any presence or residence conditions.[115] As a result, your absences from GB do not affect your entitlement to these benefits provided you satisfy the requirements relating to your work and your accident or disease.

In order to get **reduced earnings allowance (REA), constant attendance allowance** or **exceptionally severe disablement allowance** you must be present in GB when you claim.[116]

You remain entitled to constant attendance allowance and exceptionally severe disablement allowance for a period of six months (beginning with the first date on which you are absent) during which you are temporarily absent (see p247) from GB.[117] If your period of temporary absence is longer than six months the Secretary of State has a discretion to allow you to continue to receive benefit.[118]

You remain entitled to REA for a period of three months (beginning with the first date on which you are absent) during which you are temporarily absent from GB.[119] If your period of temporary absence is longer than three months, then the Secretary of State has a discretion to allow you to continue to receive benefit.[120] For constant attendance allowance or exceptionally severe disablement allowance, as well as for REA, the Secretary of State in exercising this discretion will consider the reasons for your absence and any other relevant matters. To be entitled to REA:[121]

- your absence from GB must *not* be in order to work or engage in any other economic activity; *and*
- your claim must have been made before you leave GB; *and*
- you must have been entitled to REA before going abroad.

You count as present in GB for the purposes of REA while you are employed as a mariner or airman or woman.[122] It has not been possible to make new claims for REA since 1990, unless the accident or illness to which the claim refers occurred before then. This means that if you lose your entitlement to your current claim by a longer period of absence abroad you will lose this benefit and not be able to re-claim it on your return.

15. **Disability benefits**

These benefits are disability living allowance (DLA), attendance allowance (AA) and carer's allowance (CA). For details of the presence and residence conditions in relation to these benefits and for the circumstances in which you may be treated as present because of either your occupation or that of another member of your family, see Chapter 11. Your absences abroad are likely to affect your ability to satisfy the initial and past presence requirements for these benefits.

Disability living allowance and attendance allowance

If you are coming to Great Britain (GB) and are unable to satisfy the residence rule that you have been present in GB for a total of 26 weeks in the last 52 weeks (13 weeks for children under six months of age), you only get these benefits if you are terminally ill.[123] If you are terminally ill, you still need to be present and ordinarily resident in GB in order to be entitled.[124] However, if your earnings or those of your spouse/civil partner are exempt from UK income tax you are subject to an extra test of having been present in GB for a total of at least 156 weeks in the last four years. This residence condition is not waived if you are terminally ill.[125]

If you have been abroad it may be difficult for you to show that you satisfy the criteria for the mobility and/or the care component for the necessary three months prior to the claim. If you experience difficulties with this you should seek advice.

If you go abroad you are still treated as present in GB and therefore entitled to benefit if you are:

- temporarily absent from GB and have not been absent for a period of more than 26 weeks *provided* the absence was intended to be temporary at the outset;[126] *or*
- temporarily absent from GB for the purpose of being treated for an incapacity or a disabling condition which began before you left GB *provided* the Secretary of State certifies that it is consistent with the proper administration of the system that you should continue to receive benefit;[127] *or*
- abroad as a serving member of the forces, an airman or woman or mariner, or a continental shelf worker, or if you are living with a close relative (see p182) who is a serving member of the forces.[128]

If you satisfy any of the above requirements for any particular day, then you are also treated as present in GB for the purpose of the past presence requirement for DLA and AA – ie, you have been present in GB for a period of 26 weeks in the last 52 weeks before your claim to benefit.[129]

If by the time you wish to go abroad you have reached 66 years of age and are receiving the lower rate care component or the lower rate mobility component of DLA you should be aware that if you break your claim you may not re-qualify for benefit when you return.[130] This is because claims must be made by the age of 65, and an absence longer than the period for which benefit can continue to be paid will mean you will be too old to meet the qualifying conditions for DLA, and may be unable to satisfy the stricter tests which apply to AA.

Carer's allowance

The residence and presence conditions for CA are the same as for DLA and AA *except* that:[131]
- there is no waiver of the 26-week rule for the terminally ill; *and*
- those who receive UK tax exempt earnings are not treated differently from those who do not.

For details of these rules, see p183.

If you go abroad you remain entitled to CA (and you are still treated as present in GB for the purposes of the 26-week rule) if your absence is **temporary**[132] and:
- the absence is for a continuous period that does not exceed four weeks and was always intended to be temporary (in practice the disabled person would need to travel with you or you would fail to satisfy the ordinary conditions of entitlement, but see below); *or*
- the absence is for the specific purpose of caring for the disabled person who is also absent from GB and who remains entitled while absent to AA, DLA at the highest or middle rate, or constant attendance allowance. 'Specific' here does not have to mean sole purpose but the major purpose of the absence.[133]

You also remain entitled to benefit if you go abroad without the person for whom you care provided:[134]
- the absence is for a continuous period that does not exceed four weeks and was always intended to be temporary; *and*
- you have only temporarily stopped providing care of at least 35 hours a week; *and*
- you have provided the necessary amount of care for at least 14 weeks in the period of 26 weeks before you go abroad *and* you would have provided that care for at least 22 weeks in that period but were unable to because either yourself or the person for whom you care had to go into a hospital or a similar institution for medical treatment. However, you lose your benefit if the person for whom you care loses her/his entitlement to AA or DLA after s/he has been in hospital or care home for four weeks, or 12 weeks if s/he is under 16 years of age and in receipt of DLA.

You are therefore able to take a four-week temporary holiday from caring every six months in which either you or the person for whom you care is abroad and you are still able to receive benefit for this period.

16. **Statutory sick pay and statutory maternity, paternity and adoption pay**

There are no requirements of presence or residence for any of these benefits. You remain entitled to these benefits wherever you are based, provided you meet the normal entitlement rules (see p184).[135]

17. **Maternity allowance**

To get maternity allowance (MA) you need to have been in employment either as an employed or a self-employed person for at least 26 weeks in the 66 weeks before the week in which your baby is due. Maternity allowance is payable for a period of 39 weeks starting at any time from the beginning of the 11th week before the week in which your baby is due to the week following the week in which you actually give birth to your baby.[136]

However, in order to satisfy the 'recent work' test you have to have been employed or self-employed in GB.[137] As a result, a lengthy recent absence abroad may mean that you fail to establish your entitlement to MA. You may, however, still be able to claim MA if you:[138]

- have been working abroad and you return to GB; *and*
- remained ordinarily resident in GB during your period of absence; *and*
- have received earnings at least equal to the threshold figure.

The rules dealing with whether you remain entitled to MA when you are temporarily absent from GB are nearly the same as for incapacity benefit (see p261). The only differences are that the test of treatment for an incapacity arising as the result of an industrial injury does not apply and that MA is only payable for a period of 39 weeks.

Your pregnancy alone is not sufficient for the purposes of remaining entitled to benefit during your period of temporary absence. You need to show a further specific incapacity.[139] It is advisable to obtain backdated medical certificates before going abroad.

18. **Premiums and absence abroad**

Premiums are paid as part of your weekly entitlement to income support, income-based jobseeker's allowance, pension credit, housing benefit and council tax benefit. Many of these premiums are dependent on your receipt of another benefit – eg, disability living allowance, attendance allowance or carer's allowance. If your absence abroad means that you lose entitlement to the qualifying benefit, you also lose the relevant premium, although carer's premium continues to be paid for a further eight weeks. You may not be entitled to the premium as soon as you return, since you may need to satisfy again the presence test for the qualifying benefit. You may lose entitlement to a bereavement premium unless you make a fresh claim within eight weeks of the end of your previous claim.[140]

If you are receiving premiums, it is important to consider the full implications of your absence abroad on your benefit entitlement. It may be possible for you to time your absences in such a way that your premiums are not affected. For more information, consult your local advice agency.

Notes

1. Introduction
1 See R(S) 5/85
2 Eg, Social Security (Northern Ireland Reciprocal Arrangements) Regulations 1976 SI No.1003

3. Temporary absence
3 *Chief Adjudication Officer v Ahmed and others* CA, 16 March 1994, *The Guardian*, 15 April 1994 per Neill LJ
4 para 070859 DMG
5 *Chief Adjudication Officer v Ahmed and others* CA, 16 March 1994, *The Guardian*, 15 April 1994 per Neill LJ
6 R(U) 16/62
7 *Chief Adjudication Officer v Ahmed and others* CA, 16 March 1994, *The Guardian*, 15 April 1994 per Neill LJ
8 R(I) 73/54
9 R(S) 1/85
10 R(S) 1/66
11 s124(1) SSCBA 1992
12 Regs 4(1), (2)(a) and (b) and 3(a) and (b) IS Regs
13 Reg 4(3)(c) and (d) IS Regs
14 Reg 4(1)(a) and (2)(a)-(c) IS Regs as amended

5. Income-based jobseeker's allowance
15 s1(2)(I) JSA 1995
16 Reg 50 JSA Regs
17 Reg 50(2)(a), (3)(c) and (5)(c) JSA Regs
18 Reg 50(2)-(6) JSA Regs
19 s1(2)(a) and (c) JSA 1995
20 Regs 14, 19 and 50 JSA Regs, as amended by the Social Security (Jobseeker's Allowance and Mariners' Benefits) (Miscellaneous Amendment) Regulations 1997 No. 563
21 Regs 14(1)(m), 19(1)(m) and 50(6)(c) JSA Regs
22 Reg 14(1)(c) JSA Regs
23 Reg 19 JSA Regs
24 Reg 50(2)(c), (3)(b) and (5)(b) JSA Regs
25 Reg 50(6)(b) and (d) JSA Regs
26 Reg 50(5)(d) and (e) JSA Regs
27 Reg 14(1)(e) and (g) and 19(1)(e) and (g) JSA Regs
28 Reg 19(1)(e) and (g) JSA Regs
29 Reg 170 JSA Regs
30 Reg 50(1) and (4) JSA Regs
31 Reg 19(1)(p)(ii) JSA Regs
32 Sch 3 para 3(10) IS Regs

33 Sch 2 para 3(10) JSA Regs
34 Sch 3 para 3(11) IS Regs; Sch 2 para
3(10) and (11) JSA Regs

6. **Housing benefit and council tax benefit**

35 Reg 7(13) and (17) HB Regs
36 Reg 7 HB Regs
37 Reg 7(17) HB Regs
38 See also paras 3.39-3.41 GM and reg
7(9) HB Regs
39 For further details of who is treated as
occupying a dwelling see CPAG's
*Welfare Benefits and Tax Credits
Handbook.*
40 *R v HBRB ex parte Robertson* [1988] *The
Independent,* 5 March 1988
41 Reg 7 HB Regs
42 *R v Penwith DC ex parte Burt* 22 HLR 292
43 s130(1) SSCBA 1992; reg 7 HB Regs
44 See reg 7 HB Regs
45 See para A3.15 GM
46 s131(3)(a) SSCBA 1992
47 s6(5) Local Government Finance Act
1992; s99(1) Local Government Finance
(Scotland) Act 1992
48 Reg 8(3) CTB Regs
49 Art 3 Council Tax (Exempt Dwellings)
Order 1992 No. 558

7. **Pension credit**

50 s1(2) SPCA 2002
51 Reg3 SPC Regs
52 Reg 4 SPC Regs
53 Reg 4 SPC Regs
54 Reg 5 SPC Regs

8. **The social fund**

55 Reg 5(1)(a) SFM&FE Regs
56 Reg 5(1)(b) SFM&FE Regs
57 Reg 3(1) SFM&FE Regs
58 Reg 3 SFM&FE (Amdt) Regs
59 Reg 7(3) and (4) SFM&FE Regs
60 Reg 7(7) and (8) SFM&FE Regs
61 Reg 7(9)(b) SFM&FE Regs
62 Reg 7(5) SFM&FE Regs
63 Reg 7(1A) SFM&FE Regs
64 Reg 1A SFCWP Regs
65 Reg 2(a) SFWP Regs
66 Reg 4(2) SFWP Regs
67 SF Dirs 23(1)(a) and 29
68 SF Dir 8
69 *R v Social Fund Inspector and Secretary of
State for Social Security ex parte Davey*
(CO/1418/97), unreported, QBD
70 SF Dir 25
71 SF Dir 4(a)(I)

72 *R v SFI ex parte Amina Mohammed* [1992]
The Times, 25 November 1992
73 SF Dirs 14-17
74 SF Dir 16(b)
75 SF Dir 22

9. **Tax credits**

76 Reg 4 TC(R) Regs
77 s3 TCA 2002

10. **Contribution-based JSA and incapacity benefit**

78 s21 and Sch 1 para 11 JSA 1995; regs
14, 19 and 50 JSA Regs as amended by
Social Security (New Deal) Regulations
1998 (SI No.1274) and Jobseeker's
Allowance (Amendment) (No. 2)
Regulations 1999 (SI No.3087)
79 ss1(2)(d)(i) and 2 JSA 1995
80 Reg 11(1A) SSB(PA) Regs as amended
81 Reg 4A SS(MB) Regs as amended
82 EC Regulation 1408/71
83 In order to qualify as a member of the
family you must be the spouse, civil
partner, son, daughter, step-son, step-
daughter, father, father-in-law, step-
father, mother, mother-in-law or
step-mother of the person serving in the
forces – see reg 2(5)(b) SSB(PA) Regs
84 Reg 2(1), (1A) and (1B) SSB(PA) Regs
85 Reg 2(1)(a) SSB(PA) Regs
86 Reg 2(1) SSB(PA) Regs
87 R(S) 2/86 and R(S) 1/90
88 R(S) 10/51
89 R(S) 1/69; R(S) 2/69; R(S) 4/80; R(S) 6/
81
90 s94(1) SSCBA 1992
91 Reg 3 SSB(PA) (Amendment)
Regulations 1994 (SI No.268)
92 Reg 11(2) SSB(PA) Regs
93 Reg 4A SS(MB) Regs

11. **Child benefit and guardian's allowance**

94 s146 SSCBA 92
95 Reg 23(1) CB Regs
96 Reg 23(4) CB Regs
97 Reg 24 CB Regs
98 Reg24 CB Regs
99 Reg 21 CB Regs
100 Reg 21(1)(b)(i)
101 Reg 5 SS(GA) Regs
102 Reg 9 SS(GA) Regs

12. **Retirement pensions**

103 Reg 10 SS(WB&RP) Regs
104 Reg 4(1) SSB(PA) Regs
105 Reg 4(3), (4), (5)(c) and (6) SSB(PA) Regs

106 See *Rotao Annette Carson v Secretary of State for Work and Pensions* [2002] EWHC 978
107 Reg 5(3)(a), (aa) and (6) SSB(PA) Regs
108 Reg 8(1) SSB(PA) Regs

13. Bereavement benefits
109 Reg 4(a) SSB(PA) Regs
110 s1(2)(a) SSAA 1992 as amended by s70 WRPA 1999; reg 19(2), (3) SS(C&P) Regs
111 ss3 and 4 SSAA 1992 as amended by s70 and Sch 8 WRPA 1999

14. Industrial injuries benefits
112 ss94(1), 108 and 109 SSCBA 1992 as amended by s65 Social Security Act 1998
113 s2(1)(a) SSCBA 1992
114 s94(5) SSCBA 1992
115 Reg 9(3) and (7) SSB(PA) Regs
116 s113 SSCBA 1992
117 Reg 9(4) SSB(PA) Regs
118 Reg 9(4) SSB(PA) Regs
119 Reg 9(5) SSB(PA) Regs
120 Reg 9(5) SSB(PA) Regs
121 Reg 9(5)(a)-(c) SSB(PA) Regs
122 Reg 5(b) SS(IIMB) Regs; for the meaning of 'mariner' and 'airman' see regs 4-7 and Sch II of SS(EEEIIP) Regs

15. Disability benefits
123 Reg 2(4) SS(DLA) Regs; reg 2(3) SS(AA) Regs
124 Reg 2(1) SS(DLA) Regs; reg 2(1) SS(AA) Regs
125 Reg 2(1)(b) SS(DLA) Regs; reg 2(1)(b) SS(AA) Regs as amended by Social Security (Immigration and Asylum) Consequential Amendment Regulations 2000 (SI No. 636)
126 Reg 2(2)(d) SS(DLA) Regs; reg 2(2)(d) SS(AA) Regs; reg 10 SSB(PA) Regs
127 Reg 2(2)(e) SS(DLA) Regs; reg 2(2)(e) SS(AA) Regs; reg 10 SSB(PA) Regs
128 Reg 2(2)(a)-(c) SS(DLA) Regs; reg 2(2)(a)-(c) SS(AA) Regs
129 Regs 2(1)(a)(iii), (2) SS(DLA) Regs; regs 1(a), 2(1)(a)(iii), (2) SS(AA) Regs
130 Reg 3 SS(DLA) Regs as amended by Social Security (DLA) Amendment Regs 1997 (SI No. 349)
131 Reg 9 SS(ICA) Regs as amended by Social Security (Immigration and Asylum) (Consequential Amendment) Regulations 2000
132 Reg 9(2) SS(ICA) Regs; reg 10B SSB(PA) Regs

133 CG/15/1993
134 Regs 4(2) and 9(2) SS(ICA) Regs

16. Statutory sick pay and statutory maternity, paternity and adoption pay
135 Reg 10 SSP(MAPA) Regs; reg 2A SMP(PAM) Regs; reg 4 SPPSAP(PAM) Regs

17. Maternity allowance
136 ss35(2) and 165 SSCBA 1992
137 s2(1)(a) and (b) SSCBA 1992
138 Reg 2 Social Security (Maternity Allowance) (Work Abroad) Regulations as amended by Social Security (Maternity Allowance)(Work Abroad)(Amendment) Regulations 2000 No. 691
139 R(S) 1/75

18. Premiums and absence abroad
140 Sch 2 para 8A(3) IS Regs, and similar provisions in JSA, HB and CTB Regs, all as amended by Social Security (Amendment) Bereavement Benefits Regulations 2000 (SI No. 2239)

Chapter 20

Getting paid while abroad

This chapter covers:
1. General rules (below)
2. Receiving benefit while abroad (below)
3. Paying national insurance contributions while abroad (p276)

1. General rules

This chapter deals with how to get your benefit paid to you when you go abroad. Because some benefits require national insurance (NI) contributions, the chapter also covers how to make voluntary NI contributions in Great Britain or Northern Ireland when you go abroad. For further details about NI contributions, see CPAG's *Welfare Benefits and Tax Credits Handbook*.

In order to find out whether you are entitled to benefit see the chapter relevant to your immigration status in Part 2 of this book. In order to find out how your absence or absences abroad affect your benefit entitlement, see Chapter 19. If a number of benefits are paid, the temporary absence rules will apply separately to each benefit.

For all benefits, if you delay for a year in cashing or collecting your benefit after it has been issued to you (whether or not this is because you have gone abroad), you will lose your right to have it paid to you even though you are strictly 'entitled' to the benefit.[1] The only exceptions to this rule are if:[2]

- you apply in writing to the Department of Work and Pensions or the Revenue for the benefit to be paid to you and you have good cause for not asking for the money earlier (for the meaning of 'good cause' see CPAG's *Welfare Benefits and Tax Credits Handbook*); *or*
- the Secretary of State is satisfied that no payment was issued; *or*
- payment was issued and returned and no duplicate payment has been issued.

2. Receiving benefit while abroad

Most people now receive benefit by direct transfer into a bank account. If you go abroad and remain entitled to benefit you can:

- ask for your benefits to be paid directly into a bank or building society account in Great Britain;[3] *or*
- ask the DWP to pay your benefits directly into a bank account abroad, although in some countries you will have to open an account with a specific bank in order to be paid in this way.

Contact your local office to get more details about the procedures.

There are specific considerations relating to particular benefits which are described below.

Income support and income-based jobseeker's allowance

If you are going abroad, you should inform your local benefits office. If you are claiming income-based jobseeker's allowance (JSA) and you are going abroad in order to attend a job interview, you should notify Jobcentre Plus who may also ask you to explain your absence in writing. Similarly, if you are taking a two-week holiday from jobseeking (see p252) you must notify Jobcentre Plus in writing and you will be asked to fill out a holiday form so you can be contacted if a job becomes available.

Housing benefit and council tax benefit

If you are going abroad you should tell your local authority about your absence and notify it of any reduction in income that may occur, for instance if your part-time earnings are going to cease. This is because such a reduction may affect the amount of benefit to which you are entitled. Housing benefit (HB) and council tax benefit (CTB) can continue in payment while you are out of the country for a period of 13 weeks and in some circumstances for 52 weeks (see p253). A new period of absence starts if you return home for even a short stay of at least 24 hours.[4] On your return home if there is a gap in your claim you should ask for backdating but would need to show that you have good cause for a late claim.[5] If you have any difficulties getting such a claim accepted, you should contact your local advice centre.

If you are going abroad for longer than you will be able to claim HB and CTB, and there is someone living in your home while you are away, then, depending on that person's circumstances, it may be possible for her/him to argue that s/he is responsible for paying the housing costs and so claim HB and CTB in her/his own right.

If you are a private or housing association tenant and your HB is paid directly to you, while you are away you may need to make arrangements with your local authority to request that the benefit is paid directly to your landlord.

Incapacity benefit, maternity allowance and contribution-based jobseeker's allowance

Incapacity benefit (IB), maternity allowance and contribution-based JSA can be paid to you while you are abroad. Before going abroad you should inform your local office of your trip and the reasons for it. You will be asked to fill out a form giving the reasons for your absence and when you intend to return to the UK. You should tell your office well in advance of your trip abroad otherwise it may not be possible to reach a decision on your claim before you go abroad.

If you have claimed IB and you are due a medical examination when you go abroad you should ask if this can be arranged abroad. If this is not agreed you will run a greater risk that the Secretary of State will refuse to pay these benefits during your absence.

Retirement pensions and bereavement benefits

Both retirement pensions and bereavement benefits can be paid to you while you are abroad. If the DWP thinks that you are entitled to retirement pension and it has an address at which to contact you, it will write to you a few months before you reach state pension age to determine whether or not you wish to claim. If you do not receive a letter but you think that you may be entitled, you should contact the DWP yourself (for address see Appendix 2).

If you are happy for your benefit to be paid in the UK you do not need to tell your local office that you are going abroad if you will not be away for more than three months. If, however, you are going abroad for more than three months, and you need your benefit transferred into an account outside the UK, you should tell your local office so that arrangements can be made to pay your benefit to you abroad. If you need to get your benefit paid into a bank account while you are abroad, you should give the DWP as much notice as possible as it is often very slow in making these arrangements. If you have not resolved this before you leave, you should authorise a friend, relative or advice agency in the UK to complete the arrangements.

Attendance allowance and disability living allowance

If you are going abroad and you are in receipt of attendance allowance (AA) or disability living allowance (DLA) you should contact your local benefits office or the Disability Contact Processing Unit (see Appendix 2). If you are in receipt of severe disablement allowance or extra premiums paid with your HB or CTB, remember that you may lose these allowances if your absence means that you will lose entitlement to DLA or AA. It may be possible for you to time your absence to avoid this situation and to ensure that you can continue to claim on your return.

Carer's allowance

If you are going abroad and are in receipt of carer's allowance (CA) you should contact your local office.

If you lose your entitlement to CA you should still be eligible for a carer's premium paid with your IS, income-based JSA, HB or CTB for a further period of eight weeks, provided you are entitled to these benefits while you are away.[6] If you lose your entitlement to CA while you are abroad and the disabled person for whom you care is staying in the UK, s/he may be able to claim a severe disability premium during your absence instead. For further information see CPAG's *Welfare Benefits and Tax Credits Handbook*.

3. **Paying national insurance contributions while abroad**

Entitlement to many benefits (the 'contributory benefits') depends on the national insurance (NI) contributions you have made. When you go abroad you can generally decide whether or not to continue to pay NI contributions voluntarily here, in order to protect your entitlement to certain benefits. The contribution rates if you go abroad are the same as if you pay in the UK.

For pensions you can obtain a 'pension forecast' by writing to the Revenue. You should receive a reply which may help you to decide whether to make voluntary contributions or not. If your pension will be so low that you will always need to claim a means-tested benefit to top it up and you are planning to stay in this country when you retire, it is probably not worth making voluntary contributions. For further details see CPAG's *Welfare Benefits and Tax Credits Handbook*.

Payments may be made in any of the following ways:[7]

- by direct debit every month in arrears;
- once a year at the end of the year for which the contributions are due;
- by a person you nominate to make the payments for you in the UK in either of the above two ways.

For further information about whether or not to make voluntary contributions and how to make them you can contact the Pensions and Overseas Benefits Directorate and obtain leaflet NI38. With this leaflet you will also be sent Form CF38 which you should fill in and return if you decide to make contributions while you are abroad.

Notes

1. General rules
1 Reg 38(1) SS(C&P) Regs as amended by
Tax Credits (Claims and Payments)
(Amendment) Regulations 1999 No.
2572

2. Receiving benefit while abroad
2 Reg 38(2A) SS(C&P) Regs
3 Reg 21 SS(C&P) Regs as amended by
SS(C&P) Amendment Regulations 1999
No. 2358 and Tax Credits (Claims and
Payments) (Amendment) Regulations
1999 No. 2572
4 *R v Penwith DC ex parte Burt* [1988] 22
HLR 292 (QBD); para A3/3.170 GM
5 Reg 83(12) HB Regs; reg 69(14) CTB
Regs
6 Sch 3 para 17 HB Regs; Sch 1 para 17
CTB Regs; Sch 1 para 17 JSA Regs – all as
amended by Social Security
(Miscellaneous Amendments)
Regulations 2000 No. 681
7 s13 SSCBA 1992

Part 4

European Community social security law

Chapter 21

European Community social security law: introduction

This chapter covers:
1. Who needs to use this section (below)
2. The foundations of the European Union (p282)
3. Using European Community law (p284)
4. Immigration outline for European Economic Area nationals (p287)
5. The different routes for claiming social security benefits and tax credits (p288)
6. Remedies (p289)

This part of the book concerns the rights and benefits to which you may be entitled if you are travelling to, from or around the European Economic Area (EEA). It describes the rights you may have as a citizen of a country within the EEA including the European Union, or as a dependant of one of these citizens.

Because this book is about benefit entitlement for migrants, this section only covers European law in respect of migrants. For information about European Community law on the equal treatment between men and women, see CPAG's *Welfare Benefits and Tax Credits Handbook*.

1. **Who needs to use this section**

If you are a European Economic Area (EEA) national (see p282) you are never a 'person subject to immigration control' for benefit purposes (see p155). This is because as an EEA national you do not require leave to enter and are not subject to the 'no recourse to public funds restriction'. This applies equally to any family members who enter the UK with you, whatever their nationality.[1] However, EEA nationals may have to satisfy the habitual residence and right to reside tests for certain benefits (see Chapter 11). If you fail these residence tests you are classified as a 'person from abroad' for benefit purposes. This means that you are not entitled to certain benefits. However, certain EEA nationals are exempt from the habitual residence and right to reside tests (see Chapter 8).

People for whom this section is particularly relevant are:

- EEA nationals who are subject to the habitual residence test;
- EEA nationals who are subject to the right to reside test;
- EEA nationals who have failed the contributions conditions for contributory benefits but who have worked in another member state;
- EEA nationals who do not meet the residence conditions for a particular benefit but who have worked or resided elsewhere in the EEA;
- EEA nationals who have family members living in other EEA states;
- spouses/civil partners and family members of EEA nationals who are not themselves EEA nationals and who wish to claim benefit;
- nationals of states which have association agreements with the European Union;
- refugees and stateless persons.

2. The foundations of the European Union

The European Union (EU) was established in 1957. It began as an economic body and this is reflected in its original name, the European Economic Community (EEC). The EU now has 27 members as follows:

Austria	Germany	The Netherlands
Belgium	Greece	Poland
Bulgaria	Hungary	Portugal
Cyprus	Ireland	Romania
Czech Republic	Italy	Slovakia
Denmark	Latvia	Slovednia
Estonia	Lithuania	Spain
Finland	Luxembourg	Sweden
France	Malta	The UK

European Community (EC) law has been extended to countries outside the EU who are covered by the European Economic Area (EEA) Agreement. EEA nationals are covered by EC law to much the same extent as nationals of EU states. There are slight differences in that EEA nationals are not able to rely on the EC Treaty. The EEA Agreement came into force in January 1994 when the EU joined another trading group, the European Free Trade Area. The Agreement mirrors the free movement of workers provisions in the EC Treaty but does not have provisions equivalent to Articles 12 or 18 of the EC Treaty. The EEA consists of the EU countries plus:

- Iceland;

- Liechtenstein;
- Norway.

> From 1 June 2002, the right to freedom of movement also applies to Switzerland. Any further references in this part to EEA nationals should be interpreted as including Switzerland.

EC law applies in all of these countries but it extends beyond the actual territory of the member states. It also applies to countries 'for whose external relations a member state is responsible'. Therefore Spain not only includes the mainland but also the Balearic and the Canary Islands. Portugal includes Madeira and the Azores.[2] However, there are certain exceptions to this general rule. In particular, in the UK Gibraltar is covered, whereas the Isle of Man and the Channel Islands are not.

Some of the newer member states to the EU do not have full EC rights. The restriction on some rights applies to eight of the member states who joined the EU in 2004 (the A8 states) and the two states who joined the EU in 2007 (the A2 states).

> The A8 states are Czech Republic, Estonia, Hungary, Latvia, Lithuania, Poland, Slovakia and Slovenia.
> The A2 states are Bulgaria and Romania.

The institutions of the European Community

The Commission

The Commission,[3] which is based in Brussels, is effectively the EU's civil service. There are 20 commissioners in charge of the various 'Directorate Generals', and they are European officials, not representatives of their states of origin. It is the Commission that makes proposals for European legislation; it therefore, has quite a different role to the UK civil service, which is supposed to have a non-political role.

The Council

The Council[4] decides whether to pass community legislation after consultation with the European Parliament (see p284). It is based in Brussels. It is made up of the representative minister from each member state with domestic responsibility for a particular policy area. In the field of social security the Council consists of the minister for social affairs from each member state. In the UK this is the minister for work and pensions.

Some EC measures require the Council to vote unanimously to pass them before they become law. However, most measures need a 'qualified majority' vote of ministers. This means that ministers cast votes according to the size of their member state. Therefore, the UK has ten votes, whereas the Republic of Ireland, with a much smaller population, has only three votes. Under this system, a proposal needs 62 votes out of 87 to pass, so if the UK wants to block such a proposal, it would need the support of two other large member states, or a number of small member states, to be successful.

The European Parliament

The European Parliament, which is based in Strasbourg, does have some participation in the adoption of EC legislation but its role is very much one of an advisory and supervisory body. Unlike the British Parliament, it cannot pass laws itself, although it can require the Council to consider its representations. Members of the European Parliament are directly elected by people of the member states and sit in political groups reflecting their political opinions rather than their nationalities. For some types of EC law, the European Parliament is only entitled to be consulted, but in many areas, it has the right to a co-decision with the Council. This gives it considerable influence over the final legislation. For example, both Articles 39 and 42 of the EC Treaty give the Parliament 'co-decision' power.

The European Court of Justice

This is the main institution you need to know about for the purposes of this book. There is more information about its procedure on p291. The European Court of Justice (ECJ) is based in Luxembourg. It has responsibility for making sure EC law is observed and applied in the same way throughout the EU. Its decisions are binding on all member states. It should not be confused with the European Court of Human Rights, which operates from Strasburg and hears cases based on the European Convention on Human Rights (see CPAG's *Welfare Benefits and Tax Credits Handbook* for more information).

Judgments of the ECJ are brief and do not offer the type of reasoning found in UK judgments, and this can often present difficulties for those seeking to interpret a case.

3. **Using European Community law**

The European Union (EU) is the product of a number of international treaties. The Treaty of Rome (the European Community (EC) Treaty) was the founding treaty and it remains in force today. However, it has been amended by a number of subsequent treaties. The important ones for this book are: the Single European Act 1986, the Treaty of European Union ('Maastricht') 1993 and the Treaty of Amsterdam 1999.

The objects of the EC Treaty as amended include:
- the promotion of economic and social cohesion through the creation of an area without frontiers;
- the prohibition of discrimination on grounds of nationality;
- the introduction of a concept of European citizenship.

Since the UK joined the EU in 1973 the EC's legal system has had an important effect on English law. There are two important principles.
- The supremacy of EC law over domestic law – EC law has higher standing than the law of the member state. If domestic law is not consistent with EC law a court or tribunal should not apply it.[5]
- 'Direct effect' (see below).

'Direct effect' means that EC law forms a part of our national legal system, as if it had been adopted by the UK Parliament. As a result, individuals can claim rights under that law in national courts or tribunals. Not all EC measures have direct effect. In order to have 'direct effect', an EC law must be:
- clear;
- precise; *and*
- unconditional.

The European Court of Justice (ECJ) applies this test generously, with the consequence that many provisions of EC law are directly effective. Most EC law relevant to this book is directly effective.

Purposive interpretation of European Community law

The European legal system and its terminology differ from domestic law. The relationship between EC law and the domestic law of member states is complex. This is inevitable, as EC law has to deal with many different legal systems. There are different principles of interpretation for EC law and UK law. This causes problems as the UK judiciary does not always apply the European principles where appropriate.

Interpretation of European law takes a 'purposive' approach. That means you interpret a legal instrument by establishing its objective. It is therefore important to interpret any EU provisions in the light of the objectives of EC law as a whole.

By contrast, UK law is interpreted by taking the literal meaning of the words and phrases used. Only if this is ambiguous, is the purpose of the legislation examined.

European legislative instruments

Most EC law relevant to social security is in the form of treaty articles or regulations (see p286).

Treaties

Treaties are the constitutional framework of the EC and they have a higher status than other EC legislation. The ECJ (see p290) regularly returns to the fundamental principles of the treaties when considering cases. Individual parts of the treaty are divided into Articles.

Regulations

'Regulation' has a different meaning in EC law to that in UK law. In UK law a 'regulation' is secondary legislation made by a minister using powers given by statute. Courts and commissioners can consider the validity of a set of regulations and in some circumstances declare them unlawful and strike them down.

In EC law a 'regulation' is not secondary legislation. It is more like UK primary legislation. It has direct effect and it overrides conflicting domestic legislation. This will be the case even if an EC regulation is in conflict with a UK statute.

Where a regulation is the legal instrument used, it lays down the content of the law itself and it is unnecessary for a member state to legislate in the same field. Therefore, unlike a directive there is no need for a member state to transpose regulations in domestic law.

Directives

A directive is an instrument of EC law which is addressed to the governments of member states. It is akin to an instruction to member states to change the law in a particular area. For example, there is a new Race Directive that requires member states to remove race discrimination in areas such as access to social security. The directive is binding upon the member state as to the result to be achieved, but it leaves the individual member states with discretion as to how to achieve it.[6] Directives are transposed into domestic law via a statute or statutory instrument (confusingly also called a 'regulation' in the UK). Member states are usually given a period of two years to incorporate the directive into domestic legislation.

The relationship between directives and national law is quite complex. In particular, member states do not always interpret directives accurately. Therefore although a directive has been adopted you may still find some areas that appear to be incompatible with EC law. If there is any doubt it is important to compare the directive with the domestic law to see whether the directive has been properly implemented.

Decisions

Decisions are in some ways similar to directives. It is an individual act designed to be addressed to a specified person(s) or state. A decision does not require any further measures to be taken to implement it. It is a binding act with the force of law. However, it is only binding on the parties to whom it is addressed.[7]

Chapter 21: European Community social security law: introduction
4. Immigration outline for European Economic Area nationals

21

Recommendations

Recommendations and opinions form part of what is known as 'soft law'. They are not binding on anybody, but courts and tribunals should take them into account in reaching their decisions.[8]

4. Immigration outline for European Economic Area nationals

UK immigration law is governed by a series of Acts of Parliament,[9] which provides a framework under which secondary legislation, in the form of immigration rules, set out the specific detail.[10] However, these Acts and rules cannot be applied to people entitled to rely on rights of entry and residence in the UK under European Community (EC) law.[11]

If you have a right to enter and live in the UK under EC law, you cannot be prevented from doing so by national law. Three categories of people have rights of entry, residence and to engage in economic activities in the UK as a result of EC law. They are:

- European Union (EU)/European Economic Area (EEA) nationals;
- family members, *of any nationality*, of EU/EEA nationals;
- nationals of states outside the EU/EEA to whom rights are granted by agreements between their state and the EU/EEA (see Part 5).

If EC law gives you a right to enter and reside in the UK, national law cannot affect that right by requiring, for instance, that you ask for permission to enter the UK or to reside here.[12] However, you can be required to let the UK authorities know that you have taken up residence here. If you are exercising your EC rights you are able to enter and reside in another member state freely. You are not admitted subject to a period of leave and consequently you can remain in that state for as long as you choose. These rights apply equally to your family whatever their nationality. For example, an EEA national who is married to a Nigerian citizen will not have to get entry clearance for her/his spouse. S/he does not have to fulfil the UK immigration conditions for a spouse and s/he will not be given limited leave. This applies to all EEA nationals, including UK nationals. However, in order for a UK national to bring in a spouse avoiding UK immigration rules the UK national must first engage EC law. S/he will, therefore, need to have moved within the EEA exercising EC rights.

Your right of residence in the UK can only come to an end if you cease to qualify under EC law, or your personal activities constitute a threat to public policy, public security or public health.[13] You cannot be removed for claiming benefits. If the UK authorities wish to expel you from the UK, you are entitled to a right of appeal against that decision.[14] The issue of residence has taken on great

21

Chapter 21: European Community social security law: introduction
4. Immigration outline for European Economic Area nationals

significance for EEA nationals since the introduction of the right to reside test for certain benefits. For further details on residence, see Chapter 11.

5. The routes for claiming social security benefits and tax credits

There are three main areas of European Community (EC) law that are significant for social security purposes:
- rights of residence;
- equal treatment;
- co-ordination of social security.

They are all linked to the right within the EC Treaty to freedom of movement.

It is a fundamental principle of EC social security law that nationals of member states should be able to move freely from one member state to another in order to seek work. The right to mobility is not absolute, but is generally confined to economically active groups. If you are a citizen of a European Economic Area (EEA) member state you and your dependants have rights under EC law, and therefore under UK law, to enter and reside in the UK.

EC law does not set out to make social security provisions the same in each member state. The national systems and standards of living are too different for that to be feasible. Instead EC law aims to ensure there is continuity of social protection for people who move between member states. Although the objective is clear, often the law is not.

The Treaty legislation which sets out these principles is as follows.
- Article 12 EC Treaty prohibits discrimination on nationality grounds.
- Article 17 EC Treaty states that any national of a member state is a citizen of the EU.
- Article 18 EC Treaty provides that all citizens of the EU have the right to move and reside freely within the EU subject to certain limitations and conditions laid down in the Treaty.
- Article 39 EC Treaty gives workers a right to enter and reside in another member states in order to work or to look for work.
- Article 42 EC Treaty provides the foundation for the co-ordination of social security schemes. It states that in order to ensure freedom of movement for workers migrants must be able to aggregate periods of work in other member states in order to be able to claim benefits in another and to be able to export benefits to other member states.
- Article 43 EC Treaty gives the self-employed a right to 'freedom of establishment'. This means that a self-employed person may freely enter and reside in any other member state.

- Article 49 EC Treaty gives the right to freely enter and reside in another member state in order to provide services. It also includes the right to receive services.

The detailed rules relating to these rights are spelled out in Regulations and Directives. The variety of EC rules all have the same objectives: to make it easier for workers to move freely from member state to member state. However, whether you can rely on a particular area of EC law depends whether you fit within the scope of that particular piece of legislation.

6. **Remedies**

The aim of the Treaty is to achieve economic as well as social integration, and the rules are based on the general rule against discrimination in Article 12:

'Within the scope of application of this Treaty, and without prejudice to any social provision contained therein, any discrimination on grounds of nationality shall be prohibited.'

EC law recognises that there is more to removing barriers to free movement than the abolition of immigration controls. The objective of free movement would in practice be frustrated if a migrant were to lose out on social security benefits guaranteed under the law of a member state.

Examples

A British woman may be deterred from taking up a job in France if she cannot rely on national insurance contributions made in both countries when she comes to receive her pension, whether she returns to England, or retires in France.

An Italian man may decide not to seek work in the UK if he cannot get child benefit for children living in Italy.

Appeal tribunals and social security commissioners

Remedies

If a person believes that s/he has rights under European Community (EC) law s/he can assert those rights in the appropriate tribunal or court. A social security claimant should raise the matter with the DWP when making a claim or when s/he receives a decision by the DWP. EC law binds UK courts and tribunals, it also binds the DWP. This means that you can rely on EC law in applications for revisions and supersessions and in appeals to tribunals and social security commissioners in the same way as you would use UK law. See CPAG's *Welfare*

Benefits and Tax Credits Handbook for details of how to challenge social security decisions.

It is an error of law for a tribunal to fail to address a point of European law raised in the course of an appeal.[15] If a case involves a European Economic Area (EEA) national the tribunal should make enquiries to determine whether that person can be assisted by EC law.[16]

You can ask the tribunal or commissioner to refer the matter to the European Court of Justice (ECJ – see p290) but should seek specialist help before doing so. Legal help (formerly legal aid) is available for references to the ECJ if legal assistance would have been available before the domestic court or tribunal. Although it is possible to refer cases to the ECJ from a tribunal it, is probably more sensible to refer matters from the commissioner or higher courts.[17]

In some very limited circumstances national time limits in which to lodge an appeal or to bring a judicial review do not apply as they may act as a bar to you asserting EC rights. The circumstances in which this would apply is when a member state has not fully transposed a directive into domestic legislation.[18] The time limit runs only from the time the directive is fully transposed. This does not apply to EC regulations which do not require transposing legislation by the member state. Furthermore, a national limit which restricts the backdating of benefit is not contrary to EC law.[19]

Legal help

Legal help is available for assistance with preparation for tribunals and commissioners' appeals. Public funding for representation is not generally available for hearings before tribunals and commissioners. However, solicitors with contracts for welfare benefits and tax credits can get public funding for representation for claimants under section 6(8)(b) Access to Justice Act.[20] This gives the Lord Chancellor discretion to award public funding for representation in proceedings which are otherwise excluded. You have to show in addition to the usual tests, that legal representation is the only adequate way of establishing the facts and presenting the case.

The European Court of Justice

How cases get to the court

The ECJ has the power to make preliminary rulings concerning:

- interpretation; *and*
- validity.

Actions in the ECJ refer to questions on the interpretation or validity of EC law only. The ECJ has no power to interpret national legislation. Some are direct actions – eg, an action brought by the Commission against a member state for failure to fulfil a Treaty obligation[21] or an action brought by one member state against another.[22]

More significantly for this book, the other way in which cases reach the ECJ is on a reference from a national court under Article 234 of the EC Treaty. Where a question of interpretation of EC law arises in any court or tribunal of a member state, that court or tribunal may request a ruling on that question if it considers that a decision on the question is necessary to enable it to give judgment.

A reference under Article 234 is not an appeal. It merely provides a means for national courts to obtain a ruling on the interpretation of an EC provision. The national court then applies the ruling to national law and decides the case itself.

A reference can be made by any 'court or tribunal' which would clearly include both social security commissioners and tribunals, and the domestic proceedings are then adjourned pending the outcome of the reference.

There is no absolute right to have your case referred to the ECJ unless you have no further judicial remedy. A final court of appeal must make a reference in relation to a question of EC law. In the UK, this is generally taken to mean the House of Lords. However, there is some authority to suggest that if leave to appeal cannot be obtained by a higher court that a reference should be made by the lower court or tribunal.[23] Once judgment has been given by the ECJ, the member state must act to give effect to it.[24]

There is also no right to a reference to the ECJ if the matter is *'acte clair'*.[25] This means that if a provision is clear, for example because the ECJ has already ruled on the question, there is no need for the court to refer.

The ECJ has held[26] that it is *not* necessary for a national court to make a reference if:

- the question of EC law is irrelevant; *or*
- the provision has already been interpreted by the ECJ; *or*
- the correct application is so obvious as to leave no room for doubt.

The Court of Appeal[27] has also ruled on this issue. The Court held that a reference would not be necessary if the ECJ had already ruled on the question, or the matter was reasonably clear and free from doubt.

Individuals cannot apply to the ECJ direct. You can ask a tribunal or commissioner to refer a question to the ECJ, but you should seek specialist advice before doing so. In view of the complexity of the law it may be more sensible to seek a referral from a commissioner than from a tribunal.

The procedure

The UK court, commissioner or tribunal drafts the question and submits it to the ECJ. It is then served on the parties, who have two months to make written submissions. There is usually an oral hearing.

The UK proceedings are adjourned pending the outcome of the reference. The ECJ often takes a very long time to give its judgments so a reference is likely to cause a considerable delay. It may be appropriate to ask the DWP to make interim payments while awaiting a decision.[28]

The advocate general's opinion

The judges of the ECJ are assisted by nine advocate generals (AGs). The AGs are not judges but they do have something of a judicial function. Once all the parties to a case have made their submissions and before the judges consider the case the AG gives an opinion. The AG's opinion offers an analysis of the legal position, much more akin to a UK judgment, and thus reading the AG's opinion often illuminates the reasoning of the ECJ. However, the opinion is not binding and it may or may not be followed by the ECJ. Where the ECJ chooses not to follow the opinion, which happens increasingly in social security law, the applicants and their advisers are often left somewhat bemused as to how the ECJ arrived at its decision.[29] The AG's opinion is given to all parties to the proceedings and is published in the *Official Journal*.

The judgment and after

Once the judgment has been given, the member state must act to give effect to it, if necessary. The UK proceedings will be re-listed for hearing in the light of the judgment.

Damages

If a member state breaches EC law by denying an individual the rights to which s/he is entitled under EC rules, it may be liable to pay damages. In order to claim damages in such cases, the individual must show three things. First, the EC law at issue must have intended to confer rights on individuals. Second, there must be a link between the damage, which the person suffered, and the breach of EC law by the member state. Finally, the breach must have been 'sufficiently serious'. The ECJ can award damages if the following can be shown:

- the EC law at issue intended to confer rights on individuals; *and*
- there is a link between the damage the person suffered and the breach of EC law by the member state; *and*
- the breach was 'sufficiently serious'.

In other words, not every breach of EC law by a member state will give individuals the right to claim damages. If a member state was diligent about attempting to apply EC law correctly it will not be liable.[30]

The precise scope of this doctrine has not yet been worked out but it has recently been held that damages can only be awarded where the state's failure was 'manifest and serious'.[31]

Costs and legal help

Generally legal help (formerly legal aid) is available if it would have been available for proceedings before the domestic courts. This includes the High Court, Court of Appeal, the House of Lords and some cases before the commissioners and tribunals.[32] The ECJ does not rule on costs. The ECJ can grant legal help itself where a party is unable to meet all or part of the costs of the case.

Notes

1. Who needs to use this section

1 EEA nationals have the right to enter another member state under EC Reg 1612/68 and have the right to bring members of their family with them. They are not subject to any periods of limited leave and therefore do not fall within the UK definition of 'person subject to immigration control' as set out in s115 IAA 1999. Furthermore the spouse of an EEA national does not lose EC law rights simply because they separate. See *Diatta*. Case C–267/83.

2 Art 227(1) EC Treaty. For a full list of countries covered see para 070040 DMG

2. The foundations of the EU

3 Arts 155-163 EC Treaty

4 Arts 145-154 EC Treaty

5 *Costa v ENEL* [1964] ECR 585; *Administrazione della Finanze delle State v Simmenthal* [1978] ECR 629

6 Art 189 EC Treaty

7 Art 189 EC Treaty

8 *Grimaldi v Fonds de maladies Professionelles* [1989] ECR 4407; see *Wadman v Carpenter Farrer Partnership* [1993] IRLR 374

4. Immigration outline for EEA nationals

9 IA 1971; Immigration (Carriers' Liability) Act 1987; IA 1988; AIAA 1993; AIA 1996

10 HC 395

11 s2 European Communities Act 1972

12 C-157/79 *Pieck* [1981] ECR 21711, [1980] 3 CMLR 378

13 Arts 39(3) and 56 Treaty of Rome

14 Art 15 I(EEA)O; Art 8 Dir 64/221

5. The two routes for claiming social security benefits and tax credits

15 R(SB) 6/91; R(S) 2/93

16 CIS/771/1997

17 Traditionally legal aid has been excluded from representation before the commissioners and tribunals. However, it was successfully argued in CF/3662/1999 that the Lord Chancellor did have the power to award legal aid under s6(8)(b) Access to Justice Act. This has now happened several times. In theory it should also be possible to secure legal aid for a hearing before a tribunal.

18 *Emmott* Case C-208/90

19 *Johnson* Cases C-410/92; *Steenhorst-Neerings* Case C-338/91

20 See note 17

21 Art 169 EC Treaty

22 Art 170 EC Treaty

23 *Hagen v Fratelli* [1980] 3 CMLR 253

24 Arts 5 and 170 EC Treaty

25 *Acte clair* is a doctrine originating in French administrative law, whereby if the meaning of a provision is clear no 'question' of interpretation arises. It was first introduced into EC law by the Advocate General in *Van Gend en Loos* Cases C-28/30/62. It was later applied in *CILFIT /srl* Case C-283/81.

26 *CILFIT /srl* Case C-283/81

27 Lord Denning in *Bulmer Ltd v Bollinger SA* [1974] Court of Appeal see also *R v ILEA (ex parte Hinde)* [1985] 1 CMLR 716

28 There is a general view that interim payments should be available pending EC cases but the DWP is rarely asked to do so. A refusal may be challengeable by judicial review but you should seek specialist advice before proceeding.

29 See for example, *Graham* Case C-92/94 involving discrimination in invalidity benefit.

30 *Francovich v Italian State* [1993] 2 CMLR 66; [1991] ECR I 5357; [1992] IRLR 84

31 *R v HM Treasury ex parte British
    Telecommunications plc* [1996] 3 WLR
    203; *Brasserie du Pecheurs SA v Federal
    Republic of Germany* [1996] QBD 404;
    [1996] 2 WLR 506
32 See note 17

Chapter 22

The co-ordination of social security: general rules and principles

This chapter covers:
1. The legal basis for the co-ordination of social security (below)
2. The personal scope of EC Regulation 1408/71 (p296)
3. The material scope of EC Regulation 1408/71 (p299)
4. The single state principle (p302)
5. The principle of non-discrimination (p305)
6. The principle of aggregation and apportionment (p306)
7. The principle of exportability (p307)
8. Overlapping benefits (p308)

1. The legal basis for the co-ordination of social security

The co-ordination rules secure and promote freedom of movement by co-ordinating the many different social security schemes within the European Economic Area (EEA). The intention is that people should not lose out on social security protection simply because they move to another member state.

The legal basis for the co-ordination of social security can be found both in Treaty Articles and Regulations. It stems from the following fundamental principle as set out in Article 39 of the Treaty.

- Freedom of movement for workers shall be secured within the Community.
- Such freedom of movement shall entail the abolition of any discrimination based on nationality between workers of the member states as regards employment, remuneration and other conditions of work and employment.

Article 42 of the Treaty is designed to secure the following safeguards for migrant workers and their dependants:

22

Chapter 22: The co-ordination of social security: general rules and principles
1. The legal basis for the co-ordination of social security

- the aggregation of all qualifying periods taken into account under the laws of the different countries, for the purpose of acquiring, retaining and calculating benefit entitlement; *and*
- payment of benefits to people resident in the territories of member states other than their state of origin.

The mechanism adopted by the European Community (EC) to achieve this is Council Regulation (EEC) 1408/71.[1] However, this Regulation has to be read together with EC Regulation 574/72, which sets out the procedure for implementing EC Regulation 1408/71. The regulations are divided into three parts.

- the general rules applying to all benefits;
- the applicable law – eg, which member state is responsible for paying you benefit;
- the special rules for each individual category of benefit.

The precise rights of people, under the co-ordination rule, vary according to the status of the particular claimant and according to the benefit claimed. It is therefore important to check the individual rules for each category of benefit. These are covered in Chapter 23. However, there are general principles that apply. In particular the regulations have four main principles:

- the single state (see p302);
- non-discrimination (see p305);
- aggregation and apportionment (p306);
- exportability (see p307).

2. **The personal scope of EC Regulation 1408/71**

The term **'personal scope'** relates to who can rely on the Regulation.[2] You fall within the personal scope of the Regulation if you are an employed or self-employed person or a student who is, or has been, subject to the legislation of one or more member states and:

- you are a national of one of the member states (including A8 and A2 states); *or*
- you are a refugee; *or*
- you are a stateless person; *or*
- you are a family member or a survivor of an European Economic Area (EEA) national, a refugee or a stateless person who has been employed or self-employed.

Insured people

The concept of an employed or self-employed person for European Community (EC) social security purposes has an EC law meaning which overrides any

Chapter 22: The co-ordination of social security: general rules and principles
2. The personal scope of EC Regulation 1408/71

22

definition in the national legislation.[3] An employed or self-employed person is defined as:

> 'any person who is insured compulsorily or on an optional continued basis, for one or more of the contingencies covered by the branches of a social security scheme for employed or self-employed persons or by a special scheme for civil servants'.[4]

The personal scope of Regulation 1408/71 is therefore defined in relation to people insured under national legislation rather than in relation to the definitions of free movement. The term 'worker' is not used in this Regulation and indeed the European Court of Justice (ECJ) has ruled that the two terms are not the same.[5]

You are included under this definition if:

- you are currently paying national insurance (NI) contributions; *or*
- you ought to be paying NI contributions (because you fulfil the statutory criteria) even if your contributions have not in fact been paid;[6] *or*
- you have, in the past, been insured under the relevant scheme of insurance;[7] *or*
- you have worked but are no longer economically active;[8] *or*
- you are a student[9] who has previously been subject to the legislation of at least one member state.[10]

If you are a part-time worker you are still covered under the co-ordination rule, no matter how much or how little time you devote to your activities.[11] However, you must still satisfy the insurance definition (see above). If you earn less than the lower earnings limit, then you are probably not covered.[12]

Family members of an insured person

The definitions of **'family member'** are slightly different under the co-ordination rule than other areas of EC law. For example, children are considered to be children until the age of 21 rather than 20 as with UK law. Equally generally in EC law your 'family' can be comprised of a much wider group than your immediate family – eg, grandparents and other relatives who are dependent. Under the co-ordination rule a member of the family is any person defined or designated as a member of the household by the legislation under which benefits are provided. This means that the decision as to whether or not you count as the family member of an insured person is largely a matter of national law. Under UK law, you are a 'member of the family' if you are a dependant.[13] This includes unmarried couples and children up to the age of 20 for whom you are treated as responsible. UK rules define the family as largely being those who are members of your household. However, EC law specifically allows for a family member to be included under the co-ordination rule even if s/he is not living in your household as long as s/he is mainly dependent on you.[14]

The rights that you gain as a family member are often referred to, particularly by the DWP, as 'derived rights'.[15] Until recently, EC law drew a clear distinction

22

Chapter 22: The co-ordination of social security: general rules and principles
2. The personal scope of EC Regulation 1408/71

between those rights which you could obtain yourself as an insured person under the co-ordination rule and the more limited rights which could be claimed as derived rights. However, an ECJ decision suggests that the scope of derived rights may be interpreted broadly, and in favour of claimants. The reasoning for this is that an insured person is likely to also be a worker (see p348) because the social security entitlement of a 'worker's' family under the co-ordination rule is a social advantage.[16] It seems that earlier decisions, which distinguished between the rights of the insured person and the rights of members of their families and survivors, are now limited to the aggregation and co-ordination rules relating to unemployment benefits[17] and that, in respect of all other social security benefits, family members and survivors of workers can benefit from the co-ordination rule on the same terms as workers themselves.

As a family member you can retain your derived rights even when you are not living permanently with the worker.[18] You only lose your EC rights if you divorce and in some cases where there are children you can retain rights even after divorce.

Survivors

You are defined as a '**survivor**' if you are a survivor in national law – eg, in the UK, a widow, widower or surviving civil partner is a survivor. Note that this is subject to the same proviso that you can be a dependant, and do not have to have been living under the same roof as the worker.[19] As a survivor you retain rights under the co-ordination rule when your spouse dies.

Refugees

A refugee is defined in Article 1(d) of the Regulation as being a person who is a refugee under Article 1 of the Convention on the Status of Refugees, signed at Geneva on 28 July 1951. This means a person who is unwilling or unable to return to the country of her/his nationality or former habitual residence because of a well-founded fear of persecution on specified grounds. It has been established that a person is a refugee within the meaning of the 1951 Refugee Convention as soon as s/he fulfils the criteria contained in the definition.[20] This would necessarily occur prior to the time at which her/his refugee status is formally determined. In other words a person is a refugee from the point s/he claims to have grounds for asylum not from the point that the Home Office grants her/him refugee status.

In theory, therefore, an asylum seeker who has worked in the UK can argue that current legislation which excludes asylum seekers from benefit are in breach of the equal treatment provision in Regulation 1408/71. A number of challenges have been made relying on this approach; as yet none have been successful.[21] (Although some asylum seekers have successfully claimed benefit under the EC association agreements – see p383.) The Court of Appeal rejected the argument on the basis that EC Regulation 1408/71 only comes into play once there has been

Chapter 22: The co-ordination of social security: general rules and principles
3. The material scope of Regulation 1408/71

22

some movement between member states. Since that decision a number of similar cases have arisen in Germany and the German courts have chosen to refer the cases to the ECJ.[22] The ECJ held in these cases that in order for a refugee to rely on EC Regulation 1408/71 s/he must have moved with the EEA.[23]

Applying the existing caselaw a refugee or an asylum seeker who has moved within the EEA should be able to rely on EC Regulation 1408/71 to override the UK exclusions from benefit. S/he must have worked in at least one EEA member state.

Stateless persons

A stateless person is someone who does not have any nationality.

3. The material scope of Regulation 1408/71

The **'material scope'** of the Regulation refers to the matters covered or the range of benefits that are within its scope. Individual social security benefits are not directly referred to. Instead the Regulation refers to any social security designed to protect against certain risks. The risks are listed in Article 4(1) of the regulation as those for:

* sickness and maternity benefits;
* invalidity benefits;
* old age benefits;
* survivors' benefits;
* benefits for accidents at work and occupational diseases;
* death grants;
* unemployment benefits;
* family benefits.[24]

In addition, the Regulation specifies that special non-contributory cash benefits are within the scope of the Regulation if they are provided under legislation which, because of its personal scope, objectives and/or conditions for entitlement has characteristics both of the social security legislation and of social assistance.

The Regulation specifically excludes from its scope 'social assistance'.

Therefore EC Regulation 1408/71 categorises benefits into one of three groups. These are:

* social security;
* special non-contributory benefits;
* social and medical assistance.

It is important to establish which category a particular benefit falls within because your rights under the Regulation vary according to this. For a detailed list of which benefits fall within each category, see Chapter 23.

22

Chapter 22: The co-ordination of social security: general rules and principles
3. The material scope of Regulation 1408/71

Social security benefits

Social security benefits are those benefits from each member state provided for the risks listed on p299. It does not matter whether these benefits are created under a general or a special social security scheme, nor whether the scheme under which they arise is contributory or non-contributory.[25] The co-ordination rule also applies to schemes where employers are liable to pay benefit.[26] Therefore schemes such as statutory maternity pay and statutory sick pay fall under the scope of the Regulation and are social security. Equally child tax credit and child benefit which are administered by the Revenue but essentially remain social security within the scope of the Regulation. Working tax credit does not fall within the scope of the Regulation.

Special non-contributory benefits

Since 1992, the co-ordination rule also covers a new category of benefits described as special non-contributory cash benefits. These are benefits provided under legislation or schemes intended:
- to provide supplementary, substitute or ancillary cover against the risks above and which guarantee the persons concerned a minimum subsistence income having regard to the economic and social situation in the member state concerned; *or*
- solely as specific protection for the disabled; *and*
- the financing comes exclusively from taxation intended to cover general public expenditure and the conditions for calculating the benefits are not dependent on any contribution in respect of the beneficiary; *and*
- it is listed in Annex II of the Regulation.[27] (Although in the past the ECJ has indicated that the fact a benefit is not listed in Annex II may not necessarily mean that it is not covered.[28])

The main distinctions between special non-contributory benefits and social security benefits listed under Article 4(1) are that special non-contributory benefits:
- are only payable in the member state in which you reside and therefore cannot be exported;
- are payable in accordance with the legislation of that member state.

Social and medical assistance

The categories of risks listed as being covered by social security benefits and special non-contributory benefits[29] are exhaustive. Any branch of social security not mentioned in the list is not covered by the co-ordination rule.[30] In addition, the co-ordination rule is specifically said not to apply to:
- social and medical assistance;
- benefit schemes for victims of war or its consequences;

Chapter 22: The co-ordination of social security: general rules and principles
3. The material scope of Regulation 1408/71

22

- special schemes for civil servants or persons treated as such.[31]

In the past the ECJ has ruled that benefits such as income support are social assistance and not covered by EC rules.

How to distinguish between benefits

Working out whether a particular type of benefit is 'social security', 'social assistance' or a 'special non-contributory benefit' is an important exercise because establishing the right category enables you to work out whether, and how the co-ordination rule applies to it.

The category into which a benefit falls depends upon factors relating to each benefit, in particular its purpose and the conditions for eligibility,[32] rather than whether or not it is described as 'social security' by the national legal system.[33]

Under EC law, a social security benefit is one which confers upon an individual a legally defined position entitling her/him to benefits in particular circumstances without any individual or discretionary assessment.[34] By contrast social assistance is a benefit or measure which makes the claimant's need one of the essential criteria for eligibility. It is usually a means-tested benefit rather than one where entitlement is linked to a particular risk.

The ECJ used to struggle with what it called 'hybrid' benefits which are those with the characteristics both of social security (ie, giving a legally defined right in the event of a defined risk occurring), and social assistance (ie, being generally available to the population as a whole provided they satisfy the 'need' criterion). However, it often tended to offer a generous interpretation to the term social security and held such hybrid benefits to be social security. For example, the ECJ had ruled that attendance allowance (AA) and mobility allowance (the predecessor to disability living allowance (DLA)) were invalidity benefits for the purpose of Regulation 1408/71.[35]

The introduction of the category of 'special non-contributory benefits' was a response to the difficulties of the Court. This is reflected in subsequent caselaw from the ECJ which held that AA and DLA are no longer invalidity benefits but fall within the category of special non-contributory benefits (see p358). However, this issue is still ongoing and more recent caselaw has called into question whether or not DLA, AA and carer's allowance remain invalidity benefits rather than special non-contributory benefits. See Chapter 23 for further details of this.

Member states' declarations

Each member state is required to list the benefits it considers to be social security benefits and those which are treated as special non-contributory benefits.[36] They do this in special declarations which you can find in an annex to Regulation 1408/71.[37] The ECJ has held that if a member state has listed a benefit as social security, then you are entitled to rely on the declaration to prove that the benefit

22

Chapter 22: The co-ordination of social security: general rules and principles
3. The material scope of Regulation 1408/71

is social security and, therefore, comes under the co-ordination rule.[38] However, the declarations are increasingly of little practical help because they are not updated. They contain references to out-of-date legislation and do not take account of changes to EC social security law.

For example, some benefits that are listed by the UK Government as social security benefits are now also listed by the UK as special non-contributory benefits. The ECJ has considered the position for such benefits in two cases, one for AA the other for DLA, and has held that since 1992 these benefits are special non-contributory benefits and thus non-exportable.[39]

The ECJ held that the listing of AA and DLA in Annex IIa of the Regulation must be accepted as establishing that the benefits were special non-contributory benefits. The fact that the UK had not removed these benefits from its declaration on social security benefits did not prejudice this position. This judgment effectively allows a member state to change an EC Regulation. The judgments may also have consequences for income-based jobseeker's allowance (JSA).

The UK Government considers income-based JSA to be a special non-contributory benefit rather than social security. However, applying EC criteria this may not be accurate. A commissioner and the Court of Appeal have held that for EC purposes income-based JSA is an unemployment benefit, although this was in respect of a different area of EC law.[40]

If a benefit is not listed in the declaration as social security it does not necessarily mean that it is not covered. The ECJ may treat it as such if, in fact, it has the characteristics of a social security benefit.[41]

How a benefit is characterised is a matter of law, which can only finally be resolved in cases of dispute by the ECJ.[42] In practice, the DWP is not likely to treat a benefit as social security unless it is in the UK declaration, so if you want to use the co-ordination rule to claim a benefit which might be treated as social security, but could also be a hybrid benefit, or social assistance, you should take legal advice.

4. The single state principle

The Regulation specifies that a person is subject to the legislation of a single member state only.[43] This is called the 'lex laboris' rule. This means that you pay contributions and you claim benefits from only one member state. The general rule[44] is that the state responsible for you is the state in which you last worked. It should be remembered that this is a general rule and there are many exceptions to the rule. The state that is responsible for you is called the '**competent state**'. The competent state's social security institution is the competent institution. The Department for Work and Pensions (DWP) is the UK's primary competent institution. You can only qualify for UK benefits and tax credits under the co-ordination rule if the UK is the competent state.

Therefore, if you last worked in Germany and have just arrived in the UK to look for work, Germany is the competent state and the German social security department is the competent institution responsible for paying you benefit, even though you are required to sign on in the UK. However, if you subsequently work in the UK the competent state becomes the UK and the competent institution the DWP. You are normally subject to the legislation of the state in which you work even if you live in another member state.[45]

In some circumstances you may be subject to the legislation of more than one member state. This only arises if you are simultaneously employed in one European Economic Area (EEA) state and self-employed in another.[46]

However this would arise only rarely and in general in order to avoid duplication of benefits, only one state can be the competent state.

Exceptions to the rule

The Regulation contains specific situations where you are not subject to the legislation of the member state where you last worked.

- If you have stopped work in a member state and have subsequently moved to another member state you become subject to the legislation of the state of residence rather than of employment.[47] This appears to allow member states to impose residence requirements for continued entitlement to benefit acquired in a member state.
- You work temporarily in another European Union (EU)/EEA member state for a UK employer.
  - If the company that employs you sends you to work in another EU/EEA member state for less than a year, then you remain subject to the legislation of the original member state. However, if you are replacing another employee whose period of posting is ending, you are subject to the legislation of that member state.[48]
  - If you are being sent to another EEA member state from the UK to work for less than a year, you should get form E101 from the DWP before you go abroad. This certifies that you remain covered by UK legislation. If the job is extended for up to a year due to unforeseen circumstances, then you can apply for an extension using form E102. Your employer must apply for this extension before the end of the first 12-month period.[49]
- You are temporarily self-employed in another EU/EEA member state.
  - The same rules apply if you are self-employed and go to work in another EEA member state for less than 12 months.[50] If you go from the UK to take up temporary self-employment in another member state you pay self-employed earner's contributions (Class 2 and 4) as if you were still in the UK. You do not have to contribute to the other member state's insurance scheme.[51]
  - You are normally accepted as self-employed if you have been self-employed for at least 12 weeks during the last two tax years or since then, although it

may be possible to classify you as self-employed even if you do not fully meet this condition. To clarify the position you should contact the National Insurance Contributions Office.

– People working in the German construction industry have, in the past, experienced difficulties when registering as self-employed in Germany. If you go to work in the construction industry in Germany you must register at the local office of the Chamber of Handicrafts (Handwerkskammer) taking your form E101 with you. In order to register with the Handwerkskammer, you need to prove that you are qualified in your trade. You must provide a 'certificate of experience' which you can obtain from the British Chamber of Commerce. If you do not register with the Handwerkskammer, you are not allowed to be self-employed in Germany.

• You are employed in two or more EU/EEA member states.[52] If you are employed in two or more EU/EEA member states, unless you are an international transport worker (see below), you are insured under the UK scheme if:

– you normally live in the UK, and the UK is one of the EU/EEA member states you work in; *or*
– you work for several companies that are based in different EU/EEA member states; *or*
– you do not normally live in any EU/EEA member state that you work in but your employer is based in the UK.

• If when you start work you are sent abroad immediately by an employer or agency, you usually carry on paying UK national insurance contributions.

• If you are taken on while abroad you are normally insured under that member state's scheme.

However, there are special rules if an agency hires you to work for a client in the Netherlands or Germany. You may have to pay UK national insurance contributions for up to nine months if you are in Germany and six months if you are in the Netherlands. After this period you are insured in the member state in which you are working. Your employer needs to get form E101 to inform the social security authority in the other member state that you remain insured in the UK, and then form CZ3822 to inform the UK National Insurance Contributions Office.

International transport workers

If you are an international transport worker and work in two or more member states, you are insured under the UK scheme if:

• your employer's registered office is in the UK; *or*
• your employer's registered office is in another EU/EEA member state and you work for a branch office in the UK; *or*
• you live in the UK and work mainly in the UK even if your employer does not have an office here.

Chapter 22: The co-ordination of social security: general rules and principles
5. The principle of non-discrimination

22

If none of these apply, you are insured under the scheme of the EU/EEA member state where your employer has its main office.

Special arrangements

In some circumstances, it may be to your advantage to remain insured in the UK even if you are working in another member state.[53] If so, the UK Contributions Office and its counterpart in the other member state must agree to this. You should write to the Contributions Office to find out about your position.

Special rules also apply to mariners, civil servants, diplomatic or consular staff and people called up for service in the armed forces. You should get advice from the appropriate authority – the Contributions Office in the UK.

5. **The principle of non-discrimination**

If you are covered by the co-ordination rule, you are entitled to enjoy the same benefits under the legislation of the competent state as a national of that state. This is often referred to as the **'equal treatment'** provisions. Equal treatment is one of the fundamental rights of EC law and the principle of non-discrimination prohibits any form of discrimination, direct or indirect, based on your nationality.

Direct discrimination arises when one person is treated less favourably than another. Indirect forms of discrimination are not so easy to identify but arise in rules which, although apparently neutral and non-discriminatory, have, in practice, a greater adverse impact on those who are not nationals of the competent state. For example, the habitual residence test and right to reside test in UK law (see Chapter 11) would appear to be a rule, which applies equally to all European Economic Area (EEA) nationals. However, British and Irish citizens are far more likely to satisfy the test than other EEA nationals. Therefore the rule could be indirectly discriminatory. Commissioners have considered this matter and have accepted that there is discrimination but presently the caselaw suggests that the discrimination is justified.

A difference in treatment can be justified but only if it is based on objective considerations that are independent of the nationality of the persons concerned and proportionate to the legitimate aim of the national provisions.[54] The justification put forward in the UK commissioners decisions[55] appears to be wholly connected to the person's nationality and therefore may not be permissible should any case reach the European Court of Justice (ECJ).

In a recent case the ECJ held that a French national who had worked for only one day in Belgium should not be excluded from claiming unemployment benefits simply because she had not completed a specified period of employment. To do so would be contrary to the equal treatment rules under Article 3 of Regulation 1408/71 and Article 39 of the EC Treaty.[56]

22

Chapter 22: The co-ordination of social security: general rules and principles
5. The principle of non-discrimination

The non-discrimination principle has also been used to extend the rights of EU/EEA claimants and their families in relation to widows' rights,[57] disabled people's allowances,[58] allowances for large families[59] and non-contributory old age allowances.[60]

6. **The principle of aggregation and apportionment**

Aggregation and apportionment of insurance periods for the purpose of acquiring and calculating entitlement to benefit are key co-ordinating mechanisms.

Aggregation

Aggregation means adding together periods of contributions, residence or employment in all the member states in which you have lived or worked. This may be necessary if the acquisition, retention or recovery of benefits is conditional upon completion of periods of residence, employment or insurance. What constitutes a period of residence, employment or insurance is determined by the legislation of the member state in which it took place.[61]

The principle is that you should not lose out if you choose to exercise your rights to move within the European Economic Area (EEA). If you were to be at a disadvantage should you need to claim benefit this may deter you from moving. The principle of aggregation effectively lifts internal borders within the EEA in respect of residence and contribution conditions. Therefore, if necessary, you should be entitled to benefits on the basis of all of the contributions that you have made to all of the social security schemes in any member states in which you have been insured. Furthermore, it provides that, where necessary, periods of residence or employment should be taken into account as if they were completed in the member state in which you are seeking benefit.

For example, a Spanish person who has worked for many years in Spain arrives in the UK and works for two weeks. S/he may rely on the contributions paid in Spain to claim contribution-based benefits such as jobseeker's allowance or incapacity benefit. S/he may also rely on the periods of residence in Spain to meet any residence conditions – eg, for child benefit or disability living allowance. S/he obviously would still need to satisfy the main conditions for the particular benefit but European Community (EC) rules allow you to overcome territorial limitations in terms of access to and the calculation of benefit. The aggregation rule can be particularly helpful for A8 and A2 nationals. For example, a Polish person who has worked for 10 months and becomes sick may try to claim income support but find that s/he is excluded under the right to reside test. If s/he had previously worked in Poland or any other EEA state the work can be aggregated to meet the

Chapter 22: The co-ordination of social security: general rules and principles
7. The principle of exportability

22

contribution conditions for entitlement to incapacity benefit in the UK. The same principle could be applied to maternity benefits.

Aggregation tends to be applied to short-term benefits like unemployment, maternity, sickness and some invalidity benefits. There are no general aggregation provisions. Each type of social security benefit to which aggregation provisions are applied has its own rules and you need to take account of these when claiming.[62] These are covered in Chapter 23.

Apportionment

Apportionment means that two, or more, European Union (EU)/EEA member states pay a proportion of your benefit. It is a technique used in relation to longer-term entitlements such as old age and survivors' benefits and some other types of invalidity benefits.

Apportionment is often coupled with aggregation. For example, if you have contributed to the state pension scheme in a number of EU/EEA member states, each state must pay a proportion of the rate to which you would have been entitled if you had spent your whole working life in that state. The proportion is calculated by dividing your working life by the length of time actually worked in each member state.

To avoid duplication of benefit entitlement, only the competent state carries out the aggregation exercise, and you only receive a pro rata amount of any aggregated benefit.[63]

---

7. **The principle of exportability**

The aim behind the principle of exportability is to abolish residence and presence conditions which may restrict entitlements to benefit, and to enable people to export certain social security benefits when they cease to be resident in the member state where the entitlement arose.

The portability mechanism means that, except where the co-ordination rule specifically provides otherwise, certain benefits may not be reduced, modified, suspended, withdrawn or confiscated just because you go to live in a different member state.[64] Not all benefits that fall under Regulation 1408/71 can be exported. The principle of exportability only applies to:

- invalidity benefits;
- old age benefits;
- survivors' cash benefits;
- pensions for accidents at work or occupational diseases;
- death grants.

Unemployment, sickness and maternity benefits can only be exported to a limited extent. You cannot export special non-contributory benefits; they are paid only

22

Chapter 22: The co-ordination of social security: general rules and principles
7. The principle of exportability

in the state that you are resident.[65] Family benefits cannot be exported but you can claim family benefits for family members who are living apart from you in another European Union/European Economic Area member state. The rules on exporting benefits vary according to the benefit concerned and are covered in Chapter 23.

8. **Overlapping benefits**

The general principle of the co-ordination rule is that a claimant should not use one period of compulsory insurance to obtain a right to more than one benefit derived from that period of insurance.[66] In general, you are only insured in one European Union (EU)/European Economic Area (EEA) member state for any one period,[67] so you cannot use insurance from that one period to obtain entitlement to benefits of the same kind from two member states. Usually, benefits are adjusted to ensure either that only one state (the competent state) pays the benefit, taking into account periods of insurance in other EU/EEA member states; or that the benefit is paid pro rata according to the lengths of periods of insurance in different member states. Aggregation or portability provisions apply, but not both.

The co-ordination rule allows a member state to introduce provisions to prevent 'double recovery'. In the UK these are contained in the Overlapping Benefits Regulations.[68]

In certain cases, however, you may be paid both the full level of a UK benefit and a proportion of the benefit from another member state, which has been accrued as a result of insurance contributions there. Following a decision of the European Court of Justice (ECJ),[69] member states are not allowed to apply provisions preventing the overlapping of their own benefits with those of other member states where it would have the effect of reducing what you would have received from your years of contribution in the first member state alone.

This means that no adjustment can be made to your benefits under the Overlapping Benefits Regulations if the 'duplicate' benefits, which you are receiving, are:

- a UK benefit based only on years of insurance in the UK (without seeking to bring in periods of insurance from work abroad) and a benefit paid by another EU/EEA member state based only on your contribution in that member state;
  or
- a UK benefit based only on years of insurance in the UK (without seeking to bring in periods of insurance from work abroad) and a benefit paid as a result of contributions in another EU/EEA member state, where entitlement to the benefit from the second member state arises on other provisions of the co-ordination rule.

For benefits – like old age and death benefits – which are paid pro rata by different member states, depending on the length of the period of insurance in each member state, the overlapping provisions do not apply so as to 'adjust' benefits downwards. Each member state must pay you either the benefit you have earned under its system, pro rata, or the rate payable under its own legislation for the years worked, whichever is higher. In such cases the single state rule does not apply.

Example

In the UK, if you have been employed for 90 per cent of the qualifying years of your working life, you are entitled to the basic rate state retirement pension at the full rate. If you have spent the remaining 10 per cent of your working life in another member state, you can now receive your full UK pension as well as the 10 per cent pro rata pension to which you are entitled from the other member state.

There are further detailed exceptions to the overlapping provisions in relation to benefits paid for invalidity, old age, occupational disease or death.[70] Broadly speaking, a member state is not allowed to apply its overlapping provisions to reduce benefits you receive from it, which are of the same kind just because you are receiving other benefits in respect of those risks from another member state.

Notes

1. **The legal basis for the co-ordination of social security**
   1 Reg 1408/71 replaced EEC Reg 3 on 1 October 1972. The principles of both Regulations are the same and earlier caselaw which refers to Regulation 3 is still good law.

2. **The personal scope of EC Regulation 1408/71**
   2 Art 2 EC Reg 1408/71
   3 *Hoekstra (ne Unger)* [1964] ECR 177; *De Cicco* [1968] ECR 473 (under Reg 3, the predecessor to Reg 1408/71)
   4 Art 1(a) Reg 1408/71
   5 Contrast *Levin v Staatssecretaris van Justitie* [1982] ECR 1035, [1982] 2 CMLR 454 with *Heissische Knappschaft v Maison Singer et fils* [1965] ECR 965

6 *Mouthaan* [1976] ECR 1901
7 *Hoekstra* (see note 3)
8 *Pierik* [1979] ECR 1917
9 Students were added to the list by Reg 1408/71 in 1999; Reg 307/99 OJ L307/99
10 Although students fall within the scope of the Regulation this does not mean that they can override UK rules which exclude students from access to certain benefits. These exclusions apply to all students and therefore are not in breach of Reg 1408/71. However, exclusion of students from income-based JSA has been found to breach EC Directive 79/7 by discriminating against women. See CJSA/1920/1999 (*65/00).
11 *Kits van Heijuningen* [1990] ECR 1753

12 *Nolte* C-317/93 (ECJ judgment 14 December 1995) suggests that a lower earnings limit cannot be displaced as constituting indirect sex discrimination, contrary to Dir 79/7, because it can be justified by objectives of social policy.

13 s137 SSCBA 1992

14 Art 1(f) Reg 1408/71

15 See *Cristini*

16 *Cabanis-Issarte* Case C-308/93 ECJ

17 *Kermaschek* [1976] ECR 1669, and see paras 23-24 and 34 of *Cabanis-Issarte* (note 16)

18 *Gul v Dusseldorf* [1980] ECR 1573; [1987] 1 CMLR 501; *Echternach* [1989] ECR 723; *Diatta v Land Berlin* [1985] ECR 567; [1986] 2 CMLR 164. The inconsistent decision of the House of Lords in *Re Sandler, The Times*, 10 May 1985, is probably wrong and should have been referred to the ECJ.

19 Art 1(f) Reg 1408/71

20 *Khaboka v Home Secretary* [1993] Imm AR. Joined cases CIS/564/1994 and CIS/7250/1995

21 *Krasniqi v CAO and Secretary of State* CA 10 November 1998; CF/3662/1999; CFC/2613/1997(*25/00); R(FC) 1/01

22 *Khali v Bundesanstalt für Arbeit* Case C-95/9; *Chaaban v Bundesanstalt für Arbeit* Case C-96/99; *Osseili v Bundesanstalt für Arbeit* Case C-97/99; *Basser v Landesshaupstadt Stuttgart* Case C-98/99. All four of these cases involve a stateless person and the ECJ has been asked to address the point as to whether Reg 1408/71 applies to stateless persons who have travelled to a member state from a non-member country. A fifth case from the Federal Social Court in the case of *Addou v Land Nordrhein-Westfalen* Case C-180/99 asks the question whether it is necessary for refugees to move within the EEA before they may rely on Reg 1408/71.

23 CF/3662/1999

3. The material scope of EC Regulation 1408/71

24 Listed in Art 4(1) Reg 1408/71

25 Art 4(2) Reg 1408/71

26 Art 4(2) Reg 1408/71

27 Art 4(2a) Reg 1408/71

28 *Beerens* [1977] ECR 2249; *Newton* Case C-356/89

29 Art 4(1)-(2a) Reg 1408/71

30 *Scrivner and Cole* [1986] I ECR 1027

31 Art 4(4) Reg 1408/71

32 *Gillard* [1978] ECR 1661 para 12; *Piscitello* [1983] ECR 1427 para 10; *Newton* C-356/89

33 *Scrivner and Cole* [1986] I ECR 1027

34 *Newton* C-356/89

35 For example, *Scrivner and Cole* (the Belgian 'minimex' (like income support) and *Newton* (mobility allowance)

36 Art 5 Reg 1408/71; the declarations are published in the *Compendium of European Social Security Law*

37 Annex IIa Reg 1408/71

38 *Beerens* [1977] ECR 2249; *Newton* C-356/89

39 *Partridge* Case C-297/96. A similar decision was made in respect of DLA in *Snare* Case C-20/96

40 This case involved a claim under EC Directive 79/7 on the equal treatment between men and women in social security. *Hockenjos v Secretary of State for Social Security* [2001] EWCA Civ 624(CA) and CJSA/1920/1999(*65/00)

41 *Beerens* [1977] ECR 2249

42 In *Newton* C-356/89 the UK Government said that mobility allowance was not social security because it was not in its declaration and was more akin to social assistance. The ECJ said that it had more of the characteristics of social security.

4. The single state principle

43 Art 13 Reg 1408/71

44 Contained in Art 13 Reg 1408/71

45 Art 13(2)(a) and (b) Reg 1408/71

46 Art 14(c) Reg 1408/71

47 Art 13(2)(f) Reg 1408/71; C-275/96 *Kuusijarvi* [1998] ECR I-3419

48 Art 14(1)(a) Reg 1408/71

49 Art 14(1)(b) Reg 1408/71

50 Art 14a(1)(a) Reg 1408/71

51 Art 14a(1)(a) Reg 1408/71

52 Art 14(2) Reg 1408/71

53 Art 17 Reg 1408/71

5. The principle of non-discrimination

54 Art 3 Reg 1408/71; case C-237/94 *O'Flynn* [1996] ECR I-2617, para 19; case C-138/02 *Collins* [2004] ECRI-2703, para 66

55 CIS/3573/05; CIS/2559/05; CIS/2680/05; CPC/2920/05; CH/2484/05

56 *Chateignier* Case C-346/05

57 *Vandeweghe* [1973] ECR 1329

58 *Costa* [1974] ECR 1251

59 *Palermo* [1979] ECR 2645

60 *Frascogna* [1987] ECR 3431

6. The principle of aggregation and apportionment

61 *Mura* [1977] ECR 1699, [1978] 2 CMLR 416; but see also *Frangiamore* [1978] ECR 725 and *Warmerdam-Steggerda* [1989] ECR 1203

62 Sickness and maternity (Art 18 Reg 1408/71), invalidity (Art 38), old age, death (survivors) and certain other invalidity benefits (Art 45(1) to (4)), occupational disease (Art 57), death grants (Art 64), unemployment (Art 67(1) and (2)), family benefit (Art 72).

63 The general overlapping provisions are contained in Arts 12 and 46 of Reg 1408/71.

7. The principle of exportability

64 Art 10(1) Reg 1408/71

65 Art 10a Reg 1408/71

8. Overlapping benefits

66 Arts 12 and 48 Reg 1408/71; see also specific provisions in relation to particular benefits: Arts 19(2), 25(1)(b), 34(2), 39(2) and (5), 68(2), 71(2), 76 and 76(3) Reg 1408/71

67 Art 13 Reg 1408/71

68 SS(OB) Regs

69 *Petroni* [1995] ECR 1149 C-24/75

70 Arts 46a, 46b and 46c Reg 1408/71

Chapter 23

Special rules for individual categories of benefits

This chapter covers:
1. Sickness and maternity benefits (below)
2. Invalidity benefits (p316)
3. Old age benefits (p320)
4. Survivors' benefits (p327)
5. Benefits for accidents at work and occupational diseases (p328)
6. Unemployment benefits (p329)
7. Family benefits (p334)
8. Special non-contributory benefits (p336)
9. Death grants (p342)

Chapter 22 identified the co-ordination arrangements of EC Regulation 1408/71 in very general terms. However, the Regulation also has very precise rules governing your rights under the co-ordination provisions. These vary according to your particular status and the particular benefit involved. It is therefore necessary to check the special rules that relate to each benefit.

This chapter covers the specific rules for the various categories of benefit. It lists the UK benefits that fall within Regulation 1408/71 and explains how those benefits are affected by the co-ordination rule.

1. Sickness and maternity benefits

The UK benefits that fall under the co-ordination rule are:
- statutory maternity pay;
- maternity allowance;
- statutory sick pay;
- short-term incapacity benefit (IB).

For details about the rules for entitlement to these benefits, see CPAG's *Welfare Benefits and Tax Credits Handbook*.

Maternity and sickness benefits are co-ordinated by Articles 18-31 of EC Regulation 1408/71. The specific rules relating to sickness and maternity benefits in EC Regulation 1408/71 are lengthy and perhaps the most complex of all those in the Regulation. This is inevitable because it has to cater for a range of different benefits but also different circumstances that may arise. For example, if you are involved in an accident while away from your place of residence you may need to claim a range of benefits or services. Therefore sickness and maternity benefits include:

- **benefits in kind** – these are comprised of health and welfare services so, for example, medical treatment would fall under this category. It also covers cash payments to reimburse the cost of these services if you have already been charged for them;
- **cash benefits** – these are benefits for compensation for loss of earnings.[1]

General rules relating to sickness and maternity benefits

There are certain general principles that can be identified.

- You claim benefit from the state in which you were last insured. This is one of the central themes of the co-ordination rule.
- Aggregation. The Regulation specifies that where a member state makes entitlement to a particular sickness or maternity benefit conditional upon the completion of periods of insurance, residence and employment, the member state shall to the extent necessary take into account any such periods completed in other states.[2] This means that a person who has worked briefly in the UK and who worked in another member state before coming to the UK (including A8 and A2 nationals) can rely on the work undertaken or contributions paid in that other member state in order to qualify for UK IB or maternity benefits.
- You should not be excluded from claiming cash benefits from the state in which you are insured simply because you reside elsewhere. However, if you are sick or pregnant you may also have to make use of health or welfare services – eg, antenatal care. It may be unrealistic to expect you to receive such treatment from the state of insurance if you are resident elsewhere. In such cases it is the place of residence that provides such treatment.
- It is the state with whom you were last insured that is liable to bear the cost of the benefit whether it is cash or in kind. This applies even if you receive treatment or benefit in another member state.

In addition to these general principles there are quite specific rules, which vary according to whether you are employed or unemployed and whether or not you are a pensioner.

Special rules for employed or self-employed people

If you are working in, and insured for sickness in, another European Economic Area (EEA) member state and you get sick, you may need to claim benefit for short-term sickness under that state's social security scheme. Periods of insurance contributions in the UK may be aggregated with periods of insurance in that member state and count towards your entitlement to such a benefit.[3] It is sometimes possible to claim benefit from a state other than the one in which you were last insured.

If you go temporarily to another EEA member state you can claim sickness and maternity benefits from that state if your condition 'necessitates immediate benefits'.[4] This includes both cash benefits and benefits in kind. This could include reimbursement of medical and pharmaceutical expenses, treatment or medication as well as weekly cash benefits. Your sickness or pregnancy does not of itself necessitate immediate benefit but if you require medical treatment the rule is engaged.

You may wish to go to another member state for treatment because it is more effective or to avoid a lengthy waiting list. If you are already entitled to benefit and go to another member state for treatment you can continue to receive benefit. You must get authorisation from the DWP in order to do this. Authorisation cannot be withheld because your home state provides the treatment necessary if the treatment cannot be provided within a reasonable time taking into account your current state of health. If you are going abroad you should give the DWP plenty of advance warning to enable it to advise you on procedures and make the necessary arrangements on your behalf.

If you have been working in and are insured in another EEA member state and become ill, you may wish to return to the UK. In these circumstances you may be entitled to the other member state's sickness benefit in the UK. However, in order to benefit, you should make your claim before you leave the other member state. If you are entitled to benefit and want to move to live in another member state or return to the state in which you habitually reside you can get benefit there if you are authorised by the DWP. Such authorisation can only be refused if removal would be prejudicial to health. It does not have to be obtained prior to departure but not having it is likely to lead to problems with the claim until you obtain it.

If you habitually reside in a state other than the competent state, you can nevertheless claim and receive benefit from the state in which you were last insured.[5]

Special rules for unemployed claimants

If you are unemployed and receiving an exportable unemployment benefit (jobseeker's allowance for UK purposes) while looking for work in another member state and you become sick or the maternity allowance period begins, you no longer get unemployment benefit but sickness or maternity benefit. This is paid for the remainder of the unemployment benefit period of three months. However, this period can be extended if you are unable to return home.[6]

If you are eligible for one state's unemployment benefit because you are habitually resident in that state rather than having last worked there, you are also eligible for that state's benefit while sick/pregnant.

Special rules for pensioners

If you receive an 'old age' benefit from more than one member state, including a pension from the state in which you reside, you receive sickness or maternity benefit from the state in which you are resident rather than the state where you were last insured.[7]

If you are entitled to a pension from more than one member state but you do not receive a pension from the state in which you reside, you can get sickness or maternity benefit from the member state that pays you a pension.[8]

If you are eligible for a pension in one state but are resident in another and you are waiting for the pension claim to be processed you are entitled to receive benefits in kind which will be paid for by the state of residence. Once the pension claim is processed and it is established who is responsible for payment of sickness benefits that state will reimburse the state which has paid for your benefits in kind.[9]

Making a claim

You generally make a claim for benefits on the usual claim form provided for that benefit by the competent institution. The competent institution is the Department for Work and Pensions (DWP) in the UK and its equivalent in any other state. If you are unsure which state you should claim from you should start your claim in the state in which you are living and it will be passed on to the competent institution. There are, however, some forms that may be useful to obtain. Again these are generally available from the competent institution.

If you have been working in another member state you should try to get a Form E104, which is a record of the social insurance that you have paid in that member state, before returning to the UK. This will help with any claims for benefit. It is not essential to have this form and if you provide evidence of your work to the DWP it will check your insurance record with the other member state. You should be able to obtain this from the competent institution of the state in which you have been working or you could ask for a copy from the DWP prior to going abroad.

You should use Form E119, available from the competent institution to obtain benefits in kind and submit evidence of incapacity to substantiate the claim.

2. Invalidity benefits

Invalidity benefits are co-ordinated by Articles 37-43 of EC Regulation 1408/71. The rules for invalidity benefits are virtually identical to those for old age and survivors' benefits. In European Community (EC) law sickness benefits and invalidity benefits are treated very differently. In the United Kingdom (UK), incapacity benefit (IB) is an earnings replacement benefit for total incapacity to work. In other states however, 'invalidity benefits' are often more akin to a disability benefit paid according to the level of your disability, similar perhaps to industrial disablement benefit.

There are no provisions in EC law defining which are sickness and which are invalidity benefits. It is decided by looking at the conditions of entitlement to each benefit and the reason for, and length of, the incapacity.

Invalidity benefits available in the UK under the co-ordination rule are:

- long-term IB; and
- attendance allowance (AA), disability living allowance (DLA) and carer's allowance (CA) if you were in receipt of benefit prior to 1 June 1992. If you claimed after that date, see p340.[10]

Increases of long-term IB for child dependants are family benefits, not invalidity benefits.

Only long-term IB, paid after 52 weeks of incapacity, is considered to be an 'invalidity benefit'. The short-term rates of IB are classified as sickness benefits for the purposes of EC regulations and cover shorter-term incapacities (see p312).

Severe disablement allowance (SDA) was considered to be an invalidity benefit but was abolished by the UK Government in April 2001. Claimants already receiving benefit remain entitled but no fresh claims can now be made. In place of SDA, the Government introduced a new type of non-contributory IB. The Government has not yet stated whether this will be an invalidity benefit within EC rules, but its similarity to SDA means that there are grounds to argue it should be treated as an invalidity benefit.

AA, DLA and CA had all been established as 'invalidity benefits'. However, on 1 June 1992 these benefits were reclassified as 'special non-contributory benefits' (see p358).

For further details on the UK rules of entitlement to all of these benefits, see CPAG's *Welfare Benefits and Tax Credits Handbook*.

General rules

- The main principles of aggregation and exportation apply to invalidity benefits. Therefore, periods of insurance in any member state must be taken into account if necessary in order for you to qualify for benefit. Once you are entitled to an invalidity benefit you can export that benefit to another member state whatever your reason for going there.[11]

- Adult dependency increases can be paid for family members even if they are living in another member state. Although you should note that such increases are family benefits rather than invalidity benefits.
- The state from which you claim benefit is the one that determines your degree of invalidity but medical reports from other states must be taken into account. In some circumstances a state can insist on having the claimant examined by a doctor of its own choice. This is rare, however, and the general rule is that any checks and medical take place in the state in which you are living rather than the one that pays you benefit. The reports are then sent back to the paying state.[12] There are special rules relating to the aggravation of an invalidity.[13] The precise rules vary according to your situation and your status. But in general if your condition gets worse the aggravation of your condition should be taken into account in the assessment of your benefit. You should raise this with the competent institution or the relevant social security department of the state in which you are living.
- If an invalidity benefit is suspended (eg, by the DWP because you failed to attend a medical) but then resumed, the same state continues to pay. If it is withdrawn but further invalidity arises the question of who pays is decided afresh.[14]
- Some types of invalidity benefits available in the European Economic Area (EEA) are paid at different levels according to the length of time that you have been insured. Different rules apply depending on whether the amount of invalidity benefit is related to the length of insurance or not.
- Invalidity benefit may change to retirement pension at different times due to differing pension ages in the member states.

Apportionment

Although all types of invalidity benefits within the EEA are subject to the aggregation principle only some are subject to apportionment. EC Regulation 1408/71 distinguishes between Type A invalidity benefits which are subject only to aggregation and Type B which are subject to both aggregation and apportionment. The UK does not have any Type B invalidity benefits.

Type A invalidity benefit

The amount of benefit you receive does not vary according to the amount of contributions paid. It is paid at a standard rate.[15] IB is a Type A invalidity benefit.

If you have worked and paid insurance contributions only in member states with Type A invalidity benefits you are entitled to invalidity benefit under one member state's legislation only. Which member state is responsible depends on:

- where you became sick; *and*
- whether you worked in that member state or, if not, in which member state you were last employed.

Type B invalidity benefit

The rate of your benefit varies according to the amount of contributions that you have paid.[16] You may be able to get Type B invalidity benefit from two or more EEA member states if you have paid insurance contributions in any of the following member states: Austria, Denmark, Finland, France (but only under the French miners' insurance scheme, or if you were self-employed in France), Germany, Greece (except under the agricultural insurance scheme), Iceland, Italy, Liechtenstein, Luxembourg, Norway, Portugal and Sweden.

How much you get from each member state is worked out according to a formula. It is calculated by two different methods and you get whichever is higher.[17]

Where you have paid contributions in member states paying Type A benefits and others paying Type B, your benefit may be calculated according to the Type B formula.

If you were paying contributions in any one of the above states and you are getting benefit from only one of those, you should ask the authorities there to send your details to the other member states where you have been subject to the legislation/paying contributions. You may be entitled to a higher level of benefit.

The co-ordination rules for invalidity benefits varies according to whether you have worked and been insured only in countries with Type A or Type B invalidity benefit or whether you have worked and been insured in states with both types of invalidity benefit.

1. A person has only worked in states where the amount of benefit is not related to length of insurance

Invalidity benefit is paid by the state where you were insured at the time incapacity began. The only exception to this, is where an unemployment benefit is being paid by the country of residence, rather than employment. In this case the state of residence pays invalidity benefits.[18] If you receive invalidity benefit from the state of residence, invalidity benefit is not paid by any other state under EC law. However, if you are not entitled under this state, there may be entitlement in one of the other states where you were insured. If you are eligible in more than one state, the state where most recently insured should pay.[19]

Adult dependency increases can be paid for family members living in another state.[20]

Claims can be made either to the competent institution, which is liable to pay you, or to the social security authority in the state of residence, which will forward it on to the competent institution. Your date of claim is the date that it is received by either authority, or the date when entitlement to sickness benefits expired, whichever is later.[21]

If entitlement depends on incapacity for work or receiving a sickness benefit for a certain period of time account can be taken of periods in receipt of another state's benefit.[22]

2. A person has only worked in states where the amount of invalidity benefit is related to the length of time insured

Invalidity benefit from each state is worked out as follows:

Calculation 1

Assess under national law alone.

Calculation 2

a) Add up total insurance in all member states and work out the amount of benefit this would give.

b) Work out the proportion of years in each state to decide the pro rata amount which is then payable by each state.

Calculation 3

The two rates of benefit produced in 1 and 2 are compared and the claimant receives the higher of the two.

3. A person has worked and been insured in states where the amount of invalidity benefit is not related to length of insurance and in states where it is

If you were insured in a country where the amount of invalidity benefit is not dependent on insurance when incapacity begins, benefit can be paid as in 1 above as long as there is no entitlement under an insurance-related scheme and you have not yet claimed retirement pension. No account is taken of insurance periods in these countries when aggregating insurance. If this does not apply, benefit is calculated as in 2 above.[23]

Claims

Generally there are no special claim forms; you simply claim benefit on the appropriate claim form provided by the competent institution – eg, IB claim form in the UK.

Claims can be made to the competent institution or to the state in which you reside which will forward it on to the competent institution. The date of your claim is the date of receipt by either authority or the date that entitlement to sickness benefits end, whichever is the later.[24]

The date of claim is the date the claim is received at either social security office. This claim will trigger payment of invalidity benefit by all states liable to pay, as the institution receiving the claim should notify all other institutions who will then assess how much each should pay.[25]

Payment of benefit could take some time if several states are involved so the state you claim from can make an interim payment. This consists of the amount payable under its national law alone. If this amounts to nil but there is entitlement in another state, that state pays. If you are eligible in several states the state where you claim pays on behalf of the other member states. Once the true amount of invalidity benefit has been assessed it can either be paid directly to the claimant by each state in which there is entitlement, or through the institution handling the claim.[26]

3. **Old age benefits**

Old age benefits available in the UK under the co-ordination rule are:
- retirement pension;
- additional pension;
- graduated retirement benefit;
- winter fuel payments;
- increments;
- adult dependency increases of retirement pension;
- age addition;
- Christmas bonuses.

The co-ordination rules for old age benefits are found in Articles 44 to 51 of EC Regulation 1408/71. In the UK, retirement pensions of any category are included. There are four types of retirement pension in the UK: Categories A, B C and D. Categories A and B are contributory while Category D carries a residence test and is paid in strictly limited circumstances (Category C is no longer relevant as it applies only to people who were of pension age in 1948). For further details of the UK rules for entitlement to these benefits, see CPAG's *Welfare Benefits and Tax Credits Handbook*.

Although incapacity benefit (IB) and child dependency increases can be paid to someone over pension age, they are not classed as old age benefits.[27]

Winter fuel payments and bus passes are not benefits listed as old age benefits for EC Regulation 1408/71. However, there have been decisions by the European Court of Justice (ECJ) which have held that these are benefits linked to old age. Therefore there are strong grounds to argue that they fall under the co-ordination rule also.[28]

Increases of retirement pension for child dependants are family benefits, not old age benefits.

General rules

The provisions in the co-ordination rule in relation to entitlement to a UK pension are most likely to be of use to people who have worked in the UK but for an insufficient period to qualify for a full pension under UK rules alone, and who have also worked in another member state.
- If you have worked in more than one member state, your insurance record is preserved in each of those states until you reach pension age. You will get a

retirement pension from each member state where you have worked for a year or more, based on your insurance record in that member state or, where residence counts for benefit purposes, the length of your residence in that member state.

- If you have worked and paid contributions in more than one member state you may be entitled to a pension under EC law, even if you do not qualify for a pension under the national legislation of the country in which you are resident. Therefore a person who has paid contributions in the UK but does not qualify for a Category A or B pension under British legislation, but who worked in another European Union (EU)/European Economic Area (EEA) state may qualify for a retirement pension when those contributions are taken into account. The retirement pension is then worked out according to a formula (see p322).

- If a pension is dependent on periods of residence to qualify you for a full pension, then any periods of residence which you have completed in other member states will be taken into account.

- Retirement pensions are fully exportable. This means that your retirement pension will be paid to you regardless of where you live or stay in the EEA without any reduction or modification.[29]

- Pensionable age in the UK for a man is 65, for a woman 60. However, from 6 April 2010 the pension age for women will increase from 60 to 65 over a 10-year period. The age at which you may be entitled to a retirement pension differs from member state to member state. Because of this you may be entitled to an old age benefit in one EEA member state before you reach retirement age in another. Correspondingly, if you have been incapable of work before you reached pension age you may be entitled to pro rata invalidity benefits in the member state where you have not yet reached pension age. In the UK this is long-term IB.

- If you worked in a member state that only recently joined the EC and you were entitled to a retirement pension before that country joined, you may be able to rely on any reciprocal arrangements that exist with that state (see p375).

Claims

In general you make a claim for your pension in the state in which you are resident. If you have never been insured in that state your claim will be forwarded on to the member state in which you were last insured.[30] Alternatively, when you approach pension age, you could apply directly to the competent state to claim your pension. That state will pass details of your claim to any other EEA member state where you have been insured so that each one can do its calculation. The competent state will inform you whether you can claim more under domestic law alone or with your entitlement calculated under the co-ordination rule.[31]

Each member state decides how to pay your pension and pays it itself.

Calculating your pension

The following rules apply wherever you are in the EU/EEA. If you have been subject to the legislation of more than one member state, each of them must calculate your pension entitlement as follows in accordance with EC law. This is one field where migrants may be better off than others because of an exception in the overlapping provisions.

There are three steps to calculating your pension.

1. Each member state should calculate the pension you are entitled to (if any) under its own legislation.[32] For example, if you have been insured in the UK for 20 years you would be entitled to a UK pension of approximately 50 per cent of the standard rate. On the other hand, under UK domestic legislation, if you had only worked for eight years in the UK you would have no entitlement.

2. Each member state should then calculate a theoretical pension as if your entire career in the EU/EEA had been spent in that member state.[33] This theoretical amount is then reduced in proportion to the actual time you worked in that state compared with the time worked in the EU/EEA as a whole. The resulting amount is known as your pro rata entitlement.

3. Each member state then pays you whichever is the greater of the amount you are entitled to under its own domestic legislation, and the pro rata amount of its benefit which you are entitled to from that member state calculated in accordance with the co-ordination rule.[34]

Example

Mr Coiro from Italy has worked for 43 years in different member states:

8 years in the UK

15 years in Italy

20 years in Ireland

His entitlement in the UK based on UK domestic legislation (based on periods of insurance) amounts to nothing. However, if his entitlement to a UK pension was calculated as if his entire EU/EEA career of 43 years' work had been carried out in the UK, he would be eligible for 100 per cent of the UK standard rate (this is his 'theoretical entitlement'). He can therefore claim the pro rata amount of this entitlement in respect of his years of work in the UK.

His pro rata entitlement is worked out as follows:

$$\frac{\text{his theoretical rate} \times \text{his UK period of insurance}}{\text{his EU/EEA period of insurance}}$$

which is:

$$\frac{100\% \times 8 \text{ years}}{43 \text{ years}}$$

Answer: 19%

So Mr Coiro will be entitled to the pro rata rate of 19 per cent of the UK standard rate. Since the alternative amount which he could claim from the UK based on his eight years' contributions is nil, the pro rata amount is the higher of the two possible entitlements to a UK pension and that is what Mr Coiro can claim.

In this example, Italy and Ireland would perform similar calculations and Mr Coiro would receive a pension from each on the same basis. It could be that for either or both of these member states the calculation based on their domestic legislation turned out to be higher, and Mr Coiro would receive that larger pension.

Because of the way the calculation rules work for UK pensions, entitlement under domestic legislation alone will almost invariably be equal to or higher than the pro rata amount calculated in accordance with the co-ordination rule.[35] (For example, you may qualify for a Category D pension – see p324.) In order to be considered in this way, you must have paid sufficient contributions to qualify you for a UK pension.

If you have worked for a period of less than one year in an EU/EEA member state, your pension is calculated differently and you receive no pension from that state.[36] But the period is included in the calculation of your total period of employment in the EU/EEA.[37]

Graduated retirement benefit in the UK is not included in the pro rata rate calculation, but your UK entitlement is added on after the calculation under the co-ordination rule has been carried out.[38]

The pro rata equation is not recalculated when benefits are uprated. But the rate of retirement pension is increased.[39]

Extra retirement pension for your dependants

If you are entitled to a retirement pension from an EU/EEA member state you are also entitled to an extra amount for a dependent adult. Adult dependency increases are paid at the same pro rata rate as the basic pension.[40] You can claim this benefit even if the person who depends on you is in another EU/EEA member state.

If you are living in the EU/EEA member state that pays your pension, it will also pay any benefits to which you are entitled for your children. In the UK this would be child benefit or extra pension or both. A child dependency increase is a family benefit. It is not paid at a pro rata rate, but in full.

If you are living in a member state that does not pay you a retirement pension, then the member state that is paying your retirement pension will pay the benefits for your children.

If you are getting a retirement pension from two or more member states, then the member state where you were insured for the longest time will pay any benefits you are entitled to for your children.

Receiving your UK pension in another member state

You can be paid a UK pension in any other EU/EEA member state at the same rate as you would get if you were living in the UK or at the rate calculated in accordance with the formula in the co-ordination rule.[41] The calculation as to what you are entitled to will be carried out as above. Your pension may be paid directly into a bank in the member state you are living in, or in the UK. Alternatively, the pension can be paid by payable order normally issued every four weeks. Payment is always made in sterling.

Receiving income-based benefit pending payment of your pension in the UK

If you get paid arrears these will usually be sent directly to you. However, you should bear in mind that if you have claimed income support (IS) while waiting for your pension to arrive from another member state, you will have to repay that amount when your pension arrives. Similarly, if you have been getting an IS type benefit in another EU/EEA member state while waiting for your UK retirement pension, you may have to pay that amount back when your UK pension arrives.

Category D retirement pension

You may be entitled to this if you are 80 years of age or over, but it is paid only in limited circumstances. Residence in another EU/EEA member state can count towards satisfying the 10-year residence conditions for a Category D pension provided that either:

- residence in the other EU/EEA member state counts towards entitlement to old age benefits in that member state; *or*
- you were insured in the other member state and you have at some time been subject to UK legislation. For example, you have been liable to pay UK Class 1 or Class 2 national insurance contributions.

If you satisfy these conditions, the period of residence in the other EU/EEA member state is added to the periods of residence in the UK and pro rata Category D retirement pension is awarded. The UK pays the percentage of benefit which is equivalent to the number of years of residence in the UK used to satisfy the 10-year residence condition.

Winter fuel payments

Winter fuel payments are considered to be old age benefits under EC Regulation 1408/71.[42] The current DWP practice is to allow a winter fuel payment to be exported only where it has already been awarded. If you have already moved to another EEA state you cannot subsequently make a first claim for a winter fuel payment.

The reason for this stance is likely to stem from the wording of Article 10(1) of EC Regulation 1408/71 which states:

'Save as otherwise provided in this Regulation invalidity, old-age or survivors' cash benefits, pension for accidents at work or occupational diseases and death grants **acquired under the legislation of one or more Member States** shall not be subject to any reduction, modification, suspension, withdrawal or confiscation by reason of the fact that the recipient resides in the territory of a Member State other than that in which the institution responsible for payment is situated.'

It seems to be the use of the word 'acquired' which has led to the DWP's position on exporting winter fuel payments because implies that only benefits already acquired are exportable. There is caselaw from the ECJ which makes clear that the scope of Article 10(1) is not confined to the right to export benefits already acquired and that it also prohibits national law from making the acquisition of benefits dependent upon residence in a member state.

This was the position taken by the ECJ in *Smieja*[43] and confirmed in *Carraciolo*[44] in which a claim for invalidity benefit under Belgium law was made by a person resident in Italy. Benefit was refused because the claimant was not present in Belgium. The ECJ, referring back to its judgment in *Smieja* held that:

'. . ..the aim of the provision contained in article 10 is to promote the free movement of workers by insulating those concerned from the harmful consequences which might result when they transfer their residence from one member state to another. It is clear from that principle not only that the person concerned retains the right to receive pensions and benefits acquired under the legislation of one or more Member States even after taking up residence in another Member State, but also that he may not be prevented from acquiring such a right merely because he does not reside in the territory of the State in which the institution responsible for payment is situated.'

In later cases the ECJ[45] confirmed its earlier rulings stating that:

'Article 10 of Regulation No 1408/71 must be interpreted as meaning that a person may not be precluded from acquiring or retaining entitlement to the benefits, pensions and allowances referred to in that provision on the sole ground that he does not reside within the territory of the Member State in which the institution responsible for payment is situated.'

The question to be addressed is whether or not in winter fuel payments cases the UK remains the state responsible and the DWP the relevant institution.

It is common ground that a winter fuel payment is an 'old age benefit' within the scope of the Regulation and that such benefits fall within Article 10 and consequently are fully exportable. The question is whether this position has changed given the amendments to Regulation 1408/71 and in particular the insertion of Article 13(2)(f).

Article 13 of Regulation 1408/71 sets out a system of conflict rules which are used to determine which member state is responsible for an insured person. The ECJ had held[46] that a person who is a worker in one member state but who ceases to carry on an activity in the territory of that member state and who goes to another state but does not take up work in that member state continues to be subject to the legislation of the member state in which he was last employed. This led to concerns that a person might move to another member state but never become eligible to receive benefits from that member state. Article 13(2)(f) was added to Regulation 1408/71 to address this gap. It specifies that:

> 'a person to whom the legislation of a Member State ceases to be applicable, without the legislation of another Member State becoming applicable to him in accordance with one of the rules laid down in the aforegoing subqaragraphs or in accordance with one of the exceptions or special provisions laid down in Articles 14 to 17 shall be subject to the legislation of the Member State in whose territory he resides in accordance with the provisions of that legislation alone.'

It is clear from the preamble to the amending regulation that the amendment was necessary to improve the Regulation in the light of the judgment in *Ten Holder*.[47] The preamble also makes clear that following the insertion of the new paragraph 13(2)(f) it was necessary to insert a further provision stipulating when and under[48] what conditions this legislation ceases to be applicable.

In a later commissioners appeal[49] it was argued by the Secretary of State that this caselaw had been substantially overturned by subsequent decisions both in national courts and ECJ judgments. The Secretary of State argued that the implication of the later judgments was that Article 10 does not have any bearing on the acquisition of a right to benefit as opposed to its retention save where the benefit in issue adds to or supplements a benefit already in payment or perhaps where the benefit in issue is a modern version of some previous benefit paid to the claimant or there is some other clear connection. Where the benefit in issue is not linked to a benefit already in payment Article 10 therefore cannot have the effect of disapplying a residence condition that is legitimately a condition of entitlement to the benefit in issue.

A commissioner[50] held that this change in the way Article 13 is applied to those who have ceased employment necessarily changes the way Article 10 must be construed. In the light of Article 13(2)(f) a person who has ceased employment becomes entitled to benefit in the country that s/he has taken up residence and it is therefore logical that Article 10 should be construed so as not to permit her/him also to qualify for new benefits in the member state where s/he formerly lived. Article 10 permits retention of entitlement to benefits s/he has already acquired together with any new supplements to them.

The commissioner consequently found that as the winter fuel payment is not a supplement to a retirement pension it must be acquired prior to going abroad. However, this issue has not been fully resolved and is likely to remain unclear unless a case is brought to the ECJ.

4. **Survivors' benefits**

Survivors' benefits available in the United Kingdom (UK) under the co-ordination rule are:
- bereavement benefits;
- widowed parent's allowance.

Survivors' benefits are 'death benefits' under EC Regulation 1408/71. The rules for survivors' benefits are found in Articles 44 to 51 of the Regulation which are the same as those for old age benefits. Therefore the general co-ordination arrangements for survivors' benefits are the same as those for retirement pensions. The following is a summary of the main provisions for survivors' benefits. For a more detailed explanation of the rules relating to survivors' benefits, see section on old age benefits (p320).

General rules
- You can elect whether to take the amount to which you are entitled (under the co-ordination rule) from all the European Economic Area (EEA) member states in which the deceased made contributions or to take the pro rata amount from the state in which you are living.
- Survivors' benefits can be exported to any EEA member state without reduction or modification.[51] If the deceased was insured in more than one European Union (EU)/EEA member state, the pension for the surviving spouse is calculated on the same basis as would have applied to the insured person. If the person was drawing pensions under the legislation of two or more member states, the spouse will be entitled to widows' or widowers' pensions under the legislation of these member states. The rules are the same as those for retirement pensions.
- If you are bereaved and your spouse was only insured in one member state, that member state pays any benefits to which you may be entitled for your children. If your spouse was insured in more than one member state, it will normally be the member state where the child lives that will pay the benefit.

23

Chapter 23: Special rules for individual categories of benefits
5. Benefits for accidents at work and occupational diseases

5. Benefits for accidents at work and occupational diseases

Benefits for accidents at work and occupational diseases available in the UK under the co-ordination rule are:

- disablement benefit;
- constant attendance allowance, which you may receive if you are getting 100 per cent disablement benefit and need somebody to look after you;[52]
- exceptionally severe disablement allowance, which you may receive if you are getting constant attendance allowance at one of the two highest rates, and your need for constant attendance is likely to be permanent;[53]
- reduced earnings allowance, which you may receive if you are assessed at least 1 per cent for disablement benefit and your accident occurred or your disease started before 1 October 1990, and you cannot do your normal job as a result.[54]

The rules for industrial accidents and diseases can be found in Articles 52 to 63 of EC Regulation 1408/71.

General rules

- Benefits for accidents and occupational diseases covers both cash benefits and benefits in kind (see p312).
- Although EC Regulation 1408/71 applies to both employed and self-employed people you should remember that UK industrial injury benefits are only available to employed earners and not to self-employed people.[55]
- The general co-ordination rules for injury benefits are the same as those for retirement pensions.[56] Periods of insurance, residence and employment can be aggregated in order to qualify for benefit.
- Disablement benefit and related allowances are payable if you go to another European Economic Area (EEA) member state. If you are intending to travel, you should consult the office which pays you benefit well in advance so that arrangements can be made for payment in the other member state.
- A person who has suffered an industrial accident or contracted an occupational disease and who goes to stay temporarily in another member state can continue to get benefits in cash and in kind.[57] This also applies if you go to another member state for medical treatment.
- If you live in a state different to the one liable to pay you benefit you can nevertheless claim from abroad and be paid.[58]
- If you were insured in another EEA member state, you will be paid directly by the appropriate institution of that state according to its rules for determining whether or not you are eligible and how much you should be paid. That institution may arrange for the DWP to make your payments, but this will not alter the amount you receive.

- If your condition deteriorates and you are getting, or used to get, benefit from an EEA member state, then that state will be responsible for carrying out any necessary further medical examinations and paying any additional benefit.

Special rules

Accidents while travelling abroad in another member state can be deemed to have occurred in the state liable to pay industrial injury benefit. This also applies while in transit between member states.[59]

If you have worked in two or more European Union (EU)/EEA states in a job that gave you a prescribed industrial disease, you will only get benefit from the member state where you last worked in that job.

Previous accidents or diseases that arose in other member states can be taken into account in determining industrial injury benefits where this is necessary to decide the extent of the disablement. Similarly later accidents or diseases can affect the assessment of disablement but only if:

- no industrial injury benefit was payable for the original accident or disease; *and*
- there is no entitlement in the state in which the subsequent accident occurred.[60]

Claims

Generally claims should be made on the usual claim form provided by the competent institution. In all cases, benefits in kind are provided by the state where the person is staying or living. Benefits in cash are provided by the state liable to pay though it can arrange for the other state to pay on its behalf. Both benefits are financed by the state liable to pay.

Benefits in kind are secured by producing form E123. Benefits in cash can be paid when you become incapable of work.

6. **Unemployment benefits**

The only unemployment benefit[61] available in the UK is jobseeker's allowance (JSA). Furthermore, the Government position is that only contribution-based JSA is an unemployment benefit. However, a commissioner and the Court of Appeal in a separate case have both held that income-based JSA is an unemployment benefit for the purposes of EC Directive 79/7.[62] This Directive specifies that there must be equal treatment in social security between men and women. Although the decision relates to a different area of European Community (EC) law there are clearly strong grounds to argue that income-based JSA is also an unemployment benefit. The European Commission has also stated that income-based JSA is an unemployment benefit.[63]

The co-ordination rules for unemployment benefits can be found in Articles 67 to 71 of EC Regulation 1408/71. The general rule of aggregation applies to unemployment benefits but the principle of exportation applies in a much more restrictive way.

General rules

- The general rule is that you are paid unemployment benefit by the member state in which you were last employed.[64]
- An exception to this general rule is where you reside in one member state but you are working or paying contributions in another. In this case you can claim from either the member state you reside or the member state in which you pay contributions.
- If you are potentially entitled to unemployment benefit both from the member state where you last worked and the member state in which you reside you must choose where to register for work and claim unemployment benefit.[65]
- There is a limited provision for exporting unemployment benefit. If you are receiving unemployment benefit from one member state and you go to another member state you continue to be entitled to unemployment benefit from the competent state for a period of up to three months. After three months you must return to the competent state to continue receiving unemployment benefit (see below).
- The general rules of aggregation apply. Contribution-based JSA requires you to have paid contributions in the two years prior to your claim. You can use periods of insurance or employment completed as an employed person under the legislation of any other member state to satisfy the contribution conditions, provided that you were subject to UK legislation immediately before claiming contribution-based JSA. Each week of employment completed as an employed person in any other member state is treated as a contribution paid into the UK scheme on earnings of two-thirds of the present upper earnings limit for contribution purposes.
- If members of your family are living in another EEA member state and the amount of your unemployment benefit is determined by the number of people in your family, then they are taken into account as if they were living in the member state that pays your benefit.[66] If your dependant lives in another member state you need form E302 from the employment institution of the member state in which your dependant lives.

What happens if you go to another member state

If you are going to look for work in another EU/EEA member state you are entitled to contribution-based JSA abroad if:

- you are wholly unemployed immediately before you leave the UK. This means you are without any employment except for partial and intermittent unemployment.[67] Partial unemployment means you are short-time (not part-time) working. Intermittent unemployment means you are temporarily laid off; *and*

- you satisfy the conditions for contribution-based JSA before you leave the UK.[68] You qualify even if you have claimed contribution-based JSA but no decision has been made yet on your entitlement, but you are getting JSA hardship payments pending the decision; *and*
- your entitlement to contribution-based JSA arises from aggregating insurance payments you made in different member states.[69] Your entitlement to contribution-based JSA must not arise as a result of a reciprocal convention between the UK and a state that is not a member of the EU/EEA (for how to determine this, see p375);[70] *and*
- you are going to the other EU/EEA member state to seek work.[71] You are not entitled to exportable contribution-based JSA if you are going on holiday, visiting a sick relative or accompanying your spouse. If you give up work to accompany your spouse or partner on a posting abroad it is very unlikely that you will be able to export your UK contribution-based JSA. In order to establish entitlement you must show that:
  - there was just cause for voluntarily leaving your employment; *and*
  - you were capable of, available for and actively seeking work.

  Usually it is accepted that if you left work to accompany your partner on a foreign posting, you have just cause as long as you left no earlier than was reasonable to organise your affairs before travelling.[72] However, you may still lose entitlement because you will find it difficult to establish that you were available for work during this time. If, on the other hand, you were already unemployed and you accompany your spouse or partner abroad to seek work, you may be accepted as satisfying this condition; *and*
- you have been registered as available for work for at least four weeks in the UK.[73] In exceptional circumstances you may be allowed to leave the UK before the four weeks is up and still qualify. You must get authority in advance to do so from Pensions and Overseas Benefits Directorate in Newcastle; *and*
- you are registered for work in another EEA member state.[74] If you are looking for work in another member state, you must register for work there within seven days of leaving the UK and comply with that member state's regulations unless there are exceptional circumstances;[75] *and*
- the employment services of that member state will pay contribution-based JSA in accordance with its own legislation. This includes the method and frequency of payment.[76] The requirement to attend at a Jobcentre Plus is satisfied if:
  - you attend at an equivalent office in the other member state; *or*
  - you comply with that member state's control procedures, showing that you are available for work as its rules require.

That member state will carry out checks on entitlement to JSA in accordance with its own procedures. If there is doubt about whether you meet the registration and availability conditions of the member state in which you are living this will be reported to the DWP in the UK. On the advice of the other EEA state, the DWP will make a decision about whether you continue to be entitled or not. While the question is referred to the DWP your benefit may be suspended by the other state. It is important that the decision is made in the UK because you have the right to appeal. In some EU/EEA states there is no right of appeal against the decision of a decision maker.

If all of the above conditions are met, you are entitled to UK JSA abroad in an EEA member state for one of the following periods, whichever is the shortest:[77]

- three months from the date when you ceased to be available to the UK employment services;[78] *or*
- until your entitlement to UK JSA is exhausted after six months/26 weeks;[79] *or*
- if you are a seasonal worker (see below), until the end of the season.[80]

A **'seasonal worker'** is a person who:
- is 'habitually resident' in one member state and goes to work in another EEA member state; *and*
- does seasonal work in that second member state for a period of up to eight months; *and*
- remains in that member state for the whole period of that season's work.[81]

Seasonal work is work which happens every year and is linked to a particular season of the year.

On request a statement will be issued to you by the Pensions and Overseas Benefits Directorate for you to give to the employment services of the member state where you are going to look for work.[82] The statement will give:
- the rate of contribution-based JSA that is payable;
- the date from which JSA can be paid;
- the time limit for registration in the other EEA member state;
- the maximum period of entitlement;
- any other relevant facts that might affect your entitlement.

You can export JSA to more than one EU/EEA member state during the same period of absence from the UK.

But JSA can only be exported once from the UK during any one period of unemployment. You cannot return to the UK and then go abroad a second time in the same period until you have worked and paid more contributions in the UK.[83]

If you have not found a job within three months and return to the UK before the three-month period is up, you will continue to get contribution-based JSA in the UK, assuming that the six-month period for which JSA can be paid is not exhausted.[84]

If you are sick or become pregnant while looking for work in another EU/EEA member state, you may be entitled to UK short-term incapacity benefit or a maternity benefit but only for the period until your contribution-based JSA entitlement runs out.[85] For example, if you have already used up four months' while in the UK, you are only be entitled to two months' contribution-based JSA abroad. To claim these benefits you will need form E119.

If you become unemployed while working abroad and are insured in that member state's unemployment insurance scheme, then that member state is responsible for paying unemployment benefit. If you were previously insured in the UK you are normally able to use periods during which you paid national insurance and aggregate them with periods of insurance in the member state you last worked in, to enable you to get the unemployment benefit of the member state where you have been working.[86]

If you are entitled to receive JSA while in another EEA member state, you should get a letter from your Jobcentre Plus to help register for work in the other member state.

If you are going to look for work in Austria, Belgium, Finland, France, Germany, Greece, Iceland, Italy, Norway, Portugal, Spain or Sweden, you will be given Form E303. If you are going to look for work in another EU/EEA member state, then Form E303 will be sent directly to that member state.

What happens if you come to the UK and are unemployed

If you are a returning resident or an EU/EEA national coming to the UK to work or to seek work, the following applies to you.

If you have worked and paid insurance contributions under the legislation of another EU/EEA member state the periods of insurance in that state may count towards your entitlement to contribution-based JSA on your return to the UK. This will apply if, after your return to the UK, you get employment, pay Class 1 contributions but then become unemployed again.[87] You are then subject to UK legislation (ie, the UK is the competent state) and the UK is responsible for paying you the appropriate amount of contribution-based JSA.

If you were not subject to another member state's legislation while abroad (because you were an exception to the rule that the competent state is the state where you work – see p303) the unemployment insurance you paid while abroad may nevertheless still be taken into account when assessing your entitlement to contribution-based JSA if it is decided that, while you were abroad, you remained 'habitually resident' in the UK.

If you are coming to or returning to the UK to look for work and have been insured in another EU/EEA member state, you may be able to get the other member state's unemployment benefit for up to three months if:[88]
- you were getting that member state's unemployment benefit immediately before coming to the UK;[89] *and*

- you have been registered as available for work for four weeks (or less if the member state's rules allow) in the other member state;[90] *and*
- you register and claim UK JSA within seven days after you were last registered in the other member state;[91] *and*
- you satisfy the UK's availability for work rules.[92] The DWP will carry out checks and pay benefit where unemployment benefit has been exported from another EU/EEA member state to the UK. However, the DWP cannot decide whether or not there is entitlement to the other member state's unemployment benefit. If a doubt arises about your continuing entitlement, the DWP will inform the employment authorities of the other member state and, if appropriate, may suspend payment of your unemployment benefit while awaiting a reply. Before you leave the other member state you must get Form E303.[93]

7. Family benefits

Family benefits available in the UK under the co-ordination rule are:
- child benefit;
- child tax credit;
- guardian's allowance.

The co-ordination rules for family benefits are found in Articles 72 to 76 of EC Regulation 1408/71.

General rules
- The general principle of aggregation applies to family benefits although this is limited to aggregating periods of insurance or employment. No mention is made of aggregating periods of residence.
- The principle of exportation does *not* apply to family benefits. However, it is possible to receive benefits for family members who are not living with you but reside elsewhere in the European Economic Area (EEA). For example, a Spanish person working in the UK can claim child benefit for her/his children living in Spain or elsewhere in the European Community (EC). This is despite the fact that generally it is not possible to receive child benefit for children who do not reside with you. This is an example of how you can be put in a better position under EC law.
- Generally you are entitled to benefit from the state in which you last worked. However, there are exceptions to this.
- If you are posted to work in another European Union (EU)/EEA member state for less than 12 months you remain subject to the legislation of the member state from which you have been posted. (The 12-month period can be extended for a further 12 months in certain circumstances.) The member state from which you are posted will therefore be responsible for paying family benefits.[94]

If you are a member of the armed forces serving in another EEA member state, you remain subject to UK legislation.

- If you have worked outside the EEA but remain subject to the legislation of an EEA member state (see p302), you may retain the right to family benefits.[95]

In addition to the general rules there are also special rules relating only to family benefits. These rules vary according to whether you are employed, unemployed or a pensioner.

Employed persons[96]

If you are employed in a member state you claim from the state in which you are working even if your family is living in another member state. Therefore, it is possible to claim a benefit such as child benefit even though the child is not living with you.

Unemployed persons[97]

If you were previously employed or self-employed; and you are getting unemployment benefit from an EU/EEA member state you are then entitled to family benefits from that member state for members of your family who are living in any EU/EEA member state. Therefore it is possible to claim benefits even though the child does not reside with you.

If you are wholly unemployed, you are entitled to family benefits from your state of residence *only* for members of your family who are residing with you if:[98]

- you are unemployed; *but*
- you were previously employed; *and*
- during your last period of employment you were resident in a different EU/EEA member state to the one you were working in; *and*
- you are receiving unemployment benefit from the member state where you are living.

Family benefits for children of pensioners

Under EC law, family benefits are payable for the dependent children of pensioners. To qualify you must be claiming:[99]

- an old age benefit; *and*
- an invalidity benefit; *or*
- a benefit for an accident at work or an occupational disease.

If you are getting your pension from only one EU/EEA member state, family benefits are payable by that member state regardless of where in the EU/EEA you or your children are living.

If you are receiving a pension from more than one member state, family benefits are payable by the member state where you live, provided there is entitlement under that member state's scheme. If there is no entitlement under its scheme, then the member state to which you have been subject to the legislation for the longest period, and under which you have entitlement to family benefits, will be responsible for paying you.[100]

Overlapping benefit rules

Migrant workers may often be separated from family members while they search for work or establish themselves in another member state. This, combined with the fact that different member states have different conditions for benefits, some based on residence, some on employment, others on contributions, means that there is great scope for duplication of payments. Therefore, EC law has rules which seek to prevent a person being able to claim family benefits from more than one member state.

For employed and unemployed persons if there is entitlement in two different states any non-contributory benefit is suspended in preference to a contributory one. However, if a person is working in the state which pays the non-contributory benefit the other benefit is suspended. In either case if the suspended benefit is higher, that state must pay an amount equal to the difference.[101]

Claims

Claims should be made to the state liable to pay on the appropriate claim form for that benefit. A certificate proving that the children are your dependants must be obtained. There is a duty to notify any changes in the size of your family, the fact that you have moved to a different state, that your partner is working and due to get family benefits from another member state and any other change that might affect entitlement.[102]

If the family benefits are not used for the benefit of the family it can be paid to another person who will apply it to this end.[103]

---

8. **Special non-contributory benefits**

The United Kingdom (UK) benefits available are:[104]
- attendance allowance (AA);
- carer's allowance (CA);
- disability living allowance (DLA);
- income support (IS);
- income-based jobseeker's allowance (JSA);
- pension credit (PC).

In 1992, EC Regulation 1408/71 was amended to include a new category of benefits, that of special non-contributory benefits. There are no special rules relating to these benefits and the only Articles dealing with them are Articles 4(2a) and 10a of EC Regulation 1408/71. The absence of these detailed rules and the lack of caselaw in this area means that special non-contributory benefits remain something of an unknown, or at least unexplored, quantity. This is further exacerbated by the grouping together of benefits which have little in common but actually cover the multitude of benefits found throughout the rest of the Regulation.

The inclusion of this category was largely a response to the problems encountered by the European Court of Justice (ECJ) in making the distinction between 'social security benefits' which were within the scope of the Regulation and 'social assistance benefits' which were not. It is not clear however, that this problem is resolved. If anything it has perhaps added to the burden in that the ECJ must now distinguish social security from both social assistance and special non-contributory benefits.

General rules

- The crucial factor in determining the competent state for special non-contributory benefits is that of residence. The Regulation further defines residence as 'habitual residence'. Habitual residence for European Community (EC) purposes is slightly different to the habitual residence test in UK law. See p338 for further details.
- Article 10a(1) specifies that special non-contributory benefits shall be granted to people exclusively in the territory of the member state in which they reside, in accordance with the legislation of that state. Therefore, you can only receive special non-contributory benefits from the state in which you are habitually resident and these benefits may not be exported. However, there are some transitional rules for people entitled to AA, DLA or CA prior to 1 June 1992 (see p340).
- Special non-contributory benefits are subject to the principle of aggregation. Article 10a(2) specifies that a member state whose legislation makes entitlement to its own special non-contributory benefits subject to the completion of periods of employment, self-employment or residence shall regard where necessary, periods of employment, self-employment or residence completed in the territory of another member state as though they were completed in its own. However, this only applies once it is established that you are habitually resident in the member state from which you seek to claim benefit. Therefore, you can add together residence in another member state to enable you to meet the six-month residence condition for DLA or AA but you cannot use that residence to claim habitual residence in the UK for IS.
- Special non-contributory benefits are covered where they provide supplementary, substitute or ancillary cover against the social risk set out in the Article, or are specific protection for disabled people.

- Each member state has to specify which of their national benefits falls within the category of special non-contributory benefits. The UK currently lists these as AA, DLA, CA, IS, income-based JSA and PC.
- Once it is decided that you are habitually resident in a member state you may rely on the co-ordination provisions of EC Regulation 1408/71 to satisfy any residence or contribution conditions. Therefore, if you need to claim benefit the state in which you are habitually resident must add together periods of residence or employment in order that you can qualify for benefit.

The meaning of habitual residence under EC Regulation 1408/71

You are entitled to claim special non-contributory benefits from a member state in which you are habitually resident rather than the state where you last worked. In *Snares*[105] the ECJ considered the position of DLA since the introduction of special non-contributory benefits. The ECJ held that entitlement to special non-contributory benefits was not conditional on the claimant having previously been subject to the social security legislation of the state in which s/he applies for the benefit. The crucial factor for this type of benefit was the place of habitual residence.

There is often a great deal of confusion over the term 'habitual residence'. This is because it also appears in UK regulations. Furthermore, the House of Lords has given a definition on habitual residence for domestic law purposes which does not precisely follow caselaw from the ECJ. In *Nessa* the House of Lords held that in order to satisfy the habitual residence test a person must satisfy a period of residence.[106] This follows earlier caselaw that held that it was necessary to complete an appreciable period of residence before you became habitually resident.

However, a person who is able to rely on Regulation 1408/71 does not have to complete any period of residence.

The leading judgment on habitual residence in respect of this regulation is *Di Paolo*[107] which held that the key factors in determining a person's habitual residence are:

'the length and continuity of residence before the person concerned moved, the length and purpose of his absence, the nature of the occupation found in the other member state and the intention of the person concerned as it appears from all the circumstances.'

This case was concerned with unemployment benefits and is more concerned with past rather than future events. For this reason a commissioner has warned that great caution should be used in terms of applying this definition.[108] However, later judgments of the ECJ have cited *Di Paolo* as authoritative. In the case of *Swaddling* the ECJ considered both the UK and EC term of habitual residence test. It cites the *Di Paolo* test as being authoritative for IS and found that an employed person who has gone to another member state to work, who then returns to her/his country of origin and has no close relationships or ties in the state which s/he has left, is habitually resident in her/his country of origin. Consequently Mr Swaddling was habitually resident in the UK.

Once it is established a person is habitually resident and an insured person s/he may claim a special non-contributory benefit. Consequently Mr Swaddling could not be refused benefit because he failed to satisfy the appreciable period under the UK habitual residence test.

Although the *Swaddling* case involved a British citizen the decision can also apply to other EEA nationals although non-British EEA nationals who are not economically active are likely to have problems showing that they are resident in the UK.

For further details on the UK habitual residence test, see p338.

What is a special non-contributory benefit

Article 4(2)(a) of the Regulation provides that for a benefit to be a special non-contributory benefit a benefit must be:

- special;
- non-contributory;
- intended to provide supplementary, substitute or ancillary cover against one of the social security risks covered by the Regulation.

AA, DLA and CA are clearly non-contributory but it is not clear that the other two criteria are necessarily fulfilled.

'Special'

Guidance as to the meaning of this term is available by a resolution of the Administrative Commission.[109] It states that the following cumulative criteria are particularly relevant in determining whether a benefit is 'special'.

- The benefit has the characteristics of a social security benefit of a 'mixed type', in that it gives the beneficiary a legally defined right to benefit which is a characteristic of a social security benefit but also contains features of social assistance, in that the particular financial and/or other needs of the individual are taken into account.
- The characteristics of the category of benefit are closely linked to a particular social and economic context in the member state where the beneficiary resides.
- In the case of insufficient economic resources, the benefit is designed to provide assistance.
- The award could be subject to means testing, although due to its general nature it is not always necessary to examine the specific circumstances of each individual case. Means testing is an important, though not an essential criterion, which may, in particular, take into account income from gainful activity or other social security benefits.

Intended to provide cover against one of the social security risks

There is very little guidance as to the meaning of this. It is possible to see that a benefit such as income-based JSA is intended as a replacement for people with insufficient contributions for unemployment benefits or that PC steps in to replace retirement pensions. It is not so clear that this is the case with AA, CA or DLA. They appear to be unique benefits that stand alone.

Entitlement to AA, DLA and CA before 1 June 1992

If you were entitled to AA, DLA or CA before 1 June 1992 you can export your benefit if you take up 'habitual residence' (see p338) in another EU/EEA member state, provided that:

- you satisfy all the other conditions of entitlement, except the 'residence' and 'presence' conditions; *and either*
- you are working in the UK (this counts whether or not you are paying national insurance contributions); *or*
- you have worked in the UK as an employed or self-employed person.[110]

In some circumstance if you live in the UK and you go to live in a care home you will lose your AA or DLA. Because of the wording of the UK regulations this does not apply if you go into a care home in another EEA state.

Entitlement to AA, DLA and CA after 1 June 1992

If you became entitled to AA, DLA or CA after 1 June 1992 the benefits are treated as special non-contributory benefits and cannot be exported. They are payable only in, and at the expense of, the member state of 'habitual residence'. You may, however, claim a similar special non-contributory benefit from the EU/EEA member state where you are 'habitually resident' if there is an equivalent benefit there.

EC Regulation 1408/71 is an important provision for people moving within the EEA. One of its key functions is to allow certain benefits to be exported to another member state.[111] Generally benefits that can be exported for an indefinite period are long-term benefits, paid for retirement, bereavement, invalidity or industrial injury.

Prior to 1 June 1992 it was possible to export AA, DLA and CA to another EEA state because they were considered to be 'invalidity benefits' and consequently were fully exportable under Article 10 of the Regulation.

This position had been confirmed in *Newton*[112] where the ECJ held that mobility allowance was an invalidity benefit for the purpose of 1408/71 and was fully exportable.[113]

In June 1992 Regulation 1408/71 was amended to include a new category of 'special non-contributory' benefits.[114] Following this change member states were required to list the benefits considered to fall within this category in Annex IIa to

Regulation 1408/71. The UK listed AA, DLA and CA[115] to be special non-contributory benefits and consequently from that date would not allow exporting, other than for people covered by the transitional protection rules available.

Caselaw developments

The change in classification was the subject of a legal challenge in *Snares*.[116] However, the challenge failed with the ECJ holding that DLA was a special non-contributory benefit and no longer exportable. In *Partridge* the ECJ made a similar judgment in respect of AA.[117]

However, a number of subsequent decisions by the ECJ have cast doubt upon the validity of these decisions. In particular, in *Jauch*[118] the ECJ rejected that the listing of a benefit in Annex IIa was conclusive of its nature as a special non-contributory benefit. It therefore declined to follow its earlier decision in *Snares*.

The ECJ held in *Jauch* that given the importance accorded by the EC Treaty to the principle of freedom of movement for workers, any provisions which derogate from the principle of exportability of social security benefits must be interpreted strictly. A special non-contributory benefit not only has to be listed within Annex IIa but it also has to be 'special' and 'non contributory'. Applying these principles the Court held that an Austrian care allowance was not a 'special non contributory benefit' within Article 10a even though it had been listed as such in Annex IIa.

Shortly after the *Jauch* decision, the Court held that the inclusion of a maternity allowance by a member state in Annexe IIa was invalid.[119] The point was reiterated in the more recent case of *Hosse*[120] and there are a number of cases pending on a similar point.

It is clear from the emerging caselaw that the mere inclusion of a benefits in Annexe IIa is not conclusive of it being a special non-contributory benefit. The crucial question is whether or not a benefit can be said to have the characteristics of a special non-contributory benefit. The ECJ makes the point in *Jauch* that in the cases of *Snares*, *Partridge* and the later UK case of *Swaddling*.[121]

'. . .the special non-contributory character of the benefits in question was not discussed.'

Action by the European Commission

In the light of the developing caselaw the European Commission put forward draft legislation intended to reflect the judgments.[122] Although not entirely clear, it appears that the likely effect of the amendment Regulation would be that all three benefits would be fully exportable. In order for the Regulation to take effect all member states must agree to its introduction but three member states appear to have blocked the new legislation. This has led to the European Commission beginning infringement proceedings.

Advising clients

The final outcome of all of this activity remains unknown but clients who intend to move abroad to another EEA state should be advised to make a request to do so to the DWP. It will inevitably be refused and the claimants should appeal. The appeal is likely to be stayed pending the outcome of the cases before the ECJ. However, by making a claim and lodging an appeal they will protect any future possible entitlement to retain their benefit should they go to live in another member state.

9. Death grants

There are no UK death grants covered under the co-ordination rule.

Notes

1. Sickness and maternity benefits
1 Case C-61/85
2 Art 18 Reg 1408/71
3 Art 18 Reg 1408/71
4 Art 22 Reg 1408/71
5 Arts 19(1) and 21 Reg 1408/71
6 Art 25 Reg 1408/71
7 Arts 27 and 31 Reg 1408/71
8 Art 28 Reg 1408/71
9 Art 26 Reg 1408/71

2. Invalidity benefits
10 Prior to June 1992 AA and DLA were considered to be invalidity benefits and therefore exportable. However from 1 June 1992 they are listed as special non-contributory benefits and are no longer exportable; *Partridge; Snares* CDLA / 913/94. However, those eligible for benefit prior to this date retain the right to export these benefits, Art 95 Reg 1408/71.
11 Art 10(1) and Annex VI O(12) Reg 1408/71
12 Art 40(4) Reg 1408/71; Arts 40 and 51 Reg 574/72
13 Arts 40(4) and 41 Reg 574/72
14 Art 42 Reg 1408/71

15 para 071684 DMG; Art 37 Reg 1408/71
16 para 071686 DMG; Art 45(1) Reg 1408/71
17 Art 46(3) Reg 1408/71
18 Art 39 Reg 1408/71
19 Art 39(2) and (3) Reg 1408/71
20 Art 39(4) Reg 1408/71
21 Art 35(1) Reg 574/72
22 Art 40(3) Reg 1408/71
23 Art 40(1) and (2) Reg 1408/71
24 Art 35(1) Reg 574/72
25 Arts 36, 41 and 43 Reg 574/72
26 Arts 45, 47 and 53 Reg 1408/71

3. Old age benefits
27 Art 77 Reg 1408/71
28 Case C-382/98 *R v Secretary of State for Social Security ex parte Taylor*
29 Arts 1(h) and (i), 10(1) and Annex VI O(12) Reg 1408/71
30 Art 36(1) Reg 574/72
31 Arts 36 and 41 and Annex 3 (O) Reg 574/72; C-108/75 *Balsamo Institut National d'Assurance Maladie Invalidite* [1976] ECR 375; R(S) 3/82
32 Art 46(1) Reg 1408/71
33 Art 46(2) Reg 1408/71

34 Art 46(2) Reg 1408/71; para 072863 DMG
35 Art 46(1) and (2) Reg 1408/71
36 Art 48 Reg 1408/71
37 Art 46(2) Reg 1408/71
38 Annex VI O(8) Reg 1408/71
39 Art 51(1) Reg 1408/71
40 Art 47(3) Reg 1408/71
41 Art 10(1) and Annex VI O(12) Reg 1408/71

4. **Survivors' benefits**
42 CIS/488/2004; CIS/1491/2004
43 Case C-51/73
44 Case C-92/81
45 *Giletti and others* Cases C-379 to 381/85 and 93/86
46 *Ten Holder* Case C-302/84
47 *Ten Holder* Case C-302/84
48 Decisions cited as authority are *Harris, Daalmijer* and *Morvin* Case C-73/99.
49 CIS/1491/2004
50 R(IS) 8/06
51 Arts 1(h) and (i) and 10(1) and Annex VI O(12) Reg 1408/71

5. **Benefits for accidents at work and occupational diseases**
52 s104(1) and (2) SSCBA 1992
53 s105 SSCBA 1992
54 Sch 7 para 11(1) SSCBA 1992
55 s95(1)-(4) SSCBA 1992
56 Art 10(1) Reg 1408/71
57 Art 55(1) Reg 1408/71
58 Arts 52 and 63 Reg 1408/71
59 Art 56 Reg 1408/71
60 Arts 61(5) and (6) Reg 1408/71

6. **Unemployment benefits**
61 Arts 67-71 Reg 1408/71
62 *Hockenjos v Secretary of State for Social Security* [2001] EWCA Civ 624 (CA) and CJSA/1920/1999 (*65/00)
63 s1(2)(i) JSA 1995. In a letter to the TUC, November 1996, Allan Larsson of the EC said that both contribution-based and income-based JSA would be treated as falling within the scope of Regs 1408/71 and 574/72. Income-based JSA is a special non-contributory benefit under Arts 4(2a) and 10(a) and Annex IIa Reg 1408/71 although, given current domestic caselaw, this probably has little significance.
64 Art 13 Reg 1408/71; C-128/83 *Caisse Primaire d'Assurance Maladie de Rouen v Guyot*; C-20/75 *Gaetano d'Amico v Landesversicherungs-anstalt Rheinland-Pfalz* [1975] ECHR 891; R(U) 4/84

65 C-227/81 *Francis Aubin v ASSEDIC and UNEDIC* [1982] ECR 1991
66 Art 68(2) Reg 1408/71
67 Art 69(1) Reg 1408/71
68 Art 69(1) Reg 1408/71
69 Arts 67(1)-(3) and 71(1)(a)(ii) and (b)(ii) Reg 1408/71
70 Annex VI section O point 7 Reg 1408/71
71 Art 69(1) Reg 1408/71
72 R(U) 2/90
73 Art 69(1)(a) Reg 1408/71
74 Art 69(1)(b) Reg 1408/71
75 Art 69(1)(b) Reg 1408/71; C-20/75 *Gaetano d'Amico v Landesversicherungs-anstalt Rheinland-Pfalz* [1975] ECHR 891. Some EU/EEA member states have more stringent conditions than the UK and may require people with children to have formal childminding arrangements in place, including a contract, before the unemployed person is treated as available for work.
76 Art 83(3) Reg 574/72
77 Art 69(1)(c) Reg 1408/71
78 Art 69(1)(c) Reg 1408/71
79 s5(1) JSA 1995; Art 69(1)(c) Reg 1408/71
80 Art 69(1)(c) Reg 1408/71
81 Art 69(1)(c) Reg 1408/71
82 Art 83(1) Reg 574/72; R(U) 5/78
83 Art 69(3) Reg 1408/71
84 Art 69(2) Reg 1408/71; s5 JSA 1995
85 Art 25 Reg 1408/71
86 Art 67 Reg 1408/71
87 Art 67 Reg 1408/71
88 Art 69(1)(a) Reg 1408/71
89 Art 69(1) Reg 1408/71
90 Art 69(1)(a) Reg 1408/71
91 Art 69(1)(b) Reg 1408/71; C-20/75 *d'Amico* (see note 75)
92 Art 69(1) Reg 1408/71
93 Art 69(1)(c) Reg 1408/71

7. **Family benefits**
94 Art 14(a) and (b) Reg 1408/71
95 C-300/84 *Van Roosmalen* [1986] ECR 3095
96 Art 73 Reg 1408/71
97 Art 74 Reg 1408/71
98 Art 72a Reg 1408/71
99 Art 77(1)(t) Reg 1408/71
100 Arts 77(2)(b)(i) and (ii) and 79(2) Reg 1408/71
101 Art 10 Reg 574/72
102 Arts 86, 88, 90 and 91 Reg 574/72
103 Art 75(2) Reg 1408/71

8. Special non-contributory benefits

104 Annexe IIa Reg 1408/71
105 *Snares* Case C-20/96
106 *Nessa v CAO* [1999], WLR 1937
(reported as R(IS) 2/00)
107 *Di Paolo* Case C-76/76
108 R(IS) 2/2000
109 Resolution 2001/C44/06 of the
Administrative Commission of 29 June
2000
110 Art 95b(8) Reg 1408/71; R(A) 5/92
111 For a fuller account of the scope of this
Regulation see CPAG's *Welfare Benefits
and Tax Credits Handbook.*
112 *Newton* Case C-356/89
113 Mobility allowance was replaced by DLA
in April 1992 but the rules were virtually
unchanged.
114 Regulation 1247/92 introduced Arts
4(2)(a) and 10a. Art 5 was also amended
so as to provide that member states
were to list the benefits considered to fall
within this category in Annex IIa to
Regulation 1408/71.
115 The UK has also listed IS and income-
based JSA as being special non-
contributory benefits.
116 *Snares* Case C-20/96
117 *Partridge* Case C-297/96
118 *Jauch* Case C-215/99
119 *Leclere and Deaconescu* (case C-43/99)
120 *Hosse* Case C-286/03
121 *Swaddling* Case C-90/97
122 EC Reg 647

Chapter 24

· ·

Rights of residence in EC law and entitlement to benefit

This chapter covers:

---

1. Who has a right of residence in EC law

Until April 2004 the issue of whether an European Economic Area (EEA) national had a right of residence in European Community (EC) law was relatively unimportant for benefit claimants. However, from that time the UK benefit system has altered to restrict access to certain benefits unless the person has a right of residence. It has therefore become crucial for those advising EEA benefit claimants to have an understanding of who has a right of residence in EC law and when and how that residence may end.

EC law provides a right of entry to all European Union (EU) nationals into any member state. It also gives rights of residence in any member state to EU nationals who are exercising Treaty rights (see p348). Many of these rights are extended to nationals of Norway, Iceland, Liechtenstein and Switzerland by virtue of agreements with the EU.[1]

In addition a person who has lawfully resided in a member state for five years has a right of permanent residence.[2] This applies not just to the EU national but also to family members whatever their nationality.

The source of the right of residence depends upon what category the EU national falls within.

The rules on EC residence were contained in a variety of EC Directives.[3] In April 2004 EC Directive 2004/38 (the Residence Directive) was issued to repeal all of these Directives and to make some amendments to EC Regulation 1612/68. EC Regulation 1251/70 which provides a right of residence to retired and incapacitated workers has also been repealed.[4] The new Directive largely consolidates the earlier legislation with many aspects remaining the same, this is because it reflects rights contained within the Treaty which are unchanged. Where changes are made it is generally to incorporate interpretation of rights made by caselaw from the ECJ.[5]

The new Directive became fully effective from 30 April 2006. It is now the main source of residence rights for EU nationals **but it is not the sole source of residence rights.** For example, a person who is signing on and looking for work has a right of residence under Article 39 of the Treaty. A tourist who is receiving services and has a right of residence under Article 49 of the Treaty. EC Regulation 1612/68 also continues to provide some rights to residence not reflected in the Directive. For example, it gives children of former workers who are in education the right of residence in order to continue with their education (see p355). Such children have a right of residence under Article 12 and the child's right of residence in turn provides a right of residence to her/his primary carer.

It is important to look at European legislation as a whole as people often have many and varied rights arising out of different areas of EC law.

Initial right of residence

Directive 2004/38 confirms that all EU nationals have an unconditional right of entry into any member state. Most EU nationals, apart from certain A8 and A2 nationals, also have an initial right of residence in any member state for the first three months of their stay. This applies whether or not they are seeking work or exercising any other economic activity.

EU nationals who have a right of residence under the Directive are generally entitled to be treated equally with nationals of the member state in which they reside. This includes equal treatment in respect of benefits.[6] However, during the initial three-month period of residence an EU national who is not economically active is not able to rely on the equal treatment rules in the Directive. Equally during this initial three-month period s/he should not become an 'unreasonable burden' on the social assistance system of the host member state. See p364 for further details of the meaning of this term.

These restrictions during the initial three-month period only apply to people who are not economically active. It cannot apply to someone who is (or has been) a worker, self-employed or a user or provider of services during the three-month period. However, there are restrictions for some A2 and A8 nationals (see p358).

Extended right of residence

In order to have an extended right of residence beyond the three-month period you must fall within one of the following categories. Most of these are set out in the Residence Directive (see p345). You must be:
- a worker;
- self-employed;
- a former worker who has a child in education;[7]
- a former worker or self-employed person who is temporarily sick;
- a former worker or self- employed person who is permanently incapable of work;
- looking for work and signing on for JSA;
- receiving or providing services;
- a student;
- economically inactive but self sufficient;
- a family member of any of the above.

Certain conditions attach to each category. For example:
- **workseekers** must sign on for jobseeker's allowance (JSA) (see p357);
- **students** are required to make a declaration at the start of their stay that they have sufficient means to support themselves (see p360);
- **economically inactive** people are required to have some means of supporting themselves throughout the period of residence (see p367);
- **former workers incapable of work** either must be temporarily ill or if permanent they must have been resident in the UK for two years and worked for 12 months unless the permanent incapacity is due to an industrial injury (see p354);
- **A8 and A2 nationals** have additional conditions attached to their right of residence (see p358).

Permanent right of residence

EU nationals are entitled to permanent residence where they have been lawfully resident in a member state for five years or more. The right to permanent residence also applies to family members of EU nationals even where the family member is not an EU national themselves.

In addition some former workers who have reached retirement age or who have become permanently sick have the right of permanent residence (see p354).

Once acquired the right of permanent residence can generally only be lost through absence from the UK for more than two consecutive years.[8]

Continuity of residence

Your continuity of residence is not affected by temporary absences of up to six months a year or 12 months for military service. Longer absences also do not affect your continuity of residence if it is for an important reason – eg, pregnancy and childbirth, serious illness, study or vocational training or a posting in another member state or a third country.[9]

Exercising treaty rights

Someone who is exercising Treaty rights gains certain rights which can assist with claims for benefit. Generally you are said to be exercising Treaty rights if you are:
- working (see below);
- self-employed (see p355);
- looking for work (p357);
- receiving services (eg, as a tourist, paying for some health care or education – see p358);
- providing services (see p356);
- a student (must be self-sufficient at the start of studies – see p356);
- economically inactive but self-sufficient (see p361).

If you are exercising Treaty rights you have a right of residence and this residence may continue even if you are no longer exercising Treaty rights. However, the rules differ according to the category in which you fall within.

2. Workers

A worker's right to enter a member state to look for, or take up, work as an employee stems from Article 39 of the EC Treaty. The principles set out in the Treaty are given further effect by a number of regulations and directives.

A national of a member state (apart from A2 or A8 nationals with restricted access to the labour market) has the right to take up an activity as an employed person and to pursue that activity within the territory of another member state. If you have the right to enter to look for work, you equally have the right to reside and claim benefits in the same way as a British citizen.[10]

A person who has **worker status** has the right to reside in the UK and the right to access all benefits in the same way as a British citizen. If you are working, part-time or full-time, you have worker status and this status is not automatically lost if you stop work. To retain worker status you must generally be signing on and looking for another job or be temporarily incapable of work.

A8 nationals (see p358) who are working in registered work have worker status in the same way as any other EU national, even within the first 12 months of work, and therefore can access benefits and housing in the same way as other EEA nationals. A2 nationals (see p358) who are in authorised work also have full worker rights while in work. However, unlike A8 nationals, A2 nationals are only authorised to work in certain very limited categories of work (see p360).

There is a significant amount of caselaw as to the meaning of the term 'worker' and the European Court of Justice (ECJ) often interprets the term generously. The ECJ has never laid down a minimum period by which you must work in order to gain worker status and it is therefore worth arguing even if you have worked for quite a short period.

Some of the most significant caselaw has held that:

- a worker is anyone who pursues 'effective and genuine work';[11]
- there must be an employment relationship where the worker accepts directions from another and the work is carried out in return for remuneration,[12] this includes part-time work even if 'topped up' with benefits;[13]
- anyone who loses a job involuntarily still has rights as a worker;[14]
- a person who becomes temporarily incapable of work retains worker status;[15]
- a worker who becomes permanently incapable of work can also retain worker status but this is dependent on the length of residence and work in a member state;[16]
- someone looking for work who has not worked in that member state is a workseeker. Workseekers have some rights but not the same as those who have worked in that state. A8 nationals who are workseekers do not have the same rights as other EEA workseekers unless they have already completed 12 months of registered work;[17]
- a person with a fixed-term contract for a short period that comes to an end retains worker status;[18]
- a commissioner held that a French national working as an au pair for six weeks, 13 hours a week for £35 a week was a worker.[19]

Genuine and effective work

The ECJ has held that an individual must be carrying out an effective and genuine economic activity to qualify as a worker. A person carrying out only marginal and ancillary activity does not qualify since this does not constitute economic activity.

The hours of work and level of remuneration

A commissioner has held that a person who has lost her/his job involuntarily does not retain worker status unless s/he is seeking work with an income which, with tax credits, would be equivalent to her/his applicable amount for income support purposes plus rent.[20]

However, existing caselaw from the ECJ states that a person in part-time employment may be covered by the free movement provisions. In one case the ECJ held that the concept of 'worker' covered those who pursued or wished to work on a part-time basis only and as a result would obtain less than the minimum wage.[21] The ECJ observed that part-time employment constituted for a large number of people an effective means of improving their living conditions. To limit the status of workers to full-time workers, earning at least the guaranteed minimum wage, would impair the effectiveness of EC law and jeopardise the achievement of Treaty objectives. Therefore no distinction could be made between those who made do with this part-time income and those who supplemented it with other income, whether from property or the income of other family members. In a later case, the ECJ accepted that the status as worker of a part-time employee could be retained even where s/he supplemented her/his income by claiming social security.[22] In another case the ECJ held that neither the level of productivity nor the origin of the funds for paying the person concerned were relevant to the question as to whether a person is a worker.[23] The ECJ states that an employment relationship is present where a person is employed under the direction of another person in return for which they receive remuneration. That conclusion is not altered by the fact that the productivity of the person is low and that consequently her/his remuneration is largely provided by subsidies from public funds. Neither the level of productivity nor the origin of the funds from which the remuneration is paid can have any consequence in regard to whether or not the person is to be regarded a s a worker.

Pregnancy

Worker's who are pregnant or who have recently given birth often have problems in terms of their worker status. If a person is still under contract and merely on maternity leave there should be no question that she remains a worker. However, women who lose their jobs and are unable to work because they are in the later stages of pregnancy or who have recently given birth are often told by benefit authorities that they no longer retain worker status. This is because a person who has become unemployed generally only retains worker status by signing on and looking for work or because they are sick. Pregnancy does not fall within these categories. EC law on workers is largely silent on the issue of pregnancy. However, brief reference is made to the protection of rights in the recent Residence Directive. A woman is treated as having continuous residence for any period that she is absent for a temporary period due to pregnancy. This provision seems to relate to absence abroad but the rule gives some support to the view that a temporary gap in work should be ignored in terms of the loss of worker status or residence rights.

Incapacity for work

If you become temporarily incapable of work you do not lose your worker status or right of residence in the member state in which you have been working.[24] Temporary illness is not defined, but if the prognosis is that you will be able to return to work, even if this will take some time, the illness should be treated as temporary. Where an illness is permanent you only retain residence if you have been resident in that state for more than two years.[25] If you have a permanent incapacity due to an industrial accident and as a result are entitled to a benefit paid by the member state you acquire the right of permanent residence immediately. This could apply, for example, where you have an industrial accident and claim disablement benefit.

What is a social advantage – EC Regulation 1612/68

EC law says that migrant workers **'shall enjoy the same social and tax advantages as national workers'**.[26] This is one of the many equal treatment rules in EC law. It means that a person who is a 'worker' cannot be discriminated in terms of access to any social security benefits or tax credits. UK regulations generally reflect this right but problems may arise if it is felt that the person is working too few hours to be considered to be a worker. There can also be problems if you stop work due to illness or pregnancy. For further details of who is a worker, see p348.

The term social advantage has been interpreted widely by the ECJ. It certainly covers all types of social security benefits but could also include items such as fare reduction cards, education grants and hospital treatment. Anything that can be construed as a social advantage will be covered.

People who are covered by the social advantage rule – EC Regulation 1612/68

In order to rely on the social advantage route, you must be an EEA national or a national of a dependent territory of an EEA state. You must also be able to show that you are, or have been in the past, a worker. If you are not working you remain a worker if you are looking for work by signing on for jobseeker's allowance. If you are no longer economically active you can still be a 'worker' if you have worked in a member state but are now incapacitated, have suffered an industrial injury or you are retired. If you have worked in the member state and become unemployed but have a child in education you retain rights as a worker.[27]

Your rights as a worker are extended to your spouse and other family members, whatever their nationality. If you die your family continues to have rights as survivors of an EEA worker.

If you are an EEA national working in the UK, you are a worker covered by Regulation 1612/68. The UK does not include the Channel Islands and Isle of Man for this purpose.[28]

The meaning of the term worker has now been considered on numerous occasions by the ECJ and the following principles have been established. For the purposes of Regulation 1612/68 a worker is anyone who pursues 'effective and genuine work'. That is services for another under their direction and in return for remuneration.[29] This includes part-time work, even if topped up with benefits. Anyone who loses a job involuntarily still has rights as a worker (see p352). Someone looking for work has certain rights under 1612/98 but does not have the right to the same social advantage.[30]

The caselaw does *not* say that for an activity to count as work there must be:
- a minimum period of work;
- a minimum number of hours per week; *or*
- minimum pay.

It does not matter if you are paid in kind rather than cash.[31] It should also be irrelevant that the income from the work is not enough to support you.[32] Although a commissioner has suggested that a person should be earning an amount that with tax credits s/he would earn more than her/his income support applicable amount plus the level of her/his rent. This case is at odds with caselaw from the ECJ.[33] Voluntary work from which you can expect no benefit is not 'work'. However, a person who works for nothing for a period of time, under an agreement that is intended to lead to payment, may qualify as a worker. Work for your rehabilitation may not count as work under this rule.

The following activities have been considered as work:
- teaching music for 12 hours a week;[34]
- work for 60 hours over 16 weeks under a contract with no fixed hours but which requires the person to be available to work;[35]
- training over the summer in a hotel school;[36]
- working as an au pair 13 hours a week for £35 and board and lodging.[37]

Voluntary and involuntary unemployment

If you are voluntarily unemployed you can lose your right of residence in a member state and the right to a social advantage. The question of whether you are voluntarily or involuntarily unemployed is decided by the Jobcentre Plus. This is likely to cause problems for people claiming benefit. Voluntary unemployment is a familiar term in UK social security rules and is applied harshly. However, EC law allows a much more generous approach to whether you are voluntarily unemployed.

If you are an EEA national who has worked in the UK you still count as a worker for the purposes of Regulation 1612/68 if *either*:
- you are genuinely seeking work,[38] whether or not your employment ceased voluntarily or involuntarily;[39] *or*
- you are studying or training and your employment ended involuntarily, *or* there is a link between your present training/studies and your previous employment.[40]

UK nationals

If you are a UK national you are also an EEA national but you do not always have EC law rights. You can only use the social advantage rule if:[41]
- you have travelled to another EEA state; *and*
- you went to that member state to use an EC right there; *and*
- you later returned to the UK to exercise an EC right here.

If you are a dual national with the nationality of another EEA state (eg, Ireland), you can use these exemptions even if you have never moved within the EEA.[42]

If you worked in another EEA state but remained living in the UK, you may count as a 'frontier worker' and so have EC law rights.[43]

The EC rights which carry the right to free movement and social advantage are:
- the right to work, including the right to seek work;
- the right to establish yourself as self-employed, including the right to seek to do that;
- the right to receive and provide services.

If you are treated as an EEA national under these rules, then the habitual residence exemptions apply to you as they apply to other EEA nationals (see p132).

People who have worked elsewhere in the European Economic Area

People who have not worked in the UK but have worked elsewhere in the EEA do have some rights under EC law but they are limited. For example, they have the right to enter a member state and (with some exceptions for A2 and A8 nationals) to look for work and to reside. They also have the right to install family members whatever their nationality. However, they do not have the right to the same tax and social advantage as members of the national state. In order to rely on the social advantage route you must actually have worked in the state in which you wish to claim the social advantage.[44] A commissioner has decided that work in the EEA outside the UK cannot exempt a person from the habitual residence test as a worker for the purposes of Regulation 1612/68.[45] The commissioner followed earlier caselaw that a person only has rights as a worker under EC law in the UK once that person has worked in the UK.[46] If the British person has worked in the UK prior to going to another EEA state s/he may be able to argue that s/he is covered by EC Regulation 1612/68 as the work is not limited to the period since they last entered the UK. A person who has not worked in the UK but has worked elsewhere in the EEA can rely on EC Regulation 1408/71.

A8 and A2 nationals

A8 nationals can rely on Regulation 1612/68 and the social advantage rule while in registered work and A2 nationals while in authorised work. They are therefore eligible to claim all benefits. However, if they become unemployed and have not yet completed 12-months registered or authorised work they are no longer are able to rely on 1612/68. This approach is very probably unlawful because EC law only allows restrictions in respect of Articles 1-6 of EC Regulation 1612/68. The social advantage rule is contained in Article 7(2) of the Regulation and EC law does not allow restrictions in respect of this rule. It is clear that the social advantage rule applies not just to the current worker but also to a person who has had worker status in the past. For further details of the position of A8 and A2 nationals, see p358.

3. Former, retired or incapacitated workers

Retired or incapacitated workers

If you have previously had worker status you may retain the rights of a worker in certain circumstances.[47] In particular it is possible for you and your family to retain the right of residence in a member state even though you are no longer working. You also have the right to equal treatment in respect of benefits or any other social advantage.[48] These rights extend to your survivors and therefore can be crucial, for example, if your spouse is not an EEA national. You have a right to remain if:

- you have reached retirement pension age in that member state. In the UK this is currently 60 for women, 65 for men,[49] *and either*:[50]
  - you had worked in the UK for at least the last 12 months before retirement and resided continuously in the UK for more than three years; *or*
  - your spouse is a British citizen (or lost that citizenship because s/he married you);[51] *or*
- stopped working because of permanent incapacity *and either*:[52]
  - at the date you stopped working you had resided continuously in the UK for more than two years; *or*
  - your incapacity was caused by an industrial injury or disease; *or*
  - your spouse is a British citizen (or lost that citizenship because s/he married you).[53]

When working out your period of 'continuous residence', include:[54]
- absences from the UK of up to six months a year;
- longer absences due to your country's rules about military service;
- longer absences due to important reasons such as pregnancy, childbirth or serious illness.

When working out your period of employment, ignore:[55]
- days of unemployment (even if you were not paid jobseeker's allowance (JSA) – eg, because of an inadequate contribution record);
- absence from work due to illness or accident.[56]

Family members of retired or incapacitated workers

If you have a right of residence as a retired or incapacitated worker these rights are extended to your family members even after your death and regardless of their nationality.[57]

If a worker dies during her/his working life before having acquired the right of residence under this Regulation members of her/his family are entitled to remain, provided that:

- the worker at the date of her/his death has resided continuously in the territory of that member state for at least two years; *or*
- her/his death resulted from an accident at work or an occupational disease; *or*
- the surviving spouse is a national of the state of residence or lost the nationality of that state by marriage to the worker.[58]

Former worker with a child in education

A former worker who has a child in education may continue to have a right to reside through the child even though they do not meet the requirements for continuing residence under other areas of EC law. This is because Article 12 of EC Regulation 1612/68 provides a right of residence for a child in education. The ECJ has held that the primary carer of such a child also has a right of residence.[59]

4. **Self-employed**

The freedoms granted to workers under Article 39 are also granted by the Treaty to the self-employed in the form of a right of establishment and a right to provide services. The principal articles are Article 43 (establishment) and Articles 49 and 50 (services). The difference between the right of establishment and the right to provide services is one of degree rather than of kind. Both apply to business or professional activity pursued for profit or remuneration. A right of establishment is a right to install yourself in another member state permanently or semi-permanently whether as an individual or a company for the purpose of performing a particular activity there. The right to provide services, on the other hand, connotes the provision of services in one state, on a temporary or spasmodic basis, by a person established in another state. In the latter case it is not necessary to reside, even temporarily, in the state in which the service is provided.

If you are self-employed in the UK, you have a right to reside in the UK under the EC Residence Directive.[60] Self-employment includes professional activity. A person who has taken preparatory steps to offer services counts as self-employed.[61] There is no minimum period of residence or of work.

The rights and the rules relating to residence are equivalent to those for employed people under Regulation 1612/68 (see p351). Your right to reside is permanent, but may be taken away if:

- you stop residing in the UK for longer than six consecutive months (ignoring any absence for military service);[62] *or*
- you stop being self-employed, unless this is because of temporary incapacity due to illness or accident.[63] Arguably this would also apply if you are temporarily unable to work due to pregnancy.

It is relatively simple to register as self-employed in the UK. You simply need to notify the Revenue that you are self-employed and then seek contracts. This could be achieved by putting up advertisements in shops or leafleting local houses or businesses. You can fall within this category while searching for self-employed work and are covered even if the work is part time.[64]

There are no special rules for self-employed A8 or A2 nationals. They have the same rights of residence and entitlement to benefit as other self-employed EU nationals.

5. Providing or receiving services

Providing services

A person providing services in the UK is likely to be very similar to someone who is self-employed. Article 49 of the EC Treaty sets out a definition of what might constitute services. Services are considered to be services within the meaning of the Treaty where they are normally provided for remuneration, in so far as they are not governed by the provisions relating to freedom of movement for goods, capital and persons.

Receiving services

The freedom provided by Article 49 is expressed in terms of the freedom to provide services. It has however been extended by the ECJ to embrace the freedom to receive services. Those falling within this category have a right of residence directly from Article 49. It applies to all EU nationals including A8 nationals.

The ECJ has held that recipients of services include tourists, people receiving medical treatment and people travelling for the purposes of education and business as long as there is a commercial aspect to the service provided. In short, if you pay for the service you are covered.[65]

If you are receiving services in the UK, you have a right to reside in the UK.[66] That right continues as long as the services are being received (see example below). Services include:
- tourism,[67] but this must be more than visiting friends;[68]
- education, except for education provided as part of the national education system;[69] and
- medical treatment.[70] The references to medical treatment and education apply only where there is some payment for these.

The ECJ[71] was asked to consider whether the term recipient of services included someone who has no fixed abode and no money or luggage but by the very fact of being in another member state provides an assumption that the person is a tourist and that services associated with short-term residence are received such as accommodation and the consumption of meals. Unfortunately the Court fails to address this rather crucial point. However, it does open up the issue as to whether apparently non-economic EU nationals are truly not economically active or whether they are in fact service users. Many EU nationals who are not in work do come to the UK with savings, may be paying for accommodation, eating out at restaurants or simply paying for other services. Such activity may well bring with them Article 49.

6. **Workseekers**

Workseekers have many rights but are not in the same privileged position as those who have actually worked in the member state in which they wish to assert their rights. There are also differences in the rights of A2 and A8 nationals who are workseekers. A workseeker has a right to reside under Article 39 of the EC Treaty. This does not apply to A8 nationals during the first 12 months of registered work but once they have completed 12 months registered work they will be in the same position as any other EU national and will have a right of residence if signing on. A2 nationals are treated in the same way as A8 nationals except those with a certificate giving them unrestricted access to the labour market have a right of residence if they are signing on (see p358).

Although a workseeker may have a right to reside s/he still has to satisfy the habitual residence test. S/he must also be signing on for jobseeker's allowance (JSA).

Article 39 of the Treaty allows for free movement of workers. This means that a person looking for work can enter any member state and while looking for work has a right of residence in that state. In order to show that there is a genuine search for work it is necessary for the person to sign on for JSA even if, for example, s/he is a lone parent who would not normally be required to sign on.

Any EU national, subject to the restrictions for A8 and A2 nationals, can sign on for JSA and will immediately gain a right of residence. By signing on a person is exercising Treaty rights and this may later give her/him the opportunity to rely on the equality of treatment rule in Article 12 of the EC Treaty.

An A8 or A2 national cannot rely on Article 39 until they have been in registered work for 12 months unless they are exempt from the requirement to register or authorise their work (see pp359 and 360).

Nationals of Iceland, Liechtenstein and Norway cannot rely on Article 39 of the EC Treaty but they have the same rights under Article 28 of the EEA Agreement.

7. **A8 and A2 nationals**

Nationals from the accession states (see p97) are European Union (EU) nationals and therefore can rely on European Community (EC) law in much the same way as any other EU national. However, the Treaties of Accession for the A8 and A2 states restrict some EC rights. The intention of these restrictions is to enable member states to limit accession state nationals from the labour market if they so wish. How member states do this is largely up to individual member states. The outcome in terms of benefit rights are much the same for A2 and A8 nationals but there are some slight differences.

Derogations from EC law for A8 and A2 nationals

Whenever new states join the EU there is a transitional period whereby some EC rights are limited. The terms of these limits, referred to as derogations, are agreed during the negotiations on accession and are set out in legislation. It is therefore important to consider relevant EC provisions, which can give access to benefits, and to consider whether there are any derogations in respect of these rights.

Individual member states cannot act unilaterally to limit these rights, this can be done only by EC law.

A8 and A2 nationals have some restrictions on their rights to take up work as an employee in other EU states. The UK decided to focus on restricting access to benefit rather than to work. A8 nationals can take up any type of work but must register their work with the Home Office. A2 nationals must get authorisation to work but they are restricted to taking employment in certain sectors of the labour market (see p360).

The Accession Treaties for A2 and A8 nationals allow for derogation from:

- Article 39 EC Treaty;
- Articles 1-6 EC Regulation 1612/68;
- Directive 68/360[72] to the extent necessary for the derogation relating to Regulation 1612/68.

Articles 1-6 of EC Regulation 1612/68 relate only to access to entry into a member state and the taking up of employment. There is no derogation in respect of any other rights contained within regulation 1612/68.

These derogations are specific and limited in their nature. However, decision makers and sometimes tribunals take the approach that A8 nationals may not rely on any areas of EC law. This is wrong.

There are no restrictions applied to:

- Article 12 EC Treaty;
- Article 18 EC Treaty;
- Article 42 EC Treaty;
- Article 43 EC Treaty;

- Article 49 EC Treaty;
- EC Regulation 1612/68 other than Articles 1-6;
- EC Regulation 1408/71.

In addition because the Accession Treaty was introduced prior to the coming into force of EC Directive 2004/38 there are no restrictions from the Residence Directive. Although this might appear to provide scope to an argument before a tribunal that an A8 national has the same rights of residence under the Directive as any other EU national. For example, if they become unemployed or sick they retain worker status. However, this is purely a technical argument. EC law is purposive and the intention is that an A8 national does not have the same rights under the Residence Directive as other EU nationals. The restrictions under Article 39 remain and the Directive is purely to give further effect or to set out the rights under Article 39. Such an argument is therefore unlikely to succeed beyond tribunal level.

Worker registration scheme for A8 nationals

Since 1May 2004 A8 nationals who wish to take up employment are required to register under the scheme. Self-employed A8 nationals are not required to register and have full EC rights immediately.

An application for registration must be made to the Worker Registration Team at the Home Office together with evidence of identity and the fee of £50. A worker registration card and certificate are then issued.

The worker registration card is only issued the first time that the worker applies to register. It continues to be valid even where an A8 national changes employment. The certificate however, is only valid for a specific employer and expires as soon as you stop working for that employer. Therefore if you change jobs you must reapply for a certificate.

The Government position is that A8 nationals who are employed, including those who are in part-time employment and who have complied with the workers registration scheme, are treated as workers. Consequently they have a right of residence and access to all benefits. Once an A8 national has worked for 12 months they are also treated as having worker status and a right of residence and will no longer have to comply with the worker registration scheme. However, if the A8 national has worked for less than 12 months and becomes unemployed the Government considers that s/he will also lose her/his right of residence and consequently the right to any benefit.

Arguably the position taken by the Government is unlawful. An EU national who has worked in another member state has worker status under EC Regulation 1612/68. Article 7(2) of that Regulation specifies that a worker has the right to non-discrimination in respect of benefits.

The Accession Treaty only allows restrictions in respect of Articles 1-6 of EC Regulation 1612/68, there is no derogation in respect of Article 7(2). It is clear that 'worker' status may be acquired in a matter of weeks. Therefore a denial of benefit unless a person has worked continuously for at least 12 months appears to be in breach of Article 7(2) of Regulation 1612/68.

A person in this situation should also be able to argue that as they have previously had a right of residence they are able to rely on Article 12 of the EC Treaty and also have a right to be treated equally in terms of access to benefit. There are no derogations in respect of Article 12.

Authorised work scheme for A2 nationals

A2 nationals (see p97) who want to work in the UK must, except where they are exempt, obtain a work authorisation document before they take up employment. They are then issued with an accession work card (AWC). Employment cannot start until the AWC has been issued and if the employee wishes to move jobs they first have to obtain another AWC specific to that employment. If a person takes up work without obtaining an AWC they may be guilty of a criminal offence.

There are two categories of work that will lead to an AWC being issued:
* highly skilled jobs which would meet the current criteria for work permits under UK immigration rules (see p36);
* workers in the food processing industry or seasonal agricultural workers.

Some A2 nationals are exempt from applying for an AWC, see p103.

8. **Students**

If you are an European Economic Area (EEA) student you have a right of residence if you:
* are enrolled as a student in a college accredited by the host member state;
* have comprehensive sickness insurance;
* provide an assurance at the start of your studies that you have sufficient resources for yourself and your family members not to become a burden on the social assistance system of the member state during the period of residence.

Under the Student Directive, the European Union (EU) citizen or student must possess sufficient resources to avoid becoming a burden on the public finances of the host member state and s/he must be adequately insured against sickness costs. However, these limitations and conditions must be applied in compliance with the general principles of European Community (EC) law, in particular the principle of proportionality.[73] One crucial difference between the rights of residence of students and those of self-supporting EU nationals is that students are only required to provide an assurance that they are self supporting at the start of their studies.

Chapter 24: Rights of residence in EC law and entitlement to benefit
9. Self-supporting European Economic Area nationals

24

In one case the European Court of Justice held[74] that a student was entitled to a minimum subsistence benefit which was only payable to non-Belgian EU nationals who were workers under EC Regulation 16122/68. The case involved a student who initially had been self-supporting but later tried to claim a social security benefit. The claim was refused on the basis that he was not an EC worker in accordance with Regulation 1612/68. The Court found that even though an EU student is required by the relevant EC Student's Directive to be self-supporting s/he cannot be refused benefit if a national of that state would have qualified for benefit because to do so is in breach of Article 12 of the EC Treaty.

9. Self-supporting European Economic Area nationals

Article 18 gives every citizen of the European Union (EU) the right to move and reside freely within the EU subject to certain limits and conditions which are set out in European Community (EC) law. This includes all A8 and A2 nationals.

Nationals of Iceland, Liechtenstein, Norway and Switzerland are not able to rely on Article 18 as they are not citizens of an EU state (see p97). There is no equivalent right in the European Economic Area (EEA) or Swiss Agreement.

The limits and conditions vary according to the activity of the person.

Economically inactive people must:

- be covered by sickness insurance in respect of all risks in the host member state; *and*
- have sufficient resources to avoid becoming an unreasonable burden on the social assistance system of the host member state during their period of residence.

For students the rule is similar but the requirement is only to make a declaration to show sufficient resources at the start of the studies (see p360).

Limits and conditions applied under Article 18

To establish what is meant by the conditions in Article 18 it is necessary to consider the growing body of caselaw on this issue. Many of the cases dealing with rights under Article 18 also consider rights under Article 12 and therefore the two sections should be read together.

In the case of *Baumbast*[75] the Court held that a citizen of the EU who no longer enjoys a right of residence as a migrant worker in the host member state can, as an EU citizen, enjoy a right of residence by direct application of Article 18 (although this is subject to the conditions set out in the Treaty).

Mr Baumbast was a German national living and working in the UK. He was married to a non-EEA national and had children. Mr Baumbast became

24

Chapter 24: Rights of residence in EC law and entitlement to benefit
9. Self-supporting European Economic Area nationals

unemployed and left the UK to work outside the EEA. The Court found that although no longer a worker with rights of residence under Article 39, Mr Baumbast did have a right of residence under Article 18. This case was slightly unusual because it was concerned with the right of a non-EEA national to live in a member state rather than claiming benefit. Mr Baumbast did have sufficient funds to support himself. He had not had recourse to the social assistance system so it could not be said that he was an unreasonable burden on that state and he had sickness insurance.

In the case of *Trojani*[76] the Court confirms that all EU nationals have a right to reside under Article 18 subject to the limits and conditions laid down in the Treaty and legislation made under the Treaty.

The Court held that for non-economically active EU nationals the condition is to have sufficient resources to avoid becoming a burden on the social assistance system of that state during the period of residence. However, when considering those limitations the issue of proportionality should be considered.

The Court goes on to say that while it may be lawful for a state to require a non-economically active EU national to be self-supporting that does not mean that such a person cannot during her/his lawful residence in the host member state benefit from the fundamental principle of equal treatment laid down in Article 12 of the EC Treaty.

The UK position is that a person who is not economically active and who seeks benefit does not have a right of residence because the claim for benefit means that they are not self-supporting. The UK Tribunal of Commissioners also takes this approach. Effectively this means that someone who is not economically active or exercising Treaty rights in any way will never have a right of residence under Article 18.

However, the preamble to the EC Residence Directive is not as unequivocal as this. It states that as long as a person in this position does not become an 'unreasonable burden' on the social assistance system of the host member state s/he should not be expelled.

The host state should take into account the duration of residence, the personal circumstances and the amount of aid granted in order to consider whether the beneficiary has become an unreasonable burden on its social assistance system.

Implicit in this is the assumption that there are envisaged some circumstances whereby people who are not economically active do have rights to access benefits in member states.

Sufficient resources

The Directive stipulates that:[77]

'Member States may not lay down a fixed amount which they regard as 'sufficient resources', but they must take into account the personal situation of the person concerned. In all cases this amount shall not be higher than the

Chapter 24: Rights of residence in EC law and entitlement to benefit
9. Self-supporting European Economic Area nationals

24

threshold below which nationals of the host Member State become eligible for social assistance or, where this criterion is not applicable, higher than the minimum social security pension paid by the host Member State.'

Some decision makers, in particular local authorities, are taking the approach that the term 'sufficient resources' means the total of the person's applicable amount for income support (IS), income-based jobseeker's allowance (JSA) or pension credit (PC) (including any premiums they might qualify for) but in addition the amount of housing benefit (HB) and council tax benefit (CTB) they would qualify for. This view has been supported by a commissioner who has held that 'sufficient resources' means the applicable amount in respect of the claimant's IS together with the amount that would be paid toward rent.[78]

The adding together of the applicable amounts of all benefits to determine sufficient resources may not be correct. The Directive refers to the threshold by which a person becomes eligible to social assistance. Furthermore, it states that the amount shall not be higher than the threshold below which nationals of the host member state become eligible for social assistance. If social assistance does mean IS, income-based JSA or PC and can also mean HB and CTB, the threshold for such benefits is not the cumulative amounts of entitlement but the applicable amount for one. As the Directive states that the amount must not exceed the threshold by which a person becomes eligible it cannot be correct to add onto this, as the commissioner has, the amount paid in rent. There is also a question mark as to whether premiums for these benefits ought to be taken into account or whether the threshold is met by the basic amount of IS, income-based JSA or PC. People whose applicable amount would include a disability or family premium would be at a disadvantage as they would be expected to have higher resources. The applicable amount for a pensioner is higher than for a person under pension age on IS. Therefore people of pension age would be required to have greater funds available to them than others below pension age. This leads to issues of disability and age discrimination.

It is no longer clear that benefits such as IS should be categorised as social assistance. Caselaw from the European Court of Justice (ECJ) had established that benefits such as IS and HB are social assistance. However, this caselaw predates changes to EC law in which benefits such as IS moved from being defined as social assistance to become special non-contributory benefits (see p358).

In the past the ECJ struggled with what it called 'hybrid' benefits which are those with the characteristics both of social security (giving a legally defined right in the event of a defined risk occurring) and social assistance (being generally available to the population as a whole provided they satisfy the 'need' criterion). The way in which the EU dealt with these difficulties was to create a new type of special non-contributory benefit. This includes IS, income-based JSA and PC.

Although the assumption remains that any references to social assistance in EC law will equate in the UK to IS and equivalent benefits it may be valid to argue

24

Chapter 24: Rights of residence in EC law and entitlement to benefit
9. Self-supporting European Economic Area nationals

that with the emergence of special non-contributory benefits this is no longer correct. Furthermore, none of the benefits are available to the population as a whole, JSA and PC being very clearly payable only in the defined risks of unemployment and old age. It is certainly arguable that instead we should rely on the latter part of Article 8(4) which states that where social assistance is not applicable the test for sufficient resources is the minimum social security pension paid by the host member state.

An unreasonable burden

In *Grzelczyk*[79] the ECJ held that the right of residence is only lost once the person becomes an unreasonable burden on the state. This obviously requires some individual investigation into the circumstances of the person and necessarily implies that there will be situations whereby people who are not economically active will be able to claim social assistance benefits.

The ECJ also held that the condition that an EU citizen must not become an unreasonable burden on the public finances of the host member state does not preclude her/him, in given circumstances, from being entitled to a social benefit.

The notion of 'unreasonable burden' is apparently flexible and, according to the ECJ, implies that the Residence Directive accepts a degree of financial solidarity between the member states in assisting each other's nationals residing lawfully on their territory.

Mr Grzelczyk had applied for a minimum subsistence allowance which was only payable to non-Belgian EU nationals who were workers under EC Regulation 1612/68. He was refused the benefit on the basis that he was not a worker but a student. The case was referred to the ECJ to determine whether the refusal to grant the allowance was compatible with Articles 12(1) and 18(1) EC Treaty.

The ECJ referred back to its earlier decision in *Martinez Sala*[80] and held that a person lawfully residing in a member state can rely on Article 12 in all situations that fall within the scope of EC law.

Those situations include 'those involving the exercise of fundamental freedoms guaranteed by the Treaty and those involving the exercise of the right to move and reside freely in another Member State, as conferred by Article 18 of the Treaty'.

Article 12(1) must be read in conjunction with Article 18(1) which provides for rights to move and reside freely within the EC, subject to conditions and limitations laid down in the Treaty and within secondary legislation.

The ECJ held that the residence directives do not prevent member states from taking the view that a student who has recourse to social assistance no longer fulfils the conditions for the right to reside or from taking measures, within the limits imposed by EC law, either to withdraw the residence permit or not to renew it. According to the ECJ, however, in no case may such measures become the automatic consequence of a student having recourse to social assistance.

The ECJ further held that the Residence Directive does provide that the right of residence is to exist for as long as beneficiaries fulfil the conditions, but the sixth recital of the preamble to the Directive envisages that beneficiaries must not become an unreasonable burden on the public finances of the host state. The ECJ concludes that the Residence Directive,[81] accepts a certain degree of solidarity between nationals of the host member state and nationals of other member states, particularly if the difficulties the individual encounters are temporary.

In conclusion, the ECJ held that Articles 12 and 17 preclude the application of national rules which make entitlement of nationals of other member states to non-contributory social benefits such as the minimex[82] conditional upon their falling within the scope of Regulation 1612/68 where no such condition is imposed on nationals of the host state.

Although this caselaw relates to a Directive no longer in force the rules are identical to the new Residence Directive 2004/38 so the law remains good.

When does residence end

Grzelczyk is significant because it deals with when a person's residence will end. It says that although member states have the power to end the lawful residence status of nationals in need of support, having recourse to social assistance is not a sufficient reason for withdrawing or renewing residence. In order to take measures to end residence member states must demonstrate that nationals of other states have or will become an 'unreasonable' burden on the social assistance scheme. The ECJ reads into those directives 'a certain degree of financial solidarity' between nationals of a host member state and nationals of other member states.

It is clear that there is not an unqualified right of residence to all EEA nationals. However, where an EU citizen has installed themselves in another member state and who initially expected or was able to support themselves they should not automatically lose their right to reside. The same would be true of someone who is working or looking for work or who is receiving or providing services. All of these groups would have had a right of residence initially. The question that follows is how and when does that residence end and who is able to end that residence. Generally there is no formal event that ends residence. A person who tries to claim benefit will be told by the DWP, local authority, the Revenue or even a tribunal that s/he does not have a right to reside. However, it may be argued that it is for the Home Office to end a person's residence not a benefit authority and therefore it can be argued that the presumption must be that the residence continues.

Degree of financial solidarity

The question of what is meant by the term 'a degree of financial solidarity' is addressed in *Bidar*.[83] The case involved a young person who was a French national. He entered the UK with his mother who was to undergo medical treatment.

24

Chapter 24: Rights of residence in EC law and entitlement to benefit
9. Self-supporting European Economic Area nationals

Following the death of his mother he lived in the UK with his grandmother as her dependant and pursued and completed his secondary education without having recourse to social assistance.

Three years later he started a university course. He applied for a student loan which was refused on the basis that he was not 'settled' in the UK, not yet having fulfilled a period of residence of four years as required by the domestic provisions. Mr Bidar challenged that decision on the grounds that the residence requirement constituted unlawful discrimination in breach of Article 12 of the EC Treaty.

The Advocate General states that the ECJ does not envisage the member states opening up the full range of their social assistance systems to EU citizens entering and residing within their territory. To do so would undermine one of the foundations of the residence directives. On the one hand, the member states are entitled to ensure that the social benefits which they make available are granted for the purposes for which they are intended. On the other hand, they must accept that EU citizens who have been lawfully resident within their territory for a period of time may equally be eligible for such assistance where they fulfil the objective conditions set for their own nationals.

In this respect, they must ensure that the criteria and conditions for granting such assistance do not discriminate directly or indirectly between their own nationals and other EU citizens, that they are clearly suited to attaining the purpose of the assistance, are made known in advance and that the application is subject to judicial review. The Advocate General added that it should also be possible to apply them with sufficient flexibility to take account of the particular individual circumstances of applicants, where refusal of such assistance is likely to affect the substantive core of a fundamental right granted by the Treaty such as the rights contained in Article 18.

Sickness insurance

There is little information regarding the issue of sickness insurance but it is generally taken to mean that a person is covered by EC Regulation 1408/71 which provides rights to the new European Health Insurance Card (EHIC). Any person who has previously worked in a member state, who is a student or who is a family member of such a person should be covered by sickness insurance. The rights to health treatment stem from rights in the Treaty so the fact that someone has not obtained the EHIC should not make a difference to the right of the person to be treated or as to whether they are insured. It simply acts as an administrative formality to ensure that individuals do not have difficulty in proving their right to treatment in other member states.

Chapter 24: Rights of residence in EC law and entitlement to benefit
11. Family members of European Economic Area nationals

24

10. Economically inactive European Economic Area nationals

An European Economic Area (EEA) national who is not economically active and not self-supporting does not have a right of residence and consequently is largely ineligible for benefits. If a person is not economically active themselves, you should check to see if they are a family member of an EEA national (see p367).

Nationals from the 'old' EEA states can change their status by signing on if possible. This also applies to A2 and A8 nationals who have completed 12 months authorised or registered work (see p359). This gives an immediate right to reside. A8 nationals who have not completed 12 months registered work can change their position by taking up registered work which will give immediate access to any benefits to which they are entitled. For A2 nationals the position is more difficult because only certain types of limited work are authorised (see p360). All EEA nationals, including A2 and A8 nationals, who become self-employed become eligible to any benefits to which they are entitled.

11. Family members of European Economic Area nationals

Family members are defined in the Residence Directive as:

- a spouse or civil partner;
- direct descendants under the age of 21;
- dependant relatives in the ascending;
- any other family members, irrespective of nationality who are dependants or members of the household of the European Economic Area (EEA) citizen or where the EEA national cares for that person;
- a person with whom the EEA national has a 'durable relationship'.

European Community (EC) law can be particularly helpful for family members who are not EEA nationals themselves. If you are a non-EEA national and you have an EC right to remain in the UK as a member of the family of an EEA national (see p296), then you do not require leave to remain so you are *not* a 'person who is subject to immigration control' for benefits purposes.[84] This applies whether or not you have an EEA residence document. A family member who has resided in a member state for five years acquires the right of permanent residence in that member state.

If you are a non-EEA national and you do *not* have an EC right to remain in the UK, your entitlement to benefit depends upon your immigration status.

24

Chapter 24: Rights of residence in EC law and entitlement to benefit
11. Family members of European Economic Area nationals

Remember that the definition of 'family member' includes not only spouse and children aged up to 21, but also other relatives – eg, a separated spouse, parents and adult children (see p369).

Family members and residence documents

A stamp in your passport or on a Home Office letter confirming your right to reside is called a 'residence document'. If you have a residence document then the DWP must accept that you do not require leave to remain and that you have a right to reside.

If you do not have a residence document, then you can still count as a person who does not require leave to remain. Your right to remain comes from EC law so you do not need to have a residence document.[85] A decision on whether you are subject to immigration control or whether you have a right to reside for benefit purposes is a DWP decision, not a Home Office one, and can be appealed to an appeal tribunal.

A person with an EC right to remain does not *require* leave to enter or remain, but can still be given it. For example, the right of permanent residence is shown by the grant of indefinite *leave* to remain. Also where a non-EEA family member seeks admission but does not have an EEA family permit (see p100), it is practice to give six months' leave to enter subject to a public funds condition.[86]

You may have leave subject to a condition that you do not have recourse to public funds or given as a result of a maintenance undertaking. Normally, a person with such leave would be subject to immigration control for benefits purposes.[87] However, this rule can only apply to a person who *requires* leave to remain. If you have an EEA right to reside (eg, because you are married to someone who is a 'worker'), then you do not require leave to remain.[88] Your rights to remain are through the EC rules set out above and these override any UK provisions.

If you do not have permission to be in the UK, or you have limited leave to be in the UK, a claim for benefit may affect your immigration position (see Chapter 7). You should seek immigration advice before claiming.

Example

Lola is a Portuguese national. She arrives at Heathrow Airport with her 18-year-old son Joao who has a Mozambican passport but no EEA family permit. Lola is admitted as an EEA national exercising Treaty rights, but Joao is given six months' leave to enter subject to a public funds condition. Lola finds permanent work. Four months later her employer goes bankrupt and she loses her job. She is awarded income-based jobseeker's allowance (JSA). Joao also claims JSA. Because he has an EC law right to reside as Lola's son he is not 'subject to immigration control' despite the stamp in his passport. He is exempt from the habitual residence test because he has a right to reside under Directive 38/2004 as the son of a worker with that right to reside.

Family members who separate, divorce or end their civil partnership

A family member of an EEA worker does not necessarily lose their right of residence if they separate, divorce or end their civil partnership. Residence is not lost if:

- prior to the initiation of the divorce or termination of the civil partnership the marriage or registered partnership has lasted at least three years including one year spent in the host member state; *or*
- the spouse or partner who is not a national of a member state has custody of the union citizen's child(ren); *or*
- the spouse or partner who is not a national of a member state has custody of the union citizen's child(ren) or has the right of access to a minor child provided the ECJ has ruled that such access must be in the host member state and for as long as is required; *or*
- this is warranted by particularly difficult circumstances, such as having been a victim of domestic violence.

However, before acquiring the right of permanent residence, the person has to show that s/he is a worker, self-employed or self-sufficient.

Notes

1. **Who has a right of residence in EC law**
   1. Nationals of Norway, Iceland and Liechenstein have rights of free movement and associated rights by virtue of the EEA Agreement. The EC Switzerland Agreement provides similar rights to nationals of Switzerland.
   2. Art 16 Dir 2004/38
   3. These were Dirs 64/221, 68/360, 72/194, 73/148, 75/34, 75/35, 90/364, 90/365 and 93/96.
   4. Dir 635/2006
   5. This is made clear in the preamble to the Directive.
   6. Art 24 Dir 38/2004
   7. Art 12 Reg 1612/68

   8. Art 16(4) Dir 38/200. Residence of an economically active EU national or one with a right of permanent residence can also be ended on public policy, public security or public health. However, these involve serious breaches and are not regularly relied upon.

2. **Workers**
   9. Art 16 Dir 38/2004
   10. Arts 1-6 Reg 1612/68
   11. *Levin* Case 53/81
   12. *Lawrie-Blum* Case 66/85
   13. *Kempf* Case 139/85
   14. *Lair* Case 39/86
   15. Art 7 Dir 2004/38
   16. Art 17 Dir 2004/38
   17. *Lebon* Case 316/85
   18. *Ninni-Orashe* Case C-413/01
   19. R(IS) 12/98
   20. CH/3314/2005 and CIS/3315/2005

21 *Levin* Case C-53/81
22 *Kempf* Case C139/85
23 Bettray Case C344/87
24 Art 7(3) Dir 38/2004
25 Art 17(1)(b) Dir 38/2004
26 Art 7(2) Reg 1612/68
27 Art 12 Reg 1612/68
28 Art 299(6)(c) EC Treaty (formerly Art 227(6)(c); Protocol 3 to Treaty of Accession); Case C-355/89 *Barr and Montrose* [1991] I-3479
29 Case C-53/81 *Levin*; Case C-66/85 *Lawrie-Blum*
30 Case C-316/85 *Lebon*
31 Case C-196/87 *Steymann* [1988] ECR 6159
32 Case C-139/85 *Kempf* [1986] ECR 1741; CH/3314/05 and CIS/3315/05
33 CH/3314/05 and CIS/3315/05
34 Case C-139/85 *Kempf* [1986] ECR 1741
35 Case C-357/89 *Raulin*
36 Case C-27/91 *Le Manoir*
37 CIS/12909/1996 paras 14-15
38 Case C-85/96 *Martinez Sala* para 32
39 CIS/12909/1996 paras 21 and 23
40 Case C-39/86 *Lair* [1988] ECR 3161 para 37; Case C-357/89 *Raulin* [1992] ECR I-1027
41 Case C-370/90 *Surinder Singh* [1992] ECR I-4265
42 Case C-369/90 *Micheletti* [1992] ECR I-4239; Case C-292/86 *Gullung* [1988] ECR 111
43 The ECJ has been asked to decide whether a British citizen who travels on business to other EEA states but retains his home in the UK has acquired an EC right of residence in the UK (so he can benefit from EEA rules to have his wife stay here): Case C-60/00 *Carpenter*.
44 Case C-316/85 *Lebon*
45 CIS/4521/1995 para 15
46 CIS/4521/1995 para 14; *Lair* and *Raulin* (see note 40)
47 Art 17 Dir 2004/38
48 Art 24 Dir 2004/38

3. Former, retired or incapacitated workers

49 s122(1) SSCBA 1992 'pensionable age'
50 Art 17(1) Dir 2004/38
51 Art 17(2) Dir 2004/38
52 Art 17(1) Dir 2004/38
53 Art 17(2) Dir 2004/38
54 Art 17(1) Dir 2004/38
55 Art 17(2) Dir 2004/38

56 We consider that this also applies to a woman who cannot work because of pregnancy.
57 Art 17(3) Dir 2004/38
58 Art 17(2) Dir 2004/38
59 *Baumbast* Case C-314/99

4. Self-employed

60 Art 7(1)(a) para 1 Dir 2004/38
61 CIS/3559/1997
62 Art 16(3) Dir 38/2004
63 Art 16(3) Dir 38/2004
64 R(IS) 6/00

5. Providing or receiving services

65 The point was originally raised in *Watson and Belmann* where the Commission suggested that the freedom to move within the Community to receive services was the necessary corollary to the freedom to provide services. This was approved by the ECJ in *Luisi v Ministero del Tesoro* where it was held that recipients of services included tourists, persons receiving medical treatment and persons travelling for the purposes of education and business, so far as there is a commercial aspect to the service provided.
66 Art 7 Dir 38/2004
67 Case C-186/87 *Cowan* [1989] ECR 195
68 *Tisseyre*, IAT (6052)
69 Case C-263/86 *Humbel* [1988] ECR 5365
70 Cases C-286/82 and C-26/83 *Luisi and Carbone* [1988] ECR 5365
71 *Oulane* Case C-215/03 ECJ

7. A8 and A2 nationals

72 This Directive governed the residence rights of workers prior to the introduction of the consolidating Dir 2004/38.

8. Students

73 Opinion of the Advocate General *Bidar* Case C-209/03 para 32
74 *Grzelczyk* Case 184/99 ECJ

9. Self-supporting EEA nationals

75 *Baumbast* Case C413/99
76 *Trojani* Case C-456/02
77 Art 8(4) Dir 2004/38
78 CH/3314/05 and CIS/3315/05
79 *Grzelczyk* Case C-184/99
80 *Martinez Sala* Case C-85/96
81 This was the relevant residence directive for non-economically active people at the time.

82 Minimex is the equivalent to a benefit such as income support.
83 *Bidar* Case C-209/03

11. **Family members EEA nationals**
84 s115(9) IAA 1999
85 Case C-48/95 *Royer* [1976] ECR 497
86 This practice may be unlawful because the terms on which leave is granted (in particular the prohibition on employment) is inconsistent with the EC law rights of the family member.
87 s115(9)(b) and (c) IAA 1999
88 This argument has succeeded under the pre-April 2000 IS rules for persons from abroad: *Tue-Bi*, Sutton Appeal Tribunal, 14 September 2000.

Part 5

International agreements

Chapter 25

International agreements

This chapter covers:
1. Reciprocal agreements (below)
2. Council of Europe conventions and agreements (p380)
3. European Community agreements with non-European Economic Area countries (p381)

1. Reciprocal agreements

Reciprocal agreements are bilateral agreements made between the UK and one other country. They are part of UK law[1] and their purpose is to protect your entitlement to benefits if you move from one country which is a party to the agreement to the other. Like European Community (EC) law a reciprocal agreement can help you to qualify for certain benefits by allowing periods of residence and contributions paid in each of the two states to be aggregated. Furthermore they often specify that you must receive equal treatment with nationals of the state to which you have moved.

The scope of reciprocal agreements differs greatly, not only in terms of which benefits are covered and the provisions made but also in respect of which people are covered. It is therefore crucial to check the individual agreement at issue.

The UK has reciprocal agreements with European Economic Area (EEA) member states and with countries outside the EEA (see Appendix 6). However, EC social security provisions are more generous and therefore have largely replaced the reciprocal agreements. The general principle is that you look to EC law first and only if EC law does not assist do you go to the reciprocal agreement.

The agreements vary as to who is covered and which benefits are covered. It is therefore important to check each individual agreement. What follows is an outline of the benefits covered and the general principles relating to the agreements. You can find a list of all the countries and the benefits covered in Appendix 6. The following benefits are not covered by any of the agreements:
- child tax credit;
- working tax credit;
- social fund payments;

- income-based jobseeker's allowance (JSA); *and*
- income support (IS).

Reciprocal agreements with EU/EEA member states

The UK has reciprocal agreements with all the established European Union (EU)/ EEA member states except Greece. Of the newer member states only Cyprus, Malta and Slovenia have agreements. Reciprocal agreements may only be relied on by EEA nationals where EC provisions do not apply.[2]

You cannot qualify for benefits using reciprocal agreements if you:
- fall within the 'personal scope' of the co-ordination rule (see p296);[3] *and*
- acquired your right to benefit on, or after, the date EC provisions applied.[4]

If you are not covered by the co-ordination rule, you may be able to get benefits using the reciprocal agreements. Appendix 6 shows the countries with which Great Britain has social security agreements, and the benefits covered by each. Agreements between EEA member states continue to apply if you do not fall within the personal scope of the co-ordination rule but you do fall within the scope of the reciprocal agreement.[5]

Agreements between EU/EEA member states can also continue to apply if:
- the provisions of an agreement are more beneficial to you than the EC provisions; *and*
- your right to use the reciprocal agreement was acquired before:
  - EC provisions applied to the UK on 1 April 1973; *or*
  - the other member state joined the EU/EEA.[6]

This is likely to help nationals of member states that joined the EU/EEA only recently.

The UK's agreement with Denmark continues to apply in both the Faroes and Greenland as they are not part of the EU/EEA. Greenland left the EC on 1 February 1985.

People covered by the agreements

Some of the agreements cover nationals of the contracting parties, while others apply to 'people going from one member state to another'. This may be particularly significant if you are a non-EU/EEA national who has worked in two or more EU/EEA member states but cannot benefit under the co-ordination rule (see p296). Of the member states which now form the EU/EEA, the agreements with Belgium, Denmark, France, Italy and Luxembourg are confined to nationals only.[7] The convention with the Netherlands has recently been re-negotiated and now extends to all people moving from one member state to the other who fall within its scope.

The reciprocal agreements define who is counted as a national for the purpose of the reciprocal agreement where nationality is an issue. In all of these, a UK national is defined as a 'citizen of the United Kingdom and colonies' (see Chapter 2 for further details on nationality).[8]

The category of people termed 'citizens of the United Kingdom and Colonies' disappeared on 1 January 1983 when the British Nationality Act 1981 came into force. From that date on, a person who had previously held citizenship of the UK and colonies became:

- a British citizen;
- a British dependent territories citizen;
- a British overseas citizen; *or*
- a British subject.

For the purposes of the UK social security 'nationals only' conventions with Belgium, Denmark, France, Italy and Luxembourg a national in relation to the UK now includes anyone in one of the above four categories.

The definition of nationality contained in the agreements with Denmark, Italy and Luxembourg is simply that of a 'Danish' or 'Italian' or 'Luxemburger' national.[9] These agreements confer no rights if you are not a national of one of these member states. The agreement with Belgium, however, covers a 'person having Belgian nationality or a native of the Belgian Congo or Ruanda-Urundi'. The agreement with France refers to 'a person having French nationality' and 'any French-protected person belonging to French Togoland or the French Cameroons'.

When these agreements came into force in 1958, the Belgian Congo and Ruanda-Urundi and French Togoland and the French Cameroons were Belgian and French territories respectively. The question concerning who is presently covered by these agreements, insofar as Belgian and French nationals are concerned, is a matter for the Belgian and French authorities. If you come from one of these countries you should enquire of the Belgian or French authorities whether you are covered by these agreements.

The agreements confer equal treatment on the nationals of the contracting countries, stating that a 'national of one contracting party shall be entitled to receive the benefits of the legislation of the other contracting party under the same conditions as if he were a national of the latter contracting party'.[10]

The agreements with Finland, Iceland, Ireland, Portugal, Spain and Sweden are not confined to nationals but confer rights on:

- 'people who go from one country to another' (Ireland);
- 'a person subject to the legislation of one contracting party who becomes resident in the territory of the other party' (Portugal);
- 'a national of one contracting party, or a person subject to the legislation of that party, who becomes resident in the territory of the other contracting party' (Spain); *and*

- 'a national of the state and person deriving their rights from such nationals and other people who are, or have been, covered by the legislation of either of the states and people deriving their rights from such a person' (Sweden).

The agreements with Austria and Norway have nationality restrictions which apply to the protocol on benefits in kind (eg, medical treatment) but not to social security contributions and benefits. A national of the UK is defined as anyone who is recognised by the UK government as a UK national, provided that s/he is 'ordinarily resident' in the UK. A person can be treated as ordinarily resident from the first day of her/his stay in the UK.

The agreement with Germany is not restricted to nationals of either agreement member state insofar as social security benefits are concerned. However, a nationality provision applies to the Articles relating to contribution liability.

Even if you are not a national of one of the contracting parties to these agreements you may still be able to benefit from their provisions.

Benefits covered by the agreements

The following benefits are covered by some of the reciprocal agreements (see Appendix 6 for a full list of which benefits apply to which countries).

Unemployment benefits

The relevant benefit in the UK is contribution-based JSA.

None of the agreements allow you to receive unemployment benefits outside the country where you paid your insurance contributions. However, a number do provide for insurance that you have paid in one country to count towards satisfying the conditions of entitlement in the other. This is the case with the UK agreements with Austria, Cyprus, Finland, Iceland, Malta, New Zealand and Norway.

Sickness benefits

In the UK, the relevant sickness benefit is short-term incapacity benefit (IB). If you are entitled to sickness benefits, some of the agreements allow you to receive your benefit in the other country. In other cases, contributions that you have paid under one country's scheme may be taken into account to help you satisfy the conditions of entitlement in the other.

Maternity benefits

In the UK, the relevant maternity benefit is maternity allowance (MA). If you are entitled to maternity benefits, some of the agreements allow you to receive your benefit in the other country. You may be entitled to MA, or continue to be paid MA, if absent from the UK, under the reciprocal agreements with the following non-EU/EEA countries: Barbados, Cyprus, the Isle of Man, Jersey and Guernsey, Switzerland, Turkey and the former Republic of Yugoslavia. The circumstances under which you may be able to claim or retain MA differ from agreement to agreement.

Invalidity benefits

The relevant benefit in the UK is long-term IB. A number of the agreements allow you to receive invalidity benefits in the other country. The agreements with Austria, Cyprus, Iceland, Norway and Sweden allow you to continue to receive your long-term IB in the other country – subject to medical controls being undertaken in the agreement country. Correspondingly, you are able to receive the other country's invalidity benefit in the UK. The agreement with Barbados allows a certificate of permanent incapacity to be issued, permitting you to receive long-term IB without medical controls.

Benefits for industrial injuries

The relevant benefits in the UK are disablement benefit (including any additional components of it), reduced earnings allowance and retirement allowance.

Most of the agreements include industrial injuries benefits. The arrangements determine which country's legislation will apply to new accidents or diseases depending on where you are insured at the time. Many of the agreements allow you to combine the industrial injuries suffered in each country when assessing the degree of your latest injury. Furthermore, if you work in one country and remain insured under the other country's scheme and you suffer an industrial injury you can be treated as though the injury arose in the country in which you are insured. Most agreements include arrangements to allow you to receive all three of the UK benefits for industrial injuries indefinitely in the other country.

Retirement pensions and bereavement benefits

All the agreements include retirement pensions and bereavement benefits. In the UK, the relevant benefits are retirement pensions, bereavement allowance and widowed parent's allowance. In most cases, you can receive a retirement pension or bereavement benefit in the agreement country at the same rate you would be paid in the country where you are insured. This is the case under all of the agreements except those with Canada and New Zealand, which do not permit the up-rating of these benefits. If you go to live in one of these countries, your retirement pension (and any other long-term benefit) will be 'frozen' at the rate payable either when you left the UK, or when you became entitled to your pension abroad.

If you do not qualify for a retirement pension or bereavement benefit from either country, or you qualify for a pension or bereavement benefit from one country but not the other, the agreements with the following countries allow you to be paid basic old age and bereavement benefits on a pro rata basis, with your insurance under both schemes taken into account: Austria, Barbados, Bermuda, Cyprus, Finland, Iceland, Israel, Jamaica, Malta, Mauritius, Norway, the

Philippines, Sweden, Switzerland, Turkey, the USA and the former Republic of Yugoslavia.

Family benefits

In the UK, the relevant family benefits are child benefit and guardian's allowance. The provisions concerning these two benefits enable periods of residence and/or presence that you may have spent in the other country to be treated as residence and/or presence spent in Great Britain. The extent to which reciprocity exists varies, however, according to the particular agreement. For example, residence or contributions paid in the following countries count towards your satisfying UK residence conditions for guardian's allowance: Cyprus, Israel, Jamaica, Jersey/Guernsey, Mauritius and Turkey.

Dependants' benefits

In the UK a dependant's benefit is an increase of benefit covered by the agreement. Dependants' increases can be paid if the dependant is in either country to the agreement.

Of the agreements with countries which are not EU/EEA member states, those with Bermuda, Cyprus, Jamaica, Mauritius, New Zealand and the USA make provision for a person 'subject to the legislation of one member state', who becomes resident or takes up employment in the other.

The agreements with Israel, Switzerland, Turkey and the former Yugoslavia refer to nationals, in each case the respective member state's nationals and citizens of the United Kingdom and colonies.

2. Council of Europe conventions and agreements

There are numerous European conventions and agreements. These are prepared and negotiated within the Council of Europe. The most famous perhaps is the European Convention on Human Rights. The purpose of these Conventions is to address issues of common concern in economic, social, cultural, scientific, legal and administrative matters and in human rights. However, such agreements and conventions are not legally binding. They are statements of intent of the individual countries that are signatories. The UK is a signatory to a number of these agreements, two of which are significant for social security.

The European Convention on Social and Medical Assistance

The European Convention on Social and Medical Assistance (ECSMA) has been in force since 1954. It requires that ratifying states provide assistance in cash and in kind to nationals of other ratifying states, who are lawfully present in their territories and without sufficient resources, on the same conditions as their own nationals. It also prevents ratifying states repatriating lawfully present nationals of other ratifying states simply because the person is in need of assistance.

The countries that have signed this agreement are all the European Economic Area (EEA) countries (see p282) plus Macedonia and Turkey. European Community (EC) rules are more generous than this Convention, so it would not usually apply to EEA nationals. You may only benefit from this agreement if you are lawfully present in this country. These rights are recognised in UK law and if you are a person who is covered by the Convention you are not a 'person subject to immigration control' (PSIC – see p155) for means-tested benefits.[11] This therefore has potential for asylum seekers and others who would otherwise be excluded from benefit. The House of Lords has recently held that an asylum seeker on temporary admission is lawfully present.[12]

The 1961 Council of Europe Social Charter

This agreement is similar in nature to the ECSMA agreement. The signatory states are all EEA countries (see p282) plus Macedonia and Turkey. If you are a national of one of these states and you are lawfully present you are not a PSIC for means-tested benefits.

A subsequent Council of Europe Social Charter has been signed and the later agreement includes most of the above countries as well as Switzerland and the Ukraine. However, if you are a national of the later convention you are not exempt from the definition of PSIC. This is because UK regulations make reference only to the 1961 Convention.

Although the Council of Europe agreements stem from Europe they are not part of EC law. Therefore, they are of little practical use unless recognised by UK law. This is highlighted by the fact that the exemption from the definition of PSIC applies only to nationals of the signatory states to the 1961 agreement. This is because the UK regulations expressly refer to the 1961 Agreement.

3. European Community agreements with non-European Economic Area countries

The co-operation and association agreements

The European Community (EC) Treaty provides for agreements to be made with so-called third countries outside the European Union (EU).[13] The co-operation and association agreements are of far more significance than the agreements outlined in section 2 above. This is because they are part of EC law and therefore have the potential to override UK rules.

At present, the only agreements which directly affect benefits in the UK are those with Algeria, Morocco, Tunisia and Turkey.

All of these agreements contain provisions which specify that there must be equal treatment for those covered by the agreement in matters of 'social security'. The UK regulations go some way to recognise these rights but they do not fully recognise them and there is, therefore, scope for challenges before the commissioners and courts.

UK regulations specify that if you are a national of one of these states and you are lawfully working in the UK you are exempt from the definition of 'person subject to immigration control' but only for the purposes of attendance allowance, child benefit, disability living allowance, child tax credit (CTC), carer's allowance and the social fund.

However, these agreements offer equal treatment in a much wider range of benefits. In *Surul* the European Court of Justice (ECJ) equated the Turkish agreement with EC Regulation 1408/71 and held that the benefits covered were the social security benefits in EC Regulation 1408/71. Social security in this context has a distinct meaning. It refers to certain benefits intended for the risks of unemployment, sickness, maternity, old age, bereavement, industrial injury and death (see p299 for a full list of these benefits). It is clear that these benefits are covered and it has been established that income-based jobseeker's allowance (JSA) is an unemployment benefit for EC purposes.[14] It should be noted that housing benefit and council tax benefit are not covered by EC Regulation 1408/71 and consequently do not fall within the scope of the co-operation and association agreements.

Furthermore, there is caselaw to support the view that all of the benefits covered by EC Regulation 1408/71 also fall within the scope of some of the co-operation and association agreements. In *Babahenini*[15] the ECJ considered whether a disability allowance was a benefit within the scope of the Algerian agreement. As in earlier caselaw its decision was based on the principle that you look to EC Regulation 1408/71 for guidance. However, in this case the ECJ appears to extend the scope of the agreements. The effect of this judgment is that the special non-contributory benefits also fall within the agreements (see p336 for a full list of special non-contributory benefits).

The personal scope of the agreements

To be within the personal scope of the agreements you must be a national of Algeria, Morocco, Tunisia or Turkey and you must be lawfully working. This has been equated with being an 'insured person'. An insured person has the meaning given in EC Regulation 1408/71 (see p296). In broad terms this means that you have worked in the UK and you have, or you ought to have, paid national insurance contributions. A commissioner has held that an asylum seeker who had worked in the UK was covered by the Turkish Association Agreement and was therefore eligible for family credit as a family benefit under that agreement.[16] The same argument can be applied to working tax credit.

Asylum seekers and the co-operation and association agreements

There is significant potential for asylum seekers under these agreements. By applying all of this caselaw an asylum seeker from Algeria, Morocco, Tunisia or Turkey who has worked in the UK could qualify for income-based JSA as an unemployment benefit, child benefit or CTC as family benefits.

Furthermore, *Babahenini* would appear to have established that income support (IS) and all other special non-contributory benefits are covered by at least some of the agreements. Therefore an asylum seeker who has worked could qualify for IS despite the restriction of UK rules. As the agreement provides for equal treatment s/he would be eligible for full-rate IS rather than an urgent cases payment. It should, however, be noted that an asylum seeker who wishes to rely on the agreements would then have to satisfy the usual rules to be eligible for IS. This means they would only qualify, for example, if they are a lone parent or sick or a pensioner. See CPAG's *Welfare Benefits and Tax Credits Handbook* for full details of who can get IS. It should also be noted that a commissioner has held that 'special non-contributory benefits' (see p336) such as IS are not covered by the Turkish Agreement.

Notes

1. **Reciprocal agreements**
   1 s179(2) SSAA 1992
   2 Art 6 Reg 1408/71
   3 Art 2 Reg1408/71
   4 Cases C-82/72 *Walder* and C-4758/93 *Thevenon*
   5 Art 2 Reg 1408/71; Case C-99/80 *Galinsky*; R(P) 1/81
   6 Cases C-227/89 *Ronfeldt* and C-4758/93 *Thevenon*
   7 Art 3 to each of the relevant reciprocal agreements
   8 Art 1 to each of the relevant reciprocal agreements
   9 Art 1 to each of the relevant reciprocal agreements
   10 Art 1 to each of the relevant reciprocal agreements

2. **Council of Europe conventions and agreements**
   11 Sch 1 Part 1 Immigration and Benefits (Consequential Amendment) Regulations
   12 *Szoma v Secretary of State for Work and Pensions* [2005] UKHL 64, [2006] 1 All ER 1 (reported as R(IS) 2/06)

3. **European Community agreements with non-European Economic Area countries**
   13 Art 310 EC Treaty
   14 *Hockenjos v Secretary of State for Social Security, Times Law Report,* 17 May 2001; CJSA/1920/1999 (*65/00)
   15 Case C113/97 – in a recent commissioner's decision, however, the commissioner held that the Turkish Agreement did not apply to income support.
   16 CFC/2613/1997

Part 6

NASS support

Chapter 26
The NASS scheme

This chapter covers:

1. Introduction to NASS

The **National Asylum Support Service** (NASS) is part of the Home Office and is responsible for the provision of support to destitute asylum seekers. It has been operational since 3 April 2000 at which point it became responsible for the support of certain new asylum applicants.[1]

Before 5 February 1996 asylum seekers without funds received income support at the urgent cases rate of 90 per cent and housing benefit; those without accommodation in priority need were entitled to homeless housing. In February 1996 the Government decided that providing benefits was a 'pull factor' attracting asylum seekers to the UK. Initially benefits were simply withdrawn with nothing put in their place. Asylum seekers therefore sought to draw on the safety net provisions from local authorities in particular by relying on the National Assistance Act 1948 (NAA 1948) and also section 17 of the Children Act 1989.

From 6 December 1999[2] restrictions were placed on asylum seekers' ability to access support from local authorities. These restrictions have been extended[3] so that they now apply to the following local authority support:

- sections 21 and 29 of the NAA 1948;
- section 2 of the Chronically Sick and Disabled Persons Act 1970;
- section 21 and Schedule 8 of the National Health Service Act 1977;
- sections 17, 23C, 24A and 24B of the Children Act 1989;
- section 2 Local Government Act of the 2002.

It should be noted that the exclusions do not prevent a local authority from providing support under the above provisions if failing to do so would result in a breach of an asylum seeker's human rights.

Further, asylum seekers were not generally entitled to benefits and other welfare provisions because they were 'persons subject to immigration control' (see p155).[4] They were to be provided for under two new schemes of interim asylum support where assistance was provided by the local authority and NASS. On 31 March 2005 a further set of regulations were introduced detailing entitlement to support under section 4 Immigration and Asylum Act 1999 (IAA 1999) of certain failed asylum seekers and their dependants. Prior to the regulations being introduced, the power to give failed asylum seekers support was at NASS's discretion. The regulations placed the provision of such support on a statutory footing.

NASS is a directorate of the Home Office and is based in Croydon. It has gradually taken over the responsibility of providing support for asylum seekers. The directorate is now in the process of being phased out. As from April 2007 all new asylum claims will be dealt with within the New Asylum Model (NAM) and allocated to a caseowner who will also have responsibility for deciding whether or not the asylum seeker should receive asylum support. Decisions to grant or refuse NASS will be made by NAM caseowners within the Border Immigration Agency (BIA). Failed asylum seekers who originally applied for asylum before the 1 April 2007 and whose cases are being decided under the old system will continue to apply and receive support from the current section 4 team who are to be absorbed into the legacy directorate.

Some asylum seekers continue to get help from local authorities under the interim support regulations or under the NAA 1948 or community care provisions. If an asylum seeker is destitute and 'in need of care and attention' due to age, pregnancy, a disability, mental health needs or other special reasons s/he may be able to access assistance from the local authority under section 21 NAA 1948 provided they are destitute. An asylum seeker can ask the local authority to carry out a community care assessment under section 47 of the NHS and Community Care Act 1990 to determine whether s/he needs support from the local authority. As explained above, community care is restricted in relation to asylum seekers and support from a local authority may not be provided if the person's need for care and attention arises solely from the effects or anticipated effects of being destitute.[5] Unaccompanied minor asylum seekers continue to be supported by social services.

The NASS scheme incorporates the services of various voluntary sector agencies, the Refugee Arrivals Project, Migrants Helpline, Refugee Action, the Refugee Council and the Scottish and Welsh Refugee Councils in order to identify and assess applicants for asylum support.

There are three main types of NASS support available:
- **full support** under section 95 IAA 1999;

- **temporary support** under section 98 IAA 1999 which is available for asylum seekers waiting assessment for full support;
- **section 4 support (previously known as hard cases support)** under section 4 IAA 1999 which is available to failed asylum seekers who meet certain criteria (see p395).

2. **Who is entitled to NASS support**

The general conditions of entitlement to full support (see p388) are:[6]
- you must be an asylum seeker or the dependant of an asylum seeker; *and*
- you must be destitute or likely to become destitute; *and*
- if you claimed asylum after 8 January 2003, you must have made your claim for asylum as soon as reasonably practicable.[7]

For temporary support the criteria are similar but you must be destitute, not simply likely to become destitute (see p403).

Who is an asylum seeker for support purposes

For the purposes of NASS you are an asylum seeker if you:[8]
- are 18 years or older; *and*
- have made a claim for asylum:
  - at a designated place;[9] *and*
  - the claim has been recorded by the Secretary of State; *and*
  - the claim has not been determined.

The claim may be made either under the 1951 Convention (Refugee or Geneva Convention) or for protection under Article 3 of the European Convention on Human Rights. If you have made a different type of claim, such as an Article 8 claim or a claim for indefinite leave to remain you will not be able to claim NASS support. For further details on asylum claims, see Chapter 5.

You continue to be an asylum seeker until 28 days after your claim is granted or you are granted leave to remain or your appeal is allowed. Alternatively, you continue to be an asylum seekers until 21 days after your appeal is finally dismissed (as below) or, in the absence of an appeal, 21 days after refusal by the Home Office.[10]

A claim remains undetermined if it is under appeal before an adjudicator, the Asylum and Immigration Tribunal (AIT), Court of Appeal or House of Lords or the time for further appeal has not lapsed. A claim also remains during review (of a refusal of an application for reconsideration to the AIT) in the Administrative Court but not during judicial review proceedings.

In practice, whether a claim has been recorded is more of an issue for a fresh claim. First claims are generally recorded at screening. A fresh claim is not 'recorded' until it has been accepted that representations constitute a fresh claim by the Secretary of State for the Home Department (SSHD) (see p395).

Asylum seeking families who have a minor child as a dependant remain asylum seekers for support purposes until they are removed from the UK. Families should be aware that, despite this, section 9 of the Asylum and Immigration (Treatment of Claimants) Act 2004 allows NASS to withdraw support from failed asylum seeker families who in the opinion on the SSHD have not taken steps to leave the UK voluntarily. This means that families are expected to demonstrate that they are taking steps to arrange their departure from the UK so they can return home. The new provisions in section 9 were piloted across the UK in 2005 and the power to withdraw support from families has not been used since. At the time of writing, families with children under the age of 18 continue to receive section 95 support until they leave the UK or the child reaches the age of 18. Families should be aware however that there is power to withdraw support from failed asylum seeker families who do not take steps to leave the UK. If NASS decides to withdraw your support because it says that you are not taking steps to leave the UK with your family, you have the right to appeal against this decision to an adjudicator (see Chapter 29).

Who is a dependant of an asylum seeker for support purposes

Support is provided for the asylum seeker and their dependants under section 95 of the Immigration and Asylum Act 1999 (IAA 1999) so long as they are destitute. Dependants have been defined in regulations as:

- the spouse of the asylum seeker;
- minor dependant children of the asylum seeker and their spouse;
- minor children of close family who have lived in the claimant's household for six months out of the last 12 months or since birth;
- an adult child of an asylum seeker or their spouse;
- a close family member (who has lived with the family for six months out of the last 12 months or since birth) who is disabled and in need of care and attention from a member of the household;
- a partner living with the applicant as an unmarried couple for at least two of the three years before the claim;
- a member of the household previously receiving Children Act support;
- someone who lodges a claim with the Home Office to remain on the basis of being a dependant of the asylum seeker;
- children who reach the age of 18 having been treated as dependants remain dependants.

The definition of destitute

Under section 95(3) IAA 1999 someone is destitute if:
'. . .he does not have and cannot obtain both:

(a) adequate accommodation, and

(b) food and other essential items.'

The Nationality Immigration and Asylum Act 2002 (NIAA 2002) has altered this part of the 1999 Act so that people are only regarded as 'destitute' if they had neither 'adequate accommodation, and food and other essential items', but, at the time of writing, it has yet to come into force. When this happens the support only option under NASS will disappear and it will only be possible to have a package of accommodation and support. For the purposes of this part of the Act a person is destitute if there is a likelihood of destitution within 14 days.[11] If the person already receives NASS support, s/he is regarded as destitute if there is a likelihood of destitution within 56 days.

In general terms, all assets are converted into income and reduce until they are 'used up'.

Claiming as soon as reasonably practicable

NASS support can be refused if an asylum seeker fails to claim asylum 'as soon as reasonably practicable'.[12] The rule currently only applies to asylum seekers without dependant children. However, the 2004 Act[13] allows for the restriction of support for failed asylum seekers with children.

There is no statutory definition of the term 'as soon as reasonably practicable' and this has led to substantial numbers of in-country asylum seekers being refused NASS. However, there is a presumption that any claim made within three days of arrival has been made as soon as reasonably practicable.[14]

NASS support should not be withheld if a refusal of support would be in breach of your human rights. There have been many legal challenges on this issue, the result of which is that NASS support should only be withheld from applicants who have an alternative source of support.

3. **Exclusions from NASS support**

Even if you meet the definition of a person eligible for support you can be excluded from getting NASS support if you are:[15]

- not excluded from getting social security benefits by your immigration status (see p399);
- not being treated as an asylum seeker or the dependant of an asylum seeker for immigration purposes (see p392);
- applying as part of a group where every person is excluded under any of the above rules or on the basis that they are able to get interim support.

Not treated as the dependants of asylum seekers for immigration purposes[16]

If you make an application for NASS support for yourself alone as the dependant of an asylum seeker, you will not be able to get NASS support if the Home Office is not treating you as dependent on the asylum seeker for immigration purposes.[17] There is a large gap between those who are treated as dependants of asylum seekers for NASS support purposes[18] and those who the Home Office generally treats as dependant on an asylum claim. The spouse and minor children of an asylum seeker who accompany her/him to the UK are considered by the Home Office as dependents of the asylum claim.[19] In practice, if a spouse or a minor child mentioned in the asylum application requires leave to enter or remain and has not got that leave, the Home Office assumes that they are applying for leave to enter or remain in the UK as dependants of the asylum seeker although confirmation will be sought from the asylum seeker.[20] A dependent child who reaches 18 before a decision is made on the application continues to be treated as a dependant pending the decision and during any appeal.[21] The Home Office also has a discretion to treat as dependants other relatives and those who do not arrive at the same time as the principal applicant, provided there has not yet been a decision on the asylum application.[22]

If, however, you apply for support in respect of more than one person, none of the members of the group are excluded from support under this rule unless every person in the group is not either an asylum seeker or is being considered by the Home Office as the dependant on a claim to asylum.[23]

You can also get from support under this rule, whether you are making an application for support for yourself only or as part of a group application, if you are a 'dependant' of a person who is already being supported by NASS.[24] 'Dependant' for these purposes has the same meaning as in relation to an asylum seeker for NASS purposes.[25]

There are also exclusions that apply to social service provision under section 21 and local authority interim support as well as NASS. These exclusions do not apply if the provision of support is necessary to avoid a breach your human rights or community rights and they do not apply to children.[26] Under these provisions the following groups (or classes) are excluded:

- people with refugee status granted by an EEA state or their dependants;[27]
- EEA nationals and their dependants;[28]
- failed asylum seekers and their dependants who fail to comply with removal directions;[29]
- people who are not asylum seekers and are in the UK unlawfully (ie, in breach of the immigration laws under section 11 NIAA 2002).[30] Local authorities have in the past refused to offer assistance to failed asylum seekers arguing that they fall into this category on account of being 'unlawfully in the UK'. According to current caselaw a failed asylum seeker is only unlawfully present in the UK if s/he did not claim asylum at the port of entry to the UK and is therefore not on

temporary admission.[31] Failed asylum seekers who did not claim at port of entry but who have made a fresh claim for asylum or have a human rights claim may be able to argue that a local authority should provide support to avoid a breach of their human rights in view of their outstanding application with the Home Office;

- failed asylum seekers with children in respect of whom the Secretary of State for the Home Department (SSHD) has certified that it is her/his opinion that they have failed without reasonable excuse to take reasonable steps to leave or place themselves in a position to do so – also called section 9 cases.[32]

Suspension or discontinuation of support

However, even if you fulfil all the conditions so that you fall into any of the categories listed above, NASS still has discretion to discontinue or suspend you from support.[33] This can apply if you:

- are a supported person and the SSHD has reason to believe that you or your dependant have committed a serious breach of the rules of the accommodation, if accommodated in collective accommodation.[34] Each accommodation provider is likely to have a set of 'house rules' which every person has to follow. This may be that you agree not to make any noise late at night or you agree to be respectful of other residents.
- are a supported person and the SSHD has reason to believe that you or your dependent have committed an act of seriously violent behaviour;[35]
- are a supported person or their dependant who has failed without reasonable excuse to comply with a relevant condition.[36] Again this could be a house rule or one of the other general conditions for support. If your support is withdrawn because NASS says you have breached a condition of support you can appeal to an adjudicator (see Chapter 29) and if you can show you had a reasonable excuse for breaching the condition then your support will be reinstated;
- are a supported person or their dependant who has committed an offence under Part VI of the Act.[37] This includes failing to report a change of circumstances to NASS and making a false claim to get support such as not telling NASS about a source of support you may have (known as concealing financial resources). As well as being a breach of conditions which could lead to you losing your support, an offence under Part VI of the Act is also a criminal offence and you may be prosecuted if you are found to have committed a Part VI offence;
- fail within five working days to provide information sought regarding your or your dependant's application for, or receipt of, support;[38]
- fail without reasonable excuse to attend an interview relating to your or your dependant's support;[39]
- fail within 10 working days to provide information sought regarding your or your dependant's asylum application;[40]

- are a supported person and the SSHD has reason to believe that you or your dependant has concealed financial resources and unduly benefited from asylum support;[41]
- or your dependant fail to comply with reporting requirements;[42]
- are a supported person and the SSHD has reason to believe that you or your dependant has made or attempted to make a second claim for asylum before the first claim is determined;[43]
- are a person for whom there are 'reasonable grounds' to suspect that you have abandoned the authorised address without first informing NASS or, if requested, without permission.[44] Whether you are receiving subsistence only support (meaning you have an address to live at but just need money) or whether NASS provide you accommodation, the address that you live at is your authorised address. You have to tell NASS if you need to leave this address and you are not allowed to leave the address for more than 14 days. If you do not tell NASS that you are leaving the accommodation and your support is stopped, you can appeal to an adjudicator (see Chapter 29) but you will have to show that you have an excuse for leaving your accommodation.

Discontinuation or suspension can only take effect where you are already being supported by NASS.[45] If you apply for support again once your support has been discontinued, NASS may refuse to consider the application if:[46]

- there has been no 'material change in circumstances' since the original decision to suspend or discontinue the support; this means a change of circumstances within the definition of those changes of circumstance which a claimant has to notify to NASS (see p408);[47] *and*
- there are no 'exceptional circumstances' which justify considering the application for support.

If NASS decides to consider the application for support in these circumstances it may still refuse support.[48]

For breach of conditions, separate rules make it clear that when deciding whether to continue to provide support NASS can 'take into account' the extent to which any conditions upon which support has been granted have been breached.[49] It is clear that previous breaches can be taken into account and that they are relevant to the decision as to whether to continue to provide support.

It is not automatic that support ends indefinitely as NASS may either discontinue or suspend the support. For example, NASS could decide to suspend the provision of support on the basis of 'reasonable grounds' of the conduct referred to until such time as it can confirm whether such conduct did in fact take place.

4. **Temporary NASS support**

NASS may provide support or arrange for temporary support to be provided to an asylum seeker or the dependant of an asylum seeker who it appears may be destitute (ie, not who it appears are destitute).[50] There is, however, no power to provide temporary support for a person who is likely to become destitute within a certain period of time.[51] As with full NASS support (see p389), temporary support may be provided subject to conditions but those conditions must be given in writing to the person or persons being provided with temporary support.[52]

Destitution is defined in the same way for the purposes of temporary NASS support as it is for ordinary NASS support (see p390).[53] Temporary support is designed as an emergency form of support to be provided when a person has made an application for support and can only be provided until NASS decides whether support is to be provided or not.[54] If NASS refuses support, temporary support ends at the same time.[55]

Exclusion from temporary support

You are excluded from getting temporary support under NASS if you are:[56]
- not excluded from getting social security benefits by your immigration status;
- not being treated as the dependant of an asylum seeker for immigration purposes;
- applying as part of a group where every person is excluded under any of the above rules.

5. **Section 4 support (hard cases support)**

Failed asylum seekers who have reached the end of the appeal process and exhausted any appeal rights are not entitled to support from NASS and are expected by the Home Office to return to their country of origin. If for some reason a failed asylum seeker is unable to leave the UK, s/he may be able to claim support under section 4 Immigration and Asylum Act 1999 provided s/he is destitute and meets one of five support criteria. To qualify you must:[57]
- have claimed asylum as soon as reasonably practicable, if you applied for asylum before 8 January 2003; *or*
- be able to show that a refusal of support would breach of your human rights; *and*
- be destitute[58] – this is the same test as for section 95 support. If you apply for section 4 support within 21 days of your section 95 support ending NASS will automatically consider you to be destitute. If you are a failed asylum seeker who has been destitute for some time, you will have to prove this to NASS

when you apply for support. In these circumstances you need to provide evidence such as letters from friends, family and charities explaining whether they give you any support and if that can continue and if not why not.

And:

- be taking all reasonable steps to leave the UK, including where relevant applying for a travel document.[59] Signing up for voluntary return is regarded as sufficient to satisfy this criteria. However, you may also be expected to visit your embassy or carry out other tasks in order to keep receiving support or it may eventually be withdrawn; *or*

- be unable to leave the UK by reason of physical impediment.[60] This means you are unable to make a single journey from the UK to your country of origin. It does not mean you can get support because there is no medical treatment available in your country or because it would be preferable for you to remain in the UK to continue a course of treatment. In order to get support under this criterion you must provide medical evidence from a medical professional (GP, consultant, psychiatrist, etc) explaining your medical problems, whether they prevent you from travelling and for how long. It is very important that the medical evidence discusses your ability to undertake a journey rather than whether you should be allowed to stay in the UK because of your medical problems; *or*

- be unable to leave the UK because in the opinion of the SSHD there is no viable route of return.[61] To qualify under this criterion, the SSHD has to have made a declaration that in her/his opinion there is no viable route to a particular country. At the moment there is no country to which the SSHD believes there is no viable route of return. Until recently, the SSHD said there was no viable route to Iraq but this has now changed. Because the law says that the SSHD has to formally announce there is no viable route to a country in general, you are not able to argue that there is no safe route for you in particular.[62] (There is, however, a current potential alternative section 4 support entitlement for failed Iraqi asylum seekers from outside the Kurdish Regional Governorate[63]); *or*

- have challenged a decision refusing your claim for asylum by judicial review and been granted permission[64] to proceed; *or*

- the provision of accommodation is necessary to avoid a breach of human rights.[65] For example:[66]
  - where you have made an out of time appeal (and therefore ceases to qualify for section 95 support); *or*
  - where you have made a fresh claim for asylum or an Article 3 claim that has not yet been recorded by the SSHD. This means that representations or a fresh claim or new evidence has been posted to the Home Office but they have not decided whether they are going to accept a new claim for asylum

or reject the representations on the basis that they do not constitute a fresh claim. NASS caseworkers can only refuse support under this criterion if:
- the fresh claim or representations contain no detail whatsoever – eg, if you write to the Home Office stating that you are still fearful of return but do not give any further information or explaining you have new information that you will send later;
- the evidence that you have sent as part of your fresh claim has already been seen and rejected by SSHD or the courts during your asylum claim and any appeals you may have made.

Once the SSHD looks at any further representations or fresh claim you have made, s/he will write to inform you whether s/he is accepting a new application from you. If s/he decides to accept your fresh claim this means s/he has recorded it and will consider it. At this point you become an asylum seeker again and should re-apply for full asylum support under section 95. If the SSHD rejects that your representations constitute a fresh claim, your section 4 support will ultimately be withdrawn unless you can prove that you meet one of the other criteria for support.

---

6. **Other forms of support**

National assistance/community care

Asylum seekers and other non-EEA nationals who have support needs arising other than as a result of destitution or the physical effects of destitution may still qualify for assistance from local authorities under the National Assistance Act 1948 (NAA 1948) or under community care provision.[67] However, they are not eligible for support if they fall into any of the excluded groups or classes set out above, unless it can be established that the denial of support would breach their human rights or Community rights. In-country failed asylum seekers are currently regarded as being unlawfully in the UK but failed asylum seekers on temporary admission (port applicants) are not.[68]

Local authorities have a responsibility to support destitute asylum seekers and non-excluded non-EEA nationals under section 21 NAA 1948 if they are not only destitute but also have a need of 'care and attention' not otherwise available to them due to:
- age;
- pregnancy
- illness (physical and mental);
- disability.

'Care and attention' has been given a wide interpretation by caselaw and can include moderate as well as severe physical or mental disability. However the need for 'care and attention' must arise not simply from the effects (or anticipated effects) of destitution but also for some other reason, so that if made destitute the applicant is likely to suffer more acutely than an 'able-bodied' applicant. For this reason, the test has been summarised as 'destitution plus'.

Examples of 'destitution plus' include those with HIV who require NHS treatment and although able to care for themselves are more susceptible to the adverse affects of destitution;[69] a man with a severe disability to one leg who required assistance with domestic chores and mobility;[70] and a woman considered to be vulnerable as a consequence of severe domestic violence.[71]

If you are eligible for support under NAA 1948, then it is the duty of social services to support you and not NASS. In a household where one or more adults are eligible for support but where there are children without community care needs, accommodation for the family should be provided by the local authority along with support for the eligible adults. Support for the children is provided by NASS by arrangement with social services.[72]

If you are also an 'excluded' person then you need to be able to rely on a human rights or an asylum claim that, as a minimum, is not manifestly unfounded.[73]

This is a complex area of law. For example it is not straightforward to assess whether the denial of support for an excluded person may amount to a breach of her/his human rights that could be averted by her/his departure from the UK.[74] It may be possible to argue that where you have made a fresh claim for asylum, it is not reasonable to expect you to leave the UK and therefore failing to provide you with support would breach your human rights. It may also be possible to argue entitlement to support (possibly limited support), or at least a power to support, if you fall within one of the excluded groups even where it cannot be shown that the denial of support would your breach human rights.[75] In these circumstances, seek expert advice from a community care advisor.

Support under the Children Act 1989

Generally asylum seekers are excluded from help under the Children Act 1989 (CA 1989) if they are eligible for NASS support.[76] Asylum seekers with children who have been excluded from NASS support, perhaps because they have breached conditions, may be able to get help from social services under the CA 1989. Social services only have a duty to provide support to a child but are able to provide support to the parent(s) of that child if failing to do so would result in a breach of that person's human rights.

Unaccompanied minor asylum seekers are the responsibility of the local authority. They should be placed with foster carers or have other suitable accommodation arrangements made for them. Teenagers are often given little help other than support under section 17 of the Act.

A young person who is aged 16 or 17 who has been looked after for 13 weeks or more under the CA 1989 is entitled to protection under the Children (Leaving

Care) Act 2000. This allows for a needs assessment and potential support up to the age of 21 or 24 if still in education.

Entitlement to social security and tax credits

Most asylum seekers are now excluded from social security benefits and tax credits but it is still worth checking to see if you might fall within one of the groups who remain entitled (see Part 2).

Notes

1. Introduction to NASS
1 The system of support to be provided by NASS is provided for by Part VI and Schs 8 and 10 IAA 1999. The key provisions were brought into force from 3 April 2000 (see reg 2 and Sch to IAA 1999 (Commencement No. 3) Order 2000) on which date the regulations which set out the detailed machinery of the scheme also came into force: reg 1 AS Regs; r1 ASA(P) Rules.
2 IAA 1999
3 Sch 3 para 1 NIAA 2002
4 s115(9) IAA 1999
5 *Westminster v NASS* [2002] UKHL 38
6 ss94(1), s95(1) and Sch 9 paras 1-3 IAA 1999; r2(1), 3 ASA(P) Rules; reg 3 AS Regs
7 s55 NIAA 2002
8 ss94(1), 95(1) and Sch 9 para 1(1)(2) IAA1999; r2(1) ASA(P) Rules; reg 3(1) AS Regs
9 This part of the definition is not yet in force and is likely to become *otiose* when s12 IANA 2006 comes into force.
10 s94(3) IAA 1999; regs 2 and 2A AS Regs
11 Reg 7 AS Regs
12 s55 NIAA 2002
13 s9 AI (TC)A 2004
14 NASS *Policy Bulletin 75* para 3.5

3. Exclusions from NASS support
15 s95(2) IAA 1999; reg 4 AS Regs
16 The wording relates to people have not made a 'claim for leave to enter or remain in the United Kingdom or for variation of any such leave' in which they are being considered an asylum seeker or the dependant on such. A claim to asylum or to be the dependant of an asylum seeker, provided accepted as such, in immigration terms is simultaneously a claim for leave in such capacity (see paras 327-8, 330, 335, 349 HC 395 and see 31-33 HC 395 absolving asylum seekers from the requirement to apply for leave on a prescribed Home Office form).
17 Reg 4(2)(4)(c) AS Regs; this provision also excludes persons who the Home Office is not treating as asylum seekers for immigration purposes but it is doubtful that this adds anything to the general requirement for those applying as asylum seekers that a person has made a 'claim to asylum' which has been 'recorded by the Secretary of State' as having been made (see s94(1) IAA1999). However, the exclusion does operate to prevent support being provided to the potentially large group of persons who fall within the definition of dependant for support purposes (reg 2(4) AS Regs) but are not being treated by the Home Office as dependant on the asylum claim for immigration purposes.
18 Reg 2(4) AS Regs
19 para 349 HC 395

20 ADI on dependants (this is currently being revised)
21 ADI on dependants (this is currently being revised)
22 ADI on dependants (this is currently being revised)
23 Reg 4(3), (4)(c) and (5) AS Regs
24 Reg 5 AS Regs
25 The reference here is in fact to a 'dependant of a person who is ... a supported person'; by reg 2(4) AS Regs, such a dependant is given precisely the same definition as the dependant of an asylum seeker for NASS purposes.
26 Sch 3 paras 2 and 3 NIAA 2002
27 Sch 3 para 4 NIAA 2002
28 Sch 3 para 5 NIAA 2002
29 Sch 3 para 6 NIAA 2002
30 Sch 3 para 7 NIAA 2002
31 *R(AW) v Croydon London Borough Council* [2005] EWHC 2950 currently in the Court of Appeal.
32 Sch 3 para 7A NIAA 2002 as amended by s 9 AI(ToC)A 2004
33 Reg 20(1) AS Regs provides that support 'may' be suspended or discontinued.
34 Reg 20(1)(a) AS Regs
35 Reg 20(1)(b) AS Regs
36 Reg 20 (1)(k) AS Regs
37 Reg 20(1)(c) AS Regs
38 Reg 20(1)(e) AS Regs
39 Reg 20(1)(f) AS Regs
40 Reg 20(1)(g) AS Regs
41 Reg 20(1)(h) AS Regs
42 Reg 20(1)(i) AS Regs
43 Reg 20(1)(j) AS Regs
44 Reg 20(1)(d) AS Regs
45 See the wording of reg 20(1) AS Regs which refers to support for a 'supported person' or their dependants; such a person is defined as an asylum seeker or the dependant of an asylum seeker who has applied for support and for who NASS support has been provided (s94(1) IAA 1999) and indeed the regulation refers to the 'suspension' or 'discontinuation' of the existing support which presupposes the current provision of that support.
46 Reg 21(1) AS Regs; NASS *Policy Bulletin 84*
47 Reg 21(1)(c)(2) AS Regs with reference to reg 15 AS Regs
48 Reg 21(3) AS Regs
49 Reg 19 AS Regs

4. **Temporary NASS support**
50 s98(1) IAA 1999; NASS *Policy Bulletin 73*
51 As compared to the position relating to ordinary NASS support or interim support (see s95(1) IAA 1999).
52 s98(3) IAA 1999 applying s95(11)
53 s98(3) IAA 1999 applying s95(3)(5)(6) – ie, the general test as to destitution (lack of adequate accommodation or inability to meet essential living needs) and the matters which cannot be taken into account in determining whether accommodation is adequate; the more detailed rules which are set out in AS Regs, by their wording, appear only to apply to substantive decisions under the NASS scheme
54 s98(2) IAA Act or not longer than seven days after the decision in exceptional circumstances: see NASS *Policy Bulletin 73*
55 para 319 Explanatory Notes
56 Reg 4(8)(9) AS Regs

5. **Section 4 support**
57 The Immigration and Asylum (Provision of Accommodation to Failed Asylum-Seekers) Regulations 2005 (No. 930); NASS *Policy Bulletin 71*
58 Reg 3(1)(a) IA(POAFAS) Regs
59 Regs 3(1)(b) and 2(a) IA(POAFAS) Regs; ASA 06/03/12859
60 Regs 3(1)(b) and 2(b) IA(POAFAS) Regs; *R(SSHD) v ASA and Osman, Yillah, Ahmad and Musemwa (interested parties)* [2006] EWHC 1248
61 Reg 3(1)(b) and 2(c) IA(POAFAS) Regs
62 *R(Rasul) v ASA* [2006] EWHC 435; ASA 06/03/12859
63 See *R(A Mohammed) v ASA and SSHD* CO/4845/2006; LAG January 2007 p16. There is some support for the view that Reg 3(1)(a) is made out when the failed asylum seeker obtains advice from IOM that there is no assurance of a safe route and then decides not to apply for voluntary return. NASS is agreeing to support some Iraqis from outside the KRG but appear to be doing so under reg 3(2)(e).
64 Regs 3(1)(b) and 2(d) IA(POAFAS) Regs
65 Regs 3(1)(b) and 2(e) IA(POAFAS) Regs
66 NASS *Policy Bulletin 71*

6. Other forms of support

67 NASS *Policy Bulletin 82*

68 *R(AW) v Croydon London Borough Council*
[2005]EWHC 2950 currently in the
Court of Appeal.

69 *R(N) v Lambeth LBC* [2006] EWHC 3427;
R(M) v Slough BC [2006] EWCA 655 –
this case will be heard in the Lords in late
2007.

70 *R(Mani and others) v Lambeth and others*
[2002] EWHC 735

71 *R(Khan) v Oxfordshire CC* (2003) 5 CCLR
611 and [2004] EWCA 309

72 *R(Westminster) CC v NASS* [2002] UKHL
38; *R(O) v Haringey LBC* [2004] EWCA
538

73 *R(AW) v Croydon London Borough Council*
[2005]EWHC 2950 (currently in the
Court of Appeal); *Gordon Binomugisha v
Southwark* LBC [2006] EWCH 2254

74 See *PB(Claimant) v Haringey* LBC [2006]
EWHC 2255, *Gordon Binomugisha v
Southwark LBC* [2006] EWCH 2254 and
M v Islington LBC [2004] EWCA 235. In
these cases it was accepted that support
may need to be provided by the local
authority to avoid a breach of the
applicants human rights. See also *R(K) v
Lambeth LBC* [2003] EWCA 1150 and
Lambeth LBC v Grant – in both the latter
cases it was not accepted that the denial
of support (beyond temporary short
term support in the *Grant* case) would
breach the applicants human rights.

75 Withholding and withdrawal of support
(Travel Assistance and Temporary
Accommodation) Regulations 2002

76 See NASS *Policy Bulletins 29* (on when
minors become adults) and *33* (on age
disputed cases)

Chapter 27

Claims and awards

This chapter covers:
1. Procedure for claiming NASS support (below)
2 Deciding if destitute under the NASS scheme (p403)

---

1. Procedure for claiming NASS support

Applications for support

If you are either an asylum seeker, or the dependant of an asylum seeker, for support purposes, you are able to make an application for NASS support to NASS.[1] The application may be for you or for yourself and your dependants.[2] Similar to applying for social security benefits, you must apply for NASS support using a particular form. You must either use form **NASS1**, which is attached to the Asylum Support Regulations 2000 or a form which is very similar to that form if you do not have an exact copy.[3]

If the application is for yourself and your dependants, you only need to make one application. If you wish to obtain support as the dependant of a person who is already being supported by NASS, it is not necessary to complete the application form again; NASS will consider providing additional support for you if notified of your existence.[4]

If you do not use the form, or one very similar to it, or you do not complete the form in English and in full, NASS may not consider your application.[5] There are detailed notes attached to the Asylum Support Regulations[6] which give further information about procedures and guidance about how to fill out the form. The form asks you for details of yourself and your dependants. If you are applying as the dependant of an asylum seeker, the form asks you for details of the asylum seeker of whom you are a dependant and any of her/his dependants (for who qualifies as a dependant, see p390). The form also asks for details of the stage which your asylum claim has reached, the kind of support you need, your current accommodation, any other kind of support you get including support from friends or relatives, cash, savings, investments or other property which you have, employment, state benefits you receive and also about any disabilities or special needs which you have. The details of any assistance from the voluntary organisations, solicitor or other representative who helped you to fill in the form should also be given on the form. In relation to many of the details requested, NASS requires you to send in documents to confirm what you have stated. Four passport size photographs are also required. To save time and for your application to be considered as soon as possible, the form can be faxed to NASS, otherwise it can be sent by post. If you send the form in by fax, you should also send the original by post.[7]

If you are currently detained by the immigration authorities but you are about to be released or if you have made a bail application and you are waiting for it to be heard, you may still make an application for support in the expectation of your release.[8]

NASS may make further enquiries of you in connection with any of the details contained in the application form.[9]

2. Deciding if destitute under the NASS scheme

If you apply for support for yourself and any dependants, NASS will decide whether the group taken as a whole is destitute or likely to become destitute.[10] The same approach applies when NASS is considering whether to continue to provide support for a person who is already being supported and their dependants who are also already being supported or who are being added to the application for support.[11] To determine whether you, as an applicant for support, and any dependants are 'destitute' or 'likely to become destitute', NASS must consider whether you have 'adequate accommodation' or any means of getting adequate accommodation and whether you cannot meet your other 'essential living needs'.[12]

NASS must follow special rules which set out what is and what is not relevant in deciding these questions. These rules apply both when you make an application for support and to the question of whether, at any stage, NASS should continue to provide you with support.[13] In considering whether you are destitute both in terms of whether you have adequate accommodation and whether you can meet your essential living needs, NASS must take into account any of the following which are available either to you or to any of your dependants:[14]

- any income you have or which you may reasonably be expected to have;
- any other support which is available or which may reasonably be expected to be available to you;
- any of the following assets which are available to you or which might reasonably be expected to be available to you: cash, savings, investments, land, vehicles or goods for trade or business.

This might include support from friends and relatives in the United Kingdom (UK) or from voluntary sector organisations.[15] Land may include property such as a house and other outbuildings. Investments include business investments, income bonds, life assurance policies, pension schemes, stocks and shares and unit trusts. NASS may provide you with support on a limited basis in order for you to have time to sell items of property, six months if it is a house. NASS treats the money which is received from the sale as cash or savings and takes it into account when deciding whether to provide support. If you do not consider it reasonable that you should have to sell your property, you should give your reasons for this at the time that you send in your application form.[16]

Also in deciding whether you have adequate accommodation and whether you can meet your essential living needs, NASS must ignore:

- any assets which you or your dependants have which are not referred to immediately above;[17]
- NASS support or temporary support which you or your dependants presently have or may be provided with.[18]

It has been confirmed that NASS will ignore items of jewellery, personal clothing, bedding and medical or optical items (eg, wheelchairs).[19] However, NASS asks you to disclose, in your application for support, any items of jewellery or watches belonging to you or your dependants which are worth over £1,000 at the current market value, and to inform NASS immediately if any of those items are subsequently sold and how much they were sold for.[20] The intention is that NASS may then take into account the money you have received as a result of the sale.

The further rules as to what is to be taken into account in determining destitution deal separately with the questions of accommodation and essential living needs.

Meeting essential living needs

For the purposes of deciding whether you can meet your essential living needs, certain items are not treated as essential living needs. Your inability to provide for yourself any of the following items is not relevant for the purpose of deciding whether you are destitute:[21]

- the costs of sending or receiving faxes, photocopying or buying or using computer facilities;
- travelling expenses.

However, although the above expenses cannot be taken into account at this stage, if you are found to be destitute, they may be met by NASS either under the category of expenses incurred in connection with your asylum claim or if your case is exceptional (see p405).

The rules therefore appear to exclude any travelling requirements which you may have. However, the regulations expressly exempt from this exclusion the costs of your initial journey from any place in the UK where you happen to be to accommodation which is being provided for you by NASS or your journey to accommodation not being provided by NASS but to an address where you are intending to live where you have notified the Home Office or NASS of your intention to live there.[22] This is normally accommodation at which it is a condition of your temporary admission to the UK that you reside (see p40). Although the rules do not expressly state that these journeys are to be taken into account in considering destitution, the fact that they are exempt from being excluded indicates that NASS should both take them into account and, if it finds that you do not have the means to pay for this travel, provide support in order that you can travel to your accommodation. The fact that any other need that you have is not referred to by these rules, does not automatically convert that need into being an 'essential living need' so that your inability to meet it must be taken into account by NASS in deciding whether you are destitute.[23] In relation to any other need, NASS must decide for itself whether that need is indeed essential for your living. In determining this question, the individual circumstances of any particular applicant for support are important.

Clothing

In deciding whether you can meet your essential living needs as regards your clothing, NASS cannot take into account your personal preferences.[24] This rule is designed to prevent complaints based on your inability to provide for yourself particular clothing which is more expensive than that which is reasonably required – eg, particularly fashionable clothes or designer wear. However, NASS is not prevented from taking into account your individual circumstances when it comes to deciding whether you can meet your clothing requirements.[25] We suggest that the following factors are all relevant to deciding whether you can meet this essential living need: whether you can afford to provide for yourself clothes suitable for the different weather conditions in the UK; whether you have enough changes of clothes required for cleanliness; and whether you have clothes which are suitable to any particular health or other individual needs that you have.

Adequate accommodation

If you are applying for support but you have some form of accommodation, NASS must decide whether your existing accommodation is 'adequate'. Similarly, if you are already being supported by NASS but your accommodation is not being provided by NASS, NASS may consider whether the accommodation is adequate or whether it should be providing accommodation in addition for you. In deciding either[26] of those questions, NASS must have regard to whether:[27]
- it is 'reasonable' for you to continue to occupy the accommodation;
- you can afford to pay for the accommodation;
- the accommodation is provided as temporary support under NASS or any other emergency basis while the claim for asylum support is being determined;
- you can gain entry to the accommodation;

- if the accommodation is a house-boat, a caravan or some other moveable structure which may be lived in, whether there is somewhere where you are able to place it and have permission to live in it;
- you may live in the accommodation together with your dependants;
- you or your dependants are likely to suffer harassment, threats or violence if you continue to live in the accommodation.

Accommodation may also be considered inadequate if it is unsuitable for you on account of your health needs – eg, if you have a physical disability and you are staying at a friend's house and sleeping on the floor you may be destitute if NASS accepts the accommodation is inadequate on account of you sleeping on the floor.

There may be circumstances in which, notwithstanding the above matters, you still want to stay in your existing accommodation. If you indicate to NASS that you want to stay in the accommodation then, in deciding whether the accommodation is adequate, NASS may leave out of account all of the above matters except the questions of whether you can afford the accommodation and whether the accommodation is temporary NASS or other emergency accommodation.[28]

Reasonable to continue to occupy

Regard must be had to whether it is 'reasonable' for you to continue to occupy the accommodation.[29] In deciding whether it is reasonable for you to continue to occupy accommodation, NASS may have regard to the general housing circumstances which exist in the district[30] of the local government housing authority in which the accommodation is situated.[31]

So if your accommodation is worse or more overcrowded than the other accommodation generally found in the area in which you live, it may not be reasonable for you to continue to live there.[32]

Afford to pay for the accommodation

NASS must consider whether you can afford to pay for your existing accommodation,[33] taking into account:[34]

- any income or assets (see p403), aside from NASS support or temporary support, available to you or any of your dependants or which might be expected to be available to you or your dependants;
- the costs of living in the accommodation;
- your other reasonable living expenses.

Access to the accommodation

Your accommodation is not adequate if you have been illegally evicted from the accommodation or squatters have unlawfully moved into the accommodation.

Harassment, threats or violence

NASS must consider whether it is 'probable' that your continued occupation of your accommodation will lead to domestic violence against you or any of your dependants.[35] In order to count for these purposes, the domestic violence must be:[36]

- from a person who is or has been a 'close family member'; *and*
- in the form of either actual violence or threats of violence which are likely to be carried out. There is no definition of close family member, but depending on the circumstances, it may cover married or unmarried partners and ex-partners, those to whom you have a blood relationship, in-laws, relatives of your partner and others who have lived or live in your household. It should be noted that there is no requirement that the family member actually lives with you,[37] it may be that it is the fact that your address is known to the person from whom you fear domestic violence which means that your continued occupation of that accommodation is likely to lead to domestic violence.

Although the asylum support rules do not expressly say so, it is clear that other forms of violence or threats from persons not normally associated with you which you have suffered must be taken into account in deciding whether your current accommodation is adequate.[38] This treatment may be in the form of racial harassment or attacks,[39] sexual abuse or harassment, harassment because of your religion or for other reasons.

Decisions and support pending a decision

There regulations do not require NASS to make a decision within any particular time. The Government intends that NASS makes a decision within two working days of receiving the application, although this cannot be guaranteed in all cases. If no decision has been made within seven days of making the application, NASS should write to you to explain why there is a delay in making a decision.[40]

There is a requirement to respond within five working days to any enquiry made by NASS regarding the application. NASS will not consider the application if you fail to complete the application properly or accurately or to provide evidence requested without reasonable excuse within this period.[41] While you are waiting for NASS to make a decision on your application, you should be provided with temporary support which will be provided to you directly by a voluntary agency but paid for by NASS.

If NASS decides to provide you with support, it will inform you in writing that the application has been accepted and about the package of support which will be provided. Although there are no rules requiring NASS to give reasons for its decisions, the Government intends that NASS will give you a written explanation if you are refused all support and will give you details about how you can appeal (see p423).[42]

Conditions

NASS may provide support subject to conditions.[43] The conditions might, for example, be that accommodation is not sublet or that noise is kept down to a reasonable level in the interests of neighbours. Conditions must be set out in writing[44] and given to the person who is being supported.[45] Other conditions include the requirement to reside at the address that NASS has provided and ensuring you inform NASS of any changes in your circumstances.

If you breach the conditions, NASS may take that into account in deciding whether to provide support, whether to continue to provide support and the level or kind of support which is to be provided.[46]

Dispersal

Support is provided in accommodation outside London. This is called 'dispersal'. This now applies to section 4 support as well. Most people who apply for support will be provided with accommodation outside London unless they can show a good reason for staying in London. People receiving treatment from the Medical Foundation for the Victims of Torture are usually accommodated in London. There are special provisions for those that are in the late stages of pregnancy or are receiving other medical treatment (eg, those with HIV).[47]

Health benefits

If your application for asylum support is accepted, NASS will also issue you with a certificate (HC2) enabling you to get free National Health Service prescriptions, dental treatment, sight tests and wigs.[48] You may also be able to get vouchers towards the cost of glasses and contact lenses and money back on the costs of travel to and from hospital for NHS treatment. The HC2 certificate itself tells you how to use it and what you can use it for. If you have already paid for any of the above items or travel, you may be able to claim the money back.

Changes of circumstances

If you are provided with support, you are required to notify NASS of certain relevant changes in your circumstances.[49] The changes which must be notified to NASS are where you or any or your dependants:[50]
- are joined in the UK by a dependant of yours;
- receive or get access to any money or savings, investments, land, cars or other vehicles, goods for the purposes of trade or other business which has not previously been declared to NASS;
- become employed;
- become unemployed;

- change your name;
- get married;
- begin living with another person as if you are married to them;
- get divorced;
- separate from a spouse or from a person with whom you have been living as if married to that person;
- become pregnant;
- have a child;
- leave school;
- begin to share your accommodation with another person;
- move to a different address or otherwise leave your accommodation;
- go into hospital;
- go to prison or some other form of custody;
- leave the UK;
- die.

Where there is a relevant change of circumstances a decision may be made changing the nature or level of the existing support or providing or withdrawing support for different individuals.

Eviction from accommodation

The usual security of tenure does not apply to NASS accommodation. The legislation makes provision for tenancies or licences created when NASS support is provided to come to an end before they otherwise would when the time comes for support to be terminated. These rules apply in any of the following circumstances where support is to be ended:[51]

- asylum support is suspended or discontinued (see p393) on the basis of breach of conditions, criminal offences, intentional destitution, absence from address without permission or ceasing to reside at address;
- the claim for asylum has been determined;
- the asylum seeker is no longer destitute;
- the asylum seeker moves to be supported in other accommodation.

In any of the above circumstances, any tenancy or licence which you have obtained during the period of support can be brought to an end at the end of the period specified in a 'notice to quit' which is given to you.[52]

Further applications for support and appeals

If you are refused support, then in most cases, there is nothing to prevent you from making a further application for support at any time and your application must be considered. For the criteria to make a new application after support has been discontinued or suspended and for the circumstances in which you may appeal against a negative decision by NASS and the procedures for appealing see Chapter 29.

Notes

1. Procedure for claiming NASS support
1 Reg 3(1) AS Regs
2 Reg 3(2) AS Regs
3 Reg 3(3) AS Regs
4 Reg 3(6) AS Regs
5 Reg 3(3)(4) AS Regs
6 Contained in Sch AS Regs with the application form and statement of confidentiality.
7 Explanatory notes in Sch AS Regs
8 Notes to NASS1 Form in Sch AS Regs 'Do you live in any other kind of accommodation?'
9 Reg 3(5) AS Regs

2. Deciding if destitute under the NASS scheme
10 s95(4) IAA 1999; reg 5(1) AS Regs
11 Reg 5(2) AS Regs
12 s95(1)(3) IAA 1999
13 Reg 6(1)(a)(b) AS Regs
14 Reg 6(4)(5) AS Regs
15 para 280 Explanatory Notes
16 Notes to Form NASS1 in Sch AS Regs 'Property'
17 Reg 6(6) AS Regs
18 Reg 6(3) AS Regs
19 Notes to NASS1 Form in Sch AS Regs 'Cash, savings and assets'
20 Notes to Form NASS1 'Jewellery'
21 s95(8) IAA 1999; reg 9(3)(4) AS Regs
22 Reg 9(5) AS Regs
23 Reg 9(6) AS Regs
24 s95(7)(b) IAA1999; reg 9(1)(2) AS Regs
25 Reg 9(2) AS Regs
26 That these rules apply to either situation is set out in reg 8(1)(a)(b) AS Regs.
27 s95(5)(a) IAA 1999 Act; reg 8(1)(a)-(b) and (3) AS Regs
28 Reg 8(2) AS Regs
29 Reg 8(3)(a) AS Regs

30 By reg 8(6)(b) AS Regs 'district' for these purposes is given the same meaning as in s217(3) Housing Act 1996.
31 Reg 8(4) AS Regs
32 Notes to NASS1 Form in Sch AS Regs 'General housing circumstances'
33 Reg 8(3)(b) AS Regs
34 Reg 8(5)(a)-(b) AS Regs
35 Reg 8(3)(g) AS Regs
36 Reg 8(6)(a) AS Regs; NASS *Policy Bulletin 70*
37 Although the Notes accompanying the NASS1 application form ask for information about persons who 'normally stay with you' (under 'Domestic Violence')
38 Notes to NASS1 Form in Sch AS Regs 'Violence or threats of violence'
39 See NASS *Policy Bulletin 81*
40 Notes contained in Sch AS Regs 'How long will an application take'
41 s57 NIAA 2002; reg 5A-5B AS Regs; see also NASS *Policy Bulletin 79*
42 See Notes in Sch AS Regs 'What happens next?'
43 s95(9) IAA 1999
44 s95(1) IAA 1999
45 s95(11) IAA 1999
46 Reg 19 and 20(1) AS Regs
47 See NASS *Policy Bulletin 85*
48 Notes in Sch to AS Regs
49 Reg 15(1) AS Regs
50 Reg 15(2) AS Regs
51 Reg 22(2) AS Regs
52 Reg 22(1) AS Regs

Chapter 28

Amount of NASS support

This chapter covers:
1. Support provided under NASS (below)
2. Contributions to and recovery of support (p416)

---

1. Support provided under NASS

NASS has the power to provide the following kinds of support to you as a supported asylum seeker:[1]

- the essential living needs of yourself and your dependants; *and/or*
- accommodation which is adequate for your and your dependants' needs;
- expenses, other than legal expenses, which you have in connection with your asylum claim;
- expenses that you or your dependants have in attending bail hearings where you or your dependants are detained for immigration purposes;
- services in the form of education, English language lessons, sporting or other developmental activities;[2]
- *if the circumstances of your particular case are exceptional*, any other form of support which NASS thinks necessary to enable you and your dependants to be supported.[3]

In providing for either your essential living needs or for your accommodation or other forms of support where the circumstances of your case are exceptional, NASS must provide the majority of your support otherwise than by cash payments.[4] However, this rule does not apply where the circumstances of your particular case are 'exceptional'.[5] NASS may however meet the entirety of any of the 'expenses' and 'services' referred to above by making cash payments to you and your dependants and such payments do not count for the purposes of calculating the manner in which the majority of the support is provided to meet the other needs.

In deciding the level and kind of support to make available to an applicant and their dependants or to anyone already being provided with support, NASS must take into account:[6]

- any income which you or any of your dependants have or might reasonably be expected to have;
- any support which might reasonably be expected to be available to you or any of your dependants;
- any assets (see p403) in the UK or elsewhere which are or may reasonably be expected to be available to you or any of your dependants.

Also, in deciding the level and kind of support to be provided NASS *may* take into account the question of whether you have complied with any conditions on which the support has been or is being provided (see p408).[7] For example, if you have vandalised any property provided as part your support, NASS may take account of that conduct in deciding what further support to provide.[8] The meaning of 'conditions' for these purposes is the same as for the purposes of excluding you from support entirely.[9] In deciding whether to alter the level of your support on this basis and, if so, by how much the level of support will be changed, NASS must take into account how serious or trivial the breach of your conditions was.[10]

NASS *may* generally disregard any preference which you or your dependants may have as to *how* to provide for or to arrange the provision of any of the abovementioned support.[11]

Providing essential living needs

Where NASS decides that you need support in relation to your essential living needs, the *general rule* is that you will be provided with cash on a weekly basis.[12] The total value of the support which you will be provided with is set out below.[13]

Amounts provided

The weekly amount of support is set out in the table below.[14] In cases where the application for yourself and your dependants includes a person in more than one of the categories listed below, the amounts must be added together to work out the total value of weekly support. So, for example, if a couple included within their application for support a 14-year-old dependant for support purposes, the total value of their support would be £108.65.

Person/s	Amount pw[15]
Couple	£63.07
Lone parent aged 18 or over:	£40.22
Single person aged 25 or over:	£40.22
Single person aged at least 18 but under 25:	£31.85
Person aged at least 16 but under 18	£34.60
Under 16	£45.58

In the table:
- to count as a married couple, you must be a man and a woman who are married to each other and who are members of the same household;[16]
- to count as an unmarried couple, you must be a man and a woman who, although not married, are living together as though you are married;[17]
- a 'lone parent' is a person who is not a part of a married or unmarried couple who is the parent of child who is under 18 *and* support is being provided for that child;[18]
- a 'single person' is a person who is not *either* a member of a married or unmarried couple *or* the parent of a child under 18 for whom support is being provided.[19]

Additionally, payments are made for:[20]
- pregnant women – additional payment of £3.00 a week;
- children between the ages of 1 and 3 – additional payment of £3.00 a week;
- babies under 1 – additional payment of £5.00 a week.

The amounts shown in the table are reduced in circumstances where NASS is providing you with accommodation as part of your support and included with the accommodation is some provision for your essential living needs[21]. For example, if you are being provided with bed and breakfast accommodation, the amount shown is reduced by an amount corresponding to the cost for your and your dependants' breakfasts.

The amounts shown in the table are 70 per cent of the 'applicable amounts' of income support (IS) which similarly situated adults would otherwise be entitled to if they qualified for IS and had no income.[22] The applicable amounts for IS are the total of a personal allowance, any premiums and an amount in respect of housing costs (see CPAG'S *Welfare Benefits and Tax Credits Handbook* for the calculation of applicable amounts). The amounts provided for support purposes are very deliberately less than these rates and reflect the fact that the legislation has given NASS the power to limit the level of provision for essential living needs, in any case, to a proportion of the applicable amount of IS.[23] In principle, NASS may also include in this restriction the amounts incurred in respect of expenses incurred in connection with the asylum claim (see p415) provided as part of the support package,[24] but the regulations show no intention to include them. These 'rule of thumb' levels of support are in recognition of the fact that the support is to be provided temporarily and account does not need to be taken of the cost of replacement items – eg, of furnishings or clothing.[25] NASS also assumes that the household bills are met directly by NASS. In contrast, the interim scheme contains no 'rule of thumb' figures and has no express powers of restriction to IS applicable amounts.

The above rules about provision for your essential living needs are, however, all *general* rules of thumb.[26] These rules set out what you can generally expect to receive. In appropriate cases, NASS may provide more or less or make provision in a different form to that set out in the general rules.

Maternity payment[27]

NASS also pays a one off sum of £300 on receipt of a written application between one month before the expected birth and two weeks afterwards together with the accompanying evidence: a birth certificate, form MAT B1 or other original formal evidence. This payment can also be made if a supported parent or a parent applying for support has a child under three months old who has arrived in the UK.

Providing accommodation ('dispersal')[28]

The ability of NASS to make arrangements with local authorities for the provision of support rather than providing support directly[29] is a crucial part of the dispersal scheme as it enables NASS to arrange for local authorities (in consortia in many cases with private contractors) up and down the country to provide support. In deciding upon the location and nature of the accommodation you will be given under the NASS scheme, NASS must have regard to:[30]

- the fact that you are only being provided with accommodation on a temporary basis until your claim for asylum has been dealt with including any period during which you are appealing;
- the fact that it is desirable to provide accommodation for asylum seekers in areas where there is a good supply of accommodation – eg, areas outside of London as it is the Government's view[31] that there is an acute shortage of accommodation in the London area. In making the same decision, however, NASS cannot have regard to your preferences on:
  - the area in which you wish the accommodation to be located;[32]
  - the nature of the accommodation which is to be provided;[33]
  - the nature and standard of the fixtures and fittings in the accommodation.[34]

However, in deciding upon the accommodation to be provided, NASS may still take into account your individual circumstances as they relate to your accommodation needs.[35] Your relevant individual circumstances include:[36]

- your ethnic group and/or religion as NASS should identify an area where there is an existing community of people of similar culture together with support organisations who are sensitive to your cultural background and needs;
- any special dietary needs of yourself and your dependants;
- your or your dependants' medical or psychological conditions or any disabilities which you have and any treatment you are receiving for those conditions as NASS should provide accommodation which is appropriate to

those needs.[37] (NASS has an agreement with the Medical Foundation not to disperse those being treated at the Foundation in London.)[38]

In addition, each local authority providing support may provide the accommodation outside its own area.[39] As it is NASS which is under an obligation to apply the above criteria in determining how and where support is to be provided, there is clearly a responsibility upon NASS to ensure that the above criteria is applied while keeping in mind the whereabouts in or outside the area of the local authority that you are going to be located.

Expenses in connection with asylum claim

NASS may meet your expenses which are connected with your asylum claim.[40] These expenses do not include 'legal' expenses so NASS would not, for example, meet costs of paying your lawyer to prepare your case and represent you. Included expenses are your travel expenses (or those of your witnesses) in attending your appeal or interviews or medical or other examinations in connection with your claim.[41] They also include expenses such as preparing and copying documents,[42] sending letters and faxes in order to obtain further evidence and they could extend to making disbursements for the preparation of medical reports and expert reports on your country of origin.

It should be noted that the cost of faxes, computer facilities, photocopying and travel expenses are expressly excluded as counting as 'essential living needs' for the purposes of determining destitution.[43] So while it appears that these particular expenses may not be taken into account in determining whether you are 'destitute',[44] they may still be met in providing support if you are in fact found to be destitute.

Providing services

NASS may provide the following services to any person who is receiving NASS support:[45]
- education (including the provision of English language lessons);
- sporting or other developmental activities.

The services are not provided automatically to those receiving NASS support but may *only* be provided in order to 'maintain good order' among supported asylum seekers.[46] This does not mean that good order must have broken down before these services are provided but that NASS is able to anticipate that, without the stimulation of education, language lessons and developmental activities and the general access to and integration into the wider community that such allow, 'good order' is less likely to be maintained.

2. **Contributions to and recovery of support**

Contributions to support

In deciding what level of support to provide to a destitute asylum seeker, NASS must take into account the income, support and assets which are available or might reasonably be expected to be available to you.[47] *However*, under the contributions rule, NASS may decide not to reduce the level of support provided so as to take account of your income etc but instead require you to make a contribution to the cost of providing you with the support.[48] In these circumstances, you are required to make payments directly to NASS of amounts which will be notified to you by NASS.[49] Where support is provided with a requirement that you make a contribution towards the costs of the support, NASS may make it a condition of the provision of your support that you make prompt payments of your contributions.[50]

Recovery of support

There are four circumstances in which you may be required to repay asylum support provided to you. In the first two cases, NASS *itself* may directly require you to repay support which it has provided to you. These are where:

- you later become able to convert into money, assets which you had at the time of your application for support;[51]
- you have been provided with an overpayment of support as a result of an error.[52]

The rules relating to the recovery of overpayments of support as a result of an error apply to both temporary *and* ordinary NASS support,[53] however recovery as a result of assets becoming realisable may only be of ordinary NASS support and not temporary support. If you are unable to pay, then, where recovery is being made from ordinary NASS support, the recovery may be by making a deduction from your existing asylum support[54] or NASS could recover the money through the civil courts as though it were a 'debt' which you owe to NASS.[55] Where NASS is recovering temporary support (which is only possible in overpayment cases), it may *only* proceed through the civil courts and not by way of deduction.[56] In both cases, NASS has a discretion to waive recovery even if the relevant conditions are met.[57]

In the third case, NASS may apply to the county court (or, in Scotland, the sheriff's court) for an order that you repay temporary or ordinary support obtained as a result of a misrepresentation or failure to disclose a material fact.[58]

Fourthly,[59] NASS may require the refund of any support paid to a supported person whom it transpires was not destitute.

In addition, and under yet a different procedure, NASS may try to recover from a person who has sponsored your stay in the United Kingdom (UK), ordinary support which has been provided to you.[60]

Convertible assets

In order to require you to repay the value of any asylum support which has been paid to you:[61]

- at the time of your application for asylum support, you must have had assets either in the UK or elsewhere (eg, savings, investments, property, shares) which you could not at that time convert into money which was available to you; *and*
- *since* your application for asylum support, you are able to convert those assets into money which is available to you (even if you have not done so).

NASS cannot require you to repay any more than *either:*[62]

- the total 'money' value of all the support provided to you up to the time when NASS asks you to make a repayment; *or if it is a lesser amount*
- the total 'money' value of the assets which you had at the time of the application for support and which you have since been able to convert into money.

Recovery of overpayments of support as a result of error

NASS may require you to repay any temporary support or asylum support which has been provided to you as a result of an 'error' by NASS.[63] Unlike recovery of overpayments of most social security benefits, there is no need for you to be at all responsible for the overpayment in any way. In contrast to the position for housing benefit and council tax benefit, in the asylum support scheme it is the error on the part of NASS which enables recovery rather than prevents it (see CPAG's *Welfare Benefits and Tax Credits Handbook*).

NASS may recover the support from you whether you are still being supported or whether you are no longer being supported.[64] NASS can recover no more than the total money value of the support which was provided to you as a result of its error.[65]

Recovery following misrepresentation/failure to disclose

If NASS believes that you have received support as a result of a misrepresentation or failure to disclose a material fact by any person, NASS may apply to a county court for an order that the person who made the misrepresentation or who was responsible for the failure to disclose repay the support.[66] Recovery may be made from any person who made the misrepresentation/failure to disclose and not just an asylum seeker or their dependant who received the support. The total amount which the court can order the person to repay is the money value of the support which has been paid as a result of the misrepresentation or failure to disclose and which would not have been provided if it had not been for that misrepresentation or failure to disclose.[67]

Recovery from sponsor

Support may be recovered from a 'sponsor' of a person who receives asylum support.[68] A sponsor is a person who has given a written undertaking for the purposes of the immigration rules to be responsible for the maintenance and accommodation of a person seeking to enter or remain in the UK (see p94).[69] This form of recovery is intended to deal with the situation where a person obtains admission to the UK under a sponsorship agreement in a non-asylum capacity and then seeks to remain in the UK as a refugee and becomes entitled to asylum support during the process. The sponsor can only be made liable to make payments covering the period over which the undertaking has effect.[70] A sponsor should not, therefore, be liable for payments for any period of leave which was given subsequent to the original leave in relation to which the undertaking was given, unless a further undertaking was given, or any period of residence without leave since undertakings under the immigration rules are given for the purpose of the grant of leave. The procedure for recovery is that NASS must make a complaint to a magistrates' court (or, in Scotland, a sheriff's court) for an order that the sponsor make payments. The court may order the sponsor to make weekly payments to NASS of an amount which the court thinks is appropriate having regard to all the circumstances of the case and, in particular, to the sponsor's own income.[71] The weekly sum must not be more than the weekly value of the support being provided to the asylum seeker.[72] The court can order that payments be made to cover any period before the time at which NASS made the complaint to the court but, if it does so, it must have regard to the sponsor's income during the period concerned rather than her/his current income.[73] The order can be enforced in the same way as a maintenance order.[74]

Notes

1. Support provided under NASS

1. s96(1) IAA 1999
2. Sch 8 para 4 IAA 1999; reg 14 AS Regs
3. s96(2) IAA 1999
4. s96(3) IAA 1999
5. s96(3) 1999 IAA 1999; it is unclear why the legislation applies this cashless 'majority' rule to the other forms of support referred to in s96(2) IAA 1999 in the first place since, by definition, such support may only be accessed where the circumstances of a particular case are 'exceptional' which thereby leads to the simultaneous disapplication of the rule under s96(3).
6. Reg 12(3) AS Regs
7. Reg 19(1) AS Regs
8. Vandalism is the example cited in the Explanatory Notes (at para 284).
9. s95(9)-(11) IAA 1999
10. This is because reg 19(1) allows the Secretary of State to take into account the 'extent' to which conditions have been complied with.
11. s97(7) IAA 1999
12. Reg 10(1)(2) AS Regs
13. Reg 10(2) AS Regs
14. Reg 10(2) AS Regs
15. Reg 10(2) AS Regs sets out a table containing these figures, the further definitions are contained in reg 10(3)(4) AS Regs.
16. Reg 2(1) AS Regs
17. Reg 2(1) AS Regs
18. Reg 10(4)(b)(d) AS Regs
19. Reg 10(4)(c) AS Regs
20. Reg 10A AS Regs; see also NASS *Policy Bulletin 78*
21. Reg 10(5) AS Regs
22. Applicable amounts for income support purposes are provided pursuant to s124(4) SSCBA 1992.
23. s97(5) IAA 1999
24. s97(6) IAA 1999
25. para 305 of Explanatory Notes to IAA 1999
26. See the wording of regs 10(2)(6) and 11(1) AS Regs.
27. NASS *Policy Bulletin 37*
28. NASS *Policy Bulletin 31*
29. ss94(2) and 99-100 IAA 1999
30. s97(1)(a) IAA 1999 with reference to s94(3)(4) in respect of the initial decision *and* period for any subsequent appeals to be resolved; s97(1)(b) IAA 1999
31. para 303 Explanatory Notes
32. s97(2)(a) AS Regs
33. Reg 13(2)(a) AS Regs
34. Reg 13(2)(b) AS Regs
35. Reg 13(2) AS Regs
36. Notes to Form NASS1 in Sch AS Regs under 'Accommodation'
37. See NASS *Policy Bulletin 85*
38. See further NASS *Policy Bulletin 19*
39. s99(5)(a) IAA 1999
40. s96(1)(c) IAA 1999
41. These are expressly included in the interim scheme (reg 5(3) ASIP) and it would be anomalous if the same were to be left out for the purposes of NASS.
42. Explanatory Notes to the IAA 1999 at para 300
43. s95(8) IAA 1999; reg 9(4) AS Regs but see also s97(5)(6) IAA 1999 which treats such expenses as essential living needs for the specific purposes of limiting the amount of overall expenditure incurred by the Secretary of State to any particular person.
44. s95(3) IAA 1999
45. Sch 8 para 4 IAA 1999, reg 14 AS Regs
46. Reg 14(1) AS Regs

2. Contributions to and recovery of support

47. Reg 12(3) AS Regs
48. Reg 16(2) AS Regs
49. Reg 16(3) AS Regs
50. Reg 16(4) AS Regs, conditions may generally be imposed under s95(9)-(12) IAA 1999
51. Reg 17 AS Regs
52. s114 IAA 1999
53. see s114(1) IAA 1999
54. Reg 17(4), 18 AS Regs
55. s114(3) and Sch 8 para 11(2)(a) IAA 1999

56 This is because, despite the general
wording of reg 18 AS Regs, s114(4) IAA
1999 only enables the regulations to
make provision for the recovery by
deduction from support of support
provided under s95 and not s98 IAA
1999.

57 Note the word 'may' in s114(2) IAA
1999 and reg 17(2) AS Regs; in
particular in the case of the latter it is
also clear that NASS has a discretion to
recover less than the amount which is in
fact recoverable, see reg 17(3) '...a sum
not exceeding'.

58 s112 IAA 1999

59 Reg 17A AS Regs

60 s113 IAA 1999

61 Sch 8 para 11 IAA 1999; reg 17(1) AS
Regs; note that it is unclear whether
NASS can require a person who is no
longer being supported to repay the
value of the support, there is no
equivalent wording in the para 11 or reg
17 to that in s114(2) IAA 1999 which
expressly refers to both those who are
and have ceased to be supported
persons for the purposes of recovery as
result of NASS errors.

62 Reg 17(2)(3)(5) AS Regs

63 s114(1) IAA 1999; see NASS *Policy
Bulletin 67*

64 s114(2) IAA 1999

65 s114(2) IAA 1999

66 s112 IAA 1999

67 s112(2)(3) IAA 1999

68 s113 IAA 1999

69 s113(1)(a) IAA 1999

70 s113(1)(b) IAA 1999

71 s113(3) IAA 1999

72 s113(4) IAA 1999

73 s113(5) IAA 1999

74 s113(6) IAA 1999

Chapter 29

Appeals under the NASS scheme

This chapter covers:
1. Rights of appeal (below)
2. Appeal procedures (p422)
3. Powers of asylum support adjudicators (p428)

If you are dissatisfied with a decision made by NASS, you may be able to appeal against the decision to an asylum support adjudicator. Its appellate authority is also referred to as the ASA and we use this acronym for the purpose of this chapter. We refer to an asylum support adjudicator as an adjudicator. From 1 April 2007, the ASA is becoming part of the Department of Constitutional Affairs and will change its name to the Asylum Support Tribunal. It will continue to operate in the same way.

1. Rights of appeal

The circumstances in which you have the right to appeal are very limited. You may only appeal if your NASS support has been stopped or refused; for example:
- you have made an application for asylum support under section 95 or section 4 (see p388) and it has been refused;[1] *or*
- your support under section 95 has been stopped other than because you have ceased to be an asylum seeker (unless NASS has made a mistake and you are still an asylum seeker);[2] *or*
- your support under section 4 is stopped for any reason.

In relation to any other decision relating to asylum support (such as the level of support or the place of dispersal) or *any* decision relating to temporary support, the only means of challenging the decision is by way of judicial review. Equally it is not possible to appeal a decision that you have been refused support if the reason for the refusal is:

- you have failed to provide complete or accurate information for your claim; *or*
- you have failed to co-operate with enquiries made;[3] *or*
- the refusal is due to a late claim.[4]

These decisions must be challenged by judicial review although NASS will reconsider an application where information requested is later provided.

2. **Appeal procedures**

Appeals to the asylum support adjudicator should be processed with the minimum of delay.[5] The appeal procedures are not set out in great detail but the adjudicator has a general power to give directions on matters connected with the appeal where s/he considers that it is in the interests of justice to do so.[6] There is a strict timetable for the hearing and determination of appeals, a summary of which is set out below:[7]

Day	Event
Day 1	Notice of appealable decision is received by you.
Day 4 (latest)	Notice of appeal must be received by the adjudicator.

Assuming notice of appeal is received by the adjudicator on day 4...

Day	Event
Day 4 or day 5	Adjudicator faxes notice of appeal to NASS.
Day 6	Appeal bundle sent to adjudicator by fax/hand and to appellant by first class post or by hand.
Day 7	Adjudicator:
	decides whether to hold an oral hearing;
	gives notice of details of oral hearing;
	sets date for determining appeal;
	if no oral hearing to be held, if possible the adjudicator proceeds to determine appeal if possible;
	if no oral hearing and appeal determined, send to appellant and NASS both notice of decision and statement of reasons for decision.
Day 12 (latest)	Oral hearing held, appeal determined straight after hearing, adjudicator notifies decision to appellant and NASS at hearing or if not present, sends notice to appellant or NASS of the decision.
	Last day for determining appeal if no oral hearing; adjudicator sends notice of decision and statement of reasons for decision to appellant and NASS.
Day 15	Last day for adjudicator to send statement of reasons for decision to appellant and NASS if oral hearing held.

The following rules regarding timing and sending documents apply:
- unless otherwise stated in the table or below, all notices or documents to be sent by either NASS or yourself, must be sent by first class post, fax or given by hand;[8]
- where a notice or another document is sent by first class post by NASS or by the adjudicator, it is assumed that you have received it two days after the day on which it was sent unless you can prove that you did not receive it;[9]
- where a notice or a document is sent other than by first class post, there is no assumption made about when it was received and it is treated as having been received on the day on which it was in fact received;[10]
- where a time limit expires on a number of days after a particular event, time begins running on the day on which the event occurs;[11]
- where a time limit covers a Saturday, Sunday, bank holiday,[12] Christmas Day or Good Friday, that day is not counted for the purpose of the time limit;[13] similarly if the time limit expires on or the rules say that a particular act is to be carried out on one of those days, the rules are complied with if the act is done on the next working day.[14]

You may be represented throughout the appeal procedure by a representative of your choice.[15] If you are being represented, you or your representative should ensure that NASS and the adjudicator are aware of the name and address of the representative. Where NASS or the adjudicator are required to send certain documents to you as described in the procedure below, they should also send them to your representative.[16]

Notice of appeal

Any decision against which you have the right of appeal to the adjudicator must be communicated to you in writing.[17] NASS should write to you giving full reasons for its decision to stop or refuse you support. If you wish to appeal against the decision, you must send your notice of appeal to the ASA so that it is received by the adjudicator no later than three *days* after the day on which you received the notice of the decision.[18] You must give your notice of appeal by filling out the standard form which is issued by NASS or your own form which is drawn up in the same way as the NASS form.[19] The standard form itself is attached to the Asylum Support Appeals Rules.[20] The form must be signed by you or your representative if you have one.

Your representative may be any person who you ask to represent you; there is no requirement that they have any particular qualification.[21] There is no entitlement to public funding or legal aid for representation at the ASA. The vast majority of appellants are unrepresented. The Asylum Support Appeals Project (ASAP) is currently arranging free training in representation for NASS appeals for community groups and advisers.[22] ASAP currently attends ASA on Mondays and Thursdays in order to provide representation and advice.

The form asks you for personal details such as your address and daytime telephone contact number, your NASS reference number and asks you to state whether you want an oral hearing of the appeal and whether you want to attend any oral hearing that is held by the adjudicator and whether you would need an interpreter at that hearing and if so in what language. You are asked also to give details of your representative and to state the grounds upon which you appeal, in other words to state why you disagree with the decision which NASS has made. The form must be completed in full and in English.[23] You also have to include a copy of the decision you are appealing against. If the form is not completed properly the adjudicator may invalidate the appeal and return it to you. If there is any further information or evidence which you have which relates to your claim for support or your appeal, you may send copies of the relevant documents to ASA with the form.[24] It is very important that you provide the ASA with any evidence that proves you are entitled to support. For example, if NASS does not accept that you are destitute you may have to provide letters from anyone who has been providing you with support but who cannot anymore or any voluntary agencies who know you to be destitute.

If you do not appeal in time, you may ask the adjudicator to extend the time limit for appealing. The adjudicator may extend the time for appealing either before or after the time limit has expired but *only if*:[25]

- it is in the interests of justice to extend the time limit; *and*
- you (or your representative) could not comply with the time limit due to circumstances beyond your control.

The strength of your case is relevant to the question of whether it is in the interests of justice to extend time.[26] The second requirement is more difficult to meet as it means that there must have been some practical reason for which you are not responsible which meant that you could not put in your notice of appeal in time – eg, if you were ill and incapable of dealing with your affairs during the time that you received the notice and for the following two days. The adjudicator may also extend the time limit to appeal if you have been unable to get any advice in the appeal period. If you are late in putting in your notice of appeal and the adjudicator refuses to extend time, your only alternative is to seek a judicial review of the NASS decision and/or of the decision of the adjudicator to refuse to extend time.[27]

Preparation of the appeal bundle

On the same day as the adjudicator receives notice of appeal or, if that is not reasonably practicable, as soon as possible on the next day at the latest, the adjudicator must fax a copy of the notice of appeal and any supporting documents which you sent in with your form to NASS.[28]

On the second day after the day that the adjudicator received the notice of appeal (the last day on which the adjudicator had to fax the notice of appeal to

NASS), NASS must fax or deliver by hand to the adjudicator and either fax or send by first class post to you, copies of the following documents (known as the 'appeal bundle'):[29]

- *if the appeal is against a decision to refuse to provide support rather than a withdrawal of support*, the form on which you claimed support and any supporting documentation which is attached to that form;
- the decision letter refusing you support;
- any other evidence which NASS took into account in refusing you support.

Decision of the adjudicator whether to hold a hearing

On the day after NASS sends to the adjudicator the above documents, the adjudicator must consider the documents and decide whether to hold an oral hearing of the appeal or whether the appeal is going to be determined without a hearing. Whether the adjudicator decides to hold an oral hearing or not, s/he must set the date for when the appeal is going to be determined.[30] If the adjudicator decides to hold an oral hearing, s/he must, on the same day, send a notice to NASS and to you informing you of the time, date and place of the hearing.[31] The adjudicator *must* decide to hold an oral hearing of the appeal if:[32]

- you have requested an oral hearing in your notice of appeal; *or*
- the adjudicator thinks that it is necessary in order to fairly decide the appeal. It is possible to request on the appeal form that your appeal is heard on the papers (where no one attends and the adjudicator makes her/his decision based on the evidence included in the appeal bundle) but the adjudicator can decide that an oral appeal is necessary regardless of whether you ask for a paper appeal.[33]

Where the adjudicator decides to hold an oral hearing, the hearing must be held and the appeal determined five days after the day on which the adjudicator makes the decision as to whether to hold an oral hearing.[34] If the adjudicator decides not to hold an oral hearing, s/he must determine the appeal *either* on the same day as s/he decides not to hold an oral hearing *or* 'as soon as possible' after that day which must, in all cases, be within five days after the day of the decision not to hold an oral hearing.[35]

The adjudicator usually sends directions to both you and NASS to produce further evidence.[36] These directions are sent together with the notice of the appeal hearing, if there is an oral hearing. The further evidence that you are directed to produce may be, for example, evidence as to your destitution or medical evidence or copies of previous asylum determination. These documents should be faxed or copied and posted before the hearing if possible. However, due to the speed of the appeal, it may only be possible to collate the documents required and take them to the appeal hearing. It is very important to comply with directions because if you don't the adjudicator will not have all the evidence needed to make a decision on your appeal. If an agency or solicitor has helped you complete the appeal form, the directions may be sent to them so it is important to check if they have received them and ask whether they can help you respond to them.

Further evidence before determination of the appeal

If you have some more evidence in support of your appeal which you did not send in with your notice of appeal, you may send the evidence in to be considered by the adjudicator. You should send this evidence to the adjudicator before the time for her/him to determine the appeal and you must, at the same time, send a copy of this further evidence to NASS.[37] You should note that, if no oral hearing is to be held, the adjudicator will determine the appeal, at most, eight days after you gave your notice of appeal.

If NASS wished to rely on any further evidence which was not sent by NASS to the adjudicator after NASS received the notice of appeal, NASS may send this evidence to the adjudicator before the appeal is determined for her/him to consider and must send it to you at the same time.[38]

In particular, you may wish to rely upon evidence which shows a change in your circumstances after the date of the NASS decision. You should send this evidence to the adjudicator and to NASS and/or take it to any appeal hearing (see below) as the adjudicator has the power to consider that evidence.[39]

Although you are asked to state whether you want an oral hearing of the appeal on the notice of the appeal; it may be that you were not aware of all of the information or evidence relied upon by NASS which is in the appeal bundle or any further evidence subsequently sent to you and the adjudicator by NASS. If, having seen this material, you change your mind and decide that you want an oral hearing in order to make direct representations to the adjudicator, you should notify the adjudicator of your desire for an oral hearing as soon as possible by fax or telephone as s/he may take into account your later representations in determining whether the appeal can only be disposed of fairly by granting an oral hearing. Alternatively, you may wish to make written representations to the adjudicator about these matters, which you should also do as soon as possible.

Oral hearings

You are usually sent tickets for your travel to and from the ASA and overnight accommodation is arranged and paid for if you live some distance away. If tickets are not sent then a travel warrant can be requested from the NASS travel bureau.[40] Oral hearings before the adjudicator generally take place in public.[41] However, the adjudicator has the power to exclude certain members of the public or the public generally from all or part of the hearing if s/he decides that it is in the 'public interest' to do so.[42] The power to exclude the public appears to be narrower than simply your own interests or desire to have the appeal heard in private.

However, if for any reason you feel that anyone should be excluded from the hearing then you should indicate that to the adjudicator either before the date of the hearing or at the start of the hearing.

There are no rules which set out the procedure which must be adopted at the oral hearing of the appeal and the precise procedure will be for the adjudicator at the hearing to determine. However, at the hearing, you should be able to provide oral evidence to the adjudicator, call oral evidence of any witnesses in support of your case[43] and to question any witnesses which are relied upon by NASS. You or your representative must also have the opportunity of directly addressing the adjudicator as to what decision s/he should make and commenting on all of the evidence, documentary or oral, which is provided before her/him. If witnesses are called, the adjudicator may require that they give their evidence under oath or affirmation.[44] If you have any evidence which has not been presented to NASS or the adjudicator before the appeal, you should take it to the appeal. If either yourself or NASS attend at the hearing with further evidence which has not previously been provided, you must be given the opportunity of looking at that evidence and photocopying it in order to make comments upon it before the hearing proceeds.[45]

If the adjudicator has decided to hold an oral hearing, the hearing may be heard in your absence in the following circumstances:[46]

- if you stated in your notice of appeal that you did not want to be present or be represented at an oral hearing (this is likely to arise where you have not requested an oral hearing but the adjudicator decides to hold one anyway); *or*
- you did state in your notice of appeal that you wanted to be present or represented at an oral hearing and you have been sent a notice of the date, time and place of your hearing but neither yourself nor your representative attends the hearing.

The appeal may go ahead in the absence of a representative from NASS if no representative from NASS attends the hearing.[47]

You should, if you are able, take a note of what is said at the hearing. The adjudicator must ensure that a written record of what is said at the oral hearing is made either by her/himself or in some other way.[48] If you are considering challenging the decision of the adjudicator by way of judicial review after the decision, you may wish to request a copy of the adjudicator's record of proceedings.

Decision following oral hearing

Ultimately, whether an appeal is dealt with orally or without a hearing, the adjudicator must give reasons for her/his decision in writing.[49] Where the adjudicator holds an oral hearing of the appeal, s/he must tell you and the representative of NASS the decision which has been reached at the conclusion of the hearing.[50] You can expect the adjudicator to retire for a period in order to consider the decision before telling you the outcome. If neither yourself nor your representative are present at the hearing of the appeal, the adjudicator must send you notice informing you of the outcome of the appeal on the same day as the appeal is heard.[51] The same rule applies to NASS, if its representative does not attend the hearing.[52] *In addition*, whether you were at the hearing or not, not later than three days after the day of the hearing, the adjudicator must send to both yourself and NASS a statement containing reasons for her/his decision.[53] If the adjudicator decides to dismiss your appeal s/he is able to send a copy of the reason statement to you translated into your language.

Decision if no oral hearing

Where the adjudicator does not hold an oral hearing, s/he must send notice of the decision together with a statement containing the reasons for the decision on the same day as the appeal is determined.[54]

3. Powers of asylum support adjudicators

In deciding section 95 appeals, the adjudicator should first of all decide if you are an asylum seeker. If s/he finds that you are not an asylum seeker then there is no jurisdiction to hear the appeal. The adjudicator is able to take into account any changes of circumstances which take place between the date on which the decision of NASS was made and the date of the determination of the appeal.[55] In asylum support appeals the burden of proof is on you to prove that you are entitled to support and meet the relevant criteria. Adjudicators decide issues of fact on a balance of probabilities.

On deciding your appeal, the adjudicator can do one of three things. S/he can:[56]

- make NASS reconsider the question of whether you should be provided with support – this is called 'remitting the appeal';
- substitute her/his own decision for the decision which was made by NASS and allow the appeal meaning you are entitled to support;
- dismiss the appeal so that the decision of NASS stands.

The adjudicator cannot allow a section 4 appeal under section 95 if s/he decides that you are still an asylum seeker. Instead the appeal must be either dismissed as only failed asylum seekers can qualify for section 4 and you must reapply for section 95 or the adjudicator can remit the appeal for NASS to decide whether you are entitled to section 95 support. The same is true if you apply for section 95 support but are found to be a failed asylum seeker.

Although there are no express rules as to when the adjudicator's decision takes effect, the adjudicator's decision has the strength of law and NASS is obliged to provide support in law on the day the appeal is allowed although in practice this could take a couple of days. There are also no express rules as to the backdating of support or compensating an asylum seeker who has been without support as a result of an erroneous earlier decision. The High Court has held that the ASA can award backdated support in exceptional circumstances[57] and NASS has subsequently agreed to consider backdating support where there is a delay due to its error.

Procedures following an appeal

There is no further right of appeal against the decision of the adjudicator and there is no procedure for requesting that the adjudicator reconsider the decision.[58] If you are dissatisfied with the decision which the adjudicator has made, you can only challenge the decision by applying for judicial review for which you will need the help of a solicitor. If the decision of the adjudicator is to refer the matter back to NASS for reconsideration and NASS again refuses all support, then you may appeal again to the adjudicator against the second decision.

If the adjudicator dismisses your appeal following discontinuation or suspension of support, NASS is not able to consider any further application for support from you unless it is satisfied that there was a 'material' change of circumstances between the time of the appeal and the further application for support.[59] NASS defines a material change as the circumstances listed in regulation 15. Following appeals against a refusal to award support, NASS will also consider exceptional circumstances that justify a fresh application for support as is the case if there has not previously been a NASS appeal. (The approach is different where the previous refusal was following an alleged abandonment of the accommodation or a failure to report.[60])

The decision of the adjudicator is effective from the day on which it is made.

Ending the appeal by withdrawal

You may at any stage decide that you do not wish to carry on with your appeal, in which case you must notify NASS and the adjudicator that you are withdrawing the appeal as soon as possible.[61] In addition, NASS may at any time decide that it wishes to withdraw the decision against which you have appealed. If that happens, NASS must give you and the adjudicator notice of the withdrawal as soon as possible.[62] In either of these two circumstances, the appeal is treated as having come to an end.[63] If NASS withdraws the decision, it is required to make a further decision on your application for support. If that decision is of a kind which is appealable, and you are dissatisfied with the second decision, you may appeal against it again.

Notes

1. Rights of appeal

1 s103(1) IAA 1999
2 s103(2) IAA 1999; note that the legislation here provides a right of appeal where a decision is made to stop providing support 'before that support would otherwise have come to an end', the wording is ambiguous but the intention is to allow a right of appeal in any case where support is terminated before the asylum seeker has ceased to be an asylum seeker for the support purposes (see para 317 Explanatory Notes to IAA 1999 to this effect).
3 s57 NIAA 2002
4 s55 NIAA 2002

2. Appeal procedures

5 See s104(3) IAA 1999 and the preamble to the ASA(P) Rules.
6 r14 ASA(P) Rules
7 rs3, 4, 6, 7, 13 ASA(P) Rules
8 r17 ASA(P) Rules
9 r18(2) ASA(P) Rules (the same applies where NASS or the adjudicator sends documents by first class post to each other)
10 r18(1) ASA(P) Rules
11 r18(3) ASA(P) Rules
12 As defined in the Banking and Financial Dealings Act 1971, see r2(1) ASA(P) Rules.
13 rs18(4) and 2(1) 'excluded day' ASA(P) Rules
14 rs18(4)(5) and 2(1) 'excluded day' ASA(P) Rules
15 r15 ASA(P) Rules
16 r2(2)(c) ASA(P) Rules
17 There is no specific requirement in the ASR that these decisions must be communicated by letter but the ASA(P) Rules assume that they will be (see definition of 'appeal bundle' and 'decision letter' in rs2(1) and r3(3) ASA(P) Rules).
18 r3(3) ASA(P) Rules as amended
19 r3(1) ASA(P) Rules
20 See Sch ASA (Procedure) (Amendment) Rules 2003, any change in the form should be re-issued in the Sch ASA(P) Rules (see r3(1) ASA(P) Rules). This form is also available on the ASA website.
21 rs2(2)(d) and 15 ASA(P) Rules
22 ASAP are contactable on 0208 684 5873 or for advice on 0208 684 5972 or advice@asaproject.org.uk.
23 r3(1) ASA(P) Rules
24 The form itself indicates this.
25 r3(4) ASA(P) Rules
26 see *Mahli*
27 Note that, in judicial review proceedings, the Court may refuse to interfere with the decision you wish to challenge where you have failed to exercise a right of appeal, see *ex parte Mehmet Capti* COD where the Court suggested that, in these circumstances, the applicant will have to show are more serious legal error in the decision under challenge before the Court will be prepared to intervene.
28 r4(1) ASA(P) Rules
29 r4(2) ASA(P) Rules and see definition of 'appeal bundle' in r2(1)
30 r4(3)(a)(b)(4) ASA(P) Rules
31 rs4(3)(c)(4) and 7 ASA(P) Rules
32 rs4(3) and 5(1) ASA(P) Rules
33 r5(2) ASA(P) Rules
34 r6(1) ASA(P) Rules
35 r6(2) ASA(P) Rules
36 r14 ASA(P) Rules
37 r8(1)(2) ASA(P) Rules
38 r8(3)(4) ASA(P) Rules
39 r10(2) ASA(P) Rules
40 s103(9) IAA 1999; NASS *Policy Bulletin 28.* The NASS travel bureau is contactable on 020 8633 0683 or fax 020 8633 0941.
41 r12(1) ASA(P) Rules
42 r12(2) ASA(P) Rules
43 r10(5) ASA(P) Rules assumes that witnesses may be called
44 r10(4) ASA(P) Rules
45 r10(6) ASA(P) Rules
46 r9(1)(2) ASA(P) Rules
47 r(3) ASA(P) Rules
48 r11 ASA(P) Rules
49 s103(4) IAA 1999
50 r13(1) ASA(P) Rules
51 r13(1)(b) ASA(P) Rules
52 r13(1)(d) ASA(P) Rules
53 r13(1)(d)(4) ASA(P) Rules
54 r13(2)(4) ASA(P) Rules

3. **Powers of asylum support adjudicators**
   55 r10(2) ASA(P) Rules
   56 s103(3) IAA 1999
   57 *R v ASA* [2001] EWHC 881
   58 s103(5) IAA 1999
   59 Reg 21 AS Regs; see NASS *Policy Bulletin 84*
   60 See NASS *Policy Bulletin 84*
   61 r16(2) ASA(P) Rules
   62 r16(1) ASA(P) Rules
   63 r16(3) ASA(P) Rules

Appendices

Appendices

Appendix 1

Advice on immigration and social security

Those who need help with an immigration problem should seek advice from their local law centre, a solicitor specialising in immigration work or one of the agencies listed below.

Independent advice and representation on immigration issues

Joint Council for the Welfare of Immigrants
115 Old Street
London EC1V 9JR
Tel: 020 7251 8708

Immigration Advisory Service
County House
190 Dover Street
London SE1 4YB
Tel: 020 7967 1200
www.iasuk.org.uk
(There are other offices in the regions and at the ports)

Afro Asian Advisory Service
53 Addington Square
London SE5 7LB
Tel: 020 7701 0141

AIRE Centre (Advice on Individual Rights in Europe)
3rd Floor
17 Red Lion Square
London WC1R 4QH
Tel: 020 7831 4276
www.airecentre.org.uk

Greater Manchester Immigration Aid Unit
1 Delaunays Road
Crumpsall Green
Manchester M8 4QS
Tel: 0161 740 7722
www.ein.org.uk/gmiau

Asylum Aid
28 Commercial Street
London E1 6LS
Tel: 020 7377 5123
www.asylumaid.org.uk

Refugee Action
Has one-stop services throughout the country.

Refugee Arrivals Project
Room 1116
1st Floor
Queens Building
Heathrow Airport
Hounslow TW6 1DN
Tel: 020 8759 5740

Headquarters at:
41B Cross Lances Road
Hounslow TW3 2AD
Tel: 020 8607 6888

Refugee Council
Bondway House
3–9 Bondway
London SW8 1SJ

Tel: 020 7820 3000
www.refugeecouncil.org.uk

Refugee Legal Centre
Nelson House
153–157 Commercial Road
London E7 2EB
Tel: 020 7780 3200
www.refugee-legal-centre.org.uk

(For a fuller list of agencies concerned with immigration issues including policy, race relations and civil liberties see *JCWI Immigration, Nationality and Refugee Law Handbook*, 6th edition, 2006.)

Independent advice and representation on social security

It is often difficult for unsupported individuals to get a positive response from the Department for Work and Pensions. You may be taken more seriously if it is clear you have taken advice about your entitlement or have an adviser assisting you.

If you want advice or help with a benefit problem the following agencies may be able to assist.

- Citizens advice bureaux (CABx) and other local advice centres provide information and advice about benefits and may be able to represent you.
- Law centres can often help in a similar way to CABx/advice centres.
- Local authority welfare rights workers provide a service in many areas and some arrange advice sessions and take-up campaigns locally.
- Local organisations for particular groups of claimants may offer help. For instance, there are unemployed centres, pensioners' groups, centres for disabled people etc.
- Claimants' unions give advice in some areas.
- Some social workers and probation officers (but not all) help with benefit problems, especially if they are already working with you on another problem.
- Solicitors can give some free legal advice. This does not cover the cost of representation at an appeal hearing, but can cover the cost of preparing written submissions and obtaining evidence such as medical reports. However, solicitors do not always have a good working knowledge of the benefit rules and you may need to shop around until you find one who does.

Appendix 2
Useful addresses

Immigration issues

Home Office Immigration and Nationality Directorate (IND)
Lunar House
40 Wellesley Road
Croydon CR9 2BY
Tel: 020 8696 0688/0870 606 7766

Immigration and Nationality Enquiry Bureau
Tel: 0870 606 7766 (enquiries)
0870 241 0645 (application forms)
Textphone: 0800 389 8289
www.ind.homeoffice.gov.uk

Immigration Application Forms Unit
Tel: 020 7008 8308 (enquiries) 0845
010 5555 (application forms)
Textphone: 020 7008 8457
www.ukvisas.gov.uk

National Asylum Support Service (NASS)
Voyager House
30 Wellesley Road
Croydon CRO 2AD
Tel: 0845 602 1739
Fax: 0845 601 1143
Helpline: 0845 602 1739
www.ind.homeoffice.gov.uk

Asylum Support Adjudicators
Christopher Wren House
113 High Street
Croydon CR1 1QG
Tel: 020 8588 2500/0800 389 7913

Sodexho Pass Ltd
Unit 5 Albany Court
Albany Business Park
Frimley Road
Camberley GU16 7QR
01276 687 000
www.sodexho-uk.com

Office of the Immigration Services Commissioner (OISC)
5th Floor
Counting House
53 Tooley Street
London SE1 2QN
Tel: 0845 000 0046/020 7211 1500
www.oisc.go.uk

Identity and Passport Service
Globe House
89 Ecclestone Square
London SW1V 1PN
Tel: 0870 521 0410
www.passport.gov.uk

The Overseas Visitors Record Office
Brandon House
180 Borough High Street
London SE1 1LH
Tel: 020 7230 1208
www.workingintheuk.gov.uk

Work Permits (UK)
PO Box 3468
Sheffield S3 8WA
Tel: 0114 207 4074
0845 010 6677 (employers helpline)
www.workingintheuk.gov.uk

Home Office (Minister's Private Office)
2 Marsham Street
London SW1P 4DF
Tel: 020 7035 4848
Textphone: 020 7035 4742
www.homeoffice.gov.uk

European Commission
London Office
8 Storey's Gate
London SW1P 3AT
Tel: 020 7973 1992

Immigration Law Practitioners' Association
Lindsey House
40–42 Charterhouse Street
London EC1M 6JN
Tel: 020 7251 8383
www.ilpa.org.uk

Electronic Immigration Network
The Progress Centre
Charlton Place
Manchester M12 6HS
Tel: 0845 458 4151 or 0161 273 7515
www.ein.org.uk

UK Visas
Foreign Commonwealth Office
King Charles Street
London SW1A 2AH
0845 010 5555

Social security issues

Department for Work and Pensions (benefits)
Quarry House
Quarry Hill
Leeds LS2 7UA
Tel: 0113 232 4000
www.dwp.gov.uk

Department for Work and Pensions (policy)
The Adelphi
1–11 John Adam Street
London WC2 6HT
Tel: 020 7962 8000

Department for Work and Pensions (solicitor)
New Court
48 Carey Street
London WC2A 2LS
Tel: 020 7962 8000

Benefit Enquiry Line
Victoria House
9th Floor
Ormskirk Road
Preston PR1 2QP
Tel: 0800 88 22 00
Textphone: 0800 24 33 55

Pensions and Overseas Benefits Directorate
Tyneview Park
Whitley Road
Benton
Newcastle-upon-Tyne NE98 1BA
Tel: 0191 218 7878

The Decision Making and Appeal Unit
Quarry House
Quarry Hill
Leeds LS2 7UA
Tel: 0113 232 4000

Child Benefit Centre
PO Box 1
Newcastle-upon-Tyne NE88 1AA

England, Scotland and Wales
Tel: 0845 302 1444
Textphone: 0845 302 1474

Northern Ireland
Tel: 0845 603 2000
Textphone: 0845 607 6078

Disability Contact Processing Unit (DCPU)
Government Buildings
Warbreck House
Warbreck Hill
Blackpool FY2 0YJ
Tel: 0845 712 3456
Textphone: 08457 22 44 33

NHS Benefits Services Authority
Sandyford House
Archbold Terrace
Jesmond
Newcastle upon Tyne NE2 1DB
Tel: 0191 203 5555
www.ppa.nhs.uk

Department for Education and Skills
Sanctuary Buildings
Great Smith Street
London SW1P 3BT
Tel: 0870 000 2288
Textphone: 01928 794 274

HM Revenue and Customs (tax credits)
Tax Credit Office
Preston PR1 0SB
Tel: 0845 300 3900
Textphone: 0845 300 3909
www.hmrc.gov.uk

Under 18 Support Team (UEST)
Level 4
Steel City House
West Street
Sheffield S1 2GQ
Tel: 01253 848000

HM Revenue and Customs (national insurance contributions)
Benton Park View
Newcastle upon Tyne NE98 1ZZ
Tel: 0845 302 1479
Textphone: 0845 915 3296
www.hmrc.gov.uk/nic

The President of the Appeal Service
The President's Office
5th Floor
Fox court
14 Grays Inn Road
London WC1X 8HN
Tel: 020 7712 2600
www.tribunalservice.gov.uk

Offices of the Social Security and Child Support Commissioners
England and Wales
3rd Floor
Procession House
55 Ludgate Hill
London EC4M 7JW
Tel: 020 7029 9850
Minicom: 020 7029 9820
www.osscsc.gov.uk

Scotland
George House
126 George Street
Edinburgh EH2 4HH
Tel: 0131 271 4310
www.ossc-scotland.org.uk

Northern Ireland
Headline Building
10–14 Victoria Street
Belfast BT1 3GG
Tel: 028 9033 2344
www.courtsni.gov.uk/en-GB/Services/
Tribunals

**Independent Review Service for
the Social Fund**
Centre City Podium
5 Hill Street
Birmingham B5 4UB

Tel: 0800 096 1926
Textphone: 0800 096 1929
www.irs-review.org.uk

**The Parliamentary and Health
Service Ombudsman**
Millbank Tower
London SW1P 4QP
Tel: 0845 015 4033
www.ombudsman.org.uk
Tel: 028 90 233821

The Independent Adjudicator
The Adjudicator's Office
Haymarket House
28 Haymarket
London SW1Y 4SP
Tel: 020 7930 2292
Fax: 020 7930 2298
www.adjudicatorsoffice.gov.uk

Appendix 3
Useful publications

Many of the books listed here will be in your local public library. Stationery Office books are available from Stationery Office bookshops and also from many others. They may be ordered by post, telephone or fax from The Stationary Office, PO Box 29, Norwich NR3 1GN (tel: 0870 600 5522, fax: 0870 600 5533; email: customer.services@tso.co.uk; web: www.tso.co.uk) Many of the publications listed are available from CPAG – see below for order details, or order from www.cpag.org.uk. For social security information in electronic format see details of CPAG's online services given below.

1. General immigration, nationality and asylum
JCWI Immigration, Nationality and Refugee Law Handbook
6th edition, JCWI, 2006

Macdonald's Immigration Law and Practice
6th edition, Ian Macdonald and Nicholas Blake, Macdonalds, 2005

Best practise Guide to Asylum and Human Rights Appeals
M. Henderson, ILPA, 2003

2. Nationality
Fransman: British Nationality Law
2nd edition, Butterworths, 1998 (new edition due late 2007)

3. Refugees and asylum seekers
The rights of refugees under International Law
James Hathaway, Cambridge University Press, 2005

The Refugee in International Law
2nd edition, Guy Goodwin-Gill, Clarendon, 1996

Support for Asylum Seekers
Willman, Knafler and Pierce, 2nd edition, Legal Action Group, 2004

4. Human rights
Blakestone's Guide to the Human Rights Act 1998
Oxford University Press, 2003

European Human Rights Law
Starmer, Legal Action Group, 1999

5. Children
Working with children and young people subject to immigration control : Guidelines for best practice
ILPA/Heaven Crawley, November 2004

6. EEA nationals

Free movement of persons in the enlarged European Union
N. Rogers and R. Scannell, Sweet & Maxwell, 2005

7. Social security caselaw and legislation

Social Security Case Law – Digest of Commissioners' Decisions
D Neligan (Stationery Office, looseleaf in two vols).
Commissioners' decisions also at www.osscsc.gov.uk and on CPAG's online services.

CPAG's Online Information Services
These include all social security legislation, consolidated and updated throughout the year; over 2,500 commissioners' decisions, some with commentary; the *Welfare Benefits and Tax Credits Handbook updated throughout the year* with links to the relevant legislation; CPAG's *Housing Benefit and Council Tax Benefit Legislation* (with commentary updated in line with the print version); the *Child Support Handbook* and child support legislation. Three different annual subscription packages are available (plus a basic one without legislation). For more information and to get a free 7-day trial visit the online services homepage at
http://onlineservices.cpag.org.uk

The Law Relating to Social Security
(Stationery Office, looseleaf, 11 vols).
All the legislation but without any comment. Known as the 'Blue Book'.
Vols 6, 7, 8 and 11 deal with means-tested benefits.

Social Security Legislation, Volume I:
Non-Means-Tested Benefits
D Bonner, I Hooker and R White (Sweet & Maxwell). Legislation with commentary. 2007/08 edition available from CPAG if you are a member, from October 2007: £84 for the main volume.

Social Security Legislation, Volume II:
Income Support, Jobseeker's Allowance and the Social Fund
J Mesher, P Wood, R Poynter, N Wikely and D Bonner (Sweet & Maxwell). Legislation with commentary. 2007/08 edition available from CPAG if you are a member, from October 2007: £84 for the main volume.

Social Security Legislation, Volume III:
Administration, Adjudication and the European Dimension
M Rowland and R White (Sweet & Maxwell). Legislation with commentary. 2007/08 edition available from CPAG if you are a member, from October 2007: £84 for the main volume.

Social Security Legislation, Volume IV:
Tax Credits, Child Trust Funds and Employer-Paid Social Security benefits
N Wikeley and D Williams (Sweet & Maxwell). Legislation with commentary. 2007/08 edition available from CPAG if you are a member, from October 2007: £84 for the main volume.

Social Security Legislation – updating supplement to Volumes I, II, III and IV
(Sweet & Maxwell). The spring 2008 update to the 2007/08 main

volumes, available from CPAG if you are a member (£50).

CPAG's Housing Benefit and Council Tax Benefit Legislation
L Findlay, C George, R Poynter and S Wright (CPAG). Contains legislation with a detailed commentary. 2007/08 edition available from December 2007, priced £95 including Supplement from CPAG. The 19th edition (2006/07) is still available at £93 per set. This publication is also available online (see p442).

The Social Fund: Law and Practice
T Buck (Sweet & Maxwell). Includes legislation, guidance and commentary. The 3rd edition (summer 2007) is available from CPAG for £82 if you are a CPAG member.

Social Fund Directions
Available on the IRS website at www.irssf.demon.co.uk/ssdir.htm

8. Social security guidance

Decision Makers Guide
12 volumes, memos and letters available at www.dwp.gov.uk/advisers

Handbook for Delegated Medical Practitioners
(Stationery Office, 1988)

Housing Benefit and Council Tax Benefit Guidance Manual
(Stationery Office, looseleaf)
Also available at www.dwp.gov.uk/advisers

Industrial Injuries Handbook for Adjudicating Medical Authorities
(Stationery Office, looseleaf)

Income Support Guide
(Stationery Office, looseleaf, 8 vols.)
Procedural guide issued to DWP staff.

The Social Fund Guide
(Stationery Office, looseleaf 2 vols)
Also available at www.dwp.gov.uk/advisers

9. Leaflets

The DWP publishes many leaflets available free from your local DWP or Jobcentre Plus office. To order larger numbers of leaflets, or receive information about new leaflets, write to Publicity Register, Freepost NWW 1853, Manchester, M2 9LU, tel. 0845 602 44 44; email publicity-register@dwp.gsi.gov.uk.

10. Periodicals

CPAG's *Welfare Rights Bulletin* is published every two months by CPAG. It covers developments in social security law, including commissioners' decisions. The annual subscription is £30 but it is sent automatically to CPAG Rights and Comprehensive Members. For subscription and membership details contact CPAG.

Articles on social security and immigration can also be found in *Legal Action* (Legal Action Group, monthly magazine), and on social security in the *Journal of Social Security Law* (Sweet & Maxwell, quarterly).

11. CPAG handbooks

Welfare Benefits and Tax Credits Handbook 2007/2008
£35.00 (£8.50 for claimants)
Also available online (see p442).

Child Support Handbook 2007/2008
£24.00 (15th edition, July 2007)
(£6.50 for claimants).
Also available online (see p442).

Paying for Care Handbook
£18.50 (5th edition, December 2005)

Council Tax Handbook
£16.00 (7th edition, summer 2007)

Debt Advice Handbook
£18.00 (7th edition, October 2006)

Fuel Rights Handbook
£17.00 (14th edition, autumn 2007)

Student Support and Benefits Handbook: England, Wales and Northern Ireland 2007/2008
£12.00 (4th edition, autumn 2007)

Benefits for Students in Scotland Handbook 2007/2008
£12.00 (4th edition, autumn 2007)

Personal Finance Handbook
£15.00 (2nd edition, summer 2007)

A Guide to Housing Benefit and Council Tax Benefit 2007/2008
£22.50 (Shelter/CIoH, summer 2007)

Disability Rights Handbook 2007/08
£20.00 (Disability Alliance ERA, May 2007)

Young Person's Handbook
£15.95 (3rd edition, Inclusion, summer 2007)

Welfare to Work Handbook
£24.95 (3rd edition, Inclusion, summer 2007)

For CPAG publications and most of those in Sections 6 and 10 contact:
CPAG, 94 White Lion Street, London N1 9PF, tel: 020 7837 7979, fax: 020 7837 6414. Order forms are also available at: www.cpag.org.uk/publications. Postage and packing is free for orders up to £10 in value; for orders £10.01-£100 add a flat rate charge of £3.99; for orders £100.01-£500 add £5.99; for orders £500.01+ add £9.99.

Appendix 4

People admitted for temporary purposes

Category	Rule (HC 395)	Employment conditions	Additional employment requirements	Requirement that applicants and dependants are adequately maintained and accommodated without recourse to public funds	Entry clearance required for non-visa nationals entering the UK
Visitor	40-46	Employment prohibited	Must not intend to take employment in the UK or produce goods/ provide services within the UK	Yes, out of resources available to applicant without taking employment or will be maintained and accommodated by relatives or friends	No
Visitor in transit	47-50	Employment prohibited	None	None	No
Visitor seeking medical treatment	51-56	Employment prohibited	Must not intend to take employment in the UK or produce goods/ provide services within the UK	Yes, out of resources available to applicant without taking employment or will be maintained and accommodated by relatives or friends	No

Appendix 4: People admitted for temporary purposes

Category	Rule (HC 395)	Employment conditions	Additional employment requirements	Requirement that applicants and dependants are adequately maintained and accommodated without recourse to public funds	Entry clearance required for non-visa nationals entering the UK
Student	57–62	Freedom to take employment	Must not intend to engage in any business or take employment except part-time or vacation work with the consent of the Secretary of State (in practice, consent for some work is automatically granted)	Yes, is able to meet the 'costs of her/his own accommodation and maintenance without taking employment or engaging in business'	No if seeks leave to enter for six months or less. Yes for this and nearly every category where leave of over six months is sought and not a British or EEA national.
Student re-sitting exams	69A–69F	employment restricted			
Student writing a thesis	69G–69L				
Student nurse	63–69	Freedom to take employment restricted	Must not intend to take employment or engage in business other than in connection with the training course	Yes, must have 'sufficient funds available' to satisfy the requirements without engaging in business or taking employment (except in connection with the training course); a Department of Health bursary may be taken into account in determining whether the requirements are met	See above

Category	Rule (HC 395)	Employment conditions	Additional employment requirements	Requirement that applicants and dependants are adequately maintained and accommodated without recourse to public funds	Entry clearance required for non-visa nationals entering the UK
Postgraduate doctor or dentist	70–75	None	Must *either* intend to undertake pre-registration house officer employment for up to 12 months as required for full registration with the General Medical Council; *or*, if a doctor or dentist eligible for full or limited registration with the General Medical Council or with the General Dental Council must intend to undertake postgraduate training in a hospital	Yes, applicant must be able to so maintain and accommodate	See above

Category	Rule (HC 395)	Employment conditions	Additional employment requirements	Requirement that applicants and dependants are adequately maintained and accommodated without recourse to public funds	Entry clearance required for non-visa nationals entering the UK
Spouse of student/ prospective student	76-78	Employment prohibited except where the period of leave being granted is 12 months or more, in which case there are no working restrictions	Must not intend to take work other than that permitted according to the conditions of leave	Yes, the parties must be 'able' to so maintain and accommodate	See above
Child of student/ prospective student	79-81	Employment prohibited except where the period of leave being granted is 12 months or more	None	Yes, the child must show that s/he 'can and will' be so maintained and accommodated	See above
Prospective student	82-87	Employment prohibited	None	Yes, must be able to meet the costs of these requirements without working	No

Category	Rule (HC 395)	Employment conditions	Additional employment requirements	Requirement that applicants and dependants are adequately maintained and accommodated without recourse to public funds	Entry clearance required for non-visa nationals entering the UK
Student union sabbatical officer	87A–87F	Restricted to working in the sabbatical post	Must not intend to engage in business or take employment except in connection with the sabbatical post	Yes, applicant must be able to so maintain and accommodate	See students
Au pair	88–94	Prohibited from working except as an au pair	Must intend to take up an au pair placement	Yes, must be able to so maintain and accommodate her/himself	See above (although rules advise entry clearance is obtained)
Working holidaymaker	95–100	Freedom to take employment is restricted	Must intend to take employment incidental to a holiday but not to engage in business, provide services as a professional sportsman or entertainer or pursue a career in UK	Yes, must be 'able' and must 'intend' to so maintain and accommodate her/himself	Yes

Category	Rule (HC 395)	Employment conditions	Additional employment requirements	Requirement that applicants and dependants are adequately maintained and accommodated without recourse to public funds	Entry clearance required for non-visa nationals entering the UK
Child of working holidaymaker	101–103	None	None	Yes, and without parent(s) engaging in business or taking employment except as permitted as incidental to the holiday. Must show that child can and will be so maintained and accommodated	Yes
Seasonal worker at agricultural camps	104–109	Condition imposed allowing the person to take employment only up until 30 November of the year in question	Must not intend to take employment other than as a seasonal worker at an agricultural camp	Yes, applicant must be able to so maintain and accommodate	Yes, in form of a valid Home Office work card issued by the operator of the scheme approved by the Secretary of State

Category	Rule (HC 395)	Employment conditions	Additional employment requirements	Requirement that applicants and dependants are adequately maintained and accommodated without recourse to public funds	Entry clearance required for non-visa nationals entering the UK
Teacher or language assistant under approved exchange scheme	110–115	None (or may be restricted)	Must not intend to take employment other than in an established educational establishment in the UK under an exchange scheme approved by the Department for Education and Skills, or administered by the Central Bureau for Educational Visits and Exchanges or the League for the Exchange of Commonwealth Teachers	Yes, applicant must be able to so maintain and accommodate	Yes

Category	Rule (HC 395)	Employment conditions	Additional employment requirements	Requirement that applicants and dependants are adequately maintained and accommodated without recourse to public funds	Entry clearance required for non-visa nationals entering the UK
Approved training or work experience	116–121	Freedom to take or change employment restricted	Must intend to only take employment as specified in the work permit – ie, training or work experience under the scheme	Yes, applicant must be able to so maintain and accommodate	See students, but must have a work permit issued under TWES (whether a visa national or not) or if applying for leave to remain was admitted or allowed to remain as a student

Category	Rule (HC 395)	Employment conditions	Additional employment requirements	Requirement that applicants and dependants are adequately maintained and accommodated without recourse to public funds	Entry clearance required for non-visa nationals entering the UK
Spouse and child of someone with limited leave as teacher/ language assistant or in approved teaching or work experience	122–127	None	None	Yes, the parties must be able to so maintain and accommodate in accommodation which they own or occupy exclusively; the child must show that s/he can and will be so maintained and accommodated in accommodation which her/his parents own or occupy exclusively	Yes

Appendix 5

People admitted for purposes leading to settlement

Category	Rule (HC 395)	Employment conditions (before settlement is obtained)	Additional employment requirements	Requirement that applicants and dependants are adequately maintained and accommodated without recourse to public funds	Entry clearance required for non-visa nationals to enter the UK
Returning resident (immediate settlement)	18–20	None	None	None (but must show that applicant did not receive assistance from public funds towards cost of leaving the UK previously)	No, provided applicant returns to the UK within two years
Work permit employment (leads to settlement after five years), including Highly Skilled Migrant Programme and Sector/Graduate based schemes.	128–135T	Freedom to take employment restricted to the approved employment	Must not intend to take employment other than that specified in the work permit/Immigration Employment Document (IED)	Yes, applicant must be 'able' to so maintain and accommodate	No, but work permit/IED is required whether a visa national or not

Category	Rule (HC 395)	Employment conditions (before settlement is obtained)	Additional employment requirements	Requirement that applicants and dependants are adequately maintained and accommodated without recourse to public funds	Entry clearance required for non-visa nationals to enter the UK
Permit-free employment – ie, representatives of overseas media or business, diplomatic, private servants, overseas government employees, ministers of religion, overseas airline ground crews (leads to settlement after five years)	136–185	Restricted to work in particular occupation for which admitted	Must intend to work only in the occupation for which admitted	Yes, applicant must show s/he 'can' so maintain and accommodate	Yes, although those in the category of 'overseas government employee' may, as an alternative, present any satisfactory evidence of their status
Commonwealth citizens with UK ancestry (leads to settlement after five years)	186–193	None	Must intend to take or seek employment	Yes, applicant must show s/he 'will be able' to so maintain and accommodate	Yes (mandatory since 1 April 2005)

Appendix 5: People admitted for purposes leading to settlement

Category	Rule (HC 395)	Employment conditions (before settlement is obtained)	Additional employment requirements	Requirement that applicants and dependants are adequately maintained and accommodated without recourse to public funds	Entry clearance required for non-visa nationals to enter the UK
Spouse, civil partner or unmarried partner or child of person with limited leave as work permit holder, permit-free employment (as above), Commonwealth citizen with UK ancestry (leads to settlement in line with spouse/parent)	194–199 295J–295L	None	None	Yes, parties must show that they are 'able' to so maintain and that there will be such accommodation which they own or occupy exclusively; child must show s/he 'can and will' be so maintained and accommodated in accommodation owned exclusively by her/his parents	Yes

Category	Rule (HC 395)	Employment conditions (before settlement is obtained)	Additional employment requirements	Requirement that applicants and dependants are adequately maintained and accommodated without recourse to public funds	Entry clearance required for non-visa nationals to enter the UK
Person establishing her/ himself in business, including innovators (leads to settlement after five years)	200–210H	Freedom to take employment restricted	Applicant must show that s/he will be actively involved full time in the business and that s/he does not intend to take or seek employment in the UK other than work for the business	Yes, applicant must show that s/he has 'sufficient additional' funds to so maintain and accommodate until such time as the business provides her/him with an income and, thereafter, that her/his share of the profits from the business will be sufficient for such maintenance and accommodation; applicant must show that this is the case without her/his recourse to employment other than work for the business	Yes

Category	Rule (HC 395)	Employment conditions (before settlement is obtained)	Additional employment requirements	Requirement that applicants and dependants are adequately maintained and accommodated without recourse to public funds	Entry clearance required for non-visa nationals to enter the UK
Person intending to establish her/himself in business under the provisions of an EC Association Agreements (Bulgaria and Romania) (leads to settlement after five years)	211–223	Freedom to take employment restricted	Applicant must show that s/he will be actively involved in promoting/managing the company or (if self-employed or in a partnership) that s/he will be actively involved in trading or providing services and must not intend to supplement her/his business activities by taking or seeking employment in the UK other than work for the business	Yes, applicant must show that s/he has 'sufficient additional' funds to so maintain and accommodate until such time as the business provides her/him with an income and, thereafter, that her/his share of the profits from the business will be sufficient for such maintenance and accommodation; applicant must show that this is the case without her/his recourse to employment other than work for the business	Yes

Category	Rule (HC 395)	Employment conditions (before settlement is obtained)	Additional employment requirements	Requirement that applicants and dependants are adequately maintained and accommodated without recourse to public funds	Entry clearance required for non-visa nationals to enter the UK
Investor (leads to settlement after five years)	224–231	Freedom to take employment restricted	None	Yes, applicant must be 'able' to so maintain and accommodate without taking employment (other than self-employment or business)	Yes
Writer/composer/ artist (leads to settlement after five years)	232–239	Freedom to take employment restricted	Must not intend to work other than as related to self-employment as a writer, composer, artist	Yes, applicant must show that s/he has previously been so maintained and accommodated and from her/his own resources without working except as a writer/composer/artist; applicant must show that s/he 'will be able' to accommodate her/himself from her/his own resources without working except as a writer/composer/artist	Yes

Category	Rule (HC 395)	Employment conditions (before settlement is obtained)	Additional employment requirements	Requirement that applicants and dependants are adequately maintained and accommodated without recourse to public funds	Entry clearance required for non-visa nationals to enter the UK
Spouse, civil partner or unmarried partner and child of person with limited leave as a person establishing her/himself in business (under the provisions of an EC association agreement or not), investor/writer/composer/artist (leads to settlement in line with spouse/parent concerned)	240–245 295J–295L	None	None	Yes, the parties to the marriage must show that they 'will be able' to so maintain and that there will be such accommodation owned and occupied by themselves exclusively. Child must show s/he 'can and will' be so maintained and accommodated in accommodation which her/his parents own or occupy exclusively	Yes

Category	Rule (HC 395)	Employment conditions (before settlement is obtained)	Additional employment requirements	Requirement that applicants and dependants are adequately maintained and accommodated without recourse to public funds	Entry clearance required for non-visa nationals to enter the UK
Person exercising rights of access to a child resident in the UK (leads to settlement after 12 months)	246–248F	None	None	Yes, applicant must show that s/he is able to so maintain; there must be adequate accommodation in accommodation which applicant owns or occupies exclusively	Yes
Retired person of independent means (leads to settlement after five years) and her/his spouse, unmarried partner and child (leads to settlement in line with spouse/parent)	263–276 295J–295L	Employment prohibited; there is no reference in the immigration rules to prohibiting employment for unmarried partners but it is likely that they, in line with other dependants, will be given a working prohibition	None, but applicant should be 'retired'	Yes, applicant must be 'able and willing' to so maintain and accommodate from her/his own resources with no assistance from any other person and without taking employment; if the spouse or unmarried partner is admitted, the parties must show that they 'will be able' to so maintain and accommodation in accommodation which they own or occupy exclusively; a child must show that s/he 'can and will' be so maintained and accommodated in accommodation owned or occupied exclusively by her/his parent(s)	Yes

Category	Rule (HC 395)	Employment conditions (before settlement is obtained)	Additional employment requirements	Requirement that applicants and dependants are adequately maintained and accommodated without recourse to public funds	Entry clearance required for non-visa nationals to enter the UK
Spouse, civil partner or unmarried partner of settled person in UK (leave granted for probationary period initially, thereafter indefinite leave granted)	281–289C 295A–295L	None	None	Yes, the parties must show that they 'will be able' to so maintain and that there will be such accommodation owned or occupied by themselves exclusively	Yes
Bereaved spouse or unmarried partner, death occuring during the probationary period (immediate settlement)	287–289 295M–295O	None	None	None	Only granted to those applying to stay rather than enter

Category	Rule (HC 395)	Employment conditions (before settlement is obtained)	Additional employment requirements	Requirement that applicants and dependants are adequately maintained and accommodated without recourse to public funds	Entry clearance required for non-visa nationals to enter the UK
Fiancé of settled person in UK (granted limited leave initially; with a view to marriage and settlement)	290–295	Employment prohibited	None	Yes, applicant must show that there will be adequate maintenance and accommodation available to her/him until the date of the marriage and that, after the marriage, the parties to the marriage 'will be able' to so maintain and that there will be such accommodation owned or occupied by themselves exclusively	Yes
Child or adopted child of settled parent(s) or relatives in UK (indefinite leave to enter granted)	297–300 309A–313	None	None	Yes, applicant must show that s/he 'can and will' be accommodated adequately by the 'parent, parents or relative' the child is seeking to join in accommodation which the 'parent, parents or relatives' the child is joining own or occupy exclusively; applicant must also show that s/he 'can and will' be maintained adequately by the 'parent, parents or relative' the child is seeking to join.	Yes

Appendix 5: People admitted for purposes leading to settlement

Category	Rule (HC 395)	Employment conditions (before settlement is obtained)	Additional employment requirements	Requirement that applicants and dependants are adequately maintained and accommodated without recourse to public funds	Entry clearance required for non-visa nationals to enter the UK
Child or adopted child of parent(s) given limited leave to enter or remain in UK with a view to settlement (given limited leave initially with a view to settlement)	301–303 314–316F	None	None	Yes, applicant must show s/he 'can and will' be so maintained and accommodated in accommodation owned or occupied exclusively by the parent(s)	Yes
Child of fiancé (limited leave initially but will eventually obtain settlement when fiancé marries and obtains settlement)	303A–303F	None	None	Yes, applicant must show that s/he 'can and will' be so maintained and accommodated	Yes

Category	Rule (HC 395)	Employment conditions (before settlement is obtained)	Additional employment requirements	Requirement that applicants and dependants are adequately maintained and accommodated without recourse to public funds	Entry clearance required for non-visa nationals to enter the UK
Parent, grandparent and other dependent relatives of person settled in the UK (immediate settlement)	317–319	None	None	Yes, applicant must show that s/he 'can and will' be so maintained and accommodated in accommodation owned or occupied exclusively by the sponsor	Yes
Refugee and spouse or civil partner or child of a refugee	352A–F	None	None	No	Yes, if the dependant of a refugee is seeking reunion with a person who has come to the UK and been recognised as a refugee s/he must apply for entry clearance to travel to the UK

Appendix 6

Reciprocal agreements

Benefits covered in conventions with EU/EEA member states

State	Retirement pension	Bereavement benefits	Guardian's allowance	Incapacity benefit (short-term)	Incapacity benefit (long-term)	Jobseeker's allowance	Maternity allowance	Disablement benefit	Industrial injuries benefits	Child benefit	Attendance allowance	Invalid care allowance
Austria	X	X	X	X	X	X	X	X	X	X	-	-
Belgium	X	X	X	X	X	X	X	X	X	X	-	-
Cyprus	X	X	X	X	X	X	X	X	X	-	-	-
Denmark		X	X	X	X	X	X	X	X	X	X	-
Finland	X	X	-	X	X	X	X	X	X	X	-	-
France	X	X	-	X	X	X	X	X	X	X	-	-
Germany		X	X	X	X	X	X	X	X	X	X	-
Iceland	X	X	X	X	X	X	-	X	X	-	-	-
Ireland	X	X	X	X	X	X	X	X	X	-	-	-
Italy	X	X	X	X	X	X	X	X	X	-	-	-
Luxembourg	X	X	X	X	X	-	X	X	X	-	-	-
Malta	X	X	X	X	X	X	-	X	X	-	-	-
Netherlands	X	X	X	X	X	X	X	X	X	-	-	-
Norway	X	X	X	X	X	X	X	X	X	X	X	-
Portugal	X	X	X	X	X	X	X	X	X	X	-	-
Spain	X	X	X	X	X	X	X	X	X	X	-	-
Sweden	X	X	X	X	X	X	X	X	X	X	-	-

There is no agreement with Greece or Liechtenstein. The agreement with Gibraltar provides that, except for child benefit, the United Kingdom and Gibraltar are treated as separate European Economic Area countries. Although Northern Ireland is part of the United Kingdom, there is an agreement between Great Britain and Northern Ireland. This is because benefits in Northern Ireland and Great Britain are separate and administered under different social security legislation.

Benefits covered in conventions with non-EU/EEA member states

State	Retirement pension	Bereavement benefits	Guardian's allowance	Incapacity benefit (short-term)	Incapacity benefit (long-term)	Jobseeker's allowance	Maternity allowance	Disablement benefit	Industrial injuries benefits	Child benefit	Attendance allowance	Disability living allowance	Invalid care allowance
Barbados	X	X	X	X	X	-	X	X	X	X	-	-	-
Bermuda	X	X	-	-	-	-	-	X	X	-	-	-	-
Canada	X	-	-	-	-	X	-	-	-	X	-	-	-
Guernsey	X	X	X	X	X	X	X	X	X	X	X	X	-
Isle of Man	X	X	X	X	X	X	X	X	X	X	X	X	X
Israel	X	X	X	X	X	-	X	X	X	X	-	-	-
Jamaica	X	X	X	-	X	-	-	X	X	-	-	-	-
Jersey	X	X	X	X	X	-	X	X	X	X	X	X	-
Mauritius	X	X	X	-	-	-	-	X	X	X	-	-	-
New Zealand	X	X	X	X	-	X	-	-	-	X	-	-	-
Philippines	X	X	-	-	-	-	-	X	X	-	-	-	-
Philippines	X	X	-	-	-	-	-	X	X	-	-	-	-
*Switzerland	X	X	X	X	X	-	-	X	X	X	-	-	-
Turkey	X	X	X	X	X	-	X	X	X	-	-	-	-
USA	X	X	X	X	X	-	-	-	-	-	-	-	-

* From June 2002 an agreement with Switzerland allows Swiss nationals the right to rely on EC social security provisions, such as Regulation 1408/71 as if they were EEA nationals.

Appendix 7

Visa nationals

Afghanistan
Albania
Algeria
Angola
Armenia
Azerbaijan
Bahrain
Bangladesh
Belarus
Benin
Bhutan
Bosnia-Herzegovina
Burkina Faso
Burundi
Cambodia
Cameroon
Cape Verde
Central African Republic
Chad
China (People's Republic of)
Colombia
Comoros
Congo (Democratic Republic of)
Congo (Republic of)
Croatia
Cuba
Djibouti
Dominican Republic
Ecuador
Egypt
Equatorial Guinea
Eritrea
Ethiopia
Fiji
Gabon
The Gambia

Georgia
Ghana
Guinea
Guinea Bissau
Guyana
Haiti
India
Indonesia
Iran
Iraq
Ivory Coast
Jamaica
Jordan
Kazakhstan
Kenya
Korea (Democratic People's Republic)
Kuwait
Kyrgyzstan
Laos
Lebanon
Liberia
Libya
Macedonia
Madagascar
Malawi
Maldives
Mali
Mauritania
Mauritius
Moldova
Mongolia
Morocco
Mozambique
Myanmar
Nepal
Niger

Nigeria
Oman
Pakistan
Papua New Guinea
Peru
Philippines
Qatar
Russia
Rwanda
Sao Tome & Principe
Saudi Arabia
Senegal
Sierra Leone
Somalia
Sri Lanka
Sudan
Surinam
Syria
Taiwan
Tajikistan
Tanzania
Thailand
Togo
Tunisia
Turkey
Turkmenistan
Uganda
Ukraine
United Arab Emirates
Uzbekistan
Vietnam
Yemen
Federal Republic of Yugoslavia*
Zambia
Zimbabwe

*(including documents issued by the Former Socialist Republic of Yugoslavia)

Appendix 8

Passport stamps and other endorsements

Figure 1: Certificate of entitlement

Figure 2: Green uniform format visa

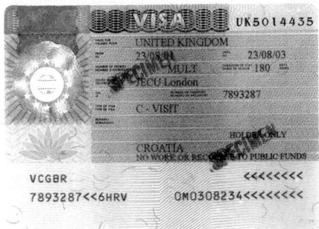

Figure 3: Red residence permit

Figure 4: Date stamp

Figure 5: Limited leave to enter (visitor or short course student)

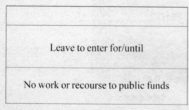

Leave to enter for/until
No work or recourse to public funds

CODE 3

Figure 6: GV3

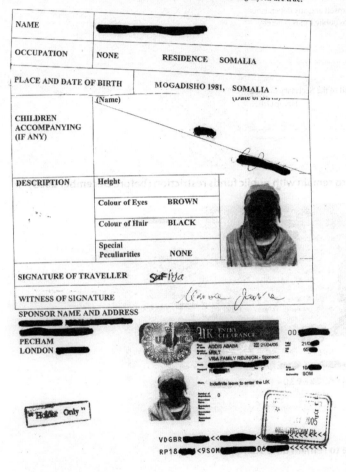

DECLARATION OF IDENTITY FOR VISA PURPOSES

I Here by declare that the following particulars concerning myself are true:

NAME	▬▬▬▬▬▬▬▬▬	
OCCUPATION	NONE	RESIDENCE SOMALIA
PLACE AND DATE OF BIRTH	MOGADISHO 1981, SOMALIA	

	(Name)	(Date of Birth)
CHILDREN ACCOMPANYING (IF ANY)		

DESCRIPTION	Height	
	Colour of Eyes	BROWN
	Colour of Hair	BLACK
	Special Peculiarities	NONE

SIGNATURE OF TRAVELLER   Safiya

WITNESS OF SIGNATURE

SPONSOR NAME AND ADDRESS

PECHAM
LONDON

UK ENTRY CLEARANCE
ADDIS ABABA   21/04/05   MULT
VISA FAMILY REUNION - Sponsor:
Indefinite leave to enter the UK
"Holder Only"

VDGBR ◄◄
RP18 ◄9SOM 06 ◄◄◄◄◄◄◄

Figure 7: Refusal of leave to enter

Figure 8: Leave to remain with public funds restriction

```
┌─────────────────────────────────────────┐
│                                          │
│                                          │
│  Leave to remain in the United Kingdom on│
│  Condition that the holder maintains and │
│  Accommodates himself and any dependants │
│  Without recourse to public funds is hereby│
│  Given                                   │
│                                          │
│  Until.................................. │
│  .........................................│
│          on behalf of the Secretary of State│
│                         Home Office      │
│                                          │
│  Date .................................. │
└─────────────────────────────────────────┘
```

CODE 1

Figure 9: Leave to remain with public funds restriction (before December 2003)

Figure 10: Leave to remain date stamp

Figure 11: Indefinite leave to remain (both before and after December 2003)

Figure 12: Application registration card

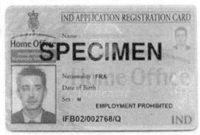

Figure 13: Residence permit confirming refugee status

Home Office
Immigration and Nationality Directorate

IMMIGRATION
STATUS
DOCUMENT

...gee Status

...ed on this document has been
...Secretary of State as a refugee
...e 1951 Geneva Convention
...Status of Refugees and its
...Protocol.

...ich leave to enter or remain in
...ngdom has been granted is
...d in the endorsement.

...d of leave indicated remains
...is able to work in the United
...t any immigration restrictions
...e of work they can undertake.

This Immigration Status Document has been endorsed in place of a valid national passport or travel document and confers upon the person named leave to enter or remain in the United Kingdom for the period indicated. It does not certify the accuracy of the personal particulars, which are those supplied by the person who made the application. It remains the property of Her Majesty's Government and may be withdrawn at any time. It should not be tampered with or passed to an unauthorised person. Any case of loss or destruction should be immediately reported to the nearest police station and to the Immigration and Nationality Directorate at the address below; only after exhaustive enquiries can a replacement be issued in such circumstances. The Immigration Status Document of a deceased person should be returned to the Immigration and Nationality Directorate for cancellation.

Enquiries about the purpose, use, or validity of this document should be made to the Immigration and Nationality Directorate at:

Lunar House, 40 Wellesley Road, Croydon, CR9 2BY (Telephone 0870 606 7766)

ACD.2151

Personal Details

Figure 14: Letter explaining refugee status

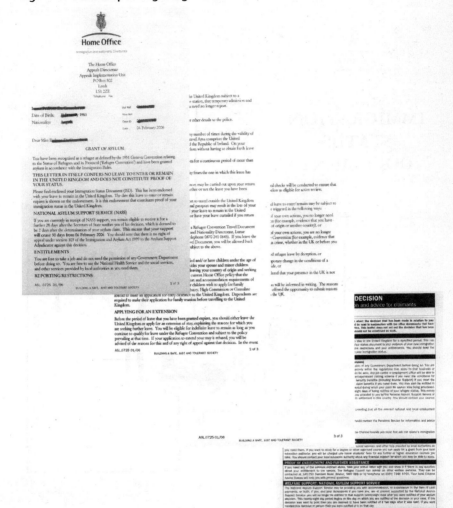

Figure 15: Residence permit confirming discretionary leave to remain

Home Office
Immigration and Nationality Directorate

IMMIGRATION STATUS DOCUMENT

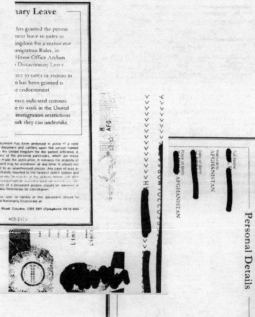

Figure 16: Letters explaining humanitarian protection or discretionary leave to remain

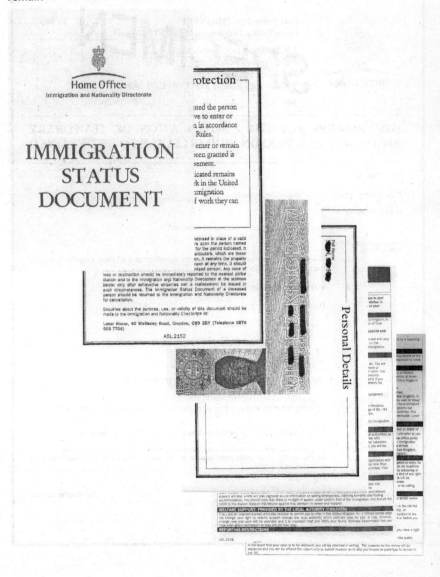

Figure 17: Notice of temporary admission

Port Reference: {MAINREF}
Home Office Reference: {HOREF}

IS 96NW

UK IMMIGRATION SERVICE
Enforcement Policy unit
Floor, Green Park House
29 Wellesley Road, CROYDON CR0 2AJ

Home Office

Tel: Fax:

IMMIGRATION ACT 1971 - NOTIFICATION OF TEMPORARY ADMISSION TO A PERSON WHO IS LIABLE TO BE DETAINED

To: {Name}

Date of Birth: {Bd1}   Nationality: {Nat1}

LIABILITY TO DETENTION

A.   You are a person who is liable to be detained*.

TEMPORARY ADMISSION RESTRICTIONS

B.   I hereby authorise your (further) temporary admission to the United Kingdom subject to the following restrictions**:

■   You **must** reside at:

{Address1}

■   You **must** report to: {Report_To}

at   {Reporting_Location}

on   {Report_On} at {Report_At}hrs.

and then on: {Report_on_2}   at   {Report_at_2}hrs.

■   You **may not** enter employment, paid or unpaid, or engage in any business or profession.

ANY CHANGE OF RESTRICTION

If these restrictions are to be changed, an Immigration Officer will write to you.

■   **Although you have been temporarily admitted, you remain liable to be detained**
■   **You have NOT been given leave to enter the United Kingdom within the meaning of the Immigration Act 1971**

Date **31 January 2002**

Immigration Officer

* Paragraph 16 of Schedule 2 to the Act
** Paragraph 21 of Schedule 2 to the Act

[IS 96NW Temporary Admission ...... VC2]

Figure 18: Notice of illegal entry/administrative removal

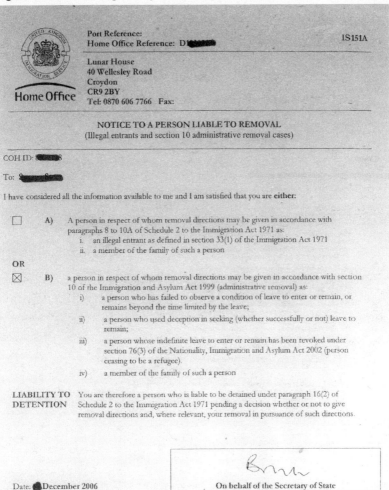

Port Reference:
Home Office Reference: D▓▓▓▓▓

IS151A

Lunar House
40 Wellesley Road
Croydon
CR9 2BY
Tel: 0870 606 7766 Fax:

Home Office

NOTICE TO A PERSON LIABLE TO REMOVAL
(Illegal entrants and section 10 administrative removal cases)

COH ID: ▓▓▓▓▓

To: ▓▓▓▓▓

I have considered all the information available to me and I am satisfied that you are **either**:

☐ A) A person in respect of whom removal directions may be given in accordance with paragraphs 8 to 10A of Schedule 2 to the Immigration Act 1971 as:
   i. an illegal entrant as defined in section 33(1) of the Immigration Act 1971
   ii. a member of the family of such a person

OR

☒ B) a person in respect of whom removal directions may be given in accordance with section 10 of the Immigration and Asylum Act 1999 (administrative removal) as:
   i) a person who has failed to observe a condition of leave to enter or remain, or remains beyond the time limited by the leave;
   ii) a person who used deception in seeking (whether successfully or not) leave to remain;
   iii) a person whose indefinite leave to enter or remain has been revoked under section 76(3) of the Nationality, Immigration and Asylum Act 2002 (person ceasing to be a refugee).
   iv) a member of the family of such a person

LIABILITY TO DETENTION You are therefore a person who is liable to be detained under paragraph 16(2) of Schedule 2 to the Immigration Act 1971 pending a decision whether or not to give removal directions and, where relevant, your removal in pursuance of such directions.

Date: ▓ December 2006

On behalf of the Secretary of State

Important notice for persons detained under the Immigration Act 1971.

You may on request have one person known to you or who is likely to take an interest in your welfare informed at public expense as soon as practicable of your whereabouts.

IS151A 04/06

Figure 19: Decision to remove for illegal entrants/those subject to administrative removal

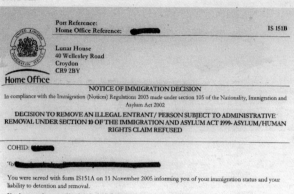

Port Reference:
Home Office Reference: ▮▮▮▮▮

IS 151B

Lunar House
40 Wellesley Road
Croydon
CR9 2BY

Home Office

NOTICE OF IMMIGRATION DECISION

In compliance with the Immigration (Notices) Regulations 2003 made under section 105 of the Nationality, Immigration and Asylum Act 2002

DECISION TO REMOVE AN ILLEGAL ENTRANT / PERSON SUBJECT TO ADMINISTRATIVE REMOVAL UNDER SECTION 10 OF THE IMMIGRATION AND ASYLUM ACT 1999- ASYLUM/HUMAN RIGHTS CLAIM REFUSED

COHID: ▮▮▮▮▮

To ▮▮▮▮▮▮▮▮▮▮▮▮▮▮▮

You were served with form IS151A on 11 November 2005 informing you of your immigration status and your liability to detention and removal.

You have made an application for indefinite leave to remain. It has been decided to refuse your claim for the reasons stated in the attached letter.

A decision has now been taken to remove you from the United Kingdom[1].

RIGHT OF APPEAL You are entitled to appeal this decision under section 82(1) of the Nationality, Immigration and Asylum Act 2002. A notice of appeal is enclosed which explains what to do and an Asylum & Immigration Tribunal leaflet which explains how to get help. The appeal must be made on one or more of the following grounds:

- That the decision is not in accordance with the immigration rules;

- That the decision is unlawful because it racially discriminates against you;

- That the decision is unlawful because it is incompatible with your rights under the European Convention on Human Rights;

- That the decision breaches rights which you have as an EEA National or member of such a person's family under Community Treaties relating to entry or residence in the United Kingdom;

- That the decision is otherwise not in accordance with the law;

- That a discretion under the immigration rules should have been exercised differently;

- That your removal from the United Kingdom as a result of the decision would:

  • breach the United Kingdom's obligations under the 1951 Refugee Convention;

  • be incompatible with your rights under the European Convention on Human Rights.

You should not appeal on grounds which do not apply to you. You must also give arguments and any supporting evidence which justifies your grounds.

---

[1] Sections 82(2)(g), 82(2)(h), 82(2)(i) of the 2002 Act.

Where a decision to remove has been made under section 10 of the Immigration and Asylum Act 1999, any leave previously granted is invalidated by the service of this notice (section 10(8) of that Act (as amended)).

[IS 151B] 06/06

Figure 20: Removal directions

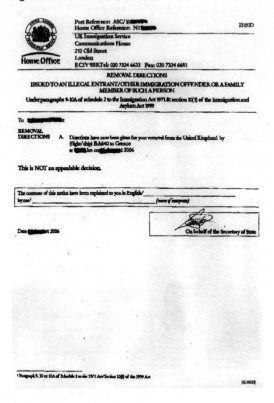

Post Reference: ASC/10
Home Office Reference: N1   IS151D

UK Immigration Service
Communications House
210 Old Street
London
EC1V 9BRTel: 020 7324 6622 Fax: 020 7324 6651

REMOVAL DIRECTIONS

ISSUED TO AN ILLEGAL ENTRANT/OTHER IMMIGRATION OFFENDER OR A FAMILY MEMBER OF SUCH A PERSON

Under paragraphs 9-10A of schedule 2 to the Immigration Act 1971 & section 10(1) of the Immigration and Asylum Act 1999

To

REMOVAL
DIRECTIONS   A.   Directions have now been given for your removal from the United Kingdom1 by
(flight/ship) BA640 to Greece
at   hrs on   2006

This is NOT an appealable decision.

The contents of this notice have been explained to you in English/
by me/ _____   (name of interpreter)

Date   2006   On behalf of the Secretary of State

1 Paragraph 9, 10 or 10A of Schedule 2 to the 1971 Act/Section 10(1) of the 1999 Act

IS151D

Figure 21: Embarkation stamp

Figure 22:

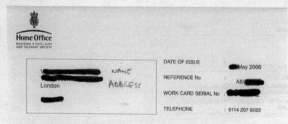

DATE OF ISSUE	: ●May 2006
REFERENCE No	: A8/●
WORK CARD SERIAL No	: ●●
TELEPHONE	: 0114 207 6022

Accession State Worker Registration Scheme

Thank you for your application to register on the Accession State Worker Registration scheme. I am
pleased to inform you that we have approved your application and that you are now registered.

Your worker registration card is attached below. If you have any queries about this document, then
please contact Work Permits (UK) on the telephone number above.

Managed Migration
Home Office
PO Box 3468
Sheffield S3 8WA

www.workingintheuk.gov.uk

Accession State Worker Registration Scheme
Registration Card

Date of Issue: ●May 2006

SURNAME	:
FORENAME(S)	:
DATE OF BIRTH	:
NATIONALITY	:
REFERENCE No	: A8/
DATE OF ISSUE	: ●May 2006

This worker registration card should be retained as evidence of your
registration with the Accession State Worker Registration Scheme.

PLEASE DO NOT LOSE - REPLACEMENTS MAY NOT BE ISSUED

WORK CARD SERIAL No ●●

●R REGISTRATION SCHEME
● CERTIFICATE

●●CEMENTS MAY NOT BE ISSUED

●n the Accession State Worker Registration
●e have approved your application.

It authorises you to work for the employer

● no longer working for the employer
●hich it is issued.

This certificate expires on the date you cease working for the specified employer.

This certificate should be retained with your worker registration card.

Name	: ●●
Date of Birth	: ● 1955
Nationality	:
Unique Reference Number:	A8/●●
Job start date	: ●●
Employer's Name	: C●●
Employer's Address	: ●●

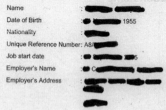

Appendix 9

Abbreviations used in the notes

AC	Appeal Cases
All ER	All England Reports
Art(s)	Article(s)
CA	Court of Appeal
CMLR	Common Market Law Reports
Crim App R	Criminal Appeal Reports
ECJ	European Court of Justice
ECR	European Court Reports
EEA	European Economic Area
ECHR	European Convention on Human Rights
EctHR	European Court of Human Rights
EHRR	European Human Rights Reports
EWCR	England and Wales Court of Appeal
EWHC	England and Wales High Court
FLR	Family Law Reports
HL	House of Lords
HLR	Housing Law Reports
IAT	Immigration Appeal Tribunal
Imm AR	Immigration Appeal Reports
INLR	Immigration and Nationality Law Reports
IRLR	Industrial Relations Law Reports
LGR	Local Government Reports
New LJ	New Law Journal
OJ	Official Journal of the European Communities
PC	Privy Council
QB	Queen's Bench Reports
QBD	Queen's Bench Division
r(s)	rule(s)
reg(s)	regulation(s)
s(s)	section(s)
Sch(s)	Schedule(s)
SJ	Solicitors' Journal
SLT	Scots Law Times
SSHD	Secretary of State for the Home Department
WLR	Weekly Law Reports

Acts of Parliament

AIA 1996	Asylum and Immigration Act 1996
AIAA 1993	Asylum and Immigration Appeals Act 1993
AI(TC)A 2004	Asylum and Immigration (Treatment of Claimants etc) Act 2004
BNA 1948	British Nationality Act 1948
BNA 1981	British Nationality Act 1981
CA 1989	Children Act 1989
FLRA 1969	Family Law Reform Act 1969
HRA	Human Rights Act 1998
IA 1971	Immigration Act 1971
IA 1988	Immigration Act 1988
IAA 1999	Immigration and Asylum Act 1999
IANA 2006	Immigration, Asylum and Nationality Act 2006
IntA 1978	Interpretation Act 1978
JSA 1995	Jobseekers Act 1995
NAA 1948	National Assistance Act 1948
NIAA 2002	Nationality, Immigration and Asylum Act 2002
SPCA 2002	State Pension Credit Act 2002
SSAA 1992	Social Security Administration Act 1992
SSCBA 1992	Social Security Contributions and Benefits Act 1992
TCA 2002	Tax Credits Act 2002

European law

Secondary legislation is made under the Treaty of Rome 1957, the Single European Act and the Maastricht Treaty in the form of Regulations (EC Reg) and Directives (EC Dir).

Regulations

Each set of regulations has a statutory instrument (SI) number and date. You ask for them by giving their date and number

AIT(P) Rules 2005	The Asylum and Immigration Tribunal (Procedure) Rules 2005 No.230
AS Regs	The Asylum Support Regulations 2000 No.704
ASA(P) Rules	The Asylum Support Appeals (Procedure) Rules 2000 No.541
AS(Amdt) Regs	The Asylum Support (Amendment) Regulations 2002 No.472
AS(IP)Amdt regs	The Asylum Support (Interim Provisions)(Amendment) Regulations 2002 No.471
CB Regs	The Child Benefit (General) Regulations 2006 No.223
CBGA(A) Regs	The Child Benefit and Guardians Allowance (Administration) Regulations 2003 No.492
CB(RPA) Regs	The Child Benefit (Residence and Persons Abroad) Regulations 1976 No.963
CB&SS(FAR) Regs	The Child Benefit and Social Security (Fixing and Adjustment of Rates) Regulations 1976 No.1267

CB&SS(FAR)Amdt Regs	The Child Benefit and Social Security (Fixing and Adjustment of Rates)(Amendment) Regulations 1998 No.1581
CF(A)O	The Consular Fees (Amendment) Order 1986 No.1881
CTB Regs	The Council Tax Benefit Regulations 2006 No.215
DWA Regs	The Disability Working Allowance (General) Regulations 1991 No.2887
FC Regs	The Family Credit (General) Regulations 1987 No.1973
HB Regs	The Housing Benefit Regulations 2006 No.213
HBCTB(CP) Regs	The Housing Benefit and Council Tax Benefit (Consequential Provisions) Regulations 2006 No.217
HBCTBIS(Amdts) Regs	The Housing Benefit, Council Tax Benefit and Income Support (Amendments) Regulations 1995 No.625
I(CERI)O	The Immigration (Control of Entry through the Republic of Ireland) Order 1972 No.1610
I(EEA)O	The Immigration (European Economic Area) Order 1994 No.1895
I(EEA) Regs 2000	The Immigration (European Economic Area) Regulations 2000 No.2326
I(EEA) Regs 2006	The Immigration (European Economic Area) Regulations 2006 No.1003
I(EC)O	The Immigration (Exemption from Control) Order 1972 No.1613
I(LER)O	The Immigration (Leave to Enter and Remain) Order 2000 No.1161
I(LR)(PFP) Regs	The Immigration (Leave to Remain) (Prescribed Forms and Procedures) Regulations 2006 No.1421
IAA(N) Regs	The Immigration Appeals (Notices) Regulations 1984 No.2040
IAA(N) Regs 2000	The Immigration Appeals (Notices) Regulations 1984 No.2246
IAA(P) Rules	The Immigration Appeals (Procedure) Rules 1984 No.2041
IA(POAFAS) Regs	The Immigration and Asylum (Provision of Accommodation to Failed Asylum Seekers) Regulations 2005 No.930
IS Regs	The Income Support (General) Regulations 1987 No.1967
JSA Regs	The Jobseeker's Allowance Regulations 1996 No.207
SFCWP Regs	The Social Fund Cold Weather Payments (General) Regulations 1988 No.1724
SFM&FE Regs	The Social Fund Maternity and Funeral Expenses (General) Regulations 1987 No.481
SFM&FE(Amdt) Regs	The Social Fund Maternity and Funeral Expenses (General) Amendment Regulations 1996 No.1443
SS(IA)CA Regs	The Social Security (Immigration and Asylum) Consequential Amendments Regulations 2000 No.636

SMP Regs	The Statutory Maternity Pay (General) Regulations 1986 No.1960
SMP(PAM) Regs	The Statutory Maternity Pay (Persons Abroad and Mariners) Regulations 1987 No.418
SPC Regs	The State Pension Credit Regulations 2002 No.1792
SPPSAP(G) Regs	The Statutory Paternity Pay and Statutory Adoption Pay (General) Regulations 2002 No.2822
SPPSAP(PAM) Regs	The Statutory Paternity Pay and Statutory Adoption Pay (Persons Abroad and Mariners) Regulations 2002 No.2821
SS(AA) Regs	The Social Security (Attendance Allowance) Regulations 1991 No.2740
SS(C&P) Regs	The Social Security (Claims and Payments) Regulations 1987 No.1968
SS(Con) Regs	The Social Security (Contributions) Regulations 2001
SS(DLA) Regs	The Social Security (Disability Living Allowance) Regulations 1991 No.2890
SS(EEEIIP) Regs	The Social Security (Employed Earners' Employment for Industrial Injuries Purposes) Regulations 1975 No.467
SS(GA) Regs	The Social Security (Guardian's Allowance) Regulations 1975 No.515
SS(IB) Regs	The Social Security (Incapacity Benefit) Regulations 1994 No.2946
SFWFP Regs	The Social Fund Winter Fuel Payment Regulations 2000 No.729
SS(IB-ID) Regs	The Social Security (Incapacity Benefit – Increases for Dependants) Regulations 1994 No.2945
SS(ICA) Regs	The Social Security (Invalid Care Allowance) Regulations 1976 No.409
SS(IIAB) Regs	The Social Security (Industrial Injuries) (Airmen's Benefits) Regulations 1975 No.469
SS(IIMB) Regs	The Social Security (Industrial Injuries) (Mariners' Benefits) Regulations 1975 No.470
SS(IIPD) Regs	The Social Security (Industrial Injuries) (Prescribed Diseases) Regulations 1985 No.967
SS(MB) Regs	The Social Security (Mariners' Benefits) Regulations 1975 No.529
SS(NIRA) Regs	The Social Security (Northern Ireland Reciprocal Arrangements) Regulations 1976 No.1003
SS(OB) Regs	The Social Security (Overlapping Benefits) Regulations 1979 No.597
SS(PFA)MA Regs	The Social Security (Persons from Abroad) Miscellaneous Amendments Regulations 1996 No.30
SS(SDA) Regs	The Social Security (Severe Disablement Allowance) Regulations 1984 No.1303
SS(WB&RP) Regs	The Social Security (Widow's Benefit and Retirement Pensions) Regulations 1979 No.642

SSB(Dep) Regs	The Social Security Benefit (Dependency) Regulations 1977 No.343
SSB(PA) Regs	The Social Security Benefit (Persons Abroad) Regulations 1975 No.563
SSB(PRT) Regs	The Social Security Benefit (Persons Residing Together) Regulations 1977 No.956
SSFA(PM) Regs	The Social Security and Family Allowances (Polygamous Marriages) Regulations 1975 No.561
SSP Regs	The Statutory Sick Pay (General) Regulations 1982 No.894
SSP(MAPA) Regs	The Statutory Sick Pay (Mariners, Airmen and Persons Abroad) Regulations 1982 No.1349
TC(Imm) Regs	The Tax Credit (Immigration) Regulations 2003 No.653
TC(R) Regs	The Tax Credit (Residence) Regulations 2003 No.654
VOLO	The Immigration (variation of Leave) Order 1976 No.1572

Other information

ADI	Asylum Directorate Instructions
API	Asylum Policy Instructions, Home Office
DMG	The Decision Makers Guide
HC 395	The last complete statement of the Immigration Rules, 23 May 1994
GM	The Housing Benefit and Council Tax Benefit Guidance Manual
IDI	Immigration Directorate Instructions

Note: There are many cases referred to in the notes. Some are followed by a bracketed number or similar reference – eg, (12573) – these are references to unreported decisions of the Immigration Appeal Tribunal.

Index

....

How to use this Index

Entries against the bold headings direct you to the general information on the subject, or where the subject is covered most fully. Sub-entries are listed alphabetically and direct you to specific aspects of the subject.